Shari'a Politics

Shari'a Politics

Islamic Law and Society in the Modern World

Edited by Robert W. Hefner

Indiana University Press
Bloomington and Indianapolis

This book is a publication of

Indiana University Press
601 North Morton Street
Bloomington, Indiana 47404-3797 USA

www.iupress.indiana.edu

Telephone orders   800-842-6796
Fax orders   812-855-7931
Orders by e-mail   iuporder@indiana.edu

Library of Congress Cataloging-in-Publication Data

Shari'a politics : Islamic law and society in the modern world / edited by Robert W. Hefner.
    p. cm.
  Includes bibliographical references and index.
   ISBN 978-0-253-35627-7 (cloth : alk. paper) — ISBN 978-0-253-22310-4 (pbk. : alk. paper) 1. Islam and politics. 2. Islam and state. 3. Islam and world politics. 4. Islamic law. I. Hefner, Robert W., [date]
   BP173.7.S5315 2011
   297.2'72—dc22

                                                    2010043161

            1 2 3 4 5   16 15 14 13 12 11

Contents

Acknowledgments

This volume is the product of a collaborative research project titled "Shari'a Politics in Muslim-Majority Countries," sponsored by the Program on Islam and Society at the Institute on Culture, Religion, and World Affairs (CURA) at Boston University. The project brought together eight leading scholars of Muslim politics, law, and society for two-day conferences in May and December 2008. In the period between the conference meetings, each team member —already with many years of research experience in the country setting— carried out additional research with the assistance of local partners, conducting interviews, organizing focus groups, and gathering textual and media materials on the circumstances of Islamic law and society.

As is inevitable with a project of this scope, the project and its researchers incurred innumerable debts in the course of our activities, too many, alas, to acknowledge here. At the very least, however, I would like to thank Peter L. Berger, the former CURA director, for his far-sighted support of this and other projects of the Program on Islam and Society at CURA, which was established in 1991. I would also like to thank the book's editor at Indiana University Press, Rebecca Tolen, for both her interest in the volume and her generous recommendations with regard to the book's editing. Last but not least, I would also like to thank Azyumardi Azra, Jajat Burhanudin, Chaider S. Bamualim, and Jajang Jahroni at the Hidayatullah State Islamic University in Jakarta, Indonesia. In the early 2000s, the counsel, conversations, and guidance of these colleagues and friends provided the inspiration for the comparative project on Islamic law and politics discussed in this book. I hope that they do not find the results of what they have inspired too disappointing.

Note on Transliteration and Spelling

The contributors to this volume draw on a broad array of languages, each with its own particular conventions of transliteration and spelling. In the interest of consistency, we have kept the transliteration of non-English terms to a minimum. With the exception of several usages of the ' to indicate the Arabic letter ʿayn (as in "shariʿa") and ' to indicate the hamza (as in "Qurʾan"), we have dispensed with most diacritical marks in this volume (including in quotations from other works). In most cases, moreover, the hamza is indicated only when it occurs within a word (as in "Qurʾan") but not when it comes at the beginning or end of a word.

Arabic-derived words are rendered in widely varying ways in non-Arabic languages. Our preference throughout the volume has been to render Arabic words used in all of the book's chapters, like shariʿa, in a uniform manner, while keeping less commonly used words in the local linguistic variety. We have also usually indicated the plural form of Arabic terms with the addition of an s to the singular form, thus "fatwas" rather than "fatawa." Finally, certain Arabic words that occur frequently throughout the volume (e.g., "madrasa," "ulama," and "shariʿa") are not italicized.

Shari'a Politics

Introduction

Shariʿa Politics—Law and Society
in the Modern Muslim World

Robert W. Hefner

One of the more striking trends in global religion during the final decades of the twentieth century was the resurgence in religious piety and observance across broad swaths of the Muslim world. This renewed religious vitality confounded those who had long forecast that, under the conditions of modernity, religion is destined to decline until, as one famous sociologist declared, it "shall disappear altogether except, possibly, in the private realm" (Mills 1959, 33). The Islamic resurgence also gave rise to a more politically ambiguous development: calls for the state to apply a uniform and codified version of *shariʿa,* or "Islamic law" (see below), to all Muslim citizens. Most activists making these appeals were mainstream Muslims intent on abiding by what they regarded as the commands of their faith. In some cases, however, as in Afghanistan, Somalia, and Pakistan in the 2000s, demands for the law were voiced by armed militants willing to carry out spectacular acts of violence to get their way.

These and other developments have raised questions about the place of the shariʿa in modern politics, and its implications for citizenship, religious tolerance, and the modern profession of Islam. Does Islam require that the state implement a uniform and comprehensive variety of shariʿa? Can the shariʿa be compatible with modern democracy and pluralist citizenship? What are the implications of the law for women, non-Muslims, and Muslims who profess a non-conforming variety of the faith? Few questions are more decisive than these for assessing the future of the Muslim world. Yet few have proved more vexing for a global public unfamiliar with the history, meanings, and politics of Islamic law.

This book aims to address the question of the place of Islamic shari'a in modern Muslim politics and civilization. Juxtaposing global trends in the law with local political histories, it examines what today's calls for the application of the shari'a mean, why the appeals have become widespread, and what the popular concern might imply for Muslim politics and world affairs in years to come.

The Shari'a and Politics

A system of ethical injunctions as much as "law" in the modern sense, the shari'a has been at the heart of Muslim religious life since the beginning of the Islamic era in the early decades of the seventh century CE. Beginning in the ninth century, the shari'a became the subject of a great jurisprudential literature, known as fiqh (Ar., literally "understanding," referring to the efforts of religious scholars to understand God's will). This body of exegesis and commentary eventually became one of the richest traditions of legal scholarship in any world civilization (Hallaq 2009a; cf. Glenn 2000). In the premodern period, most Middle Eastern states, and some but not all Asian Muslim polities, made some variety of shari'a central to their legal systems. It must be said, however, that the understanding and practice of the shari'a varied with time and place; the shari'a was also never the only normative corpus used to adjudicate local affairs. Tribal populations applied customary law in addition to Islamic. Sultans operated non-shari'a criminal courts alongside those of Islamic judges (Hallaq 2009a, 368; Vikor 2005, 191–93). From the sixteenth century on, judges in the Ottoman Empire, the greatest of the early modern era's Muslim states, applied both the shari'a and the ruler's laws (Imber 1997, 24–58). Notwithstanding this often complex legal pluralism, in most of the central Muslim lands the popular ethical imaginary remained oriented toward the symbolism and ideals, if not the fine print, of the shari'a (Johansen 1998, 61).

In the nineteenth and early twentieth centuries, the legal systems in most Muslim-majority societies turned away from shari'a-based law. Startled by the scale of the emerging European threat, Muslim rulers in Egypt and the Ottoman heartland concluded that one of the advantages enjoyed by the European powers was their centralized and codified legal systems. Eventually, most Muslim-majority states changed the status of the shari'a by replacing what had in most lands been a decentralized legal administration with a standardized and state-authorized law code. In the early decades of the twentieth century, many states did away with enforcement of the shari'a altogether, or limited its jurisdiction to family affairs and religious matters like the regulation of charitable endowments (Ar. awqaf, sing. waqf; see Kahf 1995). In the 1970s and 1980s, however, Muslim lands witnessed the emergence of great social movements calling for the state to implement Islamic law once again. Seven Muslim-majority countries introduced constitutional amendments requiring that state law conform to shari'a norms (see N. Brown 1997; Lombardi 2006, 1). Although the main currents of pro-shari'a activism were peaceful, radical social movements in several countries, including Egypt in the early 1990s and Pakistan, Indonesia, and Somalia in the 2000s, used calls for the shari'a to frame their demands for the overthrow of established Muslim governments. Some among the radicals also invoked the law to justify attacks on unveiled women, non-Muslims, and, as with the 1985 execution of the renowned Sudanese reformist Mahmud Muhammad Taha (Layish and Warburg 2002, 55–60; Mahmoud 2007, 29), those who dissent from radical understandings of the law.

These latter, radically "contentious" uses (Tarrow 1988; Wiktorowicz 2004) of Islamic law raised concerns among Muslim reformists and Western policy analysts alike. That there should be such questions among Western observers is understandable enough: the shari'a is a complex ethico-legal tradition, one with which most Westerners are unfamiliar. In addition, demands for state enforcement of religious law strike many Westerners as a violation of a core tenet of modern liberal democracy, the separation of religion and state. Further complicating Western perceptions, radical proponents of the law, from Osama bin Laden to the Jemaah Islamiyah of Indonesia, have used demands for the shari'a as a rallying cry in violent campaigns against alleged enemies, both Muslim and non-Muslim. When invoking the law in this manner, the militants often interpret the law highly selectively, highlighting aspects most at variance with the sensibilities of Muslim and Western democrats. A peculiar irony of today's cultural globalization is that the radicals' campaigns have featured calls for the mandatory veiling of women (and even the closing of girls' schools), the maiming of thieves, the stoning of adulterers, and the execution of apostates. Certainly, as will be discussed below, the regulations cited to justify such rules are in some sense "present" in classical Islamic law. But they are a small and discursively nuanced feature of one of the world's most enduring legal traditions, the ethical subtlety of which is notable by its absence from modern radicals' slogans.

Inasmuch as Islam is a religion of divine law, it should occasion no surprise that modern Muslim discussions of religion have come to focus on the question of the shari'a. As the essays in this book will make clear, however, the revival of interest in the shari'a has done little to diminish or dispel the plurality of viewpoints on the law. Indeed, as the shari'a has moved to the center of public discussion, questions concerning its meanings and applications have only become more disputatious and consequential.

One comparison illustrates the complexity of the cultural background against which this heightened interest in the shari'a has emerged. In the 1990s and 2000s media reports created the impression that the big news coming from the Muslim world was terrorist violence. The violence was indeed awful, and its impact on global affairs and Muslim politics has been harmful. From the longer-term perspective of political culture, however, the truly interesting news coming from Muslim lands concerns not just the actions of suicide bombers or airline hijackers, but also the fact that most ordinary Muslims have come to the conclusion that democracy and citizen rights are compatible with Islam. Certainly, not all Muslims subscribe to this idea. In a few countries— Saudi Arabia, Libya, several of the Gulf States—a plurality or outright majority take exception to it. In most other countries, however, survey research and ethnographic studies have confirmed that the majority of Muslims regard democracy as an appealing and legitimate form of government, and wish that it could be implemented in their own country (Esposito and Mogahed 2007; Fattah 2006; Hassan 2002; Norris and Inglehart 2004, 133–56). Although unheralded in the Western media, the Muslim public's embrace of democratic ideals ranks as one of our age's great transformations of mass political culture, not just for Muslims, but for all citizens of the modern world.

What makes this popular interest in democracy so intriguing is that it has emerged at the same time that many in those same Muslim publics have shown a growing interest in the shari'a. Analyzing data from Gallup World Poll surveys conducted between 2001 and 2007 in thirty-five Muslim-majority countries, John L. Esposito and Dalia Mogahed have noted that in most countries the majority of respondents "value a number of democratic principles" and "see no contradiction between democratic values and religious principles." More specifically, "along with indicating strong support for Islam and democracy, poll responses also reveal widespread support for *Sharia*" (Esposito and Mogahed 2007, 63, 35). The authors point out that the system of government most respondents have in mind is not theocratic: "The majority of those surveyed want religious leaders to have no direct role in crafting a constitution." Nonetheless, most "favor religious law as a source of legislation" (Esposito and Mogahed 2007, xiii). These and other studies confirm, then, that most modern Muslims "want neither a theocracy nor a secular democracy and would opt for a third model in which religious principles and democratic values coexist" (Esposito and Mogahed 2007, 35, 63; Hefner, forthcoming).

To observe that today's Muslim publics seem drawn to both the shari'a and democracy is not to suggest that public opinion is settled; nor is it to imply that accommodating the two aspirations in a workable constitutional framework is easy or even possible (cf. Abou El Fadl 2004; Ramadan 2009). The lessons offered by this volume suggest the challenge may be daunting indeed. The point that must be kept in mind, however, is that the Muslim public's preoccupation with these issues springs not from some unchanging or backward-looking civilizational impulse (cf. Huntington 1996), but from Muslims' engagement with the central political and ethical questions of our age. These questions center on "what human flourishing is: what constitutes a fulfilled life? What makes life really worth living?" (Taylor 2007, 16). What makes these questions thoroughly contemporary is that they are being posed in the context, not of neatly bounded social worlds with secure moral canopies, but of late modernity, with its trademark pluralization, social fragmentation, and heightened public debates over the common good (Casanova 1994; Salvatore and Eickelman 2004).

The adjustment of the shari'a to the modern realities of pluralism and change in gender roles, and to the widespread aspiration for public civility and participatory citizenship, is very much a work in progress, and its outcome will remain unclear for some years to come. As Tariq Ramadan (2009, 148) has recently emphasized in an important work, what is clear is that the future of Muslim politics and public ethics will hinge in part on the outcome of these efforts to bring popular understandings of the shari'a into alignment with other modern realities and other traditions of knowledge. A central aim of this book is to sift through the experience of eight important Muslim-majority countries to take the pulse of this ongoing and momentous transformation.

Mapping Shari'a Politics

It is against this backdrop, then, that the contributors to this volume came together for two meetings during 2008 to address the question of the dynamics of shari'a politics and ethics in the contemporary Muslim world. The meetings were part of a one-year project, "Shari'a Politics in Muslim-Majority Countries," sponsored by the Program on Islam and Society at the Institute on Culture, Religion, and World Affairs at Boston University. The project brought together eight leading scholars of Muslim politics, law, and society for two-day conferences in May and December. Between the meetings, each team member carried out research with the assistance of local partners in one of the eight target countries, conducting interviews, organizing focus groups, and gathering textual and media materials on the circumstances of Islamic law and society.

The case studies that have resulted from this collaboration share two general aims. First, they seek to map the politics and meanings of the shari'a in each country. In mapping the shari'a, the essays move from a simple description of the diversity of shari'a understandings to the question of how that diversity relates to broader social groupings, solidarities, and contentions. The countries included in the study are Saudi Arabia, Egypt, Iran, Turkey, Afghanistan, Pakistan, Nigeria, and Indonesia. Over the past generation, all of these countries have experienced a powerful resurgence in religious observance. In all but Turkey—which, as Hakan Yavuz's essay shows, is something of a special case when it comes to popular perceptions of the shari'a—the resurgence has been accompanied by heightened public interest in the shari'a, combined with fissiparous disagreement over just what God's law should mean today.

In carrying out this mapping, each author was asked to pay particular attention to four issues: 1) the primary currents of opinion and practice as regards the shari'a; 2) the main socio-political organizations associated with each current; 3) the relative influence of each current in the state; and 4) the way in which popular support for different currents varies according to class, gender, education, and Islamic sect, as well as in relation to political contentions in society as a whole.

If the researchers' first task looked back toward the genealogy of shari'a currents in society, their second task looked forward, to the implications of the plurality of views for politics and public ethics. More specifically, the researchers were asked to assess the implications of the main shari'a currents for four issues: democratization and citizen rights; gender relations; the place of non-Muslims and minority Muslim actors in society; and pluralist tolerance.

On Point: Shari'a and Democracy

The question of how democracy is viewed in light of the law illustrates some of the ways in which attitudes toward the shari'a interact with broader ethico-political concerns like these. Although opinion is fluid, one can broadly distinguish three viewpoints on democracy among contemporary Muslim thinkers, each grounded in a different understanding of the shari'a.

For Islamists of a radical disposition, like the influential Egyptian activist Sayyid Qutb (d. 1966; see Qutb 1953; Musallam 2005),[1] democracy and Islam are simply incompatible. The reason this is so is that democracy requires human legislation, and the very act of making law places human sovereignty above that of God, who alone is sovereign (a sovereignty referred to as *hakimiyya;* see Abou El Fadl 2004, 7; Carré 2003, 192–94; Moussalli 1992, 149–72). For strict-constructionist believers like these, there can be neither law nor legislation other than that revealed by God to humans by way of the Prophet Muhammad. To claim otherwise, and to suggest that humans can craft laws in light of the changed circumstances of the age, is to arrogate a legislative function which is God's alone (Musallam 2005).

Although many contemporary Muslim thinkers agree that some variety of shari'a should undergird Muslim politics, many take exception to the view that Islam is incompatible with democracy and legislation. Since the late nineteenth century, a long line of modernist and "neo-modernist" thinkers, including Muhammad Abduh of Egypt, Fazlur Rahman of Pakistan, and Nurcholish Madjid of Indonesia, have argued that the shari'a does not provide a fixed or all-encompassing model for politics.[2] In fact, these authors argue, God left the shari'a politically unspecific so that believers would engage in ijtihad (Ar., literally "effort," more generally, reinterpretation of the sources of the law to develop new rules) to make the general principles of God's law relevant for each age.

Scholars and activists in this tradition point out that the first generations of Muslims borrowed extensively from the Persian, Byzantine, and North African peoples they conquered, and the Prophet Muhammad enjoined Muslims to travel to the ends of the earth in search of knowledge. For much of the Islamic Middle Ages (1000–1500 CE), Muslim intellectuals also engaged with and refined the heritage of natural science and philosophy passed to them by the Greeks (Huff 2003, 53–63; Sabra 1987). In light of these precedents, and in keeping with their understandings of scripture, modernist thinkers see nothing un-Islamic about learning from other cultures. This includes adapting systems of democratic governance that happen to have been first implemented in modern times in the West.

Many modernists are quick to add that democracy for Muslims is subject to one critical ethical qualification. Even as they affirm that God has allowed humans to craft laws and construct democracy, these authors insist that the legislation that results from these activities must not contradict either of the two types of injunctions that, according to long-established scholarly understandings, lie at the heart of the shari'a. These are, first, the shari'a's "universal" rulings, rather few in number, on matters like murder, theft, fornication, inheritance, and (according to some jurists) apostasy. All of these rulings are mentioned directly in the Qur'an or in traditions of the Prophet, and, as a result, are thought to be absolutely certain and applicable for all time. The second type of provision democratic legislation must not contradict is anything related to the shari'a's goals or higher objectives (Ar. maqasid, sing. maqsad; see Auda 2008; Raysuni 2005; Weiss 1998, 54–58).

A concept implicit in Sunni Islam's Maliki school of law, the idea of the law's higher objectives has achieved far greater prominence in Islamic thought in modern times than in any previous period in Islamic history. As understood in classical scholarship, maqasid, or "higher objectives," referred to general benefits or ethically desirable circumstances that, on the basis of a holistic reading of scripture, jurists thought that God intends the shari'a to bring about (see Hallaq 1997, 180–95; Kamali 2008, 123–40; Ramadan 2009, 59–76; Raysuni 2005; Weiss 1998, 54–58). According to the celebrated jurist and theologian Abu Hamid al-Ghazali (d. 1111), the five primary aims of the law are the maintenance and protection of religion, self, property, progeny, and intellect (Hallaq

1997, 89–90; Masud 1995, 139–42). Although he believed that the *maqasid* are central features of God's law, al-Ghazali also felt that they should play only a limited role in the jurists' formulation of legal rulings. Scholars were to invoke the law's aims only where a textual injunction for the legal question at hand, or an established consensus (*ijma*) among scholars, was lacking. Some 250 years later, the Granada-born legal scholar Abu Ishaq al-Shatibi (d. 1388) developed an even more comprehensive methodology for identifying and implementing the law's higher objectives (see Masud 1995; Vikor 2005, 232, 234; Weiss 1998, 87) From the mid-twentieth century onward, al-Shatibi's scholarship played a central role in boldly comprehensive efforts to reformulate Islamic law in light of contemporary realities (see Masud 1995; Ramadan 2009, 65–70). In the classical and early modern period, however, most jurists hesitated to invoke the law's higher aims to justify their rulings. Some feared that such attempts arrogated legislative authority that was God's alone. Like critics of *maqasid*-based reasoning today, others regarded such holistic reasoning as arrogantly subjective, implying as it did a scholar's right and ability to go beyond the letter of the law.

Rather than engaging in a comprehensive meditation on God's injunctions, classical theorists, as well as many tradition-minded scholars today, preferred to limit the grounds for legal rulings to cases or rules mentioned directly in either of Islam's two scriptural sources: the Qur'an and the canonical words and deeds of the Prophet (known collectively as the Sunna [traditions] of the Prophet) as recorded in authenticated accounts known as hadith (see Kamali 2009, 1–10, and below). Where explicit rules or cases were still lacking, jurists were enjoined to reason from what they identified as an "effective cause" (Ar. *'illa*) of an already-certain rule (Hallaq 1997, 83–84; cf. Ramadan 2009, 59–60). This is to say, a jurist would resolve a legal question raised by some new case by identifying an element or feature of that case that appeared substantively equivalent to an "original" case already treated in revealed sources. In Islamic jurisprudence, this method of identifying a new case with one already known, so as to subsume it under a known ruling, is referred to as *qiyas* (often translated as "analogic reasoning," but see Hallaq 1989). In Sunni Islam, this form of juristic reasoning is regarded as one of the four main sources of the law, in addition to the Qur'an, the Sunna of the Prophet, and the consensus (*ijma*) among scholars (Hallaq 1997, 84–95; Vikor 2005, 58–65).

Most classical jurists, then, were reluctant to stray from scripturalist sources and speculate on God's deeper aims with regard to the law. On the basis of what historians and ethnographers have taught us about the legal deliberations of real-world judges (see below), in practice most seem to have been more flexible and contextual in their rulings. However, as Frank Vogel has observed, to this day tradition-minded scholars have preferred "literalism over moral substance" in their writings, as well as judgments based on preexisting rules and cases rather than some "supervening system" of higher objectives (Vogel 2000, 53; cf. Hallaq 1997, 83–104; also Lombardi 2006, 30). Notwithstanding this preference, in the modern era methodologies based on the goals of the shari'a have become a central feature of reformist legal thought. The reason this is so is that modern scholars have determined that the most effective way to establish the law's continuing relevance for ethical and political problems is, not by "piecemeal examination of . . . effective causes ('illa)" (Ramadan 2009, 60), but through a comprehensive reading aimed at determining the principles and coherence of the divine legal corpus as a whole.

It is, in any case, on grounds like these that modernist political thinkers have defended their conclusion that democracy is compatible with Islam. Democracy may not be explicitly mentioned in the Qur'an or the traditions of the Prophet. However, its scholarly proponents argue, if conducted properly it can serve the higher objectives of God's law, bringing benefit to religion, self, property, progeny, and intellect. But modernist proponents of the law's aims also emphasize that democracy must not lead to a moral free-for-all. The shari'a imposes limits on what democratic legislation may enjoin. In particular, governments cannot create legislation that runs afoul of the shari'a's universal rules or higher objectives.

There is a third ideal-typical position concerning the shari'a and democracy, one associated with what one might call "Muslim secularists" or, more neutrally, democratic pluralists (even though not all of the position's proponents would be pleased with either label). For the purposes of the present discussion, the terms "Muslim secularist" and "democratic pluralist" refer to persons who—unlike, say, an agnostic or atheist—maintain an explicit commitment to God's commands, but also believe that under modern circumstances these can best be fulfilled only if two supplementary conditions are met. The first is that government must be organized on the basis of, not the privatization of religion, but some degree of separation of religious authorities from the state (see An-Na'im 2008). The purpose of this separation is to insure that there is no state-enforced monopoly on religious conviction, and that the implementation of God's commands is not subject to abuse at the hands of state officials. The Iranian activist-turned-reformist Abdolkarim Soroush justifies the idea of a separation of powers in the following way: "The modern world has also undermined a right that has always been a source of evil and corruption . . . that is, the right to act as a God-like potentate with unlimited powers" (Soroush 2000, 64). Muslim pluralists like Soroush or Abdullahi Ahmed An-Na'im (2008) see the interweaving of religious and state authority advocated by radical Islamist authors as a threat, not just to good government, but to Islam itself.[3]

The second condition that Muslim secularists and pluralists argue must be met to fulfill God's commands under modern circumstances touches on the substance of shari'a rules. Like Muslim modernists, most (but not all; see An-Na'im 2008, 35) Muslim secularists and pluralists subscribe to the idea that modern legislation should not contradict the shari'a's universal rules or higher objectives (*maqasid*). However, secularists and pluralists tend to think of both of these normative stipulations as far less specific than do modernist or traditionalist scholars. Thus, for example, many argue that God never intended that the hudud punishments—the stoning of adulterers, the maiming of thieves, and the like—should be unchangingly applicable for all time. What God intended to be eternal is not the punishment, but the spirit of the rule, the heightened moral concern the rule inspires with regard to problems like theft or adultery. Similarly, with regard to the aims of the shari'a, Muslim pluralists and secularists tend to conceptualize these at a much higher level of generality than do traditionalist or modernist scholars. Thus, the aims of the law often include such liberal-sounding values as social justice, freedom, and equality, including gender equality (cf. Abou El Fadl 2001, 2004).

Shari'a as a Tradition of Knowledge Embedded in Forms of Life

The juxtaposition of these three perspectives on democracy highlights a creative tension long at the heart of shari'a knowledge and politics. The tension has to do with the fact that, although the shari'a is one of the world's most enduring "traditions of knowledge" (Barth 1993; cf. MacIntyre 1988, 12), the tradition's reproduction over time has always depended on its being embedded in highly particular "forms of life" (Asad 2003, 17). Inevitably, these forms of life are animated by knowledge, norms, and passions more varied than those of the shari'a alone. Moreover, rather than remaining a remote background to the law, these contextual influences color and cue actors' engagement with its meanings (cf. Ramadan 2009, 101–12).

To put the matter differently, the very moral authority of the idea of the shari'a in Muslim civilization guarantees that actors seeking public recognition will orient and legitimate their actions with reference to some representation of God's commands. Shari'a "referencing" of this sort has been a distinctive feature of Muslim politics and ethics from earliest times (Eickelman and Piscatori 1996, 7). By appealing to the shari'a in this manner, social actors help to reproduce the law's centrality in Muslim politics and discourse. This in turn may create the impression that the law's meanings are timeless and unchanging. But the paradox of the shari'a as a form of applied ethical knowledge is that, by drawing the law so deeply into their own lives, actors exert a perspectival pressure that constantly shifts and repositions the law's understanding. Equally significant, as the law moves out from textual scholarship and becomes an object of contention and "public reasoning" (Bowen 2003, 9; Taylor 2007, 185–96), much of the detail of the law's scholarly formulation is lost to lay actors. The latter's decision to subscribe to one understanding of the law as opposed to another may have as much to do with questions of social allegiance or faction, then, as with reasoned adherence to religious rules. In an important study, the anthropologist Gregory Starrett has coined the term "functionalization" to refer to instrumentalizations of this sort. By functionalization he refers to the way in which elements of a discourse like the shari'a "come to serve the strategic or utilitarian ends of another discourse" (Starrett 1998, 9). This functionalization inevitably changes the discourse's horizons and meanings, by linking its aims to those of other actors, projects, and ethical discourses.

Along with and beyond the interpretive labors of religious scholars, then, the functionalization of the law in Muslim society defines and redefines the law's meanings and relevance. Indeed, the diverse ways in which the law is embedded and instrumentalized ensure that the shari'a is far more porous in its public meanings than is scholarly discourse, which is already marked by great internal diversity (Wael Hallaq's "*ijtihadic* plurality" [2009a, 449]). The embedding and functionalization of the law continue today, and the processes raise questions as to in what sense the shari'a is "meaningful" at all. After all, how can we say the shari'a has meaning when it is invoked to justify contradictory viewpoints on the state, gender relations, and other issues?

To answer this question requires a deeper look into the development of the shari'a from earliest times to today. The history provides clues to just how the shari'a's embedding in diverse forms of life has allowed its meanings to change, even while, to borrow a phrase from the philosopher Alasdair MacIntyre (speaking of the concept of tradition generally), the law has facilitated "an argument extended through time in which certain fundamental agreements are defined and redefined" (MacIntyre 1988, 12).

From Divine Revelation to Practiced Rule

The word *shari'a* is commonly translated as "Islamic law," but the shari'a is at once greater and less specific than Western understandings of positive law imply. "The Shari'a may indeed be said to *contain* law, but one must also recognize that it embraces elements and aspects that are not, strictly speaking, law" (Weiss 1992, 1). As the anthropologist Brinkley Messick has observed, the shari'a is a "total discourse," one in which "all kinds of institutions find simultaneous expression: religious, legal, moral and economic" (Messick 1993, 3). In this regard the shari'a resembles Jewish law (*halakah*) more than it does early Christian or later canon law (see Johnson 2008, 57); it offers prescriptions on everything from prayer, diet, and dress to commerce, taxation, and warfare.

Rather than positive law, then, the shari'a is best understood as God's commanding guidance for an Islamic way of life (cf. Kamali 2008, 2–7; Ramadan 2009, 2).[4]

Establishing just what that guidance entails, of course, has never been a simple matter. The term *shari'a* appears only once in the Qur'an, where God states, "We have set you on a shari'a of command, so follow it" (Qur. 45:18). Other Qur'anic passages, however, convey an equally vivid ethico-legal spirit even without mentioning the term. In 5:48, God commands, "Judge in accordance with what God has revealed" and "We have revealed unto you the Book with the truth, confirming whatever Scripture was before it . . . we have made for each of you a law and a normative way to follow." Building on verses like these, Muslim scholars from the early period concluded that the shari'a lies at the heart of God's revelation and that it is, in some sense, all-encompassing. The methods for transforming this general ideal into practicable law, however, had yet to be devised. Indeed, it took scholars of the law (Ar. *fuqaha*, sing. *faqih*) the better part of three centuries to formulate what eventually became the classical methodology for establishing God's laws.

Centering the Tradition

The law-establishing effort passed through several phases. The first step was to delimit the divine sources. The foundational source for the shari'a is, of course, the Qur'an: God's words as revealed to the Prophet Muhammad by way of the angel Jibriel (Gabriel), a revelation that was sealed with the death of the Prophet in 632 CE. During the Prophet's lifetime, the Qur'an's various verses were never put together as a single book. A full recension was completed only after the death of the Prophet, at the initiative of the first two caliphs, Umar (r. 634–44) and Uthman (r. 644–56; see Bulliet 1994, 29; Gilliot 2006).

After establishing a canonical text, the next step was to identify and interpret the legal content of the Qur'an. This too was no simple matter. Of the Qur'an's 6,235 verses, only about 350 (or, by other counts, 500) contain discussions of direct legal relevance (Kamali 2008, 18; Hallaq 1997, 12). Even these verses "cover a relatively limited number of legal issues and, furthermore, treat of them selectively" (Hallaq 1997, 10). Of the verses with potential legal content, the greatest number (140) deal with devotional issues like ritual prayer, religious alms, fasting, and charity (Kamali 2008, 18; cf. Vikor 2005, 32–34). The second and third most common subjects are marriage and trade, each the focus of an additional seventy verses. Crime and punishment earn just thirty verses, and only five of the infractions mentioned have a punishment prescribed. These are the so-called hudud crimes: theft, highway robbery, drunkenness, fornication, and false witness with regard to fornication (Kamali 2008, 190–94; Vikor

2005, 37). Because they are mentioned directly in the Qur'an, these offenses have come to be seen as "crimes against God," and, as such, matters with which jurists are loath to tamper. Nonetheless, the general principle remains: Although the Qur'an is the "principal source of *Shari'ah*," the text as a whole contains few explicit rules, showing that "the larger part of Qur'anic legislation consists of broad and comprehensive principles" (Kamali 2008, 20).

The Qur'an, however, is not the only source of revelation. In Islamic tradition, the Prophet Muhammad is regarded as having exemplified Qur'anic ideals in a perfect manner; this simple idea is still of profound importance for Muslim thinkers today (see, e.g., Ramadan 2007). In light of the Prophet's central role in God's plan, his words and deeds came to be recognized as a second source of revelation, albeit one whose borders are less clearly delimited than the Qur'an and one that does "not command the same spiritual ranking as the text of the Qur'an" (Kamali 2009, 61). The task of gathering and verifying canonical accounts of the words and deeds of the Prophet, as expressed in hadith, took the better part of two centuries (Kamali 2009, 22–45). Today there are tens of thousands of hadith; in the early centuries of the Muslim era there were several hundred thousand more, some regarded as authoritative, others less certain. In this regard, "there was never any unified Muslim 'Talmud' which encompasses all authoritative hadith" (Vikor 2005, 43). Nonetheless, by the ninth century great collections had been compiled, and over the next two centuries dozens of these were published (Burton 1994, 119; Kamali 2009, 31–45). By the thirteenth century, Sunni Muslims recognized six canonical collections; Shi'as developed a compilation of their own (Bulliet 1994, 19; Makdisi 1981, 2–4). In addition to the established collections, others also circulated, some containing traditions of less certain authority.

As the hadith narratives were collected and authenticated, legal scholars increasingly grounded their rulings on these Prophetic traditions, in addition to passages from the Qur'an. If the products of this labor were to be consistent, however, the scholars needed a methodology for deriving rulings (Ar. *hukm*) from these two scriptural sources. Legal scholars began the difficult task of crafting this methodology during the late first and second centuries of the Muslim era, more or less in tandem with the collecting of authoritative hadith. The details of the methodology owed much to the efforts of one of the most celebrated classical scholars of the law, Muhammad b. Idris al-Shafi'i (d. 820). It was al-Shafi'i and his followers who moved hadith scholarship to the center of Muslim jurisprudence, alongside the Qur'an (see Hallaq 1993; Kamali 2008, 77–83). The effects of this methodological consolidation have reverberated in Muslim legal thought to this day.

The establishment of hadith collections and their identification as a second scriptural source had two far-reaching implications for law and authority in Islamic society. First, by comparison with the Qur'an, the hadith offered a voluminous body of legally relevant materials. The hadith collections thus facilitated a great expansion in the scope and detail of the rules derived from God's law.

The positioning of authoritative hadith at the center of the shari'a and the shari'a at the center of Islam had a second effect, related to the speed and breadth of the conquests during the first century of the Muslim era (the seventh century CE). The scale of the expansion meant that, by the middle of the eighth century, the community of Muslims extended from Spain to northern India (Kennedy 2002, 8). Yet it is estimated that, by the end of the Umayyad empire (750 CE), less than 10 percent of the non-Arab population had converted to Islam (Bulliet 1994, 40). An accelerated process of "bandwagon" conversion began shortly thereafter, however, around 790 CE in Iran and a half century later in Iraq, Syria, and Egypt (Bulliet 1994, 43). The empire's vast expanse and rapid growth meant that during these first two centuries "a dispersed and uninstitutionalized local religious authority grew up outside of caliphal jurisdiction or control" (Bulliet 1994, 36). This centrifugal dispersion threatened to replace the singularity of Islam's prophetic message with localized babble.

Studies of other so-called world religions have demonstrated that one of the greatest challenges they face as they expand geographically and demographically is how to maintain a constancy of vision as they draw in growing numbers of people from diverse cultures and territories (Fowden 1993; Hefner 1993). For eighth-century Muslims, the task of maintaining cohesion in the new multi-cultural macrocosm was complicated by two facts: the Islamic empire was one of the largest the Old World had ever seen, and Islam lacked the centralized ecclesiastical hierarchy developed by Western Christianity to stabilize its cultural message over time and space. Indeed, there was a moment in the second century of the Muslim era when it looked as if the Islamic legal community was about to splinter into a variety of localized traditions. By some estimates, there were five hundred schools of law, and many of these were prepared to make great concessions to local customs (Makdisi 1981, 2; Vikor 2005, 23). Had this process of legal regionalization continued, the result might well have been the appearance of "local Islams," each with its own ethical and legal vision (cf. Vikor 2005, 23–26; Hallaq 1997, 16–35). However, the recension of the Qur'an, the collecting of canonical hadith, and the development of a shared legal methodology all served to move the shari'a to the center of the scholarly tradition, and a relatively standardized jurisprudence (fiqh) to the center of what literate Muslims regarded as "Islam." "The development of a homogeneous corpus of authoritative Islamic texts . . . contributed greatly to a growing uniformity of Islamic belief and practice throughout the vast area in which Muslims lived" (Bulliet 1994, 21). The formula so central to Islam's civilizational vitality, that Islam is a religion of divine law and that the scholars of the law are first among its custodians, was gradually being put in place.

Elite Power and Legal Professionalization

Three other developments reinforced this centering of the Islamic ethical tradition on scripture, the law, and religious scholars. First, in 750 CE the Abbasid rulers completed their campaign to overthrow the Umayyad kings; having done so, they moved quickly to create a more efficient and unified state administration (Lapidus 2002, 56–64; Zaman 1997). The Abbasid rulers took care to lavish resources on Islam's legal scholars and, in so doing, buttress ongoing efforts to systematize legal methodologies. As Vikor has observed, with the Abbasid rise to power, "the time had come to consolidate the conquered domains into one community"; the standardization of the law through hadith-centered methodologies was "but a natural corollary of the integration of the provinces into one empire" (Vikor 2005, 30; cf. Bulliet 1994, 21).

The second development facilitating the elevation of the law and the professionalization of legal scholarship was the emergence of the madrasa, a religious college or boarding school dedicated to the intermediate and advanced study of the Islamic sciences, particularly those related to the law (Arjomand 1999; Berkey 1992; Grandin and Gaborieau 1997; Makdisi 1981). The first madrasa had been established in the tenth century in the Khurasan district of eastern Iran. Over the next century, however, the institution spread westward through Mesopotamia into Syria. It arrived in Egypt and North Africa in the twelfth century, and in Spain and northern India in the early thirteenth (Bulliet 1994, 148–49; Hefner 2007). Educating doctors, government officials, mathematicians, and astronomers as well as jurists, the madrasa became "perhaps the most characteristic religious institution of the medieval Near Eastern urban landscape" (Berkey 2003, 187).

The madrasa's institutional significance went well beyond its role in the training of elites. The spread of the madrasa accelerated the great "recentering and homogenization" of Islamic learning and authority taking place across the central Muslim lands (Berkey 2003, 189; cf. Chamberlain 1994; Bulliet 1994). In other words, the madrasa's spread was the institutional counterpart to the intellectual changes taking place in hadith scholarship and jurisprudence (fiqh) just prior to this time. The confluence of events elevated fiqh to the status of the queen of the religious sciences, accelerated the development of a fiqh-centered canon to train religious scholars, and, in principle if not always practice, ensured the recognition of legal scholars as first among Islam's religious elites (cf. Makdisi 1981, 8–9).

Together these developments ensured the centrality of God's law in Islam's civilizational imaginary. Along the way, Islamic law was transformed from a disparate variety of regional legal traditions into the large schools or guilds of law known as the *madhahib* (see Hallaq 2005, 150–77). The end result of these developments was the consolidation of the legal canon and educational complex that were to remain at the heart of Muslim politics and society until the tumultuous transformations of the modern era.

God's Law and Human Politics

Although religious scholars regularly affirmed that God's law is all-encompassing, as the corpus of classical jurisprudence took shape it began to show a distinctly uneven coverage: it was richly detailed with regard to some topics while generalized or underdeveloped with regard to others. This is of course a characteristic of law in all civilizations, for the simple reason that legal scholars devote more attention to some matters than others, as a result of the forms of life through which the law is articulated and the "concerns" to which these give rise (Glenn 2000, cf. Barth 1993). What is striking about classical Islamic law, however, is that it had a great deal to say about worship, marriage, and commerce and considerably less to say about the state and governance.

The Law in Early Polities

The relative lack of attention to questions of government is not surprising if one recalls that the hadith collections and classical jurisprudence began to take shape during the period of bandwagon conversion in the late eighth and ninth centuries CE. The hadith and the new legal scholarship both seem to have been primarily oriented toward, not setting the ship of state on a straight course, but providing the fast-growing community of believers with basic guidance on how to be Muslim (Berkey 2003; Bulliet 1994). The law's circumspectness on politics strikes us as surprising today not because of the circumstances of the early Muslim community, then, but because many of the founders of modern Islamism, like Sayyid Qutb and Sayyid Abul A'la Mawdudi, claim that Islam provides a comprehensive and specific guide to state organization. They also claim that Islam does not allow a separation of religion and state, because both must come under the commanding control of the shari'a (see Euben and Zaman 2009; Moussalli 1992, 149–72; Nasr 1996, 80–106).

On matters of state, however, it is clear that the shari'a offers a general ethical "spirit" more than it does a detailed blueprint for government organization (see Kamali 2008). The reasons for this lack of specification have to do with two things: the law's intrinsic intellectual emphases and extrinsic or contextual influences on its elaboration.

The strongest intrinsic constraint on the law's political-mindedness is, again, that the Qur'an itself offers few details on state organization. The same is true of the hadith collections. For example, one of the most widely used collections, Al-Bukhari's, contains some 7077 hadith, of which the "overwhelming" majority are devoted to "topics that were meaningful for individual Muslims in their daily lives": ritual worship (2000 hadith), marriage and divorce (286), food and drink (252), clothing (178), and medical matters (129), among others. "A meager thirty hadith touch on criminal matters (hudud), and another eighty on issues of governance (ahkam), all contained in the final portion of the collection after the topics mentioned above" (Bulliet 1994, 32).

Although the law's lack of elaboration with regard to politics owes much to the intrinsic constraints of legal methodologies, the embedding of the law in extrinsic forms of social life played a role as well. Most of the great works of classical fiqh were composed during the early to middle years of the Abbasid empire (750–1258 CE). The empire's founders had taken up arms against their Umayyad predecessors, rallying support by inveighing against the impiety of Umayyad kings (Zaman 1997). Once in power, the Abbasids took pains to demonstrate their piety by, among other things, lavishing gifts on the emerging class of professional jurists. But this generosity did not mean that the Abbasids surrendered responsibility for political matters to Islam's legal scholars. Indeed, on matters of state administration, the Abbasids drew heavily on Persian models of governance, which were more systematic, bureaucratized, and imperial-minded than the tribally inflected system the Arabs had brought to Syria and Persia a century earlier (Black 2001, 49–55; Crone 2004, 148–64).

The Abbasids' overwhelming power and their penchant for borrowing Persian forms of governance had an additional damping effect on jurists' predilection for political rule-making. Faced with powerful rulers and legal methodologies that encouraged exegetical restraint, scholars of the law focused their rulings on well-established and largely non-political topics. The resulting arrangement was of great significance for the law's subsequent development: in effect, the scholars surrendered responsibility for most of the detail of day-to-day government to state authorities. As the sociologist Sami Zubaida has observed, this tacit division of legal and political labor meant that "the shariah developed historically to rule mostly on the private affairs of the community, dealing with commercial and property transactions and family matters, as well as ritual performances. The public law provisions of the shari'a have remained largely theoretical" (Zubaida 2003, 2).[5]

One important consequence of this tacit division of legal labor was that Abbasid rulers did not hesitate to issue edicts dealing with matters on which the shari'a was silent, unspecific, or, as in criminal law, too cumbersome in its evidentiary requirements to allow for effective enforcement. Specialists of Islamic law today talk about this legal bifurcation by distinguishing the shari'a and its associated rulings (*hukm*) from rulers' edicts and statute law, which came to be known in the Ottoman period (late fifteenth century on) as *qanun* (Berkey 2003, 21; Gerber 1999; Imber 2002; Zubaida 2003, 11). *Qanun*-like law played a central role in most of the great Muslim polities of the Middle Ages and the early modern period. In principle, the ruler's edicts were supposed to be inspired by and consistent with shari'a principles. This consistency was in accordance with the doctrine of *siyasa shar'iyya*—governance in accordance with the shari'a, in matters for which there was no direct and established regulation in the shari'a itself (Kamali 2008, 7–8; Vogel 2000, 694; Vogel, this volume). Nonetheless, until the ascent of the Ottoman Empire in the sixteenth century, the ruler's statutes remained separate both in method and in substance from the shari'a, and the institutional procedures for evaluating whether they were consistent with the shari'a remained unspecific, to say the least.

Shari'a Hegemony and Pluralist Reality

The result of this arrangement was that, even while acknowledging the supremacy of the shari'a, Muslim rulers *did* make law, and in certain periods they did so through institutional mechanisms free of any direct supervision by scholars of the law. Much of the day-to-day business of trying criminals, regulating commerce, raising taxes, and conducting military campaigns was left to legislation not directly elaborated in the shari'a or its associated jurisprudence—even if, again, all parties agreed that the sultan's actions were in accord with the spirit of the shari'a, as specified by *siyasa shar'iyya*. In practice, the degree to which religious scholars influenced state legislation varied, in a manner that reflected the changing balance of power and collaboration between the state and the scholarly elite (Vikor 2005, 189–93).

Contrary to the claims of certain radical commentators today, then, from the classical period on the shari'a was not the only law in Muslim societies; all were characterized by significant legal pluralism. Although rulers encouraged the development of Islamic courts under the jurisdiction of Islamic judges (*qadis*), many also developed a system of *mazalim* tribunals in which rulers and their aides issued judgments on all manner of issues (Berkey 2003, 23; Vikor 2005, 189; Zubaida 2003, 51–52). Although some of these tribunals were advised by Muslim jurists, others were not. On criminal matters, in particular, many rulers felt that it was unrealistic to follow the strict procedures of evidence required to secure conviction in Islamic courts. The shariʻa's provisions carried such a heavy burden of proof that they made conviction for most crimes extremely difficult. Instead of the shariʻa, then, rulers' courts applied more flexible standards of evidence and prosecution: "We may say that its [the *mazalim's*] standards of justice were ad hoc and 'common sense' based on common ethics and customary standards" (Zubaida 2003, 52; cf. Vikor 2005, 192).

None of this is to say that there was a "separation of mosque and state," comparable to the so-called separation of church and state authority in Christian Europe (a characterization of religion and politics in Europe which is woefully simplistic; see Martin 1978; McLeod 2003). To whatever degree they operated independently of state control (and this varied in classical Muslim societies, and declined dramatically under the Ottomans), the judges who officiated in Islamic courts subscribed to the idea that their authority and rulings were ultimately based on the shariʻa. Equally important, both popular and scholarly opinion in Muslim lands affirmed that the ruler was obliged to "command right and forbid wrong" (Cook 2000)— even if scholars, rulers, and the lay public had different understandings of just what the norms applicable to this responsibility were. There was no high wall, then, separating state officials from scholars of the law; on the contrary, there were extensive collaborations across the state-society divide. Nonetheless, when it came to issuing regulations and applying the law, there was in practice a very real division of legal labors (Lapidus 1996). The separation preserved the ideological centrality of the shariʻa, while providing Ottoman, Mughal, and Safavid rulers with the flexibility they required for effective governance.

In modern times, the question of whether this legal pluralism was the result of the freezing or "stagnation" of Islamic jurisprudence has been a subject of debate among historians of Islamic law. Joseph Schacht (d. 1969; see Schacht 1964), one of the most influential Western scholars of the law in the mid-twentieth century, argued that after the development of Islam's schools of law (*madhahib*) in the Middle Ages the law became inflexibly conservative. Indeed, Schacht argued, the scholars' jurisprudence became so scholastically self-regarding that, rather than regulating actual legal practice, its main aim was to reference other scholarly texts (Schacht 1950). Still needing a legal system to deal with everyday affairs, rulers paid lip service to the shariʻa while leaving the heavy lifting of law-making and enforcement to non-shariʻa agencies.

More recent literature on the development of Islamic law casts doubt on Schacht's stagnation thesis. Modern historians have shown that, in both legal theory and practice, scholars of the law continued to develop their craft—albeit in a way that did not directly challenge what earlier scholars had come to view as established legal methodologies or laws (Johansen 1999). Scholars and judges allowed themselves to operate "outside the letter of the law," and this deviation from the rule was an "an accepted adaptation of the Shariʿa" (Vikor 2005, 16). This conclusion is consistent with the recent findings of anthropologists and social historians with regard to the operation of Islamic courts. They have shown that, even where drawing on traditional textual sources, judges often apply the law in a flexible and creative manner, drawing in part on local cultural understandings, including, it seems, those informing local notions of gender (see Bowen 2003; Peletz 2002; Tucker 1998).

Although, *pace* Schacht, practitioners of the law learned to apply it in an evolving and flexible manner, the fact that much of this adaptation took place "outside the letter of the law" was nonetheless consequential for the later politics of the law, especially in the nineteenth and twentieth centuries. Put simply, that kept outside the letter of the law is lost to later generations who learn the law by letter alone. In modern times, the ideal of the law to which its less lettered proponents rally shows little familiarity with the flexibility and pluralism of legal practice in Muslim history. One irony of recent efforts to restore the shariʿa, then, is that the legal imaginary to which its less scholarly proponents rally shows the imprint, not of a thousand years of Islamic legal practice, but of Western positive law and its partner in governance, the high modernist state.

God's Law and the Modern State

During the colonial and early postcolonial periods, the scope of the shariʿa in Muslim lands was progressively restricted, until its jurisdiction was limited in most countries to family law and conventional religious affairs like the pilgrimage and pious endowments (*awqaf*). European colonial governments found that the scope of Islamic law got in the way of their own imperial ambitions. Although the British in India, Nigeria, and Malaya eventually developed a synthesis of English and "Mohammadan" law (see Zaman, this volume; Lubeck, this volume; Hallaq 2009a, 377–88; Zaman 2002, 23), they and other colonial rulers sealed off the law from the broader avenues of social life.

The circumscription of Islamic law continued even after the emergence of Muslim-based movements for national restoration. During the early and middle decades of the twentieth century, nationalism, not Islamism, was the dominant political force in Muslim-majority countries, and many secular-minded nationalists wished to do away with the cumbersome plurality of legal systems once and for all (C. Brown 2000, 119; Esposito 2000). Upon assuming power in Turkey in 1924, Mustafa Kemal, the architect of modern Turkey, abolished the shariʿa courts. In 1926, his government replaced a codified variant of Islamic law known as the Mecelle, first developed in the 1870s (and implemented in

1877), with a secular legal system modeled on Belgian and Swiss law (Yavuz, this volume; Vikor 2005, 230–31). In Egypt in 1883, one year after the British occupation of the country, the shari'a courts were stripped of authority in criminal matters, which were now to be handled in state courts applying laws modeled on the French legal code (Vikor 2005, 239). In 1956, reforms initiated under Egypt's socialist and nationalist president, Gamel Abdul Nassir, took the state-imposed secularization further, doing away with most of the country's Islamic legal edifice (N. Brown 1997, 85; Lombardi 2006, 110–16; Brown, this volume).

The individual essays in this volume review the changes in the status of the shari'a in other Muslim lands over the course of the twentieth century. Although each country has a different story to tell, several trends stand out. First, with the notable exception of Saudi Arabia (see also Vogel 2000), the shari'a ceased to be primarily identified with a community of scholars, trained in autonomous educational institutions, and adjudicating disputes in accordance with their understanding of the law. Modern Muslims came to conceptualize law—religious and secular—not as a decentered and dynamic process whereby scholars enunciate shari'a-based rulings, but as a standardized code to be enforced by the state.

As Sami Zubaida (2003, 135; cf. Layish 2004; Peters 2002) has suggested, this étatized and codified understanding of law represented a "triumph of European models" over and against Islam's classical tradition. One might add that the model was not just European, but *continental* European at that. The common-law tradition applied in the United Kingdom and in some domains of American law operates on the basis of casuistic reasoning and legal precedent, not a centrally established legal code (see Glenn 2000, 210–48). Codification ripped the law from its roots in religious schools and the general forms of life in which it had once been embedded. The change impacted legal practice as well. As Clark Lombardi (2006, 64) has observed, "the judges who applied the code would simply apply the rule as written, and would not need to have any knowledge of how the law had been derived. Thus, moving to a system of codified law meant that people without classical legal training could serve as judges."

A second point follows closely from this first. This new understanding of law was also a triumph of modern notions of governance. In its classical form Islamic law was not the exclusive preserve of the state. It was instead "placed *between* state and civil society" (Vikor 2005, 254), and, in particular, between the ruler and legal scholars. Certainly, as Yavuz makes clear in his essay, during Ottoman times the jurists' autonomy was substantially compromised, as a result of the sultan's assertion of state authority over Islamic judges (*qadis*) and over the system of madrasas that trained them (see Gerber 1999, 58–76;

Imber 1997). But the codification and étatization effected by modern states shifted the balance of legal authority even more decisively to the state and rulers. In so doing, shariʿa politics—the processes involved in determining the place and authority of the shariʿa in society—was drawn ever more tightly into the interests, alliances, and contentions that everywhere surround state power. The shift in social location would guarantee that, in the late twentieth century, efforts to implement Islamic law would be functionalized for ends more varied than the law itself, including those related to struggles for control of the state.

The consequences of étatization need not be dire. Indeed, where the state operates on the basis of constitutionalism and procedural transparency, and where the letter of the law is read in light of the law's higher aims (*maqasid*) and public welfare, the prospects for an elevated repositioning of the law increase greatly (see Lombardi 2006; cf. Ramadan 2009, 82). However, where state politics shows the imprint of communal violence (see Lubeck, this volume), military dirigism (see Zaman, this volume), or the fractious dissolution of once-powerful elites (Hefner, this volume), the shariʿa may be functionalized for uncivil ends, including those concerned with the assertion of class, communal, and sectarian interests over the public good.

A third trend in the law and public religion in twentieth-century Muslim societies presents a qualified countercurrent to the étatist turn. In premodern times, scholarly learning was the preserve of a tiny proportion of the population. In most countries, only 2 percent of the adult public was literate (Findley 1989), and of these, an even tinier fraction had the aptitudes required to engage the details of the law. Ordinary Muslims were drawn into the direct experience of their religion primarily through daily prayer; state, calendrical, and life-cycle rituals; and the Sufi orders which provided a bridge between the ruler and the folk (see, e.g., Berkey 2003; Sanders 1994; Shoshan 1993, 67–78). For unlettered Muslims, then, the meaning of the law lay less in its technical detail than in the general idea that Islam is a religion of the divine "way" and commandment. As with the Afghan villagers Thomas Barfield describes in his essay in this volume, for many ordinary Muslims the law's meaning was determined, not by scholarly discourse, but by the pronouncements of local authorities who happened to be Muslim.

With the notable exception of agrarian societies like Afghanistan or Pakistan's northwest frontier (see Zaman, this volume), however, the programs of mass education that swept much of the Muslim world in the latter half of the twentieth century brought about a great transformation in popular engagement with the law. Religion increasingly came to be seen as, not the intellectual property of a few scholarly virtuosos, but divine guidance whose study and enactment are incumbent on all. As the essays in this volume make clear, mass education, urbanization, and, from the 1960s on, a vast expansion in Islamic predication strengthened the public appetite for a more popularized and participatory profession of the faith (cf. Eickelman 1992; Eickelman and Piscatori 1996).

The growth of mass piety followed a culture-bound learning curve. As more Muslims explored the tenets of their faith, many discovered that Islam is a religion of divine law, and the law encompasses myriad legal rulings. Popular religious culture took on a shari'a-mindedness deeper than it had ever been in modern Muslim history. However, although the concern with the shari'a became more widespread, its understanding and practice remained diverse. Indeed, with the pluralization of religious authority, discussions of the law's meanings became more fissiparous than ever. Among the legal issues that proved most contentious were three having to do with categories of actors accorded an off-center status in classical shari'a commentaries: women, non-Muslims, and Muslims who hold to non-established understandings of the faith.

Women, Non-Muslims, and Non-conformists

Although they offered few details on how the state should be organized, jurists in the classical era provided extensive commentaries on women, non-Muslims, and Muslim non-conformists. The status of women in Islamic jurisprudence was dealt with primarily through family law, touching on matters of marriage, divorce, property, and inheritance. In all of these fields, women were accorded far broader rights than they are thought to have enjoyed in pre-Islamic Arabia (Ahmed 1992, 9–25). Indeed, Muslim women were accorded greater rights than were their counterparts in medieval Europe. Although they were barred from studying in madrasas (and thus from the legal profession), some women used private study to achieve status as respected religious scholars (Berkey 1992, 161–71). Although women did not play a central role in mosque services or religious education, they did sponsor the establishment of religious schools. Adult women could also own property, register the purchase and sale of their properties in courts, and set up pious endowments (waqfs) to support schools, baths, and other institutions of public benefit. By the eighteenth century, women in Middle Eastern Muslim lands "constituted between 30 and 50 percent of waqf founders" (Hallaq 2009b, 69).

Notwithstanding these social achievements, on several matters classical interpretations of the shari'a assigned women a significantly different set of rights than Muslim men. In modern times, these legal interpretations have provided conservative Islamist scholars with a "letter-of-the-law" precedent with which to justify the claim that Islam does not allow women to play a prominent role in public life. Thus, for example, in principle women's testimony in courts counted as just half that of men. A girl's inherited share of her parents' properties was one-half her brother's. A woman's right to initiate divorce was also severely restricted compared to her husband's—although, here again, the practice of premodern courts actually provided greater opportunities than are allowed today under conservative interpretations of Islamic law (Tucker 2008, 38–174) Perhaps most problematic for modern notions of citizenship, several well-known classical commentaries stipulated that in both family and public affairs women were not to exercise authority over men. Citing Qur'an 4:34, classical jurists assigned men *qiwama* over women, an ambiguous term that most classical scholars interpreted to mean "guardianship" (cf. Brown, this volume). Later commentators went further, limiting the rights of women to appear in public or to associate with men, thereby blocking women's access to male-dominated political spheres (Mernissi 1991, 51–53; cf. An-Na'im 2008, 109; Tucker 2008, 177–217).

Reflecting the tendency to operate outside the letter of the law once more, judges in Islamic courts often ruled in ways that were far more favorable to women than these formal provisions imply. Indeed, as a number of recent studies have shown, court rulings on matters of gender and family were often informed by local notions of equity, fairness, and gender identity, in addition to shari'a prescriptions, and the former often characterized women's rights and duties more liberally than the latter (see Peletz 2002, 84–97; Hirsch 1998; cf. Tucker 1998). Nonetheless, in modern times, textual conservatives have justi- fied their understanding of gender with reference to, not the situated practices of real and existing judges, but the recorded stipulations of classical shari'a, and only certain stipulations at that. Most of these traditionalist understand- ings are in tension with modern, gender-equitable understandings of citizen- ship (see Ahmed 1992, 89–207; Ali 2006, xxv; Othman 1997).

The law's stipulations with regard to non-Muslims show a similarly dif- ferentiating tendency. Departing from the ecumenical spirit of the earlier Meccan period, revelations from the Medina period (622–632 CE) distinguish sharply between Muslims and non-Muslims. Qur'an 9:29, for example, urges believers to fight against and humble those to whom God has given revelation but who no longer forbid what God has forbidden, that is, Jews and Christians. Verses like these have led modern Muslim reformists to argue that the pas- sages in question apply only to heated contests taking place in seventh-century Medina, not to interfaith relations for all time (see Ramadan 2009, 73). Two distinguished Muslim pluralists, Abdullahi Ahmed an-Na'im and his teacher Muhammad Taha, go even further. They suggest that the earlier Meccan, and not the Medinan, revelations should be used as the basis for a reformulation of the shari'a in line with modern notions of citizenship and human rights (An-

Na'im 1990, 2008; Taha 1987). Taha and an-Na'im's proposal has its supporters, but for the moment many jurists regard it as too sharp a departure from established methodologies.

From the classical period onward, a significant number of jurists interpreted passages like Sura 29 as evidence of enduring tension between Muslims and non-Muslims. During Islam's Middle Ages, jurists from this same current extended the distinction into an elaborate set of prescriptions concerning the political standing of non-Muslim "peoples of the book" (ahl al-kitab), a category which commonly comprises Christians and Jews. As recipients of earlier divine revelations, and as the demographic majority in most of the newly conquered lands during the first 150 years of the Muslim era, the peoples of the book were accorded a "protected" status known as dhimmihood (Bulliet 1994, 39; Friedmann 2003, 58–74). Dhimmas were tolerated and given social autonomy on the condition that they submitted to Muslim rule and paid a special capitation tax, the jizya. The arrangement was far more generous than what most Christian European states offered Jews—and stood in stark contrast to the ethno-religious cleansing implemented by Christian forces in reconquista Spain. Notwithstanding this comparison, however, the letter of the law in classical jurisprudence imposed other restrictions on dhimmas, the overall effect of which was to underscore their subordination, sometimes quite starkly. For example, dhimmas were barred from serving in the military, forbidden to mount horses, obliged to wear clothing that marked them as non-Muslims, and, in general, excluded from positions of executive authority over Muslims. In legal principle, polytheists like Hindus, who (according to most but not all interpretations) were not included among peoples of the book, were subject to even more draconian restrictions.

Once again acting outside the letter of the law, many Muslim rulers set aside these jurisprudential restrictions on polytheists and peoples of the book, adopting a less discriminatory approach to their multi-religious societies. For most of their history, for example, India's great Mughal rulers chose to dispense with the shari'a provisions with regard to non-Muslims, although at first they did levy the jizya tax (Richards 1995, 39; Streusand 1989, 28). Muslim rulers in premodern Southeast Asia were also casual with regard to the shari'a's guidelines for dealing with non-Muslims (Reid 1993). Nonetheless, although often put aside in practice, the letter of the law with regard to non-Muslims was never formally rewritten. Today, then, it is easily invoked by letter-of-the-law literalists. This fact poses a special challenge for Muslims hoping to bring the interpretation of the shari'a in line with modern notions of democratic citizenship (see An-Na'im 2008; Mayer 2007; Ramadan 2009).

A similar tension has emerged in modern times on questions of religious freedom, not least with regard to non-conformist Muslims accused of doctrinal deviation or apostasy. By comparison with medieval Western Europe, the situation in Muslim lands on matters of religious non-conformity looks decidedly favorable. Islam had no counterpart to the inquisitional arrest, torture, and execution of tens of thousands of alleged heretics, witches, and non-conformists in early modern Europe (see Grell and Scribner 1996). Indeed, Muslim rulers tolerated a variety of what today would be regarded as mildly heterodox Sufi orders. Nonetheless, throughout Muslim history, there were occasional prosecutions for apostasy, some of which resulted in capital punishment (Friedmann 2003, 121–59; cf. De Jong and Radtke 1999).[6] At times rulers mounted full-blown campaigns against populist Sufis and others deemed heterodox, particularly where followers of the mystic path acquired a mass following and threatened central authority.

Notwithstanding these episodes, written jurisprudence took great care not to apply the accusation of apostasy broadly, and to require high standards of proof for a conviction. Those accused of apostasy were given repeated opportunities to revert back to a proper profession of Islam. However, if the accused chose not to recant, classical jurisprudence stipulated that he or she was to be stripped of all civil rights, including rights of inheritance and the right to marry a Muslim; an already-married apostate would see his or her marriage dissolved. If the offender persisted in his or her ways, the penalty was death or, in the case of women, indefinite imprisonment. On these points, Muslim jurisprudence developed a legal vigilance on matters of the faith that, to some modern Muslim commentators, stands in tension with the oft-cited injunction in Qur'an 2:26 that there is no compulsion in Islam.[7]

On all of these issues—women, non-Muslims, and Muslim non-conformists or apostates—the shari'a as classically transcribed preserved ethical strictures which stand in tension with the liberal principles enshrined in documents like the 1948 Universal Declaration of Human Rights. In modern times, Islamist thinkers like Sayyid Qutb and Abdu'l A'la Mawdudi have taken strong exception to liberal human rights schemes. Documents like the Universal Islamic Declaration of Human Rights (UIDHR) and the constitutions of the Islamic Republic of Iran and the Islamic Republic of the Sudan have tended to be more restrained in their objections to human rights proposals, but their basic position is similar. As with the UIDHR, most of these declarations begin by affirming two key principles based on the higher objectives of the shari'a: first, God has provided humanity with comprehensive legal and moral guidelines, and, second, human-made regulations must not contradict divine commands (see Mayer 2007, 123–24; cf. Musallam 2005; Nasr 1996).

Although these declarations might seem to open the floodgates to Muslim exceptionalism with regard to human rights, the main points of tension are actually few, typically centered on the question of women, non-Muslims, and freedom of religious expression, as well as the hudud provisions in criminal law. There is, however, one other, less commonly remarked point of tension between liberal notions of human rights and these traditionalist Muslim alternatives. Focused as it is on the defense of individual freedoms, the Universal Declaration of Human Rights says little about the need for individuals or institutions to uphold any specific idea of the good. Although Western political philosophers of communitarian or Catholic persuasion have sought to qualify this individualistic feature of liberal philosophy (MacIntyre 1988; Sandel 1996; Taylor 1989), the main current in liberal and human rights circles has advocated neutrality with regard to ethical issues other than human rights themselves, on the grounds that ethical matters are best left to the private deliberations of individuals. By contrast, the 1979 constitution of the Islamic Republic of Iran, the Universal Islamic Declaration of Human Rights, and the 1993 Cairo Declaration on Human Rights in Islam all make clear that affirmations of individual rights must be linked to the upholding of ethical norms, including most importantly believers' obligations to God.

The theme of not just defending rights but "commanding right and forbidding wrong" (see Cook 2000) runs through contemporary Muslim commentaries on human rights, including some otherwise sympathetic to democratic ideals. Indeed, over the long term tensions between "Muslim" and "Western" approaches to public ethics may have as much to do with Muslims' reservations with regard to libertarian models of public morality as their views of women, non-Muslims, and Muslim non-conformists.

Case Studies in the Law

The essays in this book map the basic currents of shari'a politics and culture in eight Muslim-majority societies. They do so in a Janus-faced manner, looking backward toward the genealogy of each country's ethico-legal currents and forward to assess those currents' implications for gender, citizenship, and politics. Although each country offers its own lessons, taken as a whole the essays offer a vivid sense of the state of shari'a politics and ethics today.

Saudi Arabia: Shari'a and Civil Empowerment

As Frank Vogel explains in his essay, the shari'a has a place in Saudi Arabia unlike that in any other Muslim-majority country. Whereas, in classical understandings, the law is "primordially binding [on] all" and serves (it is hoped) as a source of "precise guidance for everyday acts," the shari'a in most modern states has been codified and quarantined, regulating only a small number of private affairs. Seen from this angle, Saudi Arabia is unique among modern Muslim countries in the degree to which it allows no such marginalization of the law. On the contrary, in this land "shari'a is the constitution of the state, the sole formal source of political legitimacy, and the law of the land or common law." Most remarkable of all, even the general public agrees that the shari'a is "the solitary source of binding norms for the civil and private spheres."

In its uncodified and pervasive expression, the shari'a in Saudi Arabia resembles the form of the law that prevailed in much of the Middle East for the better part of a thousand years. The legal system is organized around two complementary poles. The first is that of classical jurisprudence (fiqh), neither codified nor étatized but applied in courts and public commentaries by scholars reasoning on the basis of their own knowledge of the law. The second mode of law-making is based in the laws and tribunals established by the ruler, as prescribed under the classical concept of "governance in accordance with the shari'a" (*siyasa shar'iyya*). According to the Saudi variation on this classical theme, the ruler complements the jurists' actions by making laws deemed to serve the public interest (*maslahah*), subject to the requirement that they not contradict the shari'a. Both in classical times and in Saudi Arabia today, this dual economy of legal production results in the jurists concerning themselves primarily with private law, whereas the ruler deals with what would commonly be regarded as public law. Vogel also argues that the premodern version of this legal system provided states in the Middle East with "a historically adequate" degree of checks and balances, an argument also recently made by the Harvard legal scholar Noah Feldman (2008).

The pervasiveness of shari'a knowledge among the Saudi citizenry guarantees that, although the state enforces the shari'a, it does not monopolize its implementation. "In their civil and private lives, citizens are both charged and empowered to mold shari'a and enforce it." Vogel's conclusion builds on a similar observation. He observes that Saudis today are hopeful for a brighter future, toward which they march under the banner of the shari'a. Empowered by high rates of literacy and an intimate understanding of the law, Saudi citizens recognize "how much of the immense moral, cultural, legal, and political meaning and power innate in shari'a falls into their hands." Vogel himself sees grounds for hope in the fact that King Abdullah's reliance on "an exclusivist, traditionalizing interpretation of shari'a" seems to be diminishing, while his willingness to collaborate with moderate reformists (known locally as the Sahwi; see al-Rasheed 2007, 59–101) is increasing. This shift, Vogel suggests, may allow King Abdullah to put Saudi Arabia on a course toward greater pluralism and constitutional innovation. Some Saudi citizens, and some in the political establishment, also hope that this opening may allow for fuller recog nition of the Shi'as, Sufis, women, and non-Muslims long given a lesser lot in Saudi society than their male Sunni counterparts (see Okruhlik 2005).

One might add a point here not explicitly raised in Vogel's incisive essay. The trend Vogel sees in the Saudi variety of shari'a politics is based on heightened rates of citizen participation; in this aspect it resembles processes identified in other societies with democratization. But the process here differs profoundly from democratization in its liberal varieties, in that it presupposes a thicker ethical consensus and a more pervasive practice of moral surveillance than is typical of liberal societies today. In the Saudi public sphere, citizens are increasingly active, but they are not enjoined to craft their own unique understanding of the good. The system presupposes public commitment to the shari'a, and a rather pervasive and non-liberal shari'a at that.

Egypt: From Shari'a Conflict to New Ethical Consensus?

Modern Egypt has long been a center of new ideas and movements with regard to the shari'a. It has also been a country in which struggles between proponents of the law and state officials have sometimes turned violent. Since the late 1990s, however, Egypt has established itself as a leading center for efforts to integrate Islamic shari'a into constitutional law (cf. Lombardi 2006).

In his essay on Egypt, Nathan Brown observes that in the late nineteenth and early twentieth centuries the Islamic shari'a was partially étatized and identified with three institutions: the religious educational establishment centered at the mosque-university Al-Azhar, a state-supported advisory office known as Dar al-Ifta, and courts of law that concerned themselves primarily with matters of personal status (cf. Skovgaard-Petersen 1997). All three institutions operated with state support, but they still enjoyed some autonomy. With the arrival of the British in 1882, and with the rise of Egyptian nationalism in the early twentieth century, the state undercut what remained of these institutions' autonomy. In 1929, laws of personal status were codified according to a legislated model; in 1956, the courts responsible for personal status law were folded into the regular court system.

Even as shari'a-oriented institutions were being dismantled, mass education, urbanization, and print Islam (mass-marketed Islamic publications) were opening the study of the law to a broader public (cf. Anderson and Eickelman 2003). The Muslim Brotherhood made implementation of the law one of its central political aims. In the 1950s and 1960s, the Nasser regime subjected the Brotherhood to fierce repression in the aftermath of militants' attacks on state officials. Nonetheless, in the late 1960s and 1970s calls for the application of shari'a-based law were again aired, winning broad public support. As Brown observes, this shift was "part of a gradual turn away from the Arab national-ism and socialism that had dominated the late 1950s and 1960s." Recognizing the change in public attitudes, the government responded by promoting its own Islamic agenda. One of its most important gestures was an amendment in 1971 to Article 2 of the constitution, which proclaimed that "the principles of the Islamic shari'a are a chief source of legislation." In 1979, Article 2 was again amended, this time to make shari'a principles "the" chief source of law. In public opinion surveys today, some two-thirds of Egyptians state that the shari'a should be the sole source of legislation.

Although in the 1990s the country was plagued by extremist violence, Brown sees evidence of a new consensus on the shari'a today. The consensus is grounded on four premises: 1) that the shari'a provides clear rules not to be abrogated by the state; 2) that the shari'a provides general guidance on the "aims" (*maqasid*) of the law; 3) that debate over the law is healthy and should not be condemned; and 4) that the shari'a provides a middle path of mod-eration for believers. The last two elements of the consensus represent tacit repudiations of the extremist opinions of the 1990s, when militants accused government officials of apostasy. Such accusations are today rare. Even among mainstream Islamists, there is a sense that the Egyptian state has taken serious steps to respect the shari'a, and these measures are legitimate (cf. Lombardi 2006).

As Brown makes clear, the new consensus is still characterized by areas of uncertainty and disputation. For example, the critically important question of how to determine the higher objectives (*maqasid*) of the law is "not always explored—and . . . exploration of it provokes disagreement." Some among the scholarly class worry that emphasizing "public interest" (*maslahah*) and the general aims of the law rather than specific legal rulings can lead to the neglect of long-accepted shari'a rulings—a view shared, one might add, by religious scholars in many Muslim lands. Nonetheless, Brown observes, for the public as a whole the focus of discussion has shifted away from "specific rules and enforcement to . . . how to realize the common good."

Although Brown does not directly address the topic, the implications of the new shari'a consensus for citizenship and Egypt's Christian Copt minority are less clear. The situation is also unclear for non-conformist Muslim intel-lectuals, some of whom continue to be targeted for harassment by conserva-tive Islamists. At the very least, however, the damping of extremist violence has created a climate in which public discussions of the shari'a can again be conducted in a more peaceful manner. Whether these civic seedlings will con-tinue to grow in the post-Mubarak era remains to be seen.

Iran: Guardianship of the Jurist and Growing Anti-clericalism

The only country to have experienced a mass-based Islamic revolution in modern times, Iran, the third case study in this volume, occupies a special place in contemporary discussions of shari'a politics. Iran is a Shi'a-majority country in a part of the globe dominated by Sunni majorities. However, as Bahman Baktiari makes clear in his essay, Iran's real claim to fame lies in the fact that its 1979 revolution implemented Ayatollah Khomeini's principle of "guardianship by the jurist" (vilayat-e faqih). Outlined in a series of lectures in 1979, and rejected even then by some among Iran's senior clerics, the vilayat doctrine gives the Islamic republic's senior jurist (faqih) a preeminent role in all matters of state. His powers include the right to appoint six religious scholars to the all-powerful Council of Guardians, a body which supervises national elections and can abrogate legislation deemed un-Islamic. The chief jurist also appoints senior members of the judiciary, exercises broad control over the armed forces, and has the right to commute convicts' sentences. Seen from this perspective, the Islamic republic does not so much resemble the classical model of "governance according to the shari'a" (siyasa shar'iyya) as it does a hybrid of clerical rule and the authoritarian "guided democracies" that emerged across the global south in the middle decades of the twentieth century.

As Baktiari demonstrates, on matters of Islamic law the Islamic republic has acted in a way that blends traditionalist literalism with high modernist exceptionalism. On one hand, Article 4 of the Iranian constitution makes clear that all laws "shall be based on Islamic principles." The chief jurist and Council of Guardians are given absolute authority to supervise legislation on the basis of this principle. Complicating this image of strict conformity to the shari'a, however, the constitution also authorizes the existence of an "Expediency Discernment Council of the System." Drawing on the long-established Sunni legal doctrine of "necessity" (zarurat, Ar. darurat; a concept not widely utilized in previous Shi'a jurisprudence), the Expediency Council has the right to authorize legislation contrary to the letter of Islamic law where the latter might undermine state interests. As Baktiari notes, Sunni scholars historically applied the principle of necessity to family and personal matters, not questions of state. Under Iran's Islamic republic, it has been deployed more strategically: whenever "the very existence of the state is threatened or, in Khomeini's words, where inaction would lead to 'wickedness and corruption.'"

In Iran, then, Islamic law has come to be applied in a flexibly functionalized manner rather than according to its letter. Critics of the regime, including many religious scholars, insist that the functionalization has often been used to buttress state power. On other matters, however, the Islamic republic has hewn to a strict-constructionist approach to the law. One of Khomeini's first acts after coming to power was to dismantle the Family Protection Law introduced by the Pahlavi regime. The previous law had restricted polygyny and abolished Muslim men's right to effect divorce unilaterally. Khomeini reinstated shari'a provisions for marriage and divorce, ostensibly to protect the family and bring women's status in line with Islamic legal principles. The principles that Khomeini had in mind repudiated gender-equitable understandings of Islamic family law.

As the anthropologist Ziba Mir-Hosseini (1999, 192–96) has shown, the application of the new law provoked protest even among women supporters of the revolution. The law also did not have the intended effect of lowering divorce rates in the country or reducing the growing number of unmarried women. Opposition to the law, especially in middle-class and educated circles, remained strong. During its brief existence, Iran's reformist parliament (2000–2004) sought to restore some of the rights revoked by Khomeini in 1979, including a woman's right to initiate divorce. The Council of Guardians quickly ruled the law illegitimate, however, on the grounds that its gender-equitable provisions were contrary to God's law.

As the 2009–10 turmoil surrounding Iran's presidential elections showed so clearly, the religious establishment's hold on government has not put an end to dissent. Indeed, public opposition has grown, and now includes many former supporters of the revolution. As Baktiari notes, there is an additional social influence at work here. In the nineteenth and twentieth centuries, Iran witnessed the growth of anti-clerical movements on a scale unseen anywhere in the Sunni world. The Pahlavi regime attempted to exploit this sentiment for the purposes of an imperial nationalism; this authoritarian effort eventually backfired. The heirs to Iranian anti-clericalism today come from a different background than these imperial nationalists. Some have been religiously educated. Most have their roots in the middle class, including a growing number of educated women. The repression of 2009–10 may well strengthen this anti-clerical current. In doing so, it may also broaden the influence of the pious Muslims and religious scholars committed to a more civic and ethicalized, rather than authoritarian, understanding of Islamic law.

Turkey: Ethicalizing God's Commands?

At first sight, shari'a politics in Turkey seem unlike any elsewhere in the Muslim world. As Hakan Yavuz explains, under the leadership of the founder of modern Turkey, Mustafa Kemal, the Turkish republic implemented an aggressive program of state-sponsored secularization. The Republican government abolished the caliphate, replaced Islamic madrasas with a unified educational system (in 1924), banned the fez and Islamic headscarves (1925), outlawed Sufi organizations, replaced Arabic script with the Latin alphabet, and, in 1937, declared secularism to be a principle of the Turkish constitution. According to the Kemalist variety of secularism, religion is a private, not a public, entity—and it was the state's responsibility to make sure that it remained that way. As Yavuz observes, "These radical measures were defended as the 'requirements of contemporary civilization'"—interpreted, we might add, in an exuberantly high-modernist manner. Although the state's actions provoked bitter resistance, republicanism was not without mass support. In addition to the modernizing elite, the Alevi minority—a non-Sunni, syncretic Islamic community—looked to Kemalism for relief from Sunni persecution (cf. White and Jongerden 2003).

Eight decades after the Kemalist revolution, the state still today proscribes any attempt to Islamize the legal system. Most of the public has internalized a proud sense of Turkish nationalism, one expression of which is the tendency to identify narrowly literal interpretations of Islamic law with Arab culture and "backwardness." But what makes these developments especially intriguing is that in recent years Turkey has experienced a far-reaching Islamic resurgence. In the 1950s and early 1960s, the state's success at social and economic modernization brought about the urbanization of Anatolia. A political opening during the same period led to a more vigorous system of multi-party politics. As an ironic consequence of Turgut Özol's neo-liberal economic policies, the 1980s saw the appearance of a new class of "conscious" Muslims, who took advantage of the liberal economic reforms to exert heightened influence. Finally, out of the fierce battles between leftist and rightist forces in the 1970s, there emerged a new language for public issues that drew heavily on Islamic ethical idioms even as it steered clear of calls for the implementation of the shari'a.

From a cross-national perspective, then, the most distinctive feature of Islam in contemporary Turkey is the fact that the Islamic revival has not given rise to a parallel demand for state-enforced shari'a. Yavuz comments that a 2006 survey found that a plurality of Turks (45 percent) identify as "Muslim first" rather than "Turkish first." However, the public's growing identification as Muslim has not led to calls for state implementation of the shari'a. Between 1996 and 2006, the percentage of the population advocating a shari'a-based state declined from 21 to 9 percent.

One might be tempted to dismiss these findings as no more than an effect of a continuing Kemalist hegemony. State policies are real, and their proscriptions are forceful. As Yavuz notes, the state "criminalizes any attempt to Islamicize the legal system or even propose a draft law on the basis of the Qur'an." At the same time, however, the public perception of the shari'a reflects something more positive and personal: a widespread desire to shift the center of gravity in Islamic ethics away from state mandate to citizen participation. In discussion, even pious Muslims distinguish between formal adherence to the law and a "moral core" (*ahlaki çekirdek*) defined in terms of honesty, fairness, charity, and human dignity.

The low levels of support for state-enforced shari'a, then, show the influence of both Kemalist nationalism and a popular desire to functionalize religion, not for the purposes of state legitimacy, but for an ethics of citizen decency. Whether this peculiar balance of understandings will survive in the absence of secularist controls is not entirely certain, but the signs thus far seem encouraging. What is even clearer is that this desire to implement Islamic law in a citizen-based and ethicalized, rather than formally étatized, way is by no means unique to Turkey.

Afghanistan: Sectarianizing Shari'a

In his discussion of shari'a politics in contemporary Afghanistan, Thomas Barfield draws attention to a tension, seen in all Muslim lands, between scholarly and popular understandings of Islamic law. Afghanistan is home to the Taliban, of course, and at first one might expect that popular understandings of the shari'a converge with those of religious scholars. The Taliban leadership were graduates of madrasa schools, so certainly they made a point of bringing a deeper understanding of the law to ordinary believers?

As Barfield reminds us, however, there have always been two currents to Afghan understandings of the shari'a, and this did not change under Taliban rule. The first current (itself comprising varied sub-types) is that common among jurists, referencing the Qur'an, the Sunna of the Prophet, and fiqh commentaries. The "second and more populist view holds that shari'a is a set of rules and practices that also reflect national traditions and mores." This latter understanding mixes elements of Islamic law with tribal custom. Some 80 percent of Afghans are rural, and most of the rural population sees little point to distinguishing local custom from shari'a law. The most elaborate of the customary legal systems is the Pashtunwali, the code of honor and patriarchal masculinity found among the largest of Afghanistan's ethnic groups, the Pashtun (primary supporters of the Taliban). But each region in Afghanistan has its own customary law, and "their specifics vary widely and often idiosyncratically."

The Taliban's inability to drag the general public toward a more literalist understanding of the shari'a is not for want of trying. "The ulama hold customary law systems in contempt, arguing that they violate orthodox Islamic practices." But lettered jurisprudence has always been an elite urban affair in tribal Afghanistan. Meanwhile, the foundation of politics and society lies in the nested affinity groups (*qawm*) found in the countryside. These are based on kinship, ethnicity, religious sect, and locality. As Barfield notes, "political mobilization of these groups tended to be interest-based rather than ideological. They were rarely swayed by abstract arguments of any type," including those that claimed to speak in the name of the shari'a.

The sectarian nature of Afghan Islam helps to explain some of the peculiarities of the Taliban movement. Although media reports often present the Taliban as stalwarts of shari'a piety, the Taliban's shari'a was interwoven with tribal honor and patriarchal violence. The Taliban instrumentalized the law, then, in a manner that ran roughshod over shari'a prescriptions for evidence and procedure. "The enthusiasm with which the Taliban imposed such punishments as amputation for theft, stoning for adultery, and the execution of homosexuals by collapsing mud walls over them," Barfield notes, "was not matched by an adherence to rules of evidence or legal procedure that Islamic jurisprudence normally demanded in such cases." An Egyptian delegation of Al-Azhar scholars who traveled to Kandahar in March 2001 in a vain attempt to convince Mullah Omar not to dynamite the Barniyan Buddhas accused the Taliban, not without reason, of what Barfield notes "might be termed 'shari'a malpractice.'"

In keeping with the Taliban conflation of customary and Islamic law, the status of women has been a particularly vexing problem in the country's shari'a politics. Conservative scholars portray Western notions of gender equality as un-Islamic, and play to rural people's anxieties that rich Kabul elites are trying to impose Western values. Many of the women activists whom Barfield interviewed feel that, in light of the pervasiveness of these accusations, the most prudent tack is education and cultural reform, rather than top-down legislation. This is particularly sensible, Barfield reports, because even if laws were passed women would have little access to the court system and less faith in the judges. Indeed, Barfield adds, in an effort to contain the opposition, President Karzai left many Taliban-era judges in place after 2001.

With the continuing uncertainties with regard to Afghanistan politics, it seems likely that the situation of pro-democracy reformers and women's-rights activists is likely to remain insecure. The constitution adopted under American aegis declares that Islam is the state religion and that no law may contravene the shari'a. No plaintiff has as yet challenged any law on the grounds that it does so. For the moment, "don't ask, don't tell" seems the operative principle. But if there have been few conservative challenges to government legislation, there are also as yet few instruments for scaling up to a more civic and ethicalized understanding of the shari'a. Local women's groups and legal reformists seem to have it right: changes to the law will be sustainable only with education and far-reaching social change, including the diminution of communal divisions, the containment of warlord militias, and the creation of a more equity-minded middle class.

Pakistan: Modernism Deferred

Shariʿa politics in Pakistan show some parallels with the situation in Afghanistan, but, as Muhammad Qasim Zaman demonstrates in his essay, they also differ in important regards. As in Afghanistan, the shariʿa in what is today Pakistan was never applied in a standardized or uniform fashion. Customary law is still widely used, and, also as in Afghanistan, many ordinary Pakistanis conflate it with Islamic law. As the recent rash of "honor killings" of young women shows, some of the most notorious applications of this customary-shariʿa hybrid are especially disadvantageous to women.

After taking control of the populous province of Bengal in the mid-eighteenth century, the British determined that they had to devise an effective system of judicial administration. They relied on local scholars and jurists, as well as English ideas of common law, to forge a hybrid legal system which came to be known as "Anglo-Muhammadan" law (see Hallaq 2009a, 377–79). This legal compendium represented Islamic law as timeless and unchanging, a conservative interpretation that accorded with traditionalist scholars' understandings. From the British period on, however, the Muslim community was swept by divergent currents of opinion about the law. Muslim modernists insisted that the shariʿa was flexible, dynamic, and compatible with liberal values. Neo-traditionalists like the Deobandis called for a strict and comprehensive application of the law even in the absence of a state governed by Muslims (cf. Metcalf 1982). The founding of the Islamic Republic of Pakistan did little to diminish the diversity of views. What it did do, however, was intensify competition for control of the state legal system.

Although the new nation's governing elite was a rather complex coalition, politicians of a broadly modernist orientation occupied key posts in the judiciary, military, and executive. By contrast, and notwithstanding their own deep divisions, the ulama remained largely outside government and eyed the modernist elite's initiatives warily. This legacy explains in part the enduring inability of the Pakistani political elite, elements of which have modernist sympathies, to devise a working relationship with the ulama establishment. In this essay as in other works (such as Zaman 2002), Zaman shows that a few ulama were willing to cooperate with the modernist politicians. However, many more regarded the efforts of even moderate Islamist politicians with skepticism, fearful that such measures served to promote the power of the executive more than the Islamization of society. The long-term consequence of this failure to build a collaboration across the state-ulama divide is that, still today, Pakistan's governing elite lacks an effective partner among the ulama.

This lack has meant that government reformists hoping to change public understandings of Islamic law have had to look elsewhere than the religious establishment for help. The executive branch has typically taken the lead in these efforts, as it did with the 1961 Muslim Family Laws Ordinance (which sought to restrict polygyny and provide women with greater inheritance rights). More vulnerable to outside pressure, the parliament has shied from such efforts. The executive's confidence was boosted by the fact that for much of its history Pakistan has been governed by quasi-military regimes. It was no coincidence, then, that General Ayub Khan sponsored the 1961 Muslim Family Laws Ordinance. In 2006, and with the backing of the United States, General Pervez Musharraf sponsored the Protection of Women Act, which sought to restrict earlier legislation mandating harsh punishments for extramarital sex. Reform-minded critics had pointed out that the existing laws on fornication had been used as legal weapons against estranged wives and independent-minded daughters. Notwithstanding support from women's groups and segments of the middle class, the government's campaign foundered. Even the religious scholars recruited by the government effort took to criticizing the proposed ordinance, complaining that the legislation threatened to turn Pakistan into a "free sex zone."

Since the late 1980s, the tension between reform-minded modernists and the ulama establishment has been exacerbated by the rise of armed Islamist groups, some with ties to Afghanistan's Taliban. The general elections of 2002 saw unprecedented gains by an alliance of Islamist parties. The alliance won an outright majority of the vote in Pakistan's Northwest Frontier Province. In areas under their control, Zaman reports, the Pakistani Taliban implement shari'a law in a manner "in line with tribal norms." As Barfield describes in Afghanistan, the Pakistani Taliban show greater enthusiasm for the shock and awe of stoning and maiming than they do for the careful proceduralism of classical jurisprudence.

The situation in Pakistan thus contrasts with that described by Brown in Egypt or Vogel in Saudi Arabia. Over the past generation the population in all three countries has developed a heightened interest in the shari'a. But the cultural content of the trend in each is different. The situation in Pakistan shows neither the civic consensus achieved in Egypt nor the citizen confidence apparent in Saudi Arabia. Certainly, by comparison with Afghanistan, Pakistan enjoys a proud tradition of Islamic intellectualism. The urban middle class also appears comfortable with the idea that democratic elections are compatible with Islam. No less significant, Zaman observes, "ordinary voters have often failed to be persuaded by any simple equation between the implementation of the shari'a and a vote for the religious groups." For the moment, however, no one in Pakistan seems capable of weaving these diverse threads together into a new consensus for a civic and ethicalized, rather than coercive and étatized, variety of Islamic law.

The recent escalation in violence presents Pakistan's mainstream ulama with a dilemma. Religious scholars have long been critical of the government and have thereby contributed to the delegitimation of the state. The ulama see the government's failure to implement the shari'a as the main cause of the recent progress of neo-Taliban groups. Nonetheless, outside of the northwest territories, most ulama condemn neo-Taliban violence, seeing it as contrary to Islam and their own religious interests.

In the midst of this crisis, Zaman sees one ray of hope. The scale of the violence now afflicting the country threatens not only the government but the ulama themselves. The challenge may yet provide an incentive for heightened cooperation between religious scholars and the state. But the relative weakness of Pakistan's civil organizations, the anti-pluralist sentiments of mainstream ulama, and the dark cloud of violence hanging over neighboring Afghanistan all suggest that the functionalization of the law for anti-state mobilization may remain a feature of Pakistani shari'a politics for some time to come.

Nigeria: Shari'a Imaginaries and Communal Divides

Paul Lubeck's essay on movements for state implementation of the shari'a in Nigeria provides a rich sociological perspective on the religious, political, and economic forces that led to the adoption of Islamic criminal law in twelve northern Nigerian states in 1999 and 2000. The shari'a movement in Nigeria has received unfavorable coverage in the Western media, especially after two poor rural women were sentenced to death by stoning for the crime of *zina* (adultery, fornication). The verdict sparked outrage in the West, as well as fierce exchanges between human rights groups and conservative supporters of the shari'a in Nigeria. Moderate supporters of the shari'a, most of whom had opposed the death sentences, were caught in the middle. Shari'a implementation in Nigeria was also accompanied by fierce outbreaks of Christian-Muslim violence, especially in middle-belt states between the Muslim-majority north and the Christian-majority south (cf. Harnischfeger 2008).

The timing of the northern states' implementation of Islamic law led many observers to suggest that the effort was primarily related to rising Muslim-Christian tensions. Lubeck's analysis partially confirms this point, but also shows that there was a broader confluence of events at work. Elements of shari'a law have been implemented in Kano and other northern kingdoms for five hundred years. The famous Fulani founder of the Sokoto Caliphate, Usman dan Fodio (1754–1817), waged jihad against rulers faulted for failing to enforce the shariʿa. In the years since, political crises in the northern states have regularly given rise to movements of religious purification and reform (tajdid). All decry the corruption of the existing socio-political order and see a more comprehensive observance of Islamic law as the solution. As Lubeck notes, the discourse of tajdid (Ar., "restoration," "revival," as of authentic Islamic teachings) is so deeply inscribed in northern political culture that social crises still give rise today to reform movements of a shariʿa-restorationist nature.

Lubeck presses beyond these historical details to ask, Why did the movement for the implementation of Islamic law gain momentum after 1999? He identifies several reasons. In 1999, civilian rule was restored after sixteen years of authoritarian rule by corrupt generals, most of whom hailed from the Muslim north. The newly elected president, Obasanjo, was a born-again Christian from Nigeria's Yoruba-speaking southwest. Although the return to civilian rule was welcomed in civil society and Christian circles, it caused anxiety among the long-dominant northern elite.

This shift in executive power was but one of the issues fueling Muslim concerns. Between the late 1960s and the 1990s, large numbers of mainline Christians and participants in African Independent Churches had left their churches to become Pentecostal. Whereas for much of the postcolonial period provincial politics had been organized around delicate interethnic and interreligious alliances, the combination of Islamic revival and Pentecostal surge burdened the Muslim-Christian divide with new cultural freight. Tensions were especially high in Nigeria's Middle Belt, a borderland region inhabited by Muslims, Christians, and adherents of indigenous African religions. The conversion of some in the last group to Christianity provided a new basis for unity among non-Muslim groups, many of whom had long chafed at their subordination to the region's Muslim rulers. In the 1980s and 1990s, the delicate tissue of ethno-religious relations in the region was torn, and there were outbreaks of bitter communal violence. At a national level, too, Christian-Muslim rivalries were intensified by the ascent of mass-based Christian alliances, like the Christian Association of Nigeria (CAN). The CAN leadership opposed Muslim hegemony in the borderlands and saw the implementation of Islamic law as a threat to Nigeria's tradition of multi-religious citizenship.

Two other developments contributed to the timing and scale of the movement for the implementation of the shariʿa. First, in the 1980s and 1990s, Nigeria's "demographic bulge" brought masses of youth into the job market, where they found few employment opportunities. For religiously educated urban Muslim youth, Lubeck writes, the failure of Nigeria's postcolonial development was "read through the cultural lens of tajdid rather than a secular nationalist or radical framework"; the crisis "confirmed what their cultural nationalist and anti-imperialist instincts told them was true."

The second development catalyzing the shari'a movement had to do with shifts within mass-based Muslim associations. Since the early twentieth century, the movement for Islamic purification in Nigeria had been dominated, not by Egyptian- or Saudi-influenced Salafis, but by local Sufis. Unlike their counterparts in some countries (see Bruinessen and Howell 2007), Nigeria's Sufis advocated the seclusion of women and restrictions on women's rights. Sufis also opposed religious education for women. Founded in 1954 and based in secondary and tertiary education, the Muslim Students' Society (MSS) rejected these Sufi restrictions. While promoting modesty in dress, the MSS supported women's education. Other reformist groups, like the 'Yan Izala, promote a more individualistic and egalitarian practice of Islam (see Kane 2003). They chafe at the hierarchical deference associated with Sufism, oppose costly bride wealth, and promote individual emancipation from patriarchal control. This mixture of neo-Salafi Puritanism and egalitarianism has resonated with urban youth. It is from the ranks of this segment of the population that the leadership of the shari'a movement has emerged.

Nigeria's shari'a movement thus reflects diverse social influences and functionalizations. The northern elites and student groups see the shari'a as an instrument for solidifying an Islamic identity in the face of continuing Christian advances. The Muslim poor have rallied to the shari'a in the hope that, having benefited so little from federal largesse, they might yet share in the country's prosperity as recipients of *zakat* alms. Other believers welcome the shari'a's prohibition of the gambling, alcohol, and prostitution so pervasive in urban society.

For women, it must be said, the situation is mixed. As in many other Muslim-majority countries, the shari'a movement is, as Lubeck says, "intensely focused on controlling the public behavior and opportunities of girls and women." The movement has given "extremely conservative and narrowly trained ulama" new authority over women, especially among the poor and uneducated. Nonetheless, as Lubeck shows, moderate wings of the shari'a movement, such as the Muslim Students' Society, have expanded women's opportunities for education and activism, at least within gender-segregated settings. Muslim groups dedicated to more civic and ethicalized understandings of Islamic law have also come on the scene, especially in the fields of women's health, education, and legal rights.

All this is part of what Lubeck calls a social "dialectic which is working itself out in the communities of Muslim northern Nigeria." The precise outcome of the process will depend on the efforts of moderate supporters of Islamic norms to make the law an effective force for civic equality and social justice. In the face of Nigeria's communal tensions and pervasive corruption, the likelihood of success, Lubeck concludes, remains "an open issue."

Indonesia: Shariʿa Idealism and Democratic Reform

The most striking feature of the revival of interest in the shariʿa in Indonesia is that the revival has coincided with one of the most successful transitions to electoral democracy the Muslim world has ever seen. In this Southeast Asian country, high levels of shariʿa piety do not seem to have undermined popular commitments to electoral democracy. This suggests that in Indonesia efforts to bring public-law components of the shariʿa into alignment with democratic values may yet yield a positive outcome.

The historical background to shariʿa politics in this country differs in important respects from that in the Muslim Middle East. In this region the great centering of the Islamic tradition around jurisprudence and madrasa education took place much later than in the Middle East or South Asia. The initial waves of conversion to Islam in the Indonesian archipelago occurred over a period stretching from the thirteenth to the nineteenth centuries. Although several small sultanates claimed to enforce the shariʿa during a few decades in the seventeenth century, for most of the premodern period local legal systems were organized around a bricolage of customary, Indic, and Islamic legal principles (see Hooker 1984; Reid 1993). From the sixteenth century on, a few scholars studied law digests, and some rulers sponsored study circles (*halqa*) dedicated to the reading of religious works. In striking contrast with the Middle East, however, residential colleges for advanced training in jurisprudence were not securely in place until well into the nineteenth century. Indeed, such schools were established in neighboring areas of Muslim Southeast Asia, like Cambodia, the southern Philippines, and southern Thailand, only in the middle decades of the twentieth century (see Hefner 2009; Liow 2009). Earlier, a few scholars may have traveled to Arabia for study, but their influence on religious life back in their homelands was limited (see Azra, Afrianty, and Hefner 2007).

In Indonesia, popular awareness of the shariʿa grew in the nineteenth century, as Muslims from more deeply Islamized portions of the archipelago, like Aceh, West Sumatra, and Banten, made the pilgrimage to Arabia. In the last decades of the nineteenth century, the trickle became a flood, as European steamships speeded the passage to the Middle East and commercial trade provided growing numbers of Indonesians with the funds required for travel. The late nineteenth century also saw the introduction of printing presses, soon adopted by religious reformists for the purpose of predication. These developments catalyzed growth in Islamic learning, the emergence of a new class of fiqh-trained scholars, and, in the early twentieth century, mass movements for a shari'a-minded Islam.

The middle decades of the twentieth century also witnessed a countercurrent to the new Islamic reform: the rise of socialist, communist, and secular nationalist movements opposed to state-enforced Islamic law. The question of the shari'a figured prominently in the debates leading up to the declaration of Indonesian independence in August 1945. The nationalist leadership that crafted the declaration eventually removed any reference to the state's duty to implement Islamic law for Muslim citizens. In the early 1950s, debates over the shari'a figured centrally in mobilizations that pitted socialists, communists, and secular nationalists against Islamist parties. The latter parties won more than 40 percent of the vote in the 1955 and 1957 elections, the freest and fairest in Indonesia until the post-Soeharto democratic transition (May 1998 to today).

During its first twenty years, the conservative nationalist "New Order" regime (1966–98) imposed a ban on public advocacy of the shari'a. In the late 1980s and early 1990s, however, the regime responded to the country's growing Islamic resurgence with extensive concessions to Islamic interests. The jurisdiction of Islamic courts (which dealt with domestic affairs, not criminal law) was expanded, and elements of the law were codified in a national compilation. After Soeharto's ouster, the question of the shari'a was again raised, now in a vigorously argumentative parliament. Legislation mandating state enforcement of the shari'a was turned back in 2001 and 2002, however, by a coalition that included centrist Muslims as well as secular nationalists.

National surveys conducted since the end of the Soeharto regime indicate that the great majority of Indonesian Muslims believe that the state should implement shari'a law. Indeed, from a comparative perspective, the level of support reported is as strong as or stronger than that in most Middle Eastern countries. But the results of Indonesia's elections show the need for care in interpreting these survey data. Since the end of the New Order, Indonesia has held competitive elections in 1999, 2004, and 2009. Parties promoting the implementation of Islamic law have consistently fared poorly. Parties of moderately Islamist nature have done better, but only by emphasizing clean government and the provision of welfare services rather than state enforcement of Islamic law.

Notwithstanding setbacks at the national level, proponents of the law have had some success in a few provinces. There Islamist organizations have worked with secular nationalist parties intent on shoring up their Islamic credentials to enact controls on alcohol, prostitution, and, most controversially, women's dress and mobility. Between 2001 and 2004, the drive to implement Islamic law at a district and municipal level made headway, but since then the movement has slowed.

The most unusual aspect of shari'a politics in post-Soeharto Indonesia, how-ever, has had to do, not with elections or legislation, but with the emergence of urban-based Islamist vigilantes. The largest of these lightly militarized gangs ransack bars and nightclubs in the name of the shari'a. The militants have also attacked liberal Muslims, Christians, members of the Ahmadiyah sect, and pro-democracy activists. The largest vigilante groups have had ties to *ancien régime* figures, which they have used to preempt crackdowns by the police. Although party rivalries have made a coordinated state response difficult, the government—with the backing of the major Muslim mass organizations—has slowly managed to curtail, though not stop, the vigilantes' excesses.

Although officially committed to Islamic law, the vigilante groups and their leadership show little interest in the law's careful proceduralism. The groups have instead used Islamic law as a framing mechanism and boundary marker to rally followers against political enemies. The use of shari'a sym-bols for identity politics in this manner is of course not peculiar to Indonesia. However, here in Indonesia the tactic appears to have backfired, contributing to the poor showing of conservative Islamists in national elections. Notwith-standing the tumult of the early post-Soeharto period, most of the public has concluded that the best way to functionalize Islamic values is through not reckless vigilantism, but democratic constitutionalism, albeit with a culturally conservative face.

To the Future

After all is said and done, then, where does shari'a politics seem to be going in the contemporary Muslim world? The studies in this volume suggest several conclusions. The first is cautionary: there is no single pattern to shari'a politics around the globe, not least as regards the hot-button issues of democracy, women's rights, religious tolerance, and criminal law. The modern era has witnessed a great pluralization of voices with regard to the law; the cacoph-ony is not likely to diminish any time soon.

The pluralized circumstances of today's world are particularly pronounced, but they are not entirely new. Wherever the law made the transition from an object of scholarly reflection to an instrument of public ethical discipline, its impact varied according to its embedding and functionalization in society. In the premodern age, the law was balanced between the (relatively more) settled hierarchies of court and town, where scholars of the law refined their craft at arm's-length from rulers, and the countryside or steppe, where peasants and tribespeople practiced a hybrid mix of customary and Islamic law. In the mod-ern era, the forms of life in which the law has been reembedded have been reshaped by influences on a global scale: migration, urbanization, and the decline of settled social hierarchies; Western colonialism and the postcolonial state, with its codified and étatized law; mass education and public debate; and new forms of civic association, mobilization, and contention.

The impact of these modern developments has varied by country, in a manner that reflects the local balances of power and ethics into which the law has been drawn. Nonetheless a general trend is clear, and allows a second conclusion from the case studies in this volume. It is that the law is no longer just a matter for small circles of scholarly virtuosos, but has been "public-ized" by being drawn into the circumstances and contentions of modern mass society. The public-ization of the law takes different forms in different places, but the trend is indisputable. In Saudi Arabia, responsibility for the law has come to be seen as residing, not just with the state, but with all sincere believers. The outcome in this country is public and participatory but not democratic: it does not extend equal rights of participation to all citizens, and it presupposes agreement on ethical principles democrats elsewhere would deem unacceptable. In Iran, interest in and engagement with the law have also gone public, indeed powerfully so. However, the guardians of the Islamic Republic have attempted to turn back this current, concentrating final authority over the law in the hands of a powerful elite. The resulting tension between authoritarian control and citizen desires has estranged many people from the republic's clerical establishment, as well as from official understandings of the law.

State authorities in Egypt have responded to the public's new shari'a-mindedness by attempting to strike a balance between centralized control and participatory enthusiasm. The balance has not been easy, but two of its more distinctive consequences have been a decline in extremist violence and a measured constitutionalization of shari'a law (Lombardi 2006). Such a balance has consistently eluded Pakistani authorities. Although at its founding the nation was blessed with an abundance of modernist Muslim intellectuals, an enduring collaboration across the state-ulama divide has never been achieved. None was established in neighboring Afghanistan, either. There the combination of civil war, foreign intervention, and tribal mobilization has favored a peculiarly patriarchal and sectarian application of shari'a law.

These last two countries point to a third and rather sobering conclusion on the uses of Islamic law in the Muslim world today. Where shari'a-mindedness is widespread but frameworks for civic participation weak, and where factional struggles for the state overlie deep ethno-religious divides, some actors may be tempted to functionalize the law for the purposes of identity politics and positional advantage. Rather than bringing shari'a interpretation into alignment with aspirations for equality and justice consistent with the "higher objectives and ethical goals (al-maqasid) of Islam's general message" (Ramadan

2009, 4), elites may use the shari'a to criminalize dissidence, sharpen divides between Muslims and non-Muslims, and limit the rights of women. In these circumstances, the law serves as a club to keep subjects in line. The formula provides a convenient cultural frame for radical control or mobilization (cf. Wiktorowicz 2004), but it does so at the price of Islamic civility, scholarly vitality, and, ultimately, social justice.

At first it looked as if Nigeria was on the verge of just such a sectarian and patriarchal instrumentalization of the law. Notwithstanding awful outbreaks of Christian-Muslim violence, however, the impact of shari'a-mindedness was, relatively speaking, modulated. The shift showed the steadying influence of an old Muslim establishment, as well as the openness of a new generation of Islamic reformists to women's education and matters of general social welfare. Whether this approach to the shari'a will work to the benefit of Nigerian democracy over the long term, however, is far less certain.

Of the eight countries discussed in this book, Turkey and Indonesia show the most unusual variations on shari'a politics. However, they do so in ways that speak to currents likely to become influential in at least some other Muslim lands. In Turkey, Kemalist laïcité and liberal economics have unwittingly given rise to a powerful resurgence in piety and observance. Rather than demanding a codified and étatized version of the law, however, the Muslim public has opted for an ethicalized Islam whose core values resemble those elsewhere identified with democratic citizenship: fairness, civic decency, and social justice for all rather than a few. Although, according to public opinion surveys, Indonesians seem to have a stronger sympathy for state-enforced shari'a, in the voting booth most show a disposition similar to that of their Turkish counterparts. Indonesians seem intent on bringing responsibility for the shari'a down from the commanding heights of the state into neighborhoods and sodalities of society. They want the shari'a to work with rather than against democratic citizenship, albeit in a form more culturally conservative than is typical of Western democracies today.

These two examples point to a fourth conclusion. Although the trend is by no means universal, there is a tendency for believers in countries endowed with more open and pluralistic polities to view the shari'a not as an inflexible code to be imposed by rulers, but as a general ethical guide to be implemented by communities of believers in a manner informed by the higher objectives (maqasid) of the law (cf. Ramadan 2009). One might call this the ethicalization and "citizenization" of the shari'a, as opposed to its formalization and étatization. The process is broadly hybridic, showing the influence of modern democratic ideas as well as long-held features of shari'a law. Remarkably, some of the effects of this current are apparent even in illiberal national settings, like

Saudi Arabia, as seen in the growing sense of empowerment ordinary citizens feel with regard to the law. The aspiration is heard all the more forcefully in the criticisms made by reformist religious thinkers in Iran, who have argued that the concentration of legal authority in the hands of a regime elite is a formula for the law's abuse. Elsewhere, as in Egypt and Indonesia, the citizenization of the shari'a has less to do with the rejection of a state role than with an interest in giving primary responsibility for the law's application to self-organizing individuals and associations.

A fifth point follows from this. Although the ethicalization and citizenization of the law may eventually become an important current in open Muslim societies, the process does not amount to the privatization of religion, as earlier prescribed in Western models of modernization. To say the law is being citizenized still implies that most believers see it as relevant in some sense to public affairs. As the public opinion surveys mentioned at the beginning of this chapter make clear, most modern Muslims reject theocratic rule, but support the idea that religious ethics are not purely private matters. Although this idea has fallen out of fashion in the liberal West, it is not all that different from the views of Europeans in the late nineteenth and early twentieth centuries, when European publics took religion more seriously than most do today (see Casanova 1994; Kalyvas 1996; McLeod 2003). However, the idea's continuing appeal in Muslim lands will likely mean that even politically open countries may promote values more conservative in content than many in the post-1960s West find congenial.

The sixth and last point is that the situation of Muslim women may prove to be one of the most important social drivers for further movement toward an ethicalized and citizenized practice of the law. At first glance this appears paradoxical. After all, classical shari'a assigned men "guardianship" over women, a notion at odds with the mutualistic arrangements many moderns, Western and Muslim, have come to prefer. Over the past generation, however, the movement of Muslim women into higher education has exceeded that of their Muslim male counterparts (C. Brown 2000, 129). Although obstacles to women's access to the professions remain, the trend is apparent there too: a great transformation of women's roles is under way, and it is creating realities on the ground at variance with classical shari'a's patriarchal guardianship.

One response to this tension, a secularist one, would be to discard the law entirely as an ethical referent for public affairs. But the legacy of Islamic law as a public ethical tradition guarantees that, for many believers, such a gesture is tantamount to rejecting Islam itself; it is, in other words, unthinkable. For the foreseeable future, then, the option preferred in many circles may instead resemble that recently discussed by the Muslim scholar of gender jurisprudence Kecia Ali (cf. Abu-Lughod 1998; Esack 2001). In a moving account, Ali has described the way in which the discontinuity between today's gender realities and classical legal commentaries presses many Muslims to approach the law in a new way:

> Not because the rulings of the jurists are themselves egalitarian—for the most part, they are not when it comes to matters of gender and sex—but because the ways in which jurists have related source texts to social contexts demonstrates that the law they constructed has "always already" been subjected to acts of interpretation. Their practice both authorizes by example human interpretive reasoning and provides a useful model for constructive dialogue between textual sources and social custom. (Ali 2006, 154)

The situation to which Ali refers is pervasive across the Muslim world, and, as Tariq Ramadan has recently reminded us (Ramadan 2009, 82), not just with regard to gender. The desire to bring the higher objectives of the law into ethicalized alignment with contemporary realities is a quiet but powerful force for renewed understandings of Islamic law (cf. Abou El Fadl 2001; Mir-Hosseini 1999).

There is a final lesson in this example. The moral power of the shari'a has always derived from the fact that its most gifted practitioners have never allowed it to be just an abstract dogma made consistent with its own premises, indifferent to the circumstances of the age. The shari'a acquires ethical power when believers are able to draw its message deep into their everyday lives, so that it informs and resonates with their moral circumstances. This truth may strike some readers as too general to shed light on the situation of the shari'a today. But its transformative force is being felt across the Muslim world. It is seen above all in the confidence many modern Muslims feel that a primary aim of God's law is to advance social justice and human dignity, and that these aims must be at the heart of any effort to make the shari'a speak to the quandary of modernity.

The revival and remaking of Islamic law is a work in progress, and its outcomes will vary. However, precisely because the shari'a is being drawn deep into the mobile life-worlds and circumstances of the late modern world, its interpretation and application will show the force of the modern. Where authoritarian elites or absolutist social movements deny understandings of the law other than their own, and where they turn their back on citizens' desire for dignity and mutuality, many believers will cease to view the shari'a as a compelling moral compass. Popular alienation will ensue, and the law's influence will wane.

This example points to the creative tension at the heart of shari'a politics today. Believers' efforts to make the shari'a a guiding force in their lives bring the law into contact with life-worlds and aspirations vastly different from those in which the law's early commentators lived. Over the long term, the law will remain a guiding force in Muslim affairs only by responding to and elevating the participatory and pluralistic aspirations of our age.

Notes

1. Qutb was an Egyptian journalist, writer, and activist who in the 1950s became the intellectual leader of the more militant wing of the Muslim Brotherhood, which was locked in a struggle with Egypt's nationalist leader, Gamel Abdul Nassir. Qutb was hanged by Egyptian authorities in 1966, but his ideas on Islamic law, God's unicity, and the corrupting nature of Western culture have become central referents for today's radical Islamists. See Qutb 1953 and Musallam 2005.

2. On the modernist-democratic tradition in contemporary Muslim politics, see Eickelman and Piscatori 1996; Esposito and Voll 2001; and Hefner 2005.

3. Secularists disagree, however, on just what the proper form of government in a Muslim-majority society should be. Not all see democracy as the best form of government; some suggest that a benevolent autocracy is more fitting. However, other secularists, today the majority, do regard democracy as the preferred form of government, on grounds similar to those presented by the modernists. See Abou El Fadl 2004 and An-Na'im 2008.

4. For a comparison of the Islamic legal tradition with the Western common-law and civil-law traditions, see Glenn 2000.

5. Not all analysts agree that the shari'a's influence on rulers and governance was relatively restricted. Recently the legal scholar Noah Feldman has suggested that in classical times the scholars' commitment to the law, and the rulers' willingness to implement the law, created an effective "constitutional arrangement" in which the law was "supreme." See Feldman 2008, 35. See also Vogel, this volume.

6. A particularly infamous incident of anti-heretical persecution was the execution of the tenth-century mystic al-Hallaj. See Massignon 1994.

7. According to some commentators, the capital penalty for apostates did not contradict the Qur'anic injunction against coercion, because apostasy was in fact a matter of political treason, not religion.

References Cited

Abou El Fadl, Khaled. 2001. *Speaking in God's Name: Islamic Law, Authority and Women.* Oxford: One World.

———. 2004. *Islam and the Challenge of Democracy.* Edited by Joshua Cohen and Deborah Chasman. Princeton and Oxford: Princeton University Press.

Abu-Lughod, Lila, ed. 1998. *Remaking Women: Feminism and Modernity in the Middle East.* Princeton: Princeton University Press.

Ahmed, Leila. 1992. *Women and Gender in Islam: Historical Roots of a Modern Debate.* New Haven: Yale University Press.

Ali, Kecia. 2006. *Sexual Ethics and Islam: Feminist Reflections on Qur'an, Hadith, and Jurisprudence.* Oxford: One World.

Anderson, Jon W., and Dale F. Eickelman, eds. 2003. *New Media in the Muslim World: The Emerging Public Sphere.* Bloomington: Indiana University Press.

An-Na'im, Abdullahi Ahmed. 1990. *Toward an Islamic Reformation: Civil Liberties, Human Rights, and International Law.* Syracuse: Syracuse University Press, 1990.

———. 2008. *Islam and the Secular State: Negotiating the Future of Shari'a.* Cambridge, Mass.: Harvard University Press.

Arjomand, Said Amir. 1999. "The Law, Agency, and Policy in Medieval Islamic Society: Development of the Institutions of Learning from the Tenth to the Fifteenth Century." *Comparative Studies in Society and History* 41 (2): 263–93.

Asad, Talal. 2003. *Formations of the Secular: Christianity, Islam, Modernity.* Stanford: Stanford University Press, 2003.

Auda, Jasser. 2008. *Maqasid al-Shariah as Philosophy of Islamic Law: A Systems Approach.* London and Washington: International Institute of Islamic Thought.

Azra, Azumardi, Dina Afrianty, and Robert W. Hefner. 2007. "Pesantren and Madrasa: Muslim Schools and National Ideals in Indonesia." In *Schooling Islam: The Culture and Politics of Modern Muslim Education,* ed. Robert W. Hefner and Muhammad Qasim Zaman, 172–98. Princeton: Princeton University Press.

Barth, Fredrik. 1993. *Balinese Worlds.* Princeton: Princeton University Press.

Berkey, Jonathan. 1992. *The Transmission of Knowledge in Medieval Cairo: A Social History of Islamic Education.* Princeton: Princeton University Press.

———. 2003. *The Formation of Islam: Religion and Society in the Near East, 600–1800.* Cambridge: Cambridge University Press.

Black, Anthony. 2001. *The History of Islamic Political Thought: From the Prophet to the Present.* New York: Routledge.

Bowen, John R. 2003. *Islam, Law and Equality in Indonesia: An Anthropology of Public Reasoning.* Cambridge: Cambridge University Press.

Brown, Carl. 2000. *Religion and State: The Muslim Approach to Politics.* New York: Columbia University Press.

Brown, Nathan J. 1997. *The Rule of Law in the Arab World: Courts in Egypt and the Gulf.* Cambridge: Cambridge University Press.

Bruinessen, Martin van, and Julia Day Howell, eds. 2007. *Sufism and the "Modern" in Islam.* London and New York: I. B. Tauris.

Bulliet, Richard W. 1994. *Islam: The View from the Edge.* New York: Columbia University Press.

Burton, John. 1994. *An Introduction to the Hadith.* Edinburgh: Edinburgh University Press.

Carré, Olivier, 2003. *Mysticism and Politics: A Critical Reading of "Fi Zilal al-Qur'an" by Sayyid Qutb.* Leiden and Boston: Brill.

Casanova, José. 1994. *Public Religions in the Modern World.* Chicago: University of Chicago Press.

Chamberlain, Michael. 1994. *Knowledge and Social Practice in Medieval Damascus, 1190–1350.* Cambridge Studies in Islamic Civilization. Cambridge: Cambridge University Press.

Cook, Michael. 2000. *Commanding Right and Forbidding Wrong in Islamic Thought.* Cambridge: Cambridge University Press.

Crone, Patricia. 2004. *God's Rule: Government and Islam.* New York: Columbia University Press.

De Jong, Frederick, and Bernd Radtke, eds. 1999. *Islamic Mysticism Contested: Thirteen Centuries of Controversies and Polemics.* Leiden and Boston: Brill.

Eickelman, Dale F. 1992. "Mass Higher Education and the Religious Imagination in Contemporary Arab Societies." *American Ethnologist* 19 (4): 1–13.

Eickelman, Dale F., and James Piscatori. 1996. *Muslim Politics.* Princeton: Princeton University Press.

Esack, Farid. 2001. "Islam and Gender Justice: Beyond Simplistic Apologia." In *What Men Owe to Women: Men's Voices from World Religions,* ed. John C. Raines and Daniel C. Maguire, 187–210. Albany: State University of New York Press.

Esposito, John L. 2000. "Introduction: Islam and Secularism in the Twenty-first Century." In *Islam and Secularism in the Middle East,* ed. John L. Esposito and Azzam Tamimi, 1–12. London: Hurst and Company.

Esposito, John L., and Dalia Mogahed. 2007. *Who Speaks for Islam: What a Billion Muslims Really Think.* New York: Gallup Press.

Esposito, John L., and John Voll. 2001. *Makers of Contemporary Islam.* New York: Oxford University Press.

Euben, Roxanne L., and Muhammad Qasim Zaman. 2009. *Princeton Readings in Islamist Thought: Texts and Contexts from al-Banna to Bin Laden.* Princeton: Princeton University Press.

Fattah, Moataz A. 2006. *Democratic Values in the Muslim World.* Boulder, Colo.: Lynne Rienner.

Feldman, Noah. 2008. *The Fall and Rise of the Islamic State.* Princeton: Princeton University Press.

Findley, Carter Vaughn. 1989. "Knowledge and Education in the Modern Middle East: A Comparative View." In *The Modern Economic and Social History of the Middle East in Its World Context,* ed. Georges Sabagh, 130–54. Cambridge: Cambridge University Press.

Fowden, Garth. 1993. *Empire to Commonwealth: Consequences of Monotheism in Late Antiquity.* Princeton: Princeton University Press.

Friedmann, Yohanan. 2003. *Tolerance and Coercion in Islam: Interfaith Relations in the Muslim Tradition.* Cambridge: Cambridge University Press.

Gerber, Haim. 1999. *Islamic Law and Culture, 1600–1840.* Leiden: Brill.

Gilliot, Claude. 2006. "Creation of a Fixed Text." In *The Cambridge Companion to the Qur'an,* ed. Jane Dammen McAuliffe, 41–57. Cambridge: Cambridge University Press.

Glenn, H. Patrick. 2000. *Legal Traditions of the World: Sustainable Diversity in Law.* New York: Oxford University Press.

Grandin, Nicole, and Marc Gaborieau, eds. 1997. *Madrasa: La transmission du savoir dans le monde Musulman.* Paris: Éditions Arguments.

Grell, Ole Peter, and Bob Scribner, eds. 1996. *Tolerance and Intolerance in the European Reformation.* Cambridge: Cambridge University Press.

Hallaq, Wael B. 1989. "Non-analogical Arguments in Sunni Juridical qiyas." *Arabica* 36 (3): 286–306.

———. 1993. "Was al-Shafi'i the Master Architect of Islamic Jurisprudence?" *International Journal of Middle Eastern Studies* 25 (4): 587–605.

———. 1997. *A History of Islamic Legal Theories: An Introduction to Sunni usul al-fiqh.* Cambridge: Cambridge University Press.

———. 2005. *The Origins and Evolution of Islamic Law.* Cambridge: Cambridge University Press.

———. 2009a. *Shari'a: Theory, Practice, Transformations.* Cambridge: Cambridge University Press.

———. 2009b. *An Introduction to Islamic Law.* Cambridge: Cambridge University Press.

Harnischfeger, Johannes. 2008. *Democratization and Islamic Law: The Sharia Conflict in Nigeria.* Chicago: University of Chicago Press.

Hassan, Riaz. 2002. *Faithlines: Muslim Conceptions of Islam and Society.* Karachi: Oxford University Press.

Hefner, Robert W. 1993. "World Building and the Rationality of Conversion." In *Conversion to Christianity: Historical and Anthropological Perspectives on a Great Transformation,* ed. Robert W. Hefner, 3–44. Berkeley and London: University of California Press.

———. 2005. "Muslim Democrats and Islamist Violence in Post-Soeharto Indonesia." In *Remaking Muslim Politics: Pluralism, Contestation, Democratization,* ed. Robert W. Hefner, 273–301. Princeton: Princeton University Press.

———. 2007. "Introduction: The Culture, Politics, and Future of Muslim Education." In *Schooling Islam: The Culture and Politics of Modern Muslim Education,* ed. Robert W. Hefner and Muhammad Qasim Zaman, 1–39. Princeton: Princeton University Press.

———, ed. 2009. *Making Modern Muslims: The Politics of Islamic Education in Southeast Asia.* Honolulu: University of Hawaii Press.

———. Forthcoming. "Human Rights in Islam: The Indonesian Case in Comparative Perspective." In *Religion and the Global Politics of Human Rights,* ed. Thomas Banchoff and Robert Wuthnow. Oxford: Oxford University Press.

Hirsch, Susan F. 1998. *Pronouncing and Persevering: Gender and the Discourses of Disputing in an African Islamic Court.* Chicago: University of Chicago Press.

Hooker, M. B. 1984. *Islamic Law in South-East Asia.* Singapore: Oxford University Press.

Huff, Toby. 2003. *The Rise of Early Modern Science: Islam, China, and the West.* 2nd ed. Cambridge: Cambridge University Press.

Huntington, Samuel P. 1996. *The Clash of Civilizations and the Remaking of the World Order.* New York: Simon and Schuster.

Imber, Colin. 1997. *Ebu's Su'ud: The Islamic Legal Tradition.* Stanford: Stanford University Press.

———. 2002. *The Ottoman Empire, 1300–1600: The Structure of Power.* New York: Palgrave Macmillan, 2002.

Johansen, Baber. 1999. *Contingency in a Sacred Law: Legal and Ethical Norms in the Muslim Fiqh.* Leiden: Brill.

Johnson, Luke Timothy. 2008. "Law in Early Christianity." In *Christianity and Law:*

An Introduction, ed. John Witte, Jr., and Frank S. Alexander, 53–69. Cambridge: Cambridge University Press.

Kahf, Monzer. 1995. "Waqf." In *The Oxford Encyclopedia of the Modern Islamic World*, ed. John L. Esposito, 4:312–16. New York: Oxford University Press.

Kalyvas, Stathis N. 1996. *The Rise of Christian Democracy in Europe*. Ithaca: Cornell University Press.

Kamali, Mohammad Hashim. 2008. *Shari'ah Law: An Introduction*. Oxford: One World.

———. 2009. *A Textbook of Hadith Studies: Authenticity, Compilation, Classification, and Criticism of Hadith*. Leicestershire: The Islamic Foundation.

Kane, Ousmane. 2003. *Muslim Modernity in Postcolonial Nigeria: A Study of the Society for the Removal of Innovation and Reinstatement of Tradition*. Leiden and Boston: Brill.

Kennedy, Hugh. 2002. *An Historical Atlas of Islam*. 2nd ed. Leiden and Boston: Brill.

Lapidus, Ira M. 1996. "State and Religion in Islamic Societies." *Past and Present* 151 (May): 3–27.

———. 2002. *A History of Islamic Societies*. 2nd ed. Cambridge: Cambridge University Press.

Layish, Aharon. 2004. "The Transformation of the Sharia'a from Jurists' Law to Statutory Law in the Contemporary Muslim World." *Die Welt des Islams* 44 (1): 85–113.

Layish, Aharon, and Gabriel R. Warburg. 2002. *The Reinstatement of Islamic Law in Sudan under Numayri: An Evaluation of a Legal Experiment in the Light of Its Historical Context, Methodology, and Repercussions*. Leiden: Brill.

Liow, Joseph Chinyong. 2009. *Islam, Education, and Reform in Southern Thailand: Tradition and Transformation*. Singapore: Institute of Southeast Asian Studies.

Lombardi, Clark B. 2006. *State Law as Islamic Law in Modern Egypt: The Incorporation of the Shari'a into Egyptian Constitutional Law*. Leiden: Brill.

MacIntyre, Alasdair. 1988. *Whose Justice? Which Rationality?* South Bend, Ind.: University of Notre Dame Press.

Mahmoud, Mohamed A. 2007. *Quest for Divinity: A Critical Examination of the Thought of Mahmud Muhammad Taha*. Syracuse: Syracuse University Press.

Makdisi, George. 1981. *The Rise of Colleges: Institutions of Learning in Islam and the West*. Edinburgh: University of Edinburgh Press.

Martin, David. 1978. *A General Theory of Secularization*. Oxford: Blackwell.

Massignon, Louis. 1994. *The Passion of Al-Hallaj: Mystic and Martyr of Islam*. Translated, edited, and abridged by Herbert Mason. Princeton: Princeton University Press.

Masud, Muhammad Khalid. 1995. *Shatibi's Philosophy of Islamic Law*. Kuala Lumpur: Islamic Book Trust.

Mayer, Ann Elizabeth. 2007. *Islam and Human Rights*. 4th ed. Boulder, Colo.: Westview.

McLeod, Hugh. 2003. Introduction to *The Decline of Christendom in Western Europe, 1750–2000*, ed. Hugh McLeod and Werner Usorf, 1–26. Cambridge: Cambridge University Press.

Mernissi, Fatima. 1991. *Women in Islam: An Historical and Theological Enquiry*. Oxford: Basil Blackwell.

Messick, Brinkley. 1993. *The Calligraphic State: Textual Domination and History in a Muslim Society*. Berkeley and London: University of California Press.

Metcalf, Barbara Daly. 1982. *Islamic Revival in British India: Deoband, 1860–1900*. Princeton: Princeton University Press.

Mills, C. Wright. 1959. *The Sociological Imagination*. Oxford: Oxford University Press.

Mir-Hosseini, Ziba. 1999. *Islam and Gender: The Religious Debate in Contemporary Iran*. Princeton: Princeton University Press.

Moussalli, Ahmad S. 1992. *Radical Islamic Fundamentalism: The Ideological and Political Discourse of Sayyid Qutb*. Beirut: American University of Beirut.

Musallam, Adnan A. 2005. *From Secularism to Jihad: Sayyid Qutb and the Foundations of Radical Islamism*. Westport, Conn.: Praeger.

Nasr, Vali Seyyed Reza. 1996. *Mawdudi and the Making of Islamic Revivalism*. Oxford: Oxford University Press.

Norris, Pippa, and Ronald Inglehart. 2004. *Sacred and Secular: Religion and Politics Worldwide*. Cambridge: Cambridge University Press.

Okruhlik, Gwenn. 2005. "Empowering Civility through Nationalism: Reformist Islam and Belonging in Saudi Arabia." In *Remaking Muslim Politics: Pluralism, Contestation, Democratization*, ed. Robert W. Hefner, 189–212. Princeton and Oxford: Princeton University Press.

Othman, Norani. 1997. "Grounding Human Rights Arguments in Non-Western Cultural Terms: Shari'a and the Citizenship Rights of Women in a Modern Nation-State." IKMAS Working Paper Series, no. 10. Bangi, Malaysia: Malaysian National University.

Peletz, Michael G. 2002. *Islamic Modern: Religious Courts and Cultural Politics in Malaysia*. Princeton: Princeton University Press.

Peters, Rudolph. 2002. "From Jurists' Law to Statute Law, or What Happens When the Shari'a Is Codified." *Mediterranean Politics* 7 (4): 82–95.

Qutb, Sayyid. 1953. *Social Justice in Islam*. Oneonta: Islamic Publications International.

Ramadan, Tariq. 2007. *In the Footsteps of the Prophet: Lessons from the Life of Muhammad*. Oxford and New York: Oxford University Press.

———. 2009. *Radical Reform: Islamic Ethics and Liberation*. Oxford and New York: Oxford University Press.

Rasheed, Madawi al-. 2007. *Contesting the Saudi State: Islamic Voices from a New Generation*. Cambridge: Cambridge University Press.

Raysuni, Ahmad al-. 2005. *Imam al-Shatibi's Theory of the Higher Objectives and Intents of Islamic Law*. London and Washington, D.C.: International Institute of Islamic Thought.

Reid, Anthony. 1993. *Expansion and Crisis*. Vol. 2 of *Southeast Asia in the Age of Commerce, 1450–1680*. New Haven: Yale University Press.

Richards, John F. 1995. *The Mughal Empire*. Cambridge: Cambridge University Press.

Sabra, A. I. 1987. "The Appropriation and Subsequent Naturalization of Greek Science in Medieval Islam." *History of Science* 25:223–43.

Salvatore, Armondo, and Dale F. Eickelman, eds. 2004. *Public Islam and the Common Good*. Leiden: Brill.

Sandel, Michael J. 1996. *Democracy's Discontent: America in Search of a Public Policy*. Cambridge, Mass., and London: Harvard University Press.

Sanders, Paula. 1994. *Ritual, Politics, and the City in Fatimid Cairo.* Albany: State University of New York Press.

Schacht, Joseph. 1950. *The Origins of Muhammadan Jurisprudence.* Oxford: Clarendon.

———. 1964. *An Introduction to Islamic Law.* Oxford: Clarendon.

Shoshan, Boaz. 1993. *Popular Culture in Medieval Cairo.* Cambridge: Cambridge University Press.

Skovgaard-Petersen, Jakob. 1997. *Defining Islam for the Egyptian State: Muftis and Fatwas of the Dar al-Ifta.* Leiden and Boston: Brill.

Soroush, Abdolkarim. 2000. *Reason, Freedom, and Democracy in Islam.* Oxford: Oxford University Press.

Starrett, Gregory. 1998. *Putting Islam to Work: Education, Politics, and Religious Transformation in Egypt.* Berkeley: University of California Press.

Streusand, Douglas E. 1989. *The Formation of the Mughal Empire.* Delhi: Oxford University Press.

Taha, Mahmoud Mohamed. 1987. *The Second Message of Islam.* Syracuse: Syracuse University Press.

Tarrow, Sidney. 1988. *Power in Movement: Social Movements and Contentious Politics.* 2nd ed. Cambridge: Cambridge University Press.

Taylor, Charles. 1989. "Cross-Purposes: The Liberal-Communitarian Debate." In *Liberalism and the Moral Life,* ed. Nancy L. Rosenblum, 159–82. Cambridge, Mass.: Harvard University Press.

———. 2007. *A Secular Age.* Cambridge, Mass.: Harvard University Press.

Tucker, Judith E. 1998. *In the House of the Law: Gender and Islamic Law in Ottoman Syria and Palestine.* Berkeley and Los Angeles: University of California Press.

———. 2008. *Women, Family, and Gender in Islamic Law.* Cambridge: Cambridge University Press.

Vikor, Knut S. 2005. *Between God and the Sultan: A History of Islamic Law.* Oxford: Oxford University Press.

Vogel, Frank E. 2000. *Islamic Law and Legal System: Studies of Saudi Arabia.* Leiden and Boston: Brill.

Weiss, Bernard G. 1992. *The Search for God's Law: Islamic Jurisprudence in the Writings of Sayf al-Din al-Amidi.* Salt Lake City: University of Utah Press.

———. 1998. *The Spirit of Islamic Law.* Athens: University of Georgia Press.

White, Paul J., and Joost Jongerden, eds. 2003. *Turkey's Alevi Enigma: A Comprehensive Overview.* Leiden: Brill.

Wiktorowicz, Quintan. 2004. *Islamic Activism: A Social Movement Approach.* Bloomington: Indiana University Press.

Zaman, Muhammad Qasim. 1997. *Religion and Politics under the Early ʿAbbasids: The Emergence of the Proto-Sunni Elite.* Islamic History and Civilization, Studies and Texts, vol. 16. Leiden: Brill.

———. 2002. *The Ulama in Contemporary Islam: Custodians of Change.* Princeton: Princeton University Press.

Zubaida, Sami. 2003. *Law and Power in the Muslim World.* London: I. B. Tauris.

1. Saudi Arabia

Public, Civil, and Individual Shariʿa
in Law and Politics

Frank E. Vogel

Shariʿa in Saudi Arabia

The Unique Stature and Reach of Shariʿa in Saudi Arabia

To map attitudes and projects on shariʿa in Saudi Arabia, one must start by recalling the unique position of shariʿa in Saudi Arabia. Shariʿa is the constitution of the state, the sole formal source of political legitimacy, and the law of the land or common law. It is avowed as the solitary source of binding norms for the civil and private spheres, shaping and justifying social, communal, and family mores as well as individual morality. And, most fundamentally, shariʿa is the central conception of the religion to which every Saudi citizen formally belongs, laying down the intricate rules of ritual practices, among them the monumental pilgrimage to the holy places which the kingdom directly administers. So if we are going to ask about shariʿa politics in Saudi Arabia, or to map attitudes toward shariʿa in the public sphere, we must engage a more comprehensive set of questions than we do in most countries. In Saudi Arabia "shariʿa politics" is not only one strand or subject within politics; shariʿa is implicated in all politics.

Shariʿa is also to be understood in Saudi Arabia in a somewhat different way than elsewhere, given the 275-year history of Saudi states' adherence to the Wahhabi[1] and Salafi tradition. Salafism (the larger conception within which Wahhabism falls) holds that the true Islam is what was practiced by the earliest generations (*salaf*), disregarding later accretions. But one should not understand from this that Salafis seek to return to a past fourteen centuries old. Quite to the contrary, their ideals and methods are addressed to the present. They seize not on history at all, but on the sacred texts; and their methods of interpreting them are ahistorical and textualist, devoted to discerning in the texts not only universal and eternal norms but also concrete rulings for the unique and temporal present. Their purpose is to emulate the holy texts in today's daily life and circumstances, but preeminently through the guidance, chiefly legal, that the texts purvey. In another sense also Salafis depart from history: the shari'a they uphold remains for them transcendent, in the sense that it is revealed only in the texts themselves; no human interpretation, practice, or tradition can usurp the texts' sanctity and finality. But this is no free individualist Protestantism: respect for the scriptural texts as texts historically revealed entails respect for textual scholarship. Saudis still trust the interpretations only of scholars ('ulama) trained in traditional religious sciences, particularly law (fiqh), and the scholars they trust in turn pay great respect to great scholars of the past, most of all to those who preceded them in this Salafi project.

Such a notion of shari'a—abstract and universalizing yet intensely programmatic, transcendent yet drawn from an intricate historical record, wholly contained in a canon of texts yet endlessly explored over centuries—occasions many distinctions from other Muslim countries, even neighboring Arab ones. While nowadays Salafism is a vital strand of Islam worldwide, in other countries it has never been the establishment view. And most other Muslim countries, unlike Saudi Arabia, were subjected for a century and more to Western colonization or its powerful influences, begun long before Saudi Arabia even started to modernize. In other countries, constitutions, law, politics, and various civic values and institutions gained hold in multiple forms and senses that were and remain independent of shari'a and Islam. In such countries, shari'a can assert a role in the public sphere only in competition with or as a complement to already prevailing systems. Understandings of shari'a often take on the color of those systems. For example, far from being the law primordially binding all—individual, family, social leader, government, and ruler—and disclosing (through the medium of the learned and the pious) precise guidance for everyday acts, shari'a can be talked about as if it were a known corpus of legal rules, offered as an alternative to the state's existing statutory scheme.

The Role of Shari'a in the Law and Legal System of Saudi Arabia

As another preliminary to understanding the meaning of shari'a in Saudi Arabia, it is necessary to grasp how shari'a, understood as summed up in revealed scriptures and interpreted by scholars over the centuries, comes to serve as the binding law of a modern legal system. Here again Saudi Arabia stands apart from all other Muslim countries, since it consciously preserves the basic features of a constitutional system that prevailed in most of the Muslim world for the last thousand years. The cardinal virtue of this system was that, while projecting an image of the state as upholding the eternal divine law, it brought that law into meaningful, flexible relationship to facts. It did this through the doctrine of *siyasa shar'iyya* ("governance in accordance with shari'a"; see Robert Hefner's introduction to this volume), which, in essence, divides the finding and applying of law into two complementary modes, both under the aegis of shari'a. One mode represents law as found by religious-legal scholars and applied by them in religious-legal courts. Law in this mode is fiqh, meaning Islamic jurisprudence, constituted by the opinions of scholars, ideally after diligent research in the revealed sources (ijtihad). The other, complementary mode is that of laws and tribunals dependent on the ruler and his political establishment. The ruler complements fiqh by exercising a power, termed *siyasa* (governance) and deemed delegated to him by shari'a itself, to make laws to serve the public interest (*maslaha*), subject only to the requirement that these laws not contradict basic shari'a principles. The theory of this system casts these two modes of law as distinct and complementary. In the first, a scholar, faced with a dispute or an issue, determines the applicable rule by searching the revealed texts for God-placed indicators (*dalils*) showing the divine ruling intended by God for the instance before him. In a book on the Saudi legal system (Vogel 2000, 23–32), I termed this process "microcosmic," to emphasize the singular and unitary character of its method and outcome: law becomes fixed and binding only when an individual believer, for every action, draws on the revelation to discover God's unique ruling for that action. This occurs in two contexts: when a judge issues a judgment or when an individual, either learned in his or her own right or advised by a non-binding scholarly opinion (*fatwa*), applies a ruling to his or her own action. In the second mode of law, *siyasa*, the ruler addresses himself first not to texts but to the contingent welfare of the people he rules. Opposite and complementary to fiqh, his law-making is "macrocosmic" in method and outcome: it is generated by a this-worldly institution addressing contingent collective needs, usually issuing in a rule binding many cases. This dual conception of law and its implementation, with its inherent dynamic tensions—e.g., fiqh innately suited to private law, *siyasa* to public law; *siyasa* dependent on fiqh for legitimacy, fiqh dependent on *siyasa* for worldly power—lent innumerable premodern legal systems a historically adequate degree of constitutional checks and balances and of compromise between ideal and necessity.

This system survives in modern Saudi Arabia—in fact, with greater force and consistency than in most historical systems. (The country's basic law of government, issued in 1992, acknowledges the system explicitly.[2]) The fiqh realm, administered by scholars, encompasses the bulk of the law of the land.

The general civil and criminal law is uncodified by the state; cases are adjudicated by judges, themselves scholars, applying their own understanding of shari'a. In theory judges generate a unique, microcosmic ruling for each case through their own ijtihad, but in practice they generally follow the rulings set forth in authoritative late works of the Hanbali school of Sunni law as amended and further developed by the legal opinions of their leading scholars over the years. Judicial precedents are not a source of law, and shari'a court judgments have begun to be published only recently.[3] Law derives instead from the opinions of scholars, who in this capacity are seen as acting from their knowledge and not in respect of any official position they may hold, even when they serve as judges. The king appoints scholars to all judicial and official fatwa-issuing positions, but, because of strong group loyalty and solidarity among scholars, the power of appointment does not translate into control over the substance of the law. The result is that the basic, common law remains outside the state's control, and can be learned only through the study of premodern Hanbali treatises and modern Saudi juristic opinions. Ascertaining it reliably is extremely difficult for the layman, and difficult even for the professional, especially on issues where judges exercise degrees of freedom of interpretation. Since fiqh encompasses the most basic rules governing business and investment, this situation obviously places heavy burdens and costs on Saudi and foreign business.

In the other branch of the legal system, *siyasa,* however, conditions are almost the reverse. Here law is not divinely indicated at all, but man-made (albeit under a divine delegation), and it is written, public, and intended for general application. The king, acting on drafts developed and proposed by his Council of Ministers and Consultative Council (Majlis al-Shura, a body formed by King Fahd in 1992), issues statutes (termed "regulations" or *nizams* in deference to the primacy of shari'a as "law") to supplement the fiqh. These laws are, however, of distinctly lower constitutional rank, and subject to multiple, unwritten checks from fiqh and the scholarly branch. In fact, scholar-judges have for many decades declined to apply *nizams* where in their view the king may have exceeded his constitutional powers. This problem has forced the state to include in all its more ambitious laws (such as those relating to commerce, labor, or capital markets) provision for a specialized tribunal within the executive branch to apply them, to which specialists trained in modern law and less resistant scholars are appointed.

It is difficult for moderns to grasp a legal system where law—the general law of the land—can be and is made outside the organs of the state, where the generation of law is at base a private and social enterprise. Tribal or "native" law offers some modern analogies, but modern states usually either exclude or only narrowly acknowledge such customary laws as part of their legal systems; they do not make them the very basis for their legitimacy, their constitution, or their general law.[4] In Saudi Arabia, on the other hand, any law that can claim, with credibility among religious-legal scholars, its origin in the revealed scriptures is, ipso facto, part of Saudi law and theoretically enforceable in Saudi courts (Vogel 1996). As an example, later in this chapter I discuss several novel forms of marriage in Saudi Arabia that fundamentally alter the balance of rights and duties between the spouses. It appears that these emerged among lay individuals, perhaps advised informally by scholars, in the 1980s and 1990s. They are legitimate under Saudi law and widely practiced, causing upheavals in Saudi gender relations. Yet the state itself has never been called on to speak to these marriages. The nearest thing to official sanction is a short fatwa by the late Grand Mufti of Saudi Arabia, Shaykh Bin Baz, but even that fatwa—inherently non-binding—possesses authority only because of the public's esteem for his learning. Similarly, in modern Saudi Arabia women have no right to drive automobiles. Yet, until the issue was forced, by a demonstration by women in 1990, no law or regulation existed to that effect (even though such a statute would have been constitutional); the prohibition stemmed from the opinions of scholars. Conversely, even complex legislation issued by the king can become a dead letter as a result of scholarly opposition.

So far we have sited the generation of shari'a rulings at the level of influential scholars. But independence from the state and institutions, and reliance on individual conviction, can extend much further down, to the individual lay conscience, where indeed shari'a is rooted. If we recall the microcosmic notion of law—a law that inheres in no institution but arises, universal and transcendent but at the same time concrete and particular, from the obedience of each solitary conscience—we can understand how, through their conscientious choices, individuals can both make and sense an intimate connection with an all-pervading law that supervenes the laws of any state or society. Salafism intensifies such a sense of intimacy, freedom, and power; for example, one of its characteristic doctrines encourages those with even partial knowledge to use it to choose among the opinions of those more learned than themselves. While Saudi citizens always have been surrounded by religion from birth, their knowledge of it has grown exponentially in today's environment of literacy, mass education, and proliferating media. Saudi schools teach Islamic subjects at every level, including the rudiments of fiqh. Twenty-four-hour religious channels are popular on satellite television; religious issues are hot topics of public debate; and interest in religion and shari'a mushrooms on websites and in videos, blogs, and chatrooms. Fatwas on every subject, deeply scholarly or not, proliferate in the media and on the web, vastly widening options beyond the traditional local scholarly hierarchy. All these factors can give the Saudi individual an increasing sense that he or she meaningfully participates in the shari'a enterprise (see Eickelman and Anderson 2003).

Indeed, a major interest of this article is the fact that Saudis appear to feel, both individually and civilly, a new sense of power and initiative to treat directly with the meanings and legitimacies of shari'a, and what that fact portends for Saudi shari'a politics and law. Individuals and civil society seem to be exhilarated by a realization that they may tap shari'a's vast reserves of meaning and authority without waiting for or depending on the state or even establishment scholars. In other Muslim countries, observers have studied burgeoning individual and civil lay mobilization and empowerment under the banner of shari'a and Islam. They describe the religious and social phenomenology of such trends using various terms: popular "piety" and "positive ethics" (Mahmood 2005, 118–52); "ethics of civic obligation" (Wickham 2002, 120); "moral conventions and solidarities" and "moral obligations" (White 2002, 210); and "moral economies assigning rights and responsibilities" (Carapico 1998, 60). These studies, and their parallels in Saudi Arabia today, are fascinating and useful for our purposes. But, for Saudi Arabia at least, we have to go a step beyond such descriptions and analyze such manifestations as exercises also in law— not just law as religious rite, as moral or ethical law, or as civic obligation or communal mores, but law in its ordinary sense of binding, enforceable rules. Certainly in Saudi Arabia, if not elsewhere, a shift in how people think about shari'a need not stay confined to the private religious sphere, but can easily engage, through continuous interlocking gears, the entire legal system from the individual, through civil society, up to the constitution and the ultimate legitimacy of the state. Whether this widening sense of individual, social, civil, and legal empowerment has become a major vehicle for shari'a politics in Saudi Arabia is one of the main themes of this chapter.

The Role of Shari'a in the Saudi Political System

To repeat, shari'a provides a pervasive system of norms not only for the legal but also for the political system of Saudi Arabia, given that most of the public conceives of shari'a as the axiomatic and exclusive source of political legitimacy and of rights and duties. Most outside accounts of the country's politics minimize this perspective, their task being to trace the development of modern political institutions in Saudi Arabia. But institutions brought from outside can disguise practices not at all comparable. To use the Saudi judiciary as an example, a Ministry of Justice, an extensive system of judicial appointment, promotion, and discipline, and a network of appellate courts, all similar to those in every other country of the Middle East, are the visible face of a judiciary that routinely ignores much of the duly adopted legislation of the state and hands down decisions continuous with the unwritten juristic traditions of the past. To understand the judicial branch of the country it is still vital to know in some detail the constitutional and legal theories that shari'a and fiqh laid down centuries ago. The political realm is not dissimilar. The panoply of elaborate modern institutions—a consultative council, ministries, independent agencies, a civil service, bodies of regulations and ministerial decrees—can blind an observer to ways in which the very life and meaning of these institutions diverge from those of apparently similar institutions in, say, Egypt or Syria, not to mention France or the United Kingdom. One must remember how recently in Saudi Arabia these institutions arose—essentially from the 1950s. No doubt a number of lenses are useful for understanding these institutions, such as tribalism, regionalism, and patronage networks, but clearly another is that of the conceptions and practices surrounding shari'a in past and present societies.

Conceptions of law and constitution in Western societies bring with them many fundamental expectations about politics, on matters such as the separation of powers, the prerogatives of the various branches, and the distinction between public and private. Shari'a as law and constitution also profoundly shapes political life, both intrinsically and through historical precedent, and the more so since it claims that it encompasses politics rather than the reverse. Again, this effect is particularly telling in Saudi Arabia, ruled in the name of a particular interpretation of shari'a for most of the last quarter millennium. Let me briefly point out three respects in which shari'a lends extensive structure not only to legal but also to political issues.

First, shari'a provides a structure according to which any issue, legal or political, occupies a particular space or field within religious discourse, dogma, and practice. One must ask: is the issue in question one of basic creed ('aqida), such as whether those who hold such-and-such a position on it thereby depart from the faith (kufr)? (Accusations of kufr are often made in Saudi Arabia, e.g., by some establishment scholars against the Shi'a.) Such matters are supposed to depend on rational and revealed certainties, not on mere opinion. Or is the issue one of mere credal deviation (bid'a), as to which opinions may differ without entailing disbelief? Or, to move from creed to law, does the political issue in question concern the rules for worship (fiqh al-'ibadat), which, shari'a dictates, are almost entirely fixed by revelation and beyond human rationality and reasoning? Or does it concern the rules for human interaction (fiqh al-mu'amalat), such as laws concerning contract or property, where novel practices may be accepted if they accord with more general principles? Or is the issue within the sphere of constitutional thought (siyasa shar'iyya, khilafa, or imama, ahkam sultaniyya), such as the legitimacy of rulers; whether shura, the Qur'anically enjoined consultation with the ruled, is merely advisory or compulsory; or the permissibility of various forms of public criticism or opposition to state policies? In this realm, forms of legal reasoning are a long-standing set of compromises between credal, legal, historical, and pragmatic considerations, and results are powerfully moderated by the age-old Sunni tenet, historically strongly affirmed by Wahhabis, that Muslims must support even erring rulers to avoid civil strife, i.e., that Muslims should contest power only through moral influence and legitimation or delegitimation. Or is the issue one of family or communal propriety, where private male authority often reigns, and where shari'a tacitly accommodates much communal norm-making, including customary and tribal norms? Or, finally, does the issue concern personal conduct, such as neglect of ritual performance or immoral behavior in private, where most acts are not actionable in court and where the distinction between conduct in private and in public is crucial? For all these variations and others, centuries of Islamic thought and practice extending down to present-day Saudi Arabia create differing expectations as to forms of reasoning, the ultimate authority to which an issue attaches (king, scholars, communities, families, individuals), institutional specialization within the state and social structure, and the relevance of history and customs.

To look into one case particularly important for both law and politics, let us return to the distinction between fiqh and *siyasa* realms as to how shari'a evaluates an act. As said above, if a matter is one on which texts do not speak and which addresses only a practical problem affecting general welfare, the ordinary expectation is that the king is free to regulate it under his *siyasa* authority as long as he respects universal shari'a norms and principles. Such a measure is largely unrestricted by technical shari'a reasoning and the authority of scholars. For example, the Department of Zakat and Income Tax freely determines and regulates income taxes imposed on foreigners. In contrast, the department solicits and follows the fatwas of scholars in levying the religiously mandated *zakat* tax on Saudis. As another example, matters of national security and relations with foreign powers are clear matters of *siyasa*. All such cases fall across a complex spectrum according to how directly they touch on religious-legal concerns. Both support for and opposition to government actions—if based on shari'a—depend for their meaning and relevance on this sort of analysis.

This first type of shari'a structure has concerned the field of religious theory and practice into which an issue falls. A second type of structure relates specifically to issues within fiqh proper—how the issue ranks within fiqh's hierarchy of forms of legal reasoning. Is a shari'a opinion found literally in revealed texts? If so, it is axiomatically binding on all. If it is not, and is instead derived from the revealed texts using legal reasoning (as most are), then one must ask if scholars widely disagree about it. If they do, is the disagreement only with non-Sunni scholars, with non-Wahhabi scholars, or among Wahhabi-Salafi scholars themselves? For example, the scholars of the central Najd region have long insisted that women must veil their faces, but Saudis are generally aware that this position is not unequivocally dictated by text and that indeed the majority of scholars outside Saudi Arabia do not require it. Also, if an opinion is based on legal reasoning, what type of reasoning is it? Is its source verbal indications (*dalils*) in concrete revealed texts? Or is it based on scholars' assessments of religious and social utilities and harms (*masalih wa-mafasid*) in contemporary Saudi Arabia? For example, it is well known in Saudi Arabia today that Saudi fatwas have often relied on the principle of *sadd al-dhara'i*, the "blocking of the means," by which a scholar may forbid an act otherwise innocuous out of concern that it would lead to a prohibited act. The most famous such ruling is that against women driving, mainly on the ground that it would lead easily to prohibited interactions between women and unrelated men.[5] This sort of legal reasoning, where scholars claim to take a larger view of consequences and interests to supplement or supplant narrower textual interpretation, always raises the issue of whether such judgments by scholars deserve as much respect as the conclusions they draw from texts. Scholars maintain that even when considering the practical consequences of a ruling their powers of discernment must be prized above those of others, since scholars alone are aware of all the textual indications, general and specific. The same controversy is joined from another angle in calls, increasing of late, that scholars should ask themselves whether the consequences of rulings, however sound as textual interpretations, serve the deeper aims and purposes of shari'a (*maqasid al-shari'a*). Some feel that scholars' textual literalism often causes more harm than good, undermining the profound moral and social values that, less literally but also indisputably, Islam stands for, and of which laypersons also have some appreciation. An example would be the Prophet Muhammad's multiple admonitions against religious intolerance, and especially against declaring professing Muslims unbelievers (*takfir*).

A corollary result under this heading of legal reasoning, obvious within Saudi Arabia but often ignored by outside analysts, is the simple question of whether any proposed action indisputably, by all interpretations, either accords with shari'a or contradicts it—a question to which citizens usually know the answer in general terms. If an existing or proposed practice is seen as enjoined by shari'a, then it is difficult to argue that it forms no part of the basic laws or constitution of the country. To give examples from the rights of women: women's rights to property or inheritance, to education (at least when it does not lead to undue mixing with men), to protection from spousal oppression or injury, and to equal pay for equal work are all supported by shari'a, and potentially therefore also by all informed Muslims on the basis of religion. The media now treat many of these rights and protections as undeniable, and often as Islamic, and label opposition to them as customs overdue for change. In contrast, a measure understood as clearly contradicting shari'a usually faces insuperable obstacles to its official adoption, absent some indirect route to the same goal. For example, abolishing capital punishment or other severe Qur'anic punishments is unthinkable. But insisting on the highest standards of certainty of guilt for such crimes, an unquestionable Islamic premise, could reduce convictions. As another example, official corruption, whether of rulers, judges, or bureaucrats, cannot claim legality, however strongly political and social customs have supported it throughout Islamic history and in modern Saudi Arabia. For decades Islamist activism in Saudi Arabia has made combating corruption a central plank of its programs for reform.

The third and last form of shari'a structure in Saudi Arabia has to do with the authority to which shari'a assigns jurisdiction over an issue. Most matters of private law fall within the jurisdiction of scholars, particularly through their fatwa institutions or the shari'a courts that they control. *Siyasa* issues naturally are largely controlled by the king and the agencies of his government. Other authorities are hybrid. The Agency for Ordering the Good and Forbidding the Evil (Hay'at al-Amr bi-al-Ma'ruf wa-al-Nahy 'an al-Munkar, popularly, the Hay'a or Mutawwa'in) is controlled by scholars appointed by the king, and largely applies fiqh norms but also partly dispenses a *siyasa* authority (Vogel 2003). The Board of Grievances (Diwan al-Mazalim) has the diverse responsibilities of 1) an administrative court deciding largely *siyasa*-based cases brought against the government; 2) a commercial court deciding cases by the fiqh law of obligations and some *siyasa* commercial law regulations; and 3) a criminal court trying infractions of *siyasa*-based regulations. The Agency for Ordering the Good and Forbidding the Evil and the Board of Grievances are both named after, and emulate, Islamic historical models.

In addition to such formal governmental authorities, shari'a contemplates many other legal authorities in the social and familial spheres. Scholars, whether or not employed by the government, are immensely influential on social and civil issues, freely giving advice on matters such as celebrating birthdays or vacationing in the West. Authority within the family is thoroughly structured by shari'a, and generally held by males over females and children. Analogies to the familial authority structure extend far and wide in Saudi society, and, reinforced by the substrate of tribalism, lend it an extremely strong patriarchal, paternalist, and filial flavor (see, on "familialism," Fandy 2001, 23–25, 30–31).

Shari'a also helps define the autonomous authorities of the individual. Shari'a ideas shape Saudi notions of citizenship, on the one hand casting doubt on any nationality other than that of the universal Muslim nation (*umma*) and on the other hand instilling a sense that to be a loyal Saudi Arabian citizen one must be a true Sunni. The latter view inexorably undermines the civil claims of religious minorities, Muslim and non-Muslim, and even those of adherents of other streams of piety within Sunni Islam, such as Sufism. Shari'a endows the layperson with certain guarantees of freedom. His conduct in the privacy of his home is shielded from surveillance or punishment on the grounds of shari'a. He has the primordial right to choose which scholarly fatwas he obeys in private life.

Shari'a Structurings in General

While the Saudi population may not know the technical details of these structurings of society and polity, they generally know them in outline. Any analysis of Saudi shari'a politics must take them into account; they generate powerful constraints and opportunities too easily missed by an outside observer. Their functioning—implicit and often intangible—can be glimpsed further in examples to follow. Again, my claim is not that such structurings by shari'a are exclusive or even always dominant. Acting powerfully alongside them are many forces formally extraneous to shari'a. Among these are the ideas and practices of modern state-building, such as the rule of law, a written constitution, civil rights and liberties, reception of foreign legal institutions, modern institutional and administrative forms, and participation in international treaties and organizations—these get the lion's share of commentary among external experts on Saudi Arabian politics. Also among these extraneous forces are those ancient companions of shari'a often symbiotic with it: tribalism and regional identity or nationalism.

Of course, many Saudi believers and scholars see all these shari'a structurings of Saudi society as unfolding from Islam in its pure and ancient form. Yet each, as practiced in Saudi Arabia, bears the stamp of historical specificity, particularly the imprint of Wahhabism. A crucial question for our analysis below will be the extent to which the religious peculiarities of Wahhabism, particularly its sense of credal superiority (which has, in the past, extended even to violence against neighboring Muslims), have mutually elective relationships with other noticeable traits of Saudi shari'a politics and law. For example, have Wahhabi exclusivism and doctrinal rigidity helped establishment scholars maintain their internal doctrinal discipline and institutional solidarity in the face of the king, despite their professed ideology of individual scholarly interpretive freedom? Does Wahhabism provide the essential elements of a founding ethic, a creation myth, marking the Saudi citizen as deserving not only of the lucrative benefits of the oil-rich rentier state but also of a heightened spiritual status? Have such outcomes required all past Saudi kings to turn to one particular group of scholars, the Wahhabi divines of Najd, to obtain popular legitimacy for their regime? If so, has this legitimacy—because of the narrowness of the Wahhabi calling and its condemnation of outsiders— given these kings scant purchase on the religious respect of other Muslims, apart from their custodianship of the holy places? Such a religious sociology of Saudi Arabia would reveal local details filling in the generic structurings dictated by shari'a. But even just positing this local religious sociology enables us to ask whether it is now rapidly changing, given some of the dramatic new trajectories in shari'a politics now being traced out by the key political actors in Saudi Arabia. For example, if the king deliberately questions age-old cherished prerogatives of the Wahhabi scholarly establishment, if Wahhabism itself splinters into camps, or if laypeople seem even slightly inclined to assert their own views about shari'a, how do such developments cause other components of Saudi shari'a politics to shift?

Mapping Shari'a Politics

With this as background, let us explore current developments in shari'a politics in Saudi Arabia. Some of them take place not in the specifically political sphere, but as the political consequences of citizens' engagement with shari'a in private and civil spheres. The discussion will be organized according to the political actor.

King Abdullah

Any discussion of shari'a politics in Saudi Arabia must begin by acknowledging the king's striking efforts, largely unanticipated in their scope, to advance reforms of government and society, particularly after he assumed full power in August 2005. On all accounts, the population accepts as sincere and genuine the king's persona as bold reformer, and his popularity is extraordinarily high. It has remained so even as some of the reforms have fallen short of early expectations and others have stalled. Most people seem willing to blame such failures on opposing forces in the royal family, among the scholars, or elsewhere in government rather than on the king.

Many, perhaps most, of King Abdullah's reforms directly implicate change in the basic religious temper of the country, and indeed constitute shari'a politics par excellence. We shall discuss three such reform causes that the king has dramatically made his own, even putting his own name on particular projects. Interestingly, in all of them he directly contends with the religious establishment.

First, the king has chosen to personally demonstrate, and to inculcate throughout government and society, a strikingly broadened tolerance of other religious currents within Islam and of other religions. Even as crown prince, in 2003, he inaugurated a series of national dialogue conferences. The first conference was attended by representatives of streams of thought routinely condemned as heretical by Wahhabi establishment scholars and subjected to social and economic disadvantage and even persecution: Sufis from the Hijaz region, Shi'as from the Eastern Province, and Shi'a Isma'ilis from the south (Ibrahim 2006). Immediately after becoming king he met with delegations of both the Shi'a groups, and these meetings were made public. In 2005 the king attended the funeral of a famous religious notable of Hijaz, the Sufi Shaykh Muhammad 'Alawi al-Maliki, who for years had been banned from public speaking or writing and was so maligned by mainstream believers that he could enter the holy mosque in Mecca only with a police guard. During 2008 the king took his cause of religious tolerance onto the world stage, convening with media fanfare a pan-Islamic conference in Mecca in June, a conference of all world religions in Madrid in July, and finally a UN Interfaith Conference in New York in November.

All of this took place against the broad background of the kingdom's efforts to suppress Saudi-generated or -sponsored domestic and international terrorism. These efforts require the king to confront various intolerant dogmatic positions, historically often held by Wahhabism itself, justifying violent jihad against non-Muslims and against Muslims deemed deviant. Among the first Saudi reactions to the events of September 11, 2001, were denials, official and unofficial, of the fact that fifteen of the nineteen terrorists involved were Saudis. But soon, led by Crown Prince Abdullah, Saudi Arabia acknowledged the extent to which extremists partly nurtured on Saudi support and extreme Wahhabi ideology posed a severe threat. The domestic mood turned decisively against religious terrorism after al-Qa'ida took the battle into Saudi Arabia itself in numerous incidents. The watershed was the attack on a residential compound in Riyadh in May 2003 that killed at least twenty-seven Saudis, non-Saudi Muslims, and non-Muslims. After it, Saudi security forces could count on popular support for their measures against extremists, however forceful. In this same period many reformers, liberal and conservative, found the courage to speak out forcefully against Wahhabi orthodoxy for allowing such extremism to grow, blaming Wahhabism's tendency to condemn non-Wahhabi faithful as infidels (takfir), the inclusion of extreme views in school textbooks, and the bigotry, narrow-mindedness, and ignorance of some Wahhabi scholars. In all this they seconded criticisms being voiced about Saudi Arabia abroad. After securing strong fatwas condemning terrorism, Saudis mounted a largely successful program to reeducate and rehabilitate members of terrorist groups, portraying them as misled or duped. Prominent Wahhabi scholars who had once applauded jihadist trends when these were directed outside the country now renounced their beliefs and served the government's reeducation campaign. Famous terrorist shaykhs went on television from prison to renounce their prior beliefs (Rasheed 2007, 165–71).

Another initiative by the king, also directly impinging on the religious establishment, is the reform of education, a cause that he again studded with projects bearing his name. Education has long needed urgent reform, as the nation faces the challenges of developing a workforce capable of diversifying its economy away from oil and employing the frighteningly huge number of Saudis entering the job market (38 percent of the population is under fifteen years of age). But education has historically been dominated, or at least strongly influenced, by religious leaders. This has led to a curriculum that many criticize as slanted toward religion to the neglect of needed skills. Impelled by the rise of extremism and under foreign pressure, the government has made changes to curricula and textbooks to remove passages inspiring intolerance and hatred of non-Muslims, steps some scholars condemn as weakening the religion's defenses against Westernization. Especially intense religious feelings surround the education of girls. When girls' education was inaugurated, against religious opposition, by King Faisal in the 1970s, a compromise ceded control over girls' schools to the religious establishment. Only recently has this arrangement changed, with the incorporation of girls' education into the general Ministry of Education in 2003. In February 2009 the king appointed his son-in-law as minister of education, making clear that he wanted results. At the same time he appointed a woman as deputy minister in charge of girls' education, the highest Saudi government office ever occupied by a woman. In higher education the government is eagerly encouraging and funding reforms. Leading the effort, the king lavishly endowed a new King Abdullah University for Science and Technology, an independent research university near Jeddah. Its campus, to which the government hopes world-class faculty will be attracted, is free of the social strictures applying elsewhere— the sexes are even allowed to mix in classes, a point attracting some fierce critique from religious scholars and the conservative public. The government also opened the door to the creation of private colleges and universities, a number of them for women, freeing them from some of the government restrictions and supervision that stultify public universities.

The third of King Abdullah's signature reform projects targets the judiciary, a stronghold of the scholars. As Saudi Arabia sought and gained membership in the World Trade Organization, internal and external attention focused on the long-standing problem of the opacity of Saudi laws, particularly in the commercial sphere, due to the absence of codification or published decisions.[6]

The judicial system has long been criticized by human rights organizations as well as business groups, and deficiencies in it, as judged by international standards, also came prominently before the public eye. Some particularly appalling judgments and sentences gained attention and condemnation worldwide. In 2006, for example, the victim of a gang rape, a young woman from the eastern Shiʻa town of Qatif, was sentenced to imprisonment and lashes—this on the grounds that, before she was abducted, she was sitting in a car alone with a former boyfriend. The sentence was reversed, but the court retrying the case increased the penalty. Some citizens (but not all) were appalled; local media ran complaints about other apparently heavy (or light) sentences delivered by judges. In the end, about eighteen months after the incident, the king pardoned her (Zoepf 2007).

To improve the judiciary, the king has taken action on two key fronts, both to be discussed in the next section: he has taken steps signaling his eagerness to codify fiqh laws, and launched under his own name a twenty-year project to upgrade the court system, inaugurated by replacing the old 1975 Regulation of the Judiciary (Nizam al-Qada') with a new one. The most striking innovation of the new regulation, issued in 2007, is to shift the supreme appellate function from the Supreme Council of the Judiciary, which also supervises the judiciary, to a new Supreme Court. For decades the Council, under the direction of the redoubtable Shaykh Salih al-Lahaydan, had steered the judiciary in a highly conservative direction and opposed codification. Indeed, perhaps because the new regulation so diminished the Council, Shaykh al-Lahaydan reportedly blocked its implementation.

But in 2009, after eighteen months of delay, that dam broke. On February 14, the king announced a series of appointments extensively reshuffling the scholarly establishment (Los Angeles Times 2009). Besides creating the new ten-member Supreme Court, he removed Shaykh Salih al-Lahaydan from his position as president of the Supreme Council of the Judiciary, after three decades in that office. He reconstituted the Council's membership, including, as mandated by the new regulation, ex officio representatives of the Ministry of Justice and the prosecutorial-investigative judiciary. The new president of the Council is the previous president of the Consultative Council, the widely respected scholar Shaykh Salih bin Humayd.[7] A new minister of justice was appointed: Dr. Muhammad bin ʻAbd al-Karim Al-ʻIsa, a youthful, active judge previously vice-president of the Board of Grievances. The former minister of justice, Dr. Abdullah Al al-Shaykh, was shifted to replace Bin Humayd as president of the Consultative Council. The king also altered the membership of the Board of Senior Scholars (Hayʼat Kibar al-ʻUlama), the highest fatwa-giving body, removing several members and adding even more, making the total membership now twenty-one. (Shaykh al-Lahaydan remains a member.)

Together, these three initiatives bearing the king's personal stamp—inculcating religious tolerance and inclusion, diluting government and religious control over education, and reforming the judiciary and the laws—represent not a shot but a barrage across the bow of his partners in rule, the conservative religious establishment. And they are all the more telling given that this king is esteemed as honest and patriotic; personal rectitude is a crucial determinant of a ruler's power to shake and shift the scholarly establishment. These reform measures are clearly seismic events within the world of Saudi shari'a politics.

The Wahhabi Scholarly Establishment

Most misjudgments about Saudi politics stem from underestimating the influence of the scholarly establishment, the professional Saudi religious scholars who adhere to the Wahhabi theological and juristic premises long conventional in Saudi Arabia. Most—but not all—of these scholars work for institutions that are part of or are funded by the government, discharging such functions as adjudication, notarization, fatwa-giving, ordering the good and forbidding the evil (*hisba*), instructing the public in Islam (*da'wa*), preaching and leading prayers, teaching in public schools and universities, and participating in international Islamic organizations. Because the religious establishment is so pervasively supported, even employed, by the government; because its erstwhile independent functions have been distributed among modern ministries and agencies; and because it invariably gives religious sanction to controversial acts of the regime at times of political unrest, the standard view of observers of Saudi politics is that the religious establishment has been coopted thoroughly by the government and that its sole political role is as the servile purveyor of ideological cover for regime authoritarianism (see, e.g., Rasheed 2007, 4, 25–26, 32–33; Nevo 1998, 42–44; Fandy 2001, 36–37; Teitelbaum 2000, 11–12; cf. Steinberg 2005; *contra* Hamzawy 2006; Commins 2006, 114; Obaid 1999, 51). The obviousness of this conclusion is undercut, however, when one factors in the shari'a-dictated structurings of the role and authority of scholars in a traditional Islamic state, particularly the age-old credal obligation to support rulers to avoid civil strife and the constitutional separation of powers between ruler and scholars. In other words, this conclusion is based on the tacit assumption that, since the scholars and king are avowed partners, they are equal partners in all matters, ignoring the doctrinal—and innate—divergence and complementarity of their roles. This conclusion also fails to explain how scholars could remain prestigious and powerful in guiding Saudi religious and social life if they in fact so basely betrayed their own principles out of greed for their positions and obsequiousness before the king.

Famously, Saudi Arabia was founded on a 1745 compact of mutual support between the religious reformer Ibn 'Abd al-Wahhab and the then-local ruler Ibn Saud. Ever since, the fundamental principle of government, almost a *Grundnorm,* has been that the Wahhabi scholarly establishment and the ruling family act in close partnership, neither imagining existence without the other. This in turn means that the scholars will not normally obstruct interests that the state considers vital to its success, nor will the state dare to undermine the textualist, scholar-guided Salafi religiosity that its legitimacy explicitly and traditionally depends on. But vital differences can still exist between the two arms of this partnership, along the lines of the *siyasa shar'iyya* system, with far-reaching significance for the internal and external life of the country. Certainly, the fact that most scholars accept salaries or hold government positions does not mean that they are submissive on all issues.

Long-standing trends, accelerating during the last decade not only in Saudi Arabia but throughout the Arab and Muslim world, have favored the influence of scholarly religious leadership and undermined the religious legitimacy of rulers. Thanks to these trends, the Saudi scholars have managed to maintain a better position in their partnership with the state than might have been expected, given the massive secular social and technological changes favoring the centralizing and modernizing state. Some establishment scholars, notably Shaykh Bin Baz (d. 1999) and Shaykh al-Uthaymin (d. 2001), enjoyed international influence, the very religious stringency that made them abhorrent to some rendering them powerfully credible to others.

Observers have much more frequently been wrong in concluding that the Saudi religious leadership has bowed, or will bow, before the king than they have been right. While this leadership has certainly capitulated even on some religious and moral issues—such as, in King Faisal's time, girls' education and the introduction of television—its refusals to do so on other issues are rarely noted or foreseen. To assess claims of either capitulation or resistance to the government's wishes, one must analyze each issue within the overlapping shari'a structures discussed above. Acquiescence in areas of government discretion or weak shari'a principle does not count for much, and may be offset by resistance elsewhere.

A list of matters on which establishment scholars are hindering or blocking concrete government measures or initiatives, and doing so in the name of shari'a, would be lengthy. Three, however, are particularly useful for understanding current shari'a politics.

The most telling example of scholarly resistance—and its immense potential persistence and firmness—is the scholars' absolute refusal, maintained since the founding of the country in 1932, to allow the codification of the fiqh they apply, or even to implement many of the king's decrees and statutes, despite the immense practical problems this refusal engenders. Pressure to codify the laws—as has been done in every other Muslim country, even those particularly devoted to shari'a (see the introduction)—has been increasing for decades. It is peaking now as Saudi Arabia faces towering demographic challenges and realizes that, to achieve its economic potential, it must urgently create a favorable business and investment climate. The king has taken two steps betraying his eagerness to do so—he quietly formed a committee of experts to carry out a codification, and he put the question of whether and how to do so to the Board of Senior Scholars. King Faisal had submitted the question in the 1970s, when the board opposed codification by a split vote, the decision being published only in 1991 (Vogel 2000, 338). Its current decision on the matter has now several times been postponed.

If codification is announced (and in fact goes forward), what form will it take? It now appears, judging from my interviews with a number of those involved or informed, that the laws will follow a model of legislation differing from that found elsewhere. Legal systems worldwide generally follow either the Anglo-American common-law or the European civil-law model. Saudi Arabia, however, adheres to a third form of legal system, for which the most characteristic form of law is neither judicial precedent (common law) nor national code (civil law), but the opinions of scholars (jurists' law). While absorbing elements from civil- and common-law systems, Saudi codification seems likely to honor its own form of legal system in two ways. First, it will likely be formulated by scholars and judges. Probably this group will draw on Hanbali fiqh but leaven it heavily with opinions from other fiqh schools and from modern scholars, especially opinions already followed by Saudi courts; it will no doubt borrow many rules from other legal systems where these are needed to fill gaps in fiqh and do not offend shari'a. Second, the codification will likely present itself not as strictly binding on judges, but as presumptive. A judge would be able to deviate from the code, but only on strong grounds that he could explain and defend. If on appeal his view earned the favor of higher courts, it would also become presumptively binding on judges; otherwise it would be reversed.

But even codification of this type may be too intrusive to earn scholarly support. Scholars still consider that the ijtihad ideal on which all of Islamic fiqh is based and which is echoed in the Basic Law (Article 48)—and which, as good Salafis, Saudi judges consider no distant ideal but a guide to concrete practice—demands that every judge must be free to rule microcosmically according to what his own conscience indicates is closest to God's own ruling for the case, disregarding other influences. Even recently, my interviews with judges otherwise cooperating with government revealed that they consider this case-by-case approach a fundamental principle of justice. One can be sure that all of the king's recent additions to the Supreme Court, the Board of Senior Scholars, and the Supreme Council of the Judiciary uphold this ideal at least in principle, since their careers up to now have depended on the approval of scholars such as Shaykh Salih al-Lahaydan.

A second example of resistance by scholars is their opposition to the king's initiative to reform the judiciary. Throughout the history of judicial reform, powerful leaders in the judiciary have worked to block reforms that sought to influence court judgments substantively, not administratively, but these leaders seem lately to have yielded some ground. Against long resistance, the government recently successfully invaded the realm of uncodified fiqh by issuing two *nizams* on judicial procedure, one for civil matters (2000) and one for criminal (2001)—though reportedly judges do not always acknowledge or follow them. Other recent *nizams* regularized the legal profession (*muhamah*) (2001) and created a modern land registry (2002)—although some lawyers still complain that judges ignore the former, and the latter is still a pilot project. The 2007 Regulation of the Judiciary reorganizing the court structure reiterates several initiatives earlier announced but never implemented. Among them is the project, which was actually decreed at least once, to incorporate into the regular courts the specialized tribunals set up to enforce particular *nizams*. Actually, the new regulation merges only the two largest of these tribunals: the commercial jurisdiction of the Board of Grievances and the labor commissions. The regulation's Article 14 reiterates and develops a provision from 1975 (also Article 14) to the effect that no panel at either of the two appellate levels may deviate from principles of law decided by the Supreme Court unless, after referral to the entire Supreme Court, its members vote to permit the deviation. In earlier form this provision had remained a dead letter, since leaders of the judiciary, notably Shaykh Salih al-Lahaydan, opposed it, for the same reasons that they opposed codification. It is not yet clear whether, enshrined again in legislation, these reforms will see greater success than they have in the past.

A third, and more discrete, issue on which the scholarly establishment has recently pushed back against the government, with revealing significance for shari'a politics, is the government's proposal to widen the area, termed *mas'a*, where pilgrims in Mecca run or walk between Safa and Marwa, two ancient points immediately adjacent to the holy mosque. Since this project affects the rites of the pilgrimage, which are intricately detailed in fiqh law itself and axiomatically within the jurisdiction of the scholars, the king was obliged to ask the Board of Senior Scholars for their opinion. Although the board had, years before, approved seemingly analogous improvements facilitating the pilgrimage ritual, and despite witness testimony that the widened area still fell between the age-old locations of the original hills of Safa and Marwa, in 2006 the board rejected the king's proposal, though by a split decision. Generally the king acquiesces in the board's rulings, but in this case he held with the minority and in 2008 ordered the improvements to proceed. Reportedly, scholars on the board went so far as to recruit young men to warn pilgrims that, if they ran the course on the ground widened by the government, their ritual act might be invalid. The government has not relented.[8]

What do these three instances of resistance by the religious establishment reveal about current Saudi shariʻa politics? Do they represent only the ever-recurrent struggles by the scholars to preserve and fortify their own constitutional branch of government? The long-running controversies over codification and judicial reform may fall into this category, since the chief issues and proposals under debate have been around for decades. But the *masʻa* controversy seems more akin to some individual scholars' vehemently reasserted opposition to the king's outreach to the Shiʻa, to his efforts to reform school curricula, or to coeducation in universities. They may be attempts to reassert conventional establishment Wahhabism as the exclusive ideology of the kingdom. The scholars' resistance may be a return volley, this time across the bows of the king and his reformers, reminding them that the establishment Wahhabi scholars, holding powerful positions in government and wielding great social influence, remain essential partners in government and social control, capable of extracting a high price for steps they dislike? If so, the king's response in his February 2009 measures is unmistakable. By exercising to the hilt, and dramatically, his power to determine which scholars hold office in the official legal system, and particularly in removing Shaykh al-Lahaydan, the king clearly has won the latest battle. But is the battle the war? Again, we can recall that observers, even Saudis, have often been wrong in predicting the defeat or retreat of the scholarly establishment; that the prestige of the scholars (as opposed to their worldly functions) does not depend on offices doled out by the king; and that the scholars augment their authority most when they are perceived as standing in opposition to actions by the king.

Before going on, we must make clear that the religious establishment was not unanimously opposed to these government measures. Though establishment scholars share general theological and fiqh methodological stances, they differ constantly on specific points of law, and there is no compulsory hierarchy among fatwas that can prevent a scholar from disagreeing if he has the self-confidence to buck group solidarity and his seniors. In every era there are always several prominent scholars who are given to constitutional views favoring government initiatives and whom the king appoints to high administrative positions. Thus, while the Saudi scholarly establishment does amazingly well in maintaining its solidarity on key survival issues, it hardly ever speaks in unison.

Also, it is palpably the case that change and evolution are occurring in the establishment, showing that the various divides (such as between the Wahhabis and the "awakening" ulama discussed below) are far from unbridgeable. Many examples of change could be given, such as increased instruction in law other than fiqh at the graduate Higher Judicial Institute of the Imam Muhammad University, or growing opportunities for fiqh-trained scholars and students to play powerful real-world roles in the burgeoning field of Islamic finance.

The Sahwa (Awakening) Ulama

In seeking religious sanction for his rule and actions in past, simpler times, a Saudi king would have no alternative but to turn to the establishment scholars described above—a group that, although it has no formal definition, institutionalization, or qualifications, is cohesive, disciplined, and self-aware. But the Islamic awakening occurring throughout the Muslim world since the 1970s has affected Saudi Arabia as much as other countries. Indeed, Saudi Arabia and Wahhabism were vital contributors to the awakening, not only tangibly through their petrodollar support of religious institutions but intangibly through their championship of Salafi religiosity as a response to modern times. The awakening first emerged elsewhere, most prominently in Egypt, but then rebounded on Saudi Arabia itself, ironically mutating the very Wahhabism that helped inspire it. From the 1970s and 1980s, as Muslim countries everywhere took strong measures against their ever-growing religious opposition, activists and scholars from around the Muslim world went into exile and found homes in Saudi Arabia. Among them were Muhammad Qutb (the brother of Sayyid Qutb), Muhammad Surur Zayn al-'Abidin, a scholar of activist tendencies from Syria (Rasheed 2007, 73–77), and 'Abd Allah 'Azzam, who inspired a young Osama bin Laden and left to foment jihad in Pakistan and Afghanistan. Occupying teaching positions at Saudi universities, they confronted conventional Wahhabism and began to meld it with their own tendencies into a new, "awakened" (sahwi), activist Salafi style. Like the old Wahhabism that spurred the conquests creating the Saudi state, this religiosity insisted that Islam was a program not for mere belief or morality but for action in the social and political, as well as international, spheres. But the old Wahhabism, while fierce in creed ('aqida), was conservative in law or fiqh, since the form and content of traditional fiqh was little challenged by the still-backward conditions of the Arabian peninsula. The newly awakened Salafism, in contrast, calls for programmatizing fiqh itself as a solution to all sorts of modern difficulties, not only personal and social but also political, including restoring the rule of the Islamic state and of shari'a worldwide. Madawi al-Rasheed describes it as "a state of mind and plan of action. Sahwa is built on a realization that ordinary man can be at the center of his own destiny" (Rasheed 2007, 66). Some Sahwi trends took Wahhabism in the direction of violent jihadism; others, especially since 9/11 and subsequent terrorist events in the kingdom, have been more moderate than the establishment itself.

Young Saudi scholars holding the Sahwi point of view grew up maintaining their Wahhabi identity and earning the trust of their superiors. They were appointed to posts within the religious establishment as professors, mosque imams, and judges. But the momentous events following Iraq's invasion of Kuwait in 1990—above all the decision of King Fahd and a small circle of princes to invite in Western forces to deter Iraq from invading Saudi Arabia and to restore Kuwait—revealed the distinctions between these scholars and their elders. The king's decision electrified Saudi society as a whole, jolting some into open criticism of the regime, a rare act in the kingdom. Although King Fahd was able to gain a somewhat grudging fatwa from the Board of Senior Scholars sanctioning this invitation (Fahad 2004, 514–19), many younger scholars of the Sahwi trend broke ranks on this issue, vehemently denouncing the king and government for inviting "Crusader" armies into the heartland of Islam, risking the autonomy of the holy places. It was inconceivable to them—and to many ordinary citizens—that, after such vast national treasure had been expended on defense, it was necessary to rely on outsiders to defend against a neighboring Arab country; corruption, cowardice, and obsequiousness toward the West suggested themselves as explanations. Using tape-recorded sermons and samizdat publications, these scholars stoked the fires of outrage. Their zeal awakened memories of the horrific episode of 1979 in which an extremist Wahhabi faction led by Juhayman al-'Utaybi, condemning corruption and deviance in the royal family, occupied the great mosque of Mecca and was defeated only with difficulty.

The two most famous "Sahwi shaykhs," Safar al-Hawali and Salman al-'Awda, were catapulted into prominence by their vehement opposition to the "Crusader" forces. They took leading roles in generating a series of famous petitions to the king demanding multiple reforms (taking as their model a 1990 petition by liberals). Initially the religious establishment, even the towering Bin Baz, tacitly endorsed the Sahwis' petitions, but it soon shifted against them, chastising their authors for creating sedition and social unrest. All of these events are extensively documented in many studies (e.g., Teitelbaum 2000; Fandy 2001; Rasheed 2007). The Sahwi leaders were progressively subjected to pressure, barred from speaking publicly, and finally arrested in 1994, provoking unprecedented public demonstrations in their defense.

Our story really begins with the release of Hawali and 'Awda from prison in 1999. They reemerged forbidden to speak publicly but otherwise, they state, not under restriction. Since their release they have renounced public criticism of the regime, hewing closer to the conventionally broad Wahhabi interpretation of the age-old Sunni tenet favoring, in the interests of civil peace, only private exhortation (*nasiha*) of a wrong-doing ruler, not public resistance or rebellion (*khuruj*). 'Awda in particular has transformed himself into a moderate, and acquired a large following. As was true for Bin Baz before him, a record of courageously opposing state power turned a merely learned and articulate scholar into an influential religious leader. Hawali took a more contentious course, but still directed his political activism largely toward foreign causes (he, however, suffered an incapacitating stroke in 2005). If it has abandoned its political rebelliousness, the Sahwi trend survives in its most characteristic trait—its insistence that Islam, particularly in its legal character, provides a complete template for daily life.

Nowadays 'Awda has an international audience, through his comprehensive website on contemporary Islamic thought (www.islamtoday.com), media properties, and appearances in public (Jones 2009). He writes often against violence and in support of moderation in religion, tolerance of other religions and groups, and mitigation of women's circumstances. He accepted an invitation from a Sufi-oriented group in Hijaz to speak before them, and met with a famous Shi'a leader and scholar from the Eastern Province. He has lent his support to relatively liberal legislative causes. The differences between him and conventional Wahhabism have often caused him to be denounced by prominent establishment scholars.

Stéphane Lacroix, a political scientist specializing in Saudi Arabia, has gone so far as to posit that Salman al-'Awda is grooming himself, and being groomed, as the next Bin Baz, and that 'Awda's reformed Sahwi wing of Saudi shari'a scholarship may become the new centrism. He even speaks of a "post-Wahhabi" Saudi Arabia (Lacroix 2004, 364; Lacroix 2008, 156–58; see also Rasheed 2007, 195).

Sahwi "Intellectuals"

Lacroix also has written enthusiastically about a new group of intellectuals and activists, not necessarily scholars (ulama), who make it their mission to conjoin a devout Sahwi adherence to Salafi Islam in all aspects of life with a program of action to improve Saudi politics and society (Lacroix 2004, 2008). Their program goes far beyond the core concerns of establishment religious leaders—concerns such as stamping out heresy, intensifying and purifying Islamic ritual practice, upholding adherence to received fiqh law, and protecting Muslim interests worldwide—to engage the full reach of everyday problems in the country. These intellectuals and activists believe that Islam offers an invaluable—and, given that this is Saudi Arabia, indispensable—framework for solving the country's problems. In their zeal to be pragmatic, some adopt a stance of principled rationalism, viewing Islam as providing strong guiding ethical, legal, social, and political principles but as otherwise flexible, realistic, and rational. As long as Islamic principles are respected, any attractive idea or practice, whether it comes from the West or anywhere else, can be examined, adapted, and put to work to solve the problems of a nation of believers.

A typical member of this group, also according to Lacroix, is 'Abd al-'Aziz al-Qasim.[9] Hailing from the central region of Qasim (as do many appointed judges and scholars) and descended from one of the most famous families of Wahhabi scholars, al-Qasim was a highly successful student of Islamic fiqh, and by the 1990s was well along in a successful career as a judge. But after becoming active in the political petition movement he was imprisoned from 1995 to 1999, spending time with Hawali and 'Awda in jail. He now heads a law office, allied with the international law firm Allen & Overy.

Al-Qasim seems not to devote himself solely to work for his clients. On his own initiative and aided by the staff of his firm, he has taken up sensitive issues confronting society (including ones unrelated to law), carried out studies, and distributed their results. He boldly speaks out on public platforms, attacking the status quo on issues such as public education and the judiciary and proposing sweeping solutions. For example, on the issue of the judiciary al-Qasim prepared several lengthy memoranda, based on his own interviews with lawyers and judges as well as all other available data, that documented deficiencies in the system and were widely circulated privately. They gave objective support to grievances widely mooted among citizens and consistently mentioned in the various petitions submitted by diverse groups to the king. On this issue and that of public education reform, his interventions provoked vehement rebuttals from the religious establishment. Some high judges and officials called him personally to chastise him, invoking his upbringing, education, and family traditions. But what is most striking is the government's reaction to his activities: far from censuring or restricting him, it has given him large consulting contracts.

Another long-standing social problem al-Qasim has taken on is that of home mortgages. This now-unfolding issue offers a useful case study and requires sustained attention.

The use of mortgages has long been retarded in Saudi Arabia, for many reasons. Like many other legal and administrative practices in common use elsewhere, it has been hindered in Saudi Arabia by the stultifying bifurcation of the legal system between a modern-law (qanuni, nizam) sphere and a fiqh sphere. Throughout the country's fifty years of rapid modernization, whenever the government or the private sector, typically led by Western-trained specialists, has sought to launch some practice that seemed to risk contradicting shari'a, the religious establishment has tried to ignore or block it. Typically, the establishment scholars do not offer any alternative solution of their own, neither one deriving from fiqh nor one they would accept as simply not contradicting it. Many of the basic modernizing *nizams* of the country were issued in such conditions. A particularly striking example of a modern legal institution confronting basic shari'a principles is the kingdom's sophisticated system of commercial banks, launched early in the country's development. This industry grew into a pillar of the economy despite the fact that, given Saudi scholars' unanimous view that the Qur'anic prohibition on usury (*riba*) applies to bank interest, it was certain that most everyday banking contracts would not be enforced in Saudi courts. After some judgments by Saudi shari'a courts to that effect in the 1980s, the government took measures to divert banking disputes away from the regular courts and into the jurisdiction of a special committee within the central bank.

The issue of mortgages arises as a special case of the same problem. Because mortgages are issued by commercial banks, not only the courts but also the notaries public have refused to facilitate them in any way. Even if the debt obligation itself can be enforced by action before the special committee for banking disputes, there remains the problem of recording and enforcing the mortgage lien that secures that debt, since interests in land fall within the jurisdiction of the ordinary courts and the notaries public. The result has been that since the 1980s mortgages have been difficult to obtain and have been used mainly by the wealthy. Meanwhile, as the population of the country has grown and new families have formed apace, rates of home ownership have lagged strikingly behind those in other countries.

Yet an apt solution to the crisis has long been approaching from another direction—the rapidly growing field of Islamic banking and finance. Saudi Arabia is now the largest market worldwide for Islamic finance and banking services. Bankers report that 95 percent of all retail consumer banking in Saudi Arabia is done Islamically, often through "Islamic windows" at conventional banks. Yet, somewhat ironically, all these developments have occurred in a regulatory environment slow to facilitate Islamic finance. The Saudi Arabian Monetary Authority (SAMA), the central bank, fears the religious scholars' vehement stance against bank interest; if Islamic finance were to gain a strong foothold, it could unleash a wave of popular opinion sweeping aside conventional finance and severely disrupting the financial dealings of both the public and the private sectors.

Among the transactions routinely marketed by Islamic banks worldwide is home purchase financing. "Islamic mortgages" use various mechanisms. One is a hire-purchase agreement, in which the house is leased to the consumer in return for payments that both cover rent and progressively buy out the bank's share. Since in this case the title remains with the bank until the buy-out is complete, the bank's security against default is built in. Hire-purchase transactions are now coming into use in Saudi Arabia, and some companies now specialize in financing homes Islamically.

Al-Qasim used this mechanism as the basis of his proposal to solve the mortgage crisis. Arguing that "not only liberals should get mortgages," al-Qasim proposed to the Ministry of Finance that hire-purchase contracts be used not just to finance housing but as the basis for a new finance industry. The ministry awarded him a consulting contract to research the legal aspects of this proposal, including reviewing and comparing foreign systems and analyzing Saudi court cases and fatwas.

One problem required immediate attention—the Board of Senior Scholars had previously declared the practice of hire-purchase unlawful. Al-Qasim prepared an extensive brief explaining that this fatwa was unduly general, condemning all hire-purchase contracts even though some forms fully met shari'a requirements. On the basis of this brief he was able to obtain other favorable fatwas.

Al-Qasim's study ended by drafting four laws or *nizams* creating a new lease-financing industry, fixing terms for finance leases, and creating a new system for the registration of real estate liens.[10] After review by the Ministry of Finance, the drafts entered the legislative process through the Board of Experts of the Council of Ministers. In due course the government's drafts reached the Consultative Council, where they were extensively rewritten, as described below. In particular, the council's financial committee, especially Dr. 'Abd al-Rahman al-Atram, a leading scholar in Saudi Islamic banking, worked closely with al-Qasim to refine them, making extensive amendments. The legislation is now before the Council of Ministers, which will decide whether to approve the Consultative Council's changes.

What lessons can we draw from this case study for shari'a politics in Saudi Arabia? For now let us just review the facts. First, a legal problem with large social and economic consequences had languished for decades, with no solution apparent in a legal climate bifurcated between two divergent legal cultures. Second, a solution to the problem had long been developing, but from the private sector, in the industry of Islamic banking and finance. This industry draws heavily on conventional banking and finance, but, adapting these according to the dictates of shari'a, projects a new Muslim-world business model. Because the model is both Islamic in aspiration and unconventional, the government viewed it with ambivalence. Third, the person who successfully proposed a solution to the problem was neither an establishment scholar nor a government lawyer. He was, rather, a private Sahwi intellectual, a critic of the scholarly establishment, respected for his credentials in Islamic causes and skilled in shari'a argumentation, yet eager to embrace rational, proven solutions regardless of their source.

Bureaucrats, Technocrats, Businessmen, Notables

There are many other notable figures in Saudi Arabian law and politics, of course, including bureaucrats, technocrats, and businessmen. These are large, disparate groupings, and under this heading I only draw some lessons from the case study just reviewed about two of its protagonists: the Ministry of Finance and the Consultative Council.

The Ministry of Finance is probably the most sophisticated and successful of the ministries, and its head, Dr. Ibrahim al-Assaf, is well qualified, highly regarded, and powerful. The central bank, which works closely with the ministry, has long resisted the pull of Islamic finance, even when Islamic finance provided a ready means to further pressing governmental objectives, such as mobilizing capital locally or facilitating government borrowing in times of budget deficit. The case study shows strikingly how the ministry is now receptive to an Islamically inspired solution. Other indications of a shift include the floating of Islamic bonds, or *sukuk*, by quasi-governmental corporations like the Saudi Arabian Basic Industries Corporation (SABIC), and the government's liberal funding of a huge new Islamic bank, al-Inma, offering 70 percent of its shares for sale to the public.

Acceptance of Islamically branded solutions and approaches is similarly growing among the country's technocratic and business elites, who habitually have looked to the West for solutions. One indication of this increasing acceptance is the phenomenal growth throughout the Gulf of Islamic modes of finance and business. Saudi businessmen were among the founders of the Islamic finance industry, and many are now huge investors in it.

Another indication is the Consultative Council's debates on the mortgage laws. The Consultative Council is a modern innovation, though with many precedents of the same name in Islamic history, by which the king discharges the religious and cultural imperative of consultation (*shura*) with his people, enjoined by the Qur'an itself (Aba-Namay 1998). It is an entirely appointive body, formed in 1992 with 60 members and now grown to 150. The appointments aim for representation of a broad variety of regions and social groupings. They include several Shi'as. So far not one of its members is female, though six women have been named to an advisory committee. King Fahd and now King Abdullah have appointed many of the most accomplished Saudi citizens: businessmen, ex-bureaucrats, scholars, lawyers, and professors predominate. It is said that the council boasts more Ph.D.s than any legislative body in the world. Its proceedings, highly regimented by rules giving considerable control to its president, are conducted behind closed doors, except for certain hours weekly that are televised. The council's powers are far more limited than those of the typical representative body it resembles at first glance: besides being entirely appointed, rather than elected, it is intended chiefly to review and comment on legislation, treaties, and government programs. Since 2005 it has also had the power to propose draft laws and amendments to existing laws. But its authority remains merely advisory, the king considering its advice alongside the opinion of the Council of Ministers.

Lately, the Consultative Council seems to be gaining vigor and influence greater than its narrow formal powers would indicate. It represents the modern version of what was formerly the pillar of social and political power in Islamic states: the variously and informally constituted authority of "notables" (a'yan), those who, whether through their status or their achievements, possess influence in society, often serving as intermediaries between society and government. The council is becoming more assertive and outspoken, and the public is paying increasing attention to its doings. Strikingly, in the case of the mortgage laws the council did not merely request minor changes, but extensively rewrote the government's draft, introducing wholly new ideas. It suggested further legislation to establish a new quasi-governmental institute that would set standards for sound Islamic banking practice—in particular, it would ensure that Islamic banks comply with the panoply of transparency and consumer protection requirements other banks must meet. During debate on the bills, some members put forward the contentious position that the government should order the sudden shift of the entire finance industry to an Islamic model; this was beaten back by cooler heads, including some supporters of the industry, who realized that the industry was still both too flawed and too weakly developed to take on the entire Saudi economy. Another proposal from the floor was also overruled: that the government should vet commercial transactions for compliance with shari'a, which is now done by scholars within each bank. Many apparently felt this was also premature when the industry is still rapidly innovating and evolving.

In all this we see evidence that the elite of civil society are increasingly engaging with Saudi shari'a politics, and in particular are showing zeal to develop and apply Islamic legal solutions to contemporary Saudi problems.

Women

The king has made clear his desire to advance women's legal status and rights, but has not established it among his signature causes. It is widely reported that he would like women to be allowed to drive; though a breakthrough on the issue is often declared imminent, it fails to happen. Women's school enrollment and educational achievements have been growing steadily for decades. Augmenting this trend, the government allowed private women's colleges to open, and these seek to offer superior educations and enlarge women's intellectual and professional opportunities, such as by offering degrees in law. A 2006 labor law provision omitting reference to segregation of the sexes and guardedly endorsing women's employment seems to have led, probably de facto more than de jure, to widened opportunities. Where not long ago women working in an office were hidden away and never seen, now mixed workplaces in private businesses are not even cause for comment. Educated women, certainly those speaking English, seem able to find work, particularly if they accept some mixing with men. Some women (or their male relatives) can choose the degree of mixing they find comfortable: the sexes may work in separate buildings or only in separate cubicles, and veiling may range from a full face covering to mere modest dress. Press coverage of women's issues seems to have greatly increased, with focus on undoubted evils like spousal abuse or neglect. Liberal women, while galled by their circumstances, keep up a guarded activism, the opportunities for which expand with better access to the media and means of communication, including the internet. Many women, even elite Western-educated women, reject the ideal of formal equality, believing that Islam holds the genders to be of equal worth while recognizing gender differences; they often support the status quo while identifying abuses. Many women's opportunities depend crucially on the men with whom they live; besides oppressive spouses and fathers, there are open-minded, supportive ones. Together with her religious beliefs, a woman's love for and loyalty to her parents, family, and traditions strongly influence her desire for change, tempering and channeling it.

What women report as most burdensome is not the inability to drive or to work with men, but the legal powers male relatives wield over women's persons, children, activities, work, and movements under Saudi administrative and family law. This is labeled the issue of men's *qiwama,* a contested term loosely translatable as "guardianship" (see Qur'an 4:34; cf. Hefner's introduction to this volume). Saudi women need permission from a male relative (usually a husband or father) to conduct ordinary activities, such as traveling alone, opening a bank account for a child, or even leaving the home for study or work (Human Rights Watch 2008). For all women, but especially those who are widowed or divorced, these restrictions are very burdensome. Under modern conditions, where women may be isolated in a nuclear family of marriage while their extended family of origin is dispersed, it can be difficult for them to have recourse to their own male relatives to ask them to exercise *qiwama* or to defend them from a husband's overreaching. Besides *qiwama,* husbands possess the options of easy divorce and polygyny, and wield these to their advantage. Child custody after divorce is a sore point, since men have the presumptive right to assume custody even of young children, particularly if the ex-wife has remarried.

As often in the Middle East, such issues, deeply affecting the daily lives of women of all classes, are not seen just as social problems needing a practical solution; for conservatives the religious laws and policies behind them form a final bulwark against the social corruption, rampant secularization, and Westernization threatening the Muslim family and, with it, Islam itself. The fiqh of family law is seen as, in the main, revealed explicitly in the Qur'an and Sunna, and not open to rationalization or innovation; change in it can be condemned not as innocent but as deviant change, bid'a, close to heresy. Yet, as is particularly remarked by outsiders, Saudi restrictions on women are more pervasive and exacting than shari'a (or Saudi formal law) requires, and appear to have evolved into their current form by cross-breeding between fiqh rules and local customs and traditions. Still, whether as a result of shari'a itself or of customary norms blurred with shari'a, efforts to increase the rights and freedoms of Saudi women face severe obstacles. Much has been achieved in recent years, but chiefly either by indirection, as opinions shift with greater knowledge of Islamic precepts favoring women (as in the case of women's education), or by slight administrative adjustments (such as allowing women without male permission to take rooms in hotels or, if over forty-five, to travel abroad). Indeed, during the last decade the government seems to have made a project of incremental improvements (see Doumato 2009 for numerous instances). Pressure continues to build in favor of women, if only because of the sheer significance of women as a bloc of highly educated, unutilized workers.

Given this context, it is fascinating that a dramatic change in the prevailing Saudi family law has recently occurred, one that profoundly affects many Saudi women's lives and goes right to the core of the question of what constitutes a lawful marriage. Reportedly, in the 1980s and 1990s laypersons in central Saudi Arabia developed novel forms of marriage called misyar and sadiq, which depend at root on the idea that a wife may validly waive her legal rights against her husband, particularly her rights to maintenance (nafaqa), including a marital dwelling, and to share equally with any co-wives her husband's cohabitation and resources (Arabi 2001, 147–67; Yamani 2008, 107–13, 203–204). Cleverly deploying this idea, a misyar marriage permits a couple to marry while at the same time relieving the husband of these two otherwise foundational obligations. Because care is taken to meet the formal requirements of a lawful marriage—the consent of the bride's male guardian, two witnesses, a dower payment, and a degree of publicity—prestigious fatwas were easily obtained sanctioning it. Use of this new stratagem has exploded, since it allows men to duck major burdens that discourage them from marriage: the cost and commitment of establishing a home for a wife, and, in the case of a second marriage, facing the disapproval of the first wife and sometimes of their social group. Even some women find *misyar* useful, such as single women or divorcees tired of depending on their father, brothers, or sons for support or for legal permission for various activities. Such women can keep their own residences or live with their families, while meeting up with their husband from time to time. Clever stipulations in the contract, or unwritten understandings, can ensure that a husband will provide the necessary permissions, as guardian, for a wife's activities, such as travel for professional reasons. Wives gain these advantages, however, only at the cost of supporting themselves, foregoing the prestige of conventional marriage, and (usually) becoming a second wife. Moreover, the husband still has the legal upper hand, able at any time to assert all his powers as both her husband and the legal guardian of both her and any children.

By slightly varying the terms of *misyar* marriage, individuals have created other forms of marriage, which have since acquired their own names. The *sadiq* or "friend" marriage is a variation developed for young people not established enough for conventional marriage; it allows them to meet for sexual relations from time to time without establishing a home together. *Mityar* and *misyaf* are marriages by which a man seeks a second wife, typically one whose appearance and education are superior to his first wife's, to accompany him on business trips or summer vacations abroad. *Misfar* is the marriage of a woman who needs a husband to accompany her on study abroad.

A form more controversial than any of these is a marriage entered into by a husband who has a secret intent to divorce in the future (*nikah bi-niyyat al-talaq*). This form was sanctioned by several high religious authorities in order to meet male Saudi students' needs for companionship for the duration of their studies abroad. It skirts close to the prohibited *mut'a*, the temporary marriage allowed by the Shi'a, but fatwas justify it as distinguishable from *mut'a* specifically because the husband keeps his intent to limit the term of the marriage secret. Other scholars reject this reasoning, saying that it condones deceit of the wife and of her guardian, and insist on the normal Sunni requirement that marriage be formed with the intention of permanence.

As noted above, these new marriages have become part of Saudi law and practice without any need for action by the state. By simple ingenuity private individuals have created socially transforming institutions without waiting for official action. In this respect these marriages resemble the financing techniques of the Islamic finance industry, which grew into a major modern social and economic institution by exploiting purely private ingenuity to overcome shari'a prohibitions on interest. In both cases the innovations rely heavily on the mechanism of "free" agreement or contract. But the use of this method to alter basic elements of the marriage relationship, however, is somewhat astonishing, given that marriage is a contract hedged about with social taboos, religious sanctity, and many explicit fiqh rules. It is of course incongruous that this astounding exercise in ingenuity is undertaken not to advance the legal status of women but to undermine it, since the woman gains admission to these marriages only by foregoing most of the material benefits that, under the law, are her compensation for ceding rights over her person. These marriages can be viewed as advancing women's interests only in a context in which women can lawfully secure similar privileges in no other way. The new marriages also sharply dilute the interests of any first wife and family, who sometimes learn of the second marriage only when the husband dies and unanticipated claimants on his estate materialize.

This raises the question whether similar ingenuity could reap any clearer advantages for women. Age-old doctrines, elaborately developed and practiced in medieval times, permit spouses to stipulate modifications of their subsidiary rights and duties, as long as these do not negate essential elements of the marriage relationship (Ali 2008; Sonbol 2008). Such stipulations are in fact used in Saudi Arabia, but rather sparingly, despite their promise. The culture runs largely against their use, holding that concessions from a husband, such as allowing his wife to continue her studies, should be obtained informally and enforced only by mutual familial good will (Yamani 2008, 96–97; Wynn 2008). But with the huge recent increase in divorce, which was once rare, perhaps this attitude will change. Then the issue will be whether Saudi judges will find such stipulations lawful and enforce them. Despite following the school of law which most favors such stipulations, the Hanbali, and despite having shown extreme flexibility in the case of *misyar,* they may not be willing to do so.

Regional and Minority Issues

Regions outside of Najd have long complained of diminished privilege and influence under the Saudi regime, and this is especially true of those belonging to minority religious groups, including Sunnis devoted to Sufism in the Hijaz, Twelver Shi'as mostly from al-Ahsa', and Isma'ilis from Najran. Space permits touching on only a few recent developments that are suggestive in view of the discussions above.

We have already mentioned King Abdullah's striking, unprecedented gestures toward the Sufis and Shi'a, beginning even before he became king: he included them in state-sponsored civic dialogues and elaborately publicized celebrations of religious tolerance. Religious practices previously forced into private may now be conducted in public, such as Shi'a 'Ashura rituals and the

Sufi celebration of the Prophet's birthday (Mawlid al-nabi). In the Hijaz regional cultural pride is more openly manifested in dress, architecture, music, literature, and manners, in addition to religious observance. An active culture has sprung up of weekly gatherings in private homes devoted to such themes as the celebration of leading Hijazis' accomplishments, Sufi thought and practice, or Arab nationalist ideas. Some of these gatherings boast websites with clips from their meetings and publications.

Activists for Human Rights, the Rule of Law, and Civil Society

Of all the groups discussed in this chapter, activists seem the least hopeful for the future. Looking for political openings toward democratic institutions, the rule of law, and an end to official corruption, they feel dispirited. Encouraged at first by King Abdullah's reform initiatives—pardons of jailed political activists, receptivity to a few reform petitions, relative freeing of the press, the institutionalization of civil-society dialogue, two new human rights organizations,[11] a draft law to license non-governmental organizations, and elections for provincial assemblies—activists are now disheartened as harsh measures suppressing political opposition have multiplied, such as the detention of Fouad al-Farhan, a noted blogger, in December 2007 and the re-imprisonment of once-pardoned Dr. Matrouk al-Faleh from May 2008 to January 2009. An analogy one activist used was that of the Grand Canyon: a beautiful vision shimmers in the distance, but if one takes a step toward it one falls into the vast abyss; i.e., one can hope and act, but only to a point. Activists are not comforted by arguments attributing the lapse of reform efforts to politics within the royal family rather than to King Abdullah's own intentions; they ask, why should the royal family support reform in any case?

While disappointed, this group is hardly cowed, and expresses itself as freely it can in the Saudi press and through other means. But, having faced repressions, it does not indulge in optimism about future reforms or about potentially transformative forces in civil society.

The Informal Public Sphere

Saudi society has always exhibited what one may loosely call the *majlis* phenomenon. The term can be applied to intimate gatherings of extended families; social events among men linked through friendship, kinship, profession, employment, or other networks; and general open houses held weekly by the powerful, where clients, complainants, supplicants, and well-wishers present themselves. Through all of these gatherings run currents of rumor, gossip, and opinion so potent that everyone seems to learn the same information at once. (Whether an item, however newsworthy, appears in the press is another question altogether.) The exchange of views in such gatherings, especially the less intimate ones, is semi-public: individuals are seated around the periphery of a large room and, if the conversation becomes general, must speak loudly to address all. The context rewards those who are eloquent, persuasive, and informed. From these seedbeds of opinion emerges (or fails to emerge) the consensus that often seems to be the sine qua non for social or political change in the kingdom.

In addition to such long-standing semi-social networks, weekly salon-like meetings are also burgeoning, often named after the day of the week they meet, e.g., *ithnayniyya,* "Monday gathering." As mentioned above, such meetings are prominent in the Hijaz, but they occur in the other regions as well. Informal meetings in homes for religious instruction are also highly popular, including many for young women. Email now makes it easy, without using public media, to invite many like-minded individuals to religious, cultural, or intellectual events or soirées.

I mentioned above an impression of newfound empowerment in Saudi Arabia at individual and civil levels to engage with shariʿa itself. Though the individual may experience this empowerment as an intimate conscientious response to texts and tradition, it can be much more: ideologically it claims roots in transcendence and universality, legally it creates rights and duties, and socially it connects with a rapidly burgeoning intersubjectivity among all similarly situated individuals, both Saudi and non-Saudi. Islam and shariʿa, always pervasively constitutive of Saudi life, are now the hot topic, and provide a discourse, a lingua franca, for articulating, negotiating, and evaluating claims of individual, social, legal, and political meaning, identity, authority, and power. The question arises: can we detect, participating in all the phenomena noted above, a new subjectivity, even individualism, in this approach to Islam and shariʿa, reclaiming authority earlier perceived as public and wielded by the state and the religious establishment? Do we see the emergence, even, of a Habermasian-style "public sphere" (Habermas 1989, cf. xvii–xviii; cf. Eickelman and Anderson 2003, 14–16) for debate and change in Saudi life?

Conclusion

A common theme in current outsider accounts of Saudi Arabia is that of an all-powerful regime sensitive to its abysmal standing in world opinion on political freedom and human rights but still avoiding genuine reform; the story is one of modest reforms delayed, proclaimed, and then not implemented, of modernization measures revealed later to be only window-dressing. Any actual progress is portrayed as a function of external factors like the price of oil or American pressure on Middle Eastern regimes to democratize and respect human rights. Clearly there is some truth in these accounts, and certainly Saudis are unlikely to gain Western-style political rights either easily or quickly. Such rights are dependent on the royal family's choice to bestow them, and it currently feels little pressure to do so. The country's overall record of political development, on matters such as human rights, democracy, and the rule of law, remains poor by all ordinary measures.

But with their emphasis on external or international criteria of political development, these accounts miss a big part of the picture. A wholly different analysis is demanded when we ask, as this chapter does, about shari'a politics and take into account the unique significance of shari'a in the Saudi setting and the multiple, complex ways it lends meaning and structure to Saudi politics and society. Viewed from its unique internal perspective, Saudi Arabia seems to be passing through a period of rapid change and development. Two perspectives on shari'a politics make this particularly clear.

The first perspective is from the bottom up. Civil society is generating many of the current changes, both directly and indirectly. One mechanism for this is the very pervasiveness of shari'a: while enforced most often by the state, it cannot be fully controlled or monopolized by the state. In their civil and private lives, citizens are both charged and empowered to mold shari'a and enforce it. Intangibly, and perhaps in a way not adequately conveyed by the developments so far discussed, Saudi Arabian society seems in a state of ferment, hopeful for a brighter future under the banner of shari'a. As in other Muslim countries worldwide, in Saudi Arabia Islam and shari'a tend to take center stage whenever citizens reflect on their individual, communal, and national identities, pasts, and futures. This tendency is not abating at all. Rather, the Saudi people, increasingly literate and informed on religious topics and finding new civic fora for discussion of them, are progressively realizing how much of the immense moral, cultural, legal, and political meaning and power innate in shari'a falls into their hands and the extent to which they are able to activate, direct, and deploy it. The directions they will take it cannot be predicted—but one can predict that these directions are unlikely to agree, soon or ever, with external expectations for the course of political development.

The second perspective on shari'a politics this review affords is from the top down, starting from the relationship between the king and the Wahhabi scholarly establishment. It is too early to tell, but this chapter raises the possibility that the king's dependence on an exclusivist, traditionalizing interpretation of shari'a, and on the proponents of this interpretation within the establishment, may be easing. Under the banners of tolerance and reform, he seems engaged in maneuvering to derive legitimacy from other scholars, such as moderate Sahwi scholars, and from religious trends such as the principled but flexible and pragmatic Salafi reformism of Sahwi intellectuals and much of the Saudi public. Taking this approach could earn the king greater religious-political legitimacy even among non-Saudi Muslims, especially as the Sunni world feels a need for leadership in the face of newly resurgent Shi'ism. But, more importantly for internal politics and law, such a shift may allow King Abdullah to set Saudi Arabia irrevocably on a course of greater pluralism of opinion and of political, legal, and constitutional innovation. The Saudi legal system may progress further toward its long-standing goal of dissolving its nearly century-old divide between fiqh and foreign or "man-made" law.

Viewed from the perspective of shari'a politics, the political and legal future of Saudi Arabia is not bleak but promising.

Notes

To acknowledge all whose knowledge and counsel have informed this essay (without responsibility for its errors) would be a lengthy undertaking, and I am pained to mention only some and not all. Many Saudi friends have guided me for many years (see Vogel 2000, vii–ix), and their invaluable contributions continue. The Harvard Alumni Association of Saudi Arabia and its members extended me much hospitality, support, and advice. Through this research I discovered new guides to understanding law and politics in Saudi Arabia: of these I particularly thank Dr. Turki Al Thunayan and his father, Dr. Abdel Aziz bin Abdel Rahman Al Thunayan, for hospitably arranging for me to meet members of the Consultative Council; Abdulaziz AlGasim (al-Qasim), for affording me full access to the studies and outcomes of his reform efforts; and Abdullah Alhoqail. This essay benefited from full-time research stays in Saudi Arabia totaling ten weeks during 2008 and 2009, allowing many meetings with generous learned and informed students, businessmen, lawyers, professors, scholars, religious leaders, officials, and judges, in both Riyadh and Jedda. Of particular note were a half-dozen meetings with groups of Saudi women of differing classes, ages, sects, and regions, including writers, activists, divorced women, working women, professional women, professors, and students. I thank particularly the several expatriate women who arranged these meetings for me. In the United States I was greatly aided by research assistants Shoaib Ahmed, Christen Decker, Haitham Osta, and Emad Zowawi.

1. The standard practice for scholars outside Saudi Arabia is to refer to the mainstream religious trend in Saudi Arabia as Wahhabism, while providing a footnote to justify the usage. Those called "Wahhabis" reject that designation, because Wahhabism is neither a sect nor a legal school (*madhhab*), and because—down to today—"Wahhabism" has often been a derogatory label used in polemics. I use the term "Wahhabi" to refer to believers worldwide who follow the centuries-old Salafi trend in matters of creed and law while drawing particular inspiration from the writings of Shaykh Ibn 'Abd al-Wahhab (d. 1792 CE).

2. See Basic Law of 1992, Articles 7, 23, 48, 55, 67. The Basic Law is a *nizam* or regulation, and it declares that the constitution of Saudi Arabia is the Qur'an and the Sunna of the Prophet.

3. The Ministry of Justice published three volumes of judgments in 2008; other judgments appear in its informative journal *al-'Adl*, published also in English translation. The Board of Grievances recently published several volumes of its decisions (three volumes had been published in the 1980s). Several administrative law tribunals have also published volumes of decisions.

4. In Afghanistan the tribally rooted *loya jirga* was the body ultimately sanctioning the constitution of 2005. But the Afghan constitution and state laws otherwise ignore customary law, despite its universal efficacy. Several African nations acknowledge customary or "native" laws, but as laws of groups that otherwise are subject to national constitutions.

5. Perhaps because this prohibition is so famous, the first national dialogue conference adopted a resolution calling for the principle to be less widely used.

6. Saudi Arabia announced an ambitious effort to become, by 2010, one of the ten easiest countries in the world in which to do business. On the basis of 2009 data, the World Bank Group ranked it thirteenth (out of 183) overall; it held first place for ease of registering property, but ranked only 140th for ease of enforcing commercial contracts (World Bank Group 2009).

7. Parallel changes under a separate regulation were made to the Board of Grievances as an administrative court system.

8. Another telling question, deserving observation, is whether the Agency for Ordering the Good and Forbidding the Evil will submit to reforms or persist in attempting to wrest society onto a conservative course. This subject is much followed in international news.

9. From an interview dated November 1, 2007: "[Al-Qasim] is of the opinion that the traditional Islamic approach may have caused, with all good intention, shari'a to become inoperative, insofar as it was unable to present shari'a as solutions and systems for development and reform. The natural result of this failure is to permit other projects to cross over to fill the void." Also, "the Islamic *sahwa* used to produce a dreamy discourse, far from reality. Crises came to restore consideration of the givens of reality. The events of September 11 and afterward came to return the Islamic discourse to its real-world responsibilities, local and global. It began to revert from the emotional discourse to a more responsible political reformist discourse" (http://www.awrd.net/look/article.tpl?IdLanguage=17&IdPublication=1&NrArticle=1534&NrIssue=1&NrSection=1&search_x=0&search_y=0; in Arabic, accessed March 12, 2009). According to Lacroix, Al-Qasim criticizes "the contemporary Islamic movements that absolutely rejected Western political forms. He states that it is not necessary to adopt those systems in their present form; rather they should constitute a source of inspiration for Muslim reformists" (http://www.islamonline.net/arabic/daawa/2005/02/article05a.shtm; in Arabic, accessed March 12, 2009).

10. The four draft laws are Nizam Muraqabat Sharikat al-Tamwil (Law on Supervision of Finance Companies), Nizam al-Rahn al-'Aqari al-Musajjal (Law on the Registered Real Estate Lien), Nizam al-Ijar al-Tamwili (Law on Finance Leasing), and Nizam al-Tamwil al-'Aqari (Law on Real Estate Finance). A fifth draft law (Nizam Qada' al-Tanfidh, Law on Judicial Enforcement) is relevant to the project as well.

11. These organizations were the governmental Human Rights Commission (HRC) (http://www.haq-ksa.org/) and the independent National Society for Human Rights

(NSHR). Many of the HRC's reports are available on the website of the UN Human Rights Commission, at http://ap.ohchr.org/documents/alldocs.aspx?doc_id=14860; many of the NSHR's are available on its own website (in Arabic and English): http://www.nshr.org.sa (both sites accessed July 4, 2010).

References Cited

Aba-Namay, Rashed. 1998. "The New Saudi Representative Assembly." *Islamic Law and Society* 5:235–65.

Ali, Kecia. 2008. "Marriage in Classical Islamic Jurisprudence: A Survey of Doctrines." In *The Islamic Marriage Contract: Case Studies in Islamic Family Law,* ed. Asifa Quraishi and Frank E. Vogel, 11–45. Cambridge, Mass.: Harvard University Press.

Arabi, Oussama. 2001. *Studies in Modern Islamic Law and Jurisprudence.* The Hague: Kluwer Law International.

Carapico, Sheila. 1998. *Civil Society in Yemen: The Political Economy of Activism in Modern Arabia.* Cambridge: Cambridge University Press.

Commins, David Dean. 2006. *The Wahhabi Mission and Saudi Arabia.* New York: I. B. Tauris.

Doumato, Eleanor Abdella. 2009. "Women's Rights in the Middle East and North Africa 2009—Saudi Arabia." Freedom House Special Report. Freedom House: Washington, D.C. http://www.freedomhouse.org/template.cfm?page=384&key=174&parent=16&report=76 (accessed July 20, 2009).

Eickelman, Dale, and Jon W. Anderson. 2003. "Redefining Muslim Publics." In *New Media in the Muslim World: The Emerging Public Sphere,* ed. Dale Eickelman and Jon W. Anderson, 1–16. 2nd ed. Bloomington: Indiana University Press.

Fahad, Abdulaziz H. al-. 2004. "From Exclusivism to Accommodation: Doctrinal and Legal Evolution of Wahhabism." *New York University Law Review* 79:485–519.

Fandy, Mamoun. 2001. *Saudi Arabia and the Politics of Dissent.* New York: Palgrave.

Habermas, Jürgen. 1989. *The Structural Transformation of the Public Sphere: An Enquiry into a Category of Bourgeois Society.* Translated by Thomas Burger. Cambridge, Mass.: MIT Press.

Hamzawy, Amr. 2006. "The Saudi Labyrinth: Evaluating the Current Political Opening." Carnegie Papers 68. Washington, D.C.: Carnegie Endowment for International Peace.

Human Rights Watch. 2008. *Perpetual Minors: Human Rights Abuses Stemming from Male Guardianship and Sex Segregation in Saudi Arabia.* New York: Human Rights Watch.

Ibrahim, Fouad N. 2006. *The Shi'is of Saudi Arabia.* San Francisco: Saqi.

Jones, Toby. 2009. "Religious Revivalism and Its Challenge to the Saudi Regime." In *Religion and Politics in Saudi Arabia: Wahhabism and the State,* ed. Mohammed Ayoub and Hasan Kosebalaban, 109–20. Boulder, Colo.: Lynne Reiner.

Lacroix, Stéphane. 2004. "Between Islamists and Liberals: Saudi Arabia's New 'Islamo-Liberal' Reformists." *Middle East Journal* 58 (3): 345–65.

———. 2008. "Les nouveaux intellectuels religieux saoudiens: Le Wahhabism en question." *Revue des mondes musulmans et de la Méditerranée* 123:141–59.

Los Angeles Times. 2009. "Saudi Arabia's King Abdullah Appoints Moderates to Key Posts." February 15.

Mahmood, Saba. 2005. *Politics of Piety: The Islamic Revival and the Feminist Subject.* Princeton: Princeton University Press.

Nevo, Joseph. 1998. "Religion and National Identity in Saudi Arabia." *Middle Eastern Studies* 34: 34–53.

Obaid, Nawaf E. 1999. "The Power of Saudi Arabia's Islamic Leaders." *Middle East Quarterly* 6 (3): 51–58.

Rasheed, Madawi al-. 2007. *Contesting the Saudi State: Islamic Voices from a New Generation.* New York: Cambridge University Press.

Sonbol, Amira. 2008. "A History of Marriage Contracts in Egypt." In *The Islamic Marriage Contract: Case Studies in Islamic Family Law,* ed. Asifa Quraishi and Frank E. Vogel, 87–122. Cambridge, Mass.: Harvard University Press.

Steinberg, Guido. 2005. "The Wahhabi Ulama and the Saudi State: 1745 to the Present." In *Saudi Arabia in the Balance,* ed. Paul Aarts and Gerd Nonneman, 11–34. New York: New York University Press.

Teitelbaum, Joshua. 2000. *Holier Than Thou: Saudi Arabia's Islamist Opposition.* Washington, D.C.: Washington Institute for Near East Policy.

Vogel, Frank E. 1996. "The Complementarity of Ifta' and Qada': Three Saudi Fatwas on Divorce." In *Islamic Legal Interpretation: Muftis and their Fatwas,* ed. M. Khalid Masud, Brinkley Messick, and David Powers, 262–69. Cambridge, Mass.: Harvard University Press.

———. 2000. *Islamic Law and Legal System: Studies of Saudi Arabia.* Boston: Brill.

———. 2003. "The Public and the Private in Saudi Arabia: Restrictions on the Powers of Committees for Ordering the Good and Forbidding the Evil." *Social Research* 70:749–68.

White, Jenny B. 2002. *Islamist Mobilization in Turkey: A Study in Vernacular Politics.* Seattle: University of Washington.

Wickham, Carrie Rosefsky. 2002. *Mobilizing Islam: Religion, Activism, and Political Change in Egypt.* New York: Columbia University Press.

World Bank Group. 2009. *Doing Business 2010: Saudi Arabia.* Washington, D.C.: The International Bank for Reconstruction and Development, World Bank. Summary data available at http://www.doingbusiness.org/ExploreEconomies/?economyid =163 (accessed July 2, 2010).

Wynn, Lisa. 2008. "Marriage Contracts and Women's Rights in Saudi Arabia." In *The Islamic Marriage Contract: Case Studies in Islamic Family Law,* ed. Asifa Quraishi and Frank E. Vogel, 200–14. Cambridge, Mass.: Harvard University Press.

Yamani, Maha A. Z. 2008. *Polygamy and Law in Contemporary Saudi Arabia.* Reading, UK: Ithaca Press.

Zoepf, Katherine. 2007. "Saudi King Pardons Victim of Gang Rape." *New York Times,* December 18.

2. Egypt

Cacophony and Consensus
in the Twenty-first Century

Nathan J. Brown

In Egypt, as in many Muslim societies, the twentieth
century witnessed a broad democratization of shariʻa-
based discourse, accompanied by fundamental shifts in interpretive authority
over the Islamic shariʻa. Those trends had divisive—and sometimes even politically violent—results. In recent years, political violence over shariʻa-based issues and grievances has receded and some signs of consensus on broad themes
have unmistakably emerged. But that consensus has framed rather than si-
lenced deep debates over the content of the shariʻa, its role in society, and
authority over its interpretation.

The twentieth century opened with the Islamic shariʻa established in specific legal and educational institutions in Egypt and with a broad social legitimacy. As a discourse, the shariʻa was a matter of technical expertise, specialist
scholarship, and legal reasoning. Attempts by political authorities to reconfigure its social and political role were at most gingerly advanced (except for
occasional clumsy and ineffectual forays by Egypt's British occupiers).

By the end of the twentieth century, however, the shariʻa had burst these
institutional frameworks and become part of very broad public discussions.
The democratization of shariʻa-based discourse came at a high price for Egyptian political and social relations: beginning in the 1970s, shariʻa-based debates
became a matter of bitter contention and violent action.

Yet in the current century, much of the sharpness and violence of earlier
debates has ebbed. While the Islamic shariʻa remains central to disputes among
Egyptians about proper social and political relations, a degree of consensus
has emerged around a very general set of ideas: that the Islamic shariʻa provides some clear legal rules that should not be abrogated by the state; that the

shari'a is not wholly identified with those rules but also provides more general guidance to social and political behavior; that debate about interpreting the shari'a among educated Muslims is healthy; and that the shari'a can provide a middle path that it is very much in the interest of Egyptians and Egyptian society to follow.

This general consensus emerged in part because of its generality. Unsurprisingly, therefore, what I have termed "consensus" expresses itself in paradoxically cacophonous forms. Egyptians continue to argue about which shari'a-based legal rules are fixed, what the general principles are, how they are to be applied, who is qualified to speak in shari'a-centered debates, and what role the state should play. More subtly, the Egyptian state has folded this cacophony into itself by absorbing or creating several different—and often competing—centers for shari'a-based authority within its bureaucratic apparatus and set of governing structures.

In other words, even as differences have narrowed somewhat, the multiplicity of individual and institutional voices continues. And the state has moved not only to regulate but also to subsume many of these voices. An understanding of debates over the role of the Islamic shari'a in modern Egypt best begins with a brief historical overview of its recent evolution in Egyptian society and politics. This will enable us to explore the emergence of some points of consensus in Egypt today—and the limits of that consensus. Finally, we can examine the cacophony that has arisen within the Egyptian state apparatus and the broader society even within the broad outlines of the consensus. While our attention will be largely on institutions and movements, each section of this essay will also incorporate (necessarily fairly briefly) some of the ways that Egyptians focus on the Islamic shari'a outside of these formal channels.

The Islamic Shari'a and Egyptian Society in the Twentieth Century

A century ago, the Islamic shari'a was most closely identified with three kinds of institutions in Egypt: an educational establishment, centered in Al-Azhar; an advisory office known as Dar al-Ifta; and courts of law that adjudicated matters of personal status. These institutions operated with state license and support, but they also had a degree of autonomy from high state officials. This autonomy operated not only in a narrow organizational sense but also in a broader intellectual manner—all three participated in a specialized shari'a-based discourse enabling them to see themselves as answerable not only to state authorities but also to more complete and timeless truths.

The autonomy accorded these institutions, however, was neither complete nor timeless. For instance, Dar al-Ifta was relatively new, and its creation out of its forebears in the nineteenth century was part of an attempt by Egypt's rulers to build up a state exercising something like sovereignty (by taking advice from an Egyptian mufti separate from the religious apparatus of the Ottoman Empire, especially on matters such as the death penalty, Egypt's hereditary governors implicitly asserted far greater autonomy). Yet for the most part when Egypt's rulers—and, after the entry of the British in 1882, the country's occupiers—attempted to assert control over educational and legal matters, they did so less by attempting to subordinate the shari'a-based institutions than by marginalizing them. In a sense, establishing religious knowledge as a specialized field allowed the reproduction of a body of religious scholars only by restricting their purview (Zaman 2002). An extensive educational apparatus was erected in the nineteenth and twentieth centuries largely outside of Al-Azhar; a set of courts was established over the course of the nineteenth century that gradually transformed what had been courts of general jurisdiction into specialized shari'a-based courts applying Islamic law in matters of personal status.

This trend—marginalizing shari'a-based institutions while maintaining their autonomy—was arrested and reversed in the course of the twentieth century by broad, long-term political and social trends. On a political level, state authorities increasingly sought to eliminate pockets of autonomy and moved to assert more direct control over the shari'a-based institutions. Personal status law was codified and legislated in 1929; in 1956 the personal status courts that applied that law were folded into the regular court system. Al-Azhar was transformed from a mosque and academy of Islamic learning into a large bureaucracy, the administrator of a national (and later even international) network of educational institutions, a full university, and a set of ancillary religious structures—and also brought under fairly close state control.

On a social level, the spread of education and the growing interest of some intellectual circles in matters related to Islam eroded the status of the Islamic shari'a as a specialist's discourse. Some of the public debate over Islam took on a broadly religious character, but some was specifically legal in nature. As the century wore on, discussions spilled over from general intellectual circles to the broad public, especially with the formation of the Muslim Brotherhood and its forays into religious education and advocacy.

In the late 1940s political violence arose involving the Muslim Brotherhood; in the 1950s and 1960s the new Nasserist regime employed extremely harsh repressive tools to crush the movement. This struggle was initially primarily political in nature; for most of the period it was only a few Muslim Brotherhood ideologues who saw the struggle between their movement and the regime as a dispute over the place of the shari'a. But that began to change in the 1970s and 1980s as Islamist movements—many operating outside of the Brotherhood's umbrella—increasingly began to incline toward arguments that placed the failure to base the Egyptian legal order on shari'a at the center of their political program. A host of other groups arose, some of them tracing the line of argumentation begun by Brotherhood ideologists like 'Abd al-Qadir 'Awda in the 1950s and Sayyid Qutb in the 1960s out to the most radical conclusions.

For such Islamist movements of the 1970s and 1980s—from the peaceful Muslim Brotherhood to the most revolutionary groups—an Islamic society such as Egypt was properly governed by the Islamic shari'a. While Islamists joined in the insistence that the Islamic shari'a was more than simply law in the narrow sense of a set of enforceable rules, they also used adherence to shari'a-based rules as a litmus test for the political system's credentials. In short, they insisted on the application of the Islamic shari'a by Egypt's legal system. And in this they were not alone. The call to apply shari'a-based law seemed to have popular resonance in the 1970s and 1980s. As part of a gradual turn away from the Arab nationalism and socialism that had dominated the late 1950s and 1960s, the regime increasingly worked to cultivate religious legitimacy. This reorientation was reflected in official pronouncements and documents. In 1971 a new constitution proclaimed that "the principles of the Islamic shari'a are *a* chief source of legislation," and in 1979 the text was amended to make it "*the* chief source" (emphasis added). A committee headed by Sufi Abu Talib, the speaker of parliament and a prominent law professor (who briefly also served as acting president after the assassination of Anwar Sadat)—worked to produce a new civil code based on Islamic jurisprudence.

Thus the Islamic shari'a, by the end of the twentieth century, was highly politicized in two senses. First, it was often understood as providing the proper basis for the entire political order; the increasing tendency to focus on the shari'a as the appropriate source for specific legal rules to be enforced by the state only heightened the normative connection between the shari'a and politics. Second, the shari'a was central to Egyptian political debates, as contending forces all claimed to be acting in accordance with its requirements. Sporadic violence in the 1970s and 1980s gave way to an insurgency in some neighborhoods of Cairo as well as scattered locations in upper Egypt in the 1990s.

Given this contentious history, it is indeed surprising to find a limited consensus emerging in Egypt; it is similarly surprising that there is some evidence of a lessening of the strong identification of the shari'a with law.

The Emerging Consensus and Its Limits

Very few Muslims in Egypt publicly question the idea that the Islamic shari'a should play a role in Egyptian society and governance. Of course, the degree to which the shari'a is central to Egyptians' concerns varies greatly among individuals and groups, but it is striking that those who harbor the deepest doubts about the wisdom of turning to the shari'a generally couch their public arguments in guarded terms. Egyptian politics today is about much more than the shari'a, but the salience of the shari'a has grown markedly, along with a general increase in public forms of religiosity over the past generation. This is true at multiple levels. In the constitutional, legal, political, educational, social, and commercial realms, discussions are often infused with general themes related to the shari'a, and shari'a-based discourse and arguments—ranging from the platitudinous to the technical—are often invoked.

Recent public opinion polling has affirmed the centrality of the Islamic shari'a for many Egyptians—almost two-thirds agree that it should be the sole source of legislation and only a very small minority think that it should not be used at all as a source of law (Rheault and Mogahed 2008). But these findings probe only general orientations and do not answer specific questions: What is the nature of the Islamic shari'a that has been invoked so often in Egyptian discussions? And how is it to order Egyptian politics, law, and society?

Four consensual themes have come to dominate discussions of the shari'a in the Egyptian public sphere. While we will begin answering such questions by reference to these themes, this should not be taken to imply that all (or even most) Egyptians agree with or subscribe to them—nor should it even be taken to imply that Egyptians avoid challenging them. Our current focus is only the apparent consensus in the public sphere. In private or restricted realms, of course, much more wide-ranging discussions take place. But because our initial interest is with the public sphere, we will first examine the four themes in the abstract, as if the arguments were not made by specific individuals, institutions, or groups. Very soon, however, we will explore in some detail how these themes are deployed by advocates of different visions of Egyptian society.

The first of these consensual themes is that the shari'a does encompass specific rules, which fall into two categories. One category is those that are fixed and incontrovertible, sometimes referred to as those on which all scholars concur. These are incumbent on all believers; implicitly or explicitly they also bind political authorities in an Islamic society. Put differently, the political order is required to observe and even enforce a body of shari'a-based rules. These definitive and binding rules are few in number, since the necessary scholarly consensus must span great historical and geographical ranges. But the rules in the second category are less certain and can vary considerably according to time and place. It is widely acknowledged that the shari'a encompasses a broad tradition of religious inquiry that extends far beyond the few incontrovertible shari'a-based rules. But the guidance to the faithful that emerges from this broader inquiry is generally not definitive—it is dependent on human effort and prevailing social conditions. While the shari'a itself is divinely inspired and unchanging, its application in most areas is not merely debatable and subject to multiple understandings but also quite flexible, responding to human needs.

The second consensual theme involves not specific rules but general purposes enjoined by the shari'a. While the shari'a is oriented toward prescribing (or sometimes encouraging) righteous behavior and prohibiting (or containing) iniquitous actions, it is held to do so within a framework that protects general principles. In other words, the shari'a cannot simply be understood as a set of rules; rather, it is deeply informed by a set of moral goals. There is increasing stress in public discussions on the *maqasid* (goals or purposes) of the shari'a—a term from Islamic jurisprudence that has now passed into general usage to refer to the overriding goals that the shari'a is said to pursue (see Robert Hefner's introduction to this volume). The relationship between the *maqasid* and the fixed rules of the shari'a is not always explored—and, as will be seen, exploration of it provokes disagreement. For some (especially credentialed specialists and trained professionals), an excessive or inexpert focus on the *maqasid* does not merely have a salutary effect of rendering shari'a-based discourse more relevant to contemporary needs but also carries a real danger as well, as some believers might be inclined to vague, even vapid, understandings of shari'a-based principles that bypass long-accepted rulings.[1]

Shifting the emphasis from shari'a-based rules to general goals has a marked effect—it simultaneously underscores both the relevance and the flexibility of the Islamic shari'a. Both characteristics—relevance and flexibility—are accentuated by a tendency to give great weight to the interests of society in public debates about the shari'a. By emphasizing *maslaha* (a term that generally means "public interest," though it has more specific technical connotations in Islamic legal thought), Egyptians are participating in a broader trend in the Muslim world. They are simultaneously participating in a historical discussion as well. The use of *maslaha* (and its linkage to *maqasid*) in efforts to derive legal rules in the absence of clear texts has a hoary history. And while *maslaha*'s role in broad public debates about Islamic law is a modern phenomenon, these debates betray echoes of a long-standing debate over how it should be employed. The current debates take the form of a sharp tension between those who use *maslaha* as a technique to make the shari'a more relevant and those who fear that it can be used to bend understandings of the shari'a to the whim of the users (Opwis 2007). Laid on top of this tension is a less obvious struggle over authority. As traditionally used, *maslaha* was a device for scholars. And it is still understood that way by some specialists. But the elision between the technical term *maslaha* and the broader concept of the public interest allows the populace and their secularly trained leaders to claim a role in the debate: while not expert in all aspects of Islamic law, they certainly seem to be on solid ground in demanding a role in determining the public interest.

Third, the theme of *wasatiyya*, moderation or centralism, has gained increasing resonance in public discussions. Increased interest in the theme is hardly restricted to Egypt; the theme has arisen in conferences and ideological statements throughout the Muslim world (and has figured prominently in international efforts to present Islam in a positive light). *Wasatiyya* has several different connotations in an Egyptian context, but it is often linked to calls for persuasion and dialogue and against violence and what is perceived as extremism. While "moderation" is an accurate translation, *wasatiyya* indicates something beyond political moderation as the term is used internationally and especially in the United States—some movements that would seem to be extremist by most political definitions lay claim to the *wasatiyya* label. (Indeed, few challenge the emphasis on *wasatiyya*, though some Salafis have expressed concern that it leads to immoral compromises and adulterates good with evil.) The term's religious overtones are often made explicit by reference to Qur'an 2:143, which describes the community of Muslims as a "middle nation." Most of those invoking the term *wasatiyya* engage in little textual exegesis of the Qur'anic verse (which appears at first glance to be in a very different context). Instead, the *wasatiyya* slogan is used to emphasize two points. The first is that proper interpretations of Islam should naturally incline against fanaticism or extremism, the second that those interpretations should incline toward those that are most sensible, appropriate, helpful, and even easiest for society (thus underscoring the increasing emphasis on *maqasid* and *maslaha*).

Finally, public discussions of the shari'a are often accompanied with expressions of distaste for *takfir* (making accusations of apostasy) and "changing with the hand"[2]—a very marked departure from two decades ago, when debates about such matters took place on the front pages of Egyptian newspapers. While radical groups still exist on the fringes of Egyptian society, the claim that individual believers are responsible for implementing change by force or that Egyptian society (or its rulers) has passed into a state of apostasy or unbelief is no longer heard so frequently in the public sphere as it was two decades ago (even if such claims were often made obliquely).

The overall effect of these consensual themes initially seems harmonious indeed—Egyptian Muslims publicly agree that there are some shari'a-based rules that they are all bound by and that the state should enforce. At the same time, emphasis has very much shifted away from specific rules and enforcement to proper personal and social conduct and peaceful discussion of how to understand religious teachings. Public debates focus on how to realize the common good and practice ethical behavior in a social context. And indeed Egyptian debates are calmer and more harmonious than they were two and three decades ago. But while the turn toward general principles has taken some of the sharp political edge off shari'a-based debates, it is not part of a process of converting the Islamic shari'a into a privatized ethical code; the emphasis is still very much on appropriate conduct within a social context, and the idea of a "wall of separation"—the famous Jeffersonian phrase—between the religious and state realms does not resonate in an Egyptian context.

More important, reference to these areas of general consensus should not obscure the fact that deep differences still remain. The consensus described above emerged partly out of difficult struggles and the nitty-gritty of everyday politics: the defeat of radical jihadist movements, the ubiquity of the Egyptian state, the restrictions on formal politics, and the effort by state officials to regulate Islam and appropriate religious sources of legitimacy. But it also emerged because its central themes resolve so little—they allow for many different interpretations and can be deployed by various groups in sharply different ways. Each of the areas of emerging consensus mentioned contains within it substantial ambiguity and potential for difference and debate. In fact, the consensus is really just an agreement that certain words or, at most, concepts are central—but not an agreement on what they mean, how they are applied, or, most of all, who may interpret and apply them.

If, for instance, there are a limited number of definitive shari'a-based rules, then what are they? Who determines them? Who enforces them? If the shari'a is flexible and subject to interpretation in other areas, who is qualified to offer interpretations? How is shari'a-based inquiry to be conducted? If *maqasid* and *maslaha* are to receive special emphasis, then who determines how such general ideas are applied? And are they a license for infinite flexibility, rendering the shari'a a collection of banal but pleasant sentiments? Or are they restricted and technical and thus inappropriate for public debate or less useful as tools for intellectual openness?

There are deep and abiding tensions even within these areas of emerging consensus, and many of those tensions are closely connected with different conceptions of interpretive authority. Those different conceptions vary along two dimensions.

First, there is a range of opinions on the relative importance of specialized training and personal piety in approaching the shari'a. Is interpretation of the shari'a a complex task, reserved for those with the requisite education and knowledge, or is it a task for all pious Muslims anxious to behave in accordance with God's guidance? The question is actually rarely posed this starkly. Those who stress specialized training—ensconced in official positions, bureaucratic offices, and faculty chairs, and holding formal credentials—would hardly argue that their teachings are absolutely binding, nor would they absolve individual believers of any responsibility for understanding Islamic teachings. Similarly, those who stress the role of individual believers—popular preachers, ordinary believers, political leaders, public officials, and intellectuals without formal religious training—do not deride the need for education or training or deny any need to seek guidance from those who specialize in shari'a-based inquiry.

But even if the polar positions are avoided, there is a wide range of inclinations, as is perhaps best illustrated by contemporary arguments about the issuing of fatwas. Is a rapid multiplication of those who issue interpretations of the Islamic shari'a causing a crisis in Islamic belief and practice—or, as those concerned about the phenomenon often term it, a crisis of "chaotic fatwas" (*fatawi 'ashwa'iyya*)? Or is it desirable that Muslims can look to a variety of sources for appropriate guidance? Is the individual believer likely to be misled by amateur interpretation, or the lazy Muslim let off the hook, allowed to select whatever interpretation she or he likes in an unregulated market of religious opinions? Can state officials shop, cherry-pick, cajole, and intimidate until they receive a blessing on a policy or law that is actually very dubious in religious terms? Or are pluralism and broad discussion signs of the vitality and relevance of Islamic teachings? Is the multiplicity of voices an opportunity for individual believers to educate themselves and draw on various perspectives and answers as well as a healthy sign that political, social, and religious issues are increasingly being explored in a shari'a-based idiom?

A second dimension of tension concerns the relative roles of the state and the society. Which state bodies have roles to play connected to the shari'a, and what are those roles? What are the relative roles of the individual Muslim, the religious scholar, official religious institutions, and state institutions (such as courts, the parliament, or the educational establishment) that are not primarily or even largely religious in their focus? If general principles—especially *maslaha*—are to be used in developing interpretations, then who may deploy them and how? Is this a function for scholars, a prerogative of political authorities, or a field of discussion for all believers?

The state is not a religiously neutral actor in Egypt. Few question its role in fostering religious values and knowledge and in encouraging and even enforcing some shari'a-based norms. And this role inevitably requires officials to designate specific interpretations as legally binding or authoritative as a matter of policy (though rarely of belief). But who develops these interpretations and how?

The tensions over expertise and over the state overlap, but they are not identical. Those who stress the need for specialized training and knowledge and decry chaotic fatwas, for instance, might easily posit that state-sponsored religious institutions are the answer. But they might just as easily hold the state responsible for contributing to the confusion by favoring weak interpretations and craven or unqualified authorities.

Thus the coincidence of emerging consensus and growing cacophony is less contradictory than immediately appears. And we can now go beyond characterizing the general areas of emerging consensus and disagreement and embody some of the voices that speak in shari'a-based terms in various ways.

The Growing Cacophony: Speaking for the Islamic Shari'a in Twenty-first-century Egypt

The move to more consensual, centrist general positions has done little to counteract or diminish the striking multiplication of institutions and groups that participate in shari'a-based discourse; many of these institutions and groups advance not merely interpretations but also claims to authority stemming from various combinations of legal authorization, specialist training, and professional integrity. We will turn our focus first to those institutions that are specifically religious in nature, including Al-Azhar and the state mufti's office. We will then turn our attention to state bodies whose work, though not ordinarily religious, involves them in claims of interpretive authority or at least authoritative selection among competing interpretations.

State Religious Institutions

AL-AZHAR   The premier Islamic institution in the country remains Al-Azhar. Named for a mosque and teaching center more than a thousand years old, Al-Azhar has grown into a large bureaucratic and educational apparatus comprising a university, a network of schools, administrative machinery, and a "research center" that undertakes a broad range of activities ranging from issuing fatwas to hosting conferences. (On Al-Azhar's history, see Dodge 1974, Crecelius 1972, and Rabi' 1992; on its current role, see Abdo 2000 and Zeghal 2007.) Al-Azhar is currently governed by a 1961 law that expanded the institution's scope but also greatly reduced its autonomy. Currently the institution is headed by the shaykh of Al-Azhar, a presidential appointee who reports (since the Sadat years) directly to the prime minister; he is aided in governance by the Supreme Council of Al-Azhar, a body headed by the shaykh and including two other presidential appointees, three government-appointed educators, representatives from four ministries, the deans of the university faculty, and four members of the research center.

The university is a leading center of religious education with an international student body. The 1961 law also added a large number of other, non-religious faculties (such as commerce, agriculture, and medicine), though the Egyptian cabinet is now developing plans to separate the religious and non-religious parts of the university.

The precise role and authority of the research center in delivering fatwas is not always clear, but it responds to requests when asked. The former head of its fatwa committee reports receiving four to five hundred requests per day.[3]

The 1961 reforms were viewed as asserting presidential control over Al-Azhar, and they unquestionably had that effect. Remarkably, the current head of the institution, appointed in 2010, also serves as a high official in the governing National Democratic Party. But the current role of Al-Azhar suggests a more complex picture than the institution's conversion into a mouthpiece for the country's political leadership. The top officials of Al-Azhar seem to rarely stray far from government wishes, but the critical role the institution plays in the country's religious structure allows some others within it to strike a more independent stance. (One recently retired, very high-ranking Al-Azhar official told me in a personal interview that it would be contrary to the Islamic shari'a for a head of state to pass his position on to his son as if it were private property—a remarkably direct rebuke to the sitting president's son, who was maneuvering to position himself as his father's successor.)

And the regime's growing reliance on Al-Azhar to provide ideological support—a notable development with the growth of the Islamist opposition—has allowed Al-Azhar to leverage its position. As Muhammad Qasim Zaman has written, "the dependence of the Egyptian state on the Azhar has enabled the latter to insist, with considerable effectiveness, on its own prerogative to authoritatively define the perimeter of all that would be Islamically acceptable" (Zaman 2002, 147). This double role—upholding the state but also defining Islam—has sometimes led to tension within the institution between the senior leadership and others who view their superiors as having been coopted. An association of Al-Azhar scholars dating back to the early 1960s, the Al-Azhar Ulama Front, came to be dominated by critics of the institution's leadership (and the government), leading to the formal dissolution of the group in 2000 (though some of its members carry on, issuing pugnacious statements and fatwas). And disputes within Al-Azhar have attracted external groups and commentators into the fray, as they take sides in the legal and doctrinal arguments. It is therefore quite telling that distress over "chaotic fatwas" is beginning to expand to fatwas emanating from individuals within Al-Azhar itself: leading figures in the religious establishment have increasingly sought to establish clear standards (and perhaps even a degree of supervision) over the issuing of fatwas from the ranks of trained religious scholars.

DAR AL-IFTA   While Al-Azhar sees itself as the authoritative voice of Islam for the Egyptian state, it is joined by a second institution that lays claim to the same status: Dar al-Ifta, the office of the state mufti (Skovgaard-Petersen 1997). Established in 1895, Dar al-Ifta has become a substantial bureaucratic apparatus, issuing perhaps five hundred to a thousand fatwas per year (Skovgaard-

Petersen 2004, 93, estimates the number of fatwas as only five hundred, but other estimates double this figure). When it was created, the Dar as a bureaucracy replaced the Hanafi chief mufti as the body consulted by many state agencies in various religious matters, such as declaring new months (and thus determining when the Ramadan fast begins and ends) or certifying execution orders in capital cases. Its role has not changed fundamentally since then. While its fatwas are not binding, the Dar regards itself as the ultimate authority interpreting Islamic law for Egyptian state institutions. And those institutions do indeed consult it, though some officials direct their queries instead to Al-Azhar. Conversely, those involved in issuing fatwas at Al-Azhar point with satisfaction to the far greater number of requests they receive from the general population. Dar al-Ifta is headed by the state mufti, an official appointed by the president. While the state mufti often has a public profile as significant as that of the shaykh of Al-Azhar, he is often regarded as less independent from the regime.

In addition to Al-Azhar and Dar al-Ifta, other state bodies do concern themselves with matters of shari'a, though not always so directly. For instance, the Ministry of Awqaf (religious endowments) administers the country's official mosques and employs a large number of religious officials. But it does not directly involve itself in interpreting the shari'a, except that its legal department examines issues of Islamic law relevant to affairs within the ministry's purview.

Officials involved in these state bodies tend to incline very strongly to the view that understanding the Islamic shari'a requires the training and background to participate in a highly specialized discourse. Ordinary believers may easily be led astray by the competing voices they hear; they will be subject to conflicting instructions without possessing the proper tools to sort through them. And that problem is compounded not merely by the multiplicity of voices but also by their uneven quality. Some of those offering interpretations do not possess the proper education and training;[4] others lack the independence and moral character to withstand pressure from those who wish to obtain specific interpretations for their own ends. Some officials have gone so far as to call for criminal penalties for those who issue unlicensed fatwas. Jamal Qutb, the former chair of the committee in Al-Azhar responsible for overseeing and coordinating fatwas, regularly states that he views Al-Azhar as the appropriate source of fatwas and that the multiplicity of institutions is a legacy of imperial rule in Egypt, created in a deliberate effort by the British and French to undercut the strength of religious institutions in the country by dividing them.[5]

The multiplicity of voices enables members of the society to engage in a shari'a-based equivalent of "forum shopping." Just as litigants in a legal dispute might explore bringing their case to various courts and other bodies involved in adjudication in an effort to obtain the most favorable outcome, "fatwa shopping" finds Egyptians resorting to different religious authorities to find a congenial interpretation (though Agrama 2005 found it surprisingly more common for pious Egyptians to shop when they felt uneasy because the first fatwa they received was actually too congenial to their interests). But while officials complain about the forest of fatwas, in some ways they contribute to the problem. They do this most obviously by their own divisions—their rivalries seem to be structurally induced and there are no effective efforts to contain them. Dueling official fatwas are a common feature of discussions of public issues involving the shari'a in Egypt.

But the official bodies also accentuate the trend in a less obvious way as well. Their autonomy, however limited, has allowed the emergence of what Malika Zeghal has called "peripheral ulama"—those who have some training and position in Al-Azhar but retain an independent and even critical voice. It is not unusual for members of Egypt's Islamist opposition movements to cite an Azharite in support of their positions or even count such religious officials as active supporters of their movements.

Other State Institutions

EDUCATION   With much religious education a state function in Egypt, the educational apparatus is a critical site for developing and fostering certain views of the shari'a. This has made it not simply a participant in shari'a-based discussions in the country but also a sharp object of contestation among competing visions and institutions.

There are three educational battlefields involving the Islamic shari'a. First, the official curriculum involves religious instruction for the vast majority of Egyptian students who are Muslim. Since curriculum design and textbook writing involve developing an official version of Islamic teachings, it is not surprising that they have excited some domestic—and increasingly international—debate. In Egypt, occasionally bitter public controversies have erupted over what teachings are put forth, and how. Educational material, therefore, reflects the outcome of political struggles over religious issues. On the specific issue of the shari'a, however, the textbooks that are currently used in Egyptian schools emphasize general themes rather than specific provisions (Toronto and Eissa 2007; Starrett 1998).[6] Occasionally specific issues are addressed and shari'a-based rules are invoked, such as those barring usury and those concerning female circumcision (which recent texts do not view as required). Other issues are addressed more generally—such as modesty in dress—without an attempt to put forward a specific position on a controversial issue (whether women must cover their hair). But rather than focusing on rules, whether specific or general, the texts devote far more attention to the principle that Islam, as a religion, is designed to be easy on the faithful. This principle seems designed both to develop a positive attitude toward Islam and the shari'a and to inculcate a sense of their flexibility.

A second educational battleground is the educational apparatus attached to Al-Azhar. A national network of alternative schools—with its roots in the Islamic educational system attached to Al-Azhar—encompasses eight thousand schools with a combined enrollment approaching two million students.[7] The schools follow a dual curriculum, covering the same subjects as the regular stream but adding additional study of the Arabic language and religious subjects. In recent years, some controversies have arisen over the degree to which other state structures—most notably the Ministry of Education—should be involved in oversight of the schools. To date, Al-Azhar has retained its autonomy, but periodic press reports suggest that other state bodies are working to limit enrollment in the Al-Azhar school system. A second controversy has involved the curriculum: while students have in the past been taught Islamic jurisprudence through the major works of the traditional law schools, in 2007 Al-Azhar moved to using recent texts designed to be easier for the students and more contemporary in focus.

A final locus of contestation is the university system. Egypt's extensive system of state universities has constructed numerous faculties of Islamic and shari'a studies. Faculties of law and departments of Arabic language also have specialists in the shari'a and Islamic studies. While the faculties themselves, as institutional bodies, do not challenge Al-Azhar's position as the state's premier (and sometimes authoritative) voice of Islam, they are important sources of expertise and support a number of critical intellectuals able to provide expert advice and public commentary. Some play very prominent public roles, similar to those played by the peripheral ulama; others are asked to provide technical advice to ministries and state bodies in a quieter and politically safer way. In general, such academics incline to the view that shari'a-based discourse requires specialized training and that broad public participation in it carries the risk of simplification and misunderstanding.[8]

THE JUDICIARY   The judiciary has become a party in debates over the Islamic shari'a in Egypt in three ways. First, the Egyptian civil code directs judges confronted with a case for which there is no clearly applicable text to turn first to custom and then to the principles of the Islamic shari'a. This provision would seem to give license to enterprising judges to apply the shari'a by stealth. And some judges have in fact used this provision in order to strike out jurisprudentially in some fairly bold directions in an effort to increase the role of the Islamic shari'a in the operation of Egypt's judicial system. But, some individual court decisions aside, the Egyptian judiciary as a body is simply unlikely to march very far down this road. The civil-law and highly positivist orientation of judicial training encourages judges to hew very closely to actual texts, and the centralized nature of authority within the judiciary penalizes those who stray too far from accepted interpretations (Brown 1997; Rutherford 2009; Ghobashy 2006).

Second, Egypt's law of personal status is based on a codified version of Islamic shari'a provisions. It has been claimed that the attempt to fix specific interpretations of the Islamic heritage in codified and legislated text mistakes the substance of the shari'a for its essence and perhaps even buries the classical legal tradition (Hallaq 2004). Whether or not that is the case, this complaint is rarely heard in Egypt and certainly not voiced by judges, who see themselves as applying and working wholly within shari'a-based conceptual categories and rules. And a recent ethnographic study of personal status courts finds that at least in one important respect—the courts' refusal to have their sessions public—judges operate in violation of the relevant legislated texts (Agrama 2005). Yet, however much judges see their role as grounded in religion, morality, and social responsibility, since 1956 they have operated on the basis of a civil-law training and heritage that rarely fosters great expertise in the jurisprudential heritage of Islam.[9]

Third and potentially most significant, Egypt's Supreme Constitutional Court has been thrust into a very prominent role in relation to the Islamic shari'a because of its interpretive authority over Article 2 of the Egyptian constitution, which was amended in 1980 (as mentioned above) to proclaim that "the principles of the Islamic shari'a are the chief source of legislation." The amended article could be read in a large number of ways: as a statement of fact, as a general (and perhaps unenforceable) instruction to law drafters, and as a vague platitude (because it mentioned the "principles" of the Islamic shari'a rather than referring to fiqh or shari'a-based rulings). But it has also been read as requiring all legislation to operate within the bounds of the Islamic shari'a, and that is a reading the Court has consistently endorsed.

The Court's jurisprudence on this subject has generated considerable scholarly attention and debate.[10] This is in part because the Court's approach itself could be pushed in various directions. On the one hand, its decisions are based on the widely used distinction between a few fixed, incontrovertible shari'a-based rules and a much larger body of shari'a-inspired discourse that seeks to pursue general goals but allows for a multiplicity of specific applications. That distinction would seem to undermine much of Article 2's power, especially because the laws in Egypt today that are the most obvious candidates for being struck down as violations of fixed shari'a rules are parts of the civil and penal codes, and were passed long before the amendment (and therefore, in the Court's reasoning, are not within its purview to strike down). But the Court has also claimed, for the political authorities and for itself, the authority to determine what those fixed rules are and how to implement those general principles. In short, it claims that Egyptian state structures can speak authoritatively on how the Islamic shari'a is to be applied in the legal realm. On occasion the Court does consult with external authorities (such as Al-Azhar), but it clearly assigns the task of ijtihad (analysis of the revealed sources) to itself and, more broadly, to political authorities in general. Even more remarkable than this assertion of authority is that few actors in Egypt today question the Court's approach. The judiciary finds itself empowered by the Court's jurisprudence, as do the executive and the legislature (since they are all licensed to determine the public interest and to exercise ijtihad). But so, at the same time, are various groups in society who are encouraged to resort to the Court if they find some element of Egypt's legal order offensive to Islam.

THE LEGISLATURE   If the Islamic shari'a is to be translated into legally enforced strictures under Egypt's constitutional system, the parliament must have a central role in the process. While a parliamentary debate peaked in the 1980s over the adoption of codes more closely inspired by—and consistent with—shari'a-based rules, the issue has receded somewhat in the past decade as shari'a debates have shifted focus from specific rules to general principles. In short, the constitutional structure that would seem to be most central to any effort to apply the Islamic shari'a has in large part been let off the hook, even as the number of Islamist deputies in that body has increased.

A confluence of factors led to the debate in the 1980s over the adoption of shari'a-based codes. First, the effort headed by Sufi Abu Talib—referred to at the outset of this essay—had produced a final (or nearly final) draft. The contents of that draft were never released, presumably because Abu Talib lost his patron with the assassination of President Anwar Sadat (Lombardi 2006; Gaffney 1994, 109–12). But the wide publicity his committee had attracted coincided with a mild liberalization in the country's party system—one that allowed a number of members of the Muslim Brotherhood and independent Islamists into the parliament under the banner of other parties. A 1985 decision of the Supreme Constitutional Court protected all laws passed before the 1980 amendment of Article 2 from judicial oversight but added that older laws inconsistent with the Islamic shari'a should be amended by the parliament.

The result was a public campaign by the Muslim Brotherhood and independent Islamists to take up the cause of Islamizing Egypt's laws. Given Article 2, the work of Abu Talib's committee, and—perhaps most important—the general popularity of the Islamic shari'a, it was difficult for the parliamentary leaders of Egypt's governing National Democratic Party to repudiate the idea. So they buried it in committee. Energetic Islamist deputies continued to press the matter from time to time[11] but their slim numbers made them easy to outmaneuver.

From time to time, however, an issue does arise that provokes a debate over interpretations of the shari'a. In such cases, the Egyptian People's Assembly resembles something like an eighteenth- or early nineteenth-century European parliament—a public sphere (and one to which access is very restricted) where contending voices reason and argue with each other on the basis of loose ideological orientations rather than rigid party discipline. While the Egyptian parliament—unlike its European predecessors—has a far clearer constitutional role in the legislative process on paper, in reality the critical legislative decisions seem to be made within the executive branch, with the parliament serving as an arena for contending views rather than an authoritative body. Such noisy debates are most common in areas related to the shari'a's role in regulating family relations—a modification to the personal status law in 2000 or a "law of the child" in 2008.[12] In such debates, members of the parliament hurl not only arguments and charges but also fatwas at their opponents, drawing in not only leading shari'a scholars from the traditional institutions of Islamic learning (especially Al-Azhar) but also public intellectuals and university professors. The government hardly abandons the fatwa-mongering field to parliamentarians but marshals its own set of religious authorities and arguments to persuade deputies and the broader public of its position.

Yet, such episodes aside, there is a very striking trend away from any shari'a-based discourse in parliamentary debates. In 2005, the Muslim Brotherhood secured one-fifth of the seats in parliamentary elections, and the organization's disciplined party bloc was therefore more able to raise issues and participate in debates. The looser parliamentary organization of the governing National Democratic Party could always muster the votes to prevail but found itself sometimes entangled in debates it would have preferred to avoid. Yet the Muslim Brotherhood has rarely used its position to push specific shari'a-based proposals, content instead with the claim that its call for good governance, an end to corruption, and caring for citizen needs is very much in keeping with the *maqasid* of the shari'a. This trend in Brotherhood discourse and thinking is itself worthy of exploration.

Outside of the State

THE MUSLIM BROTHERHOOD AND ISLAMIST MOVEMENTS   Perhaps nothing better illustrates the shift in public shari'a-based discourse away from specific rules and toward general principles than the recent evolution of shari'a-based claims by the Muslim Brotherhood. It was writers associated with the Brotherhood (notably 'Abd al-Qadir 'Awda in the 1950s and Sayyid Qutb in the 1960s—both of whom were executed) who laid the foundation for radical, shari'a-based opposition that ultimately took revolutionary form in the 1970s and 1980s. The Brotherhood itself pulled back from those radical ideas (though it still treats their originators with respect) and has disavowed any attempts to promote change by force; its oppositional rhetoric varies in tone but never goes so far as to reject the legitimacy of the current political system at all, much less on shari'a-based grounds.

But when the Brotherhood reemerged in public life in the 1970s and entered the political process in the 1980s (running candidates for parliament and inching toward the determination to form a political party), it initially made "application of the shari'a" central to its appeal. Brotherhood deputies in parliament raised matters of shari'a law, pressing to bring Egypt's legal framework into compliance with fixed shari'a-based rules.

The Brotherhood has never repudiated the call to "apply" the shari'a. Neither its leaders nor its rank and file would wish to move in such a direction. But talk of "application" has dropped from its daily lexicon nevertheless. Instead, its leaders speak of the *maqasid* of the shari'a and of the shari'a's flexibility.[13] The phrase that is now repeated almost ritually by Brotherhood leaders is not "application of the shari'a" but instead "an Islamic reference" (*marja'iyya islamiyya*), a far less demanding yardstick by which to measure Egypt's political institutions and laws. The Islamic shari'a is to serve as a general guide and a heritage from which to draw, but there is much less emphasis on specific rules. The head of the Brotherhood's parliamentary bloc explains that matters related to the shari'a rarely come up in parliamentary work—and the Brotherhood deputies do not rush to place specific shari'a-based proposals on the agenda.[14] (A leading member of the governing National Democratic Party concurs that shari'a-based arguments are rarely raised in parliamentary work.[15]) The shari'a still carries tremendous symbolic weight for the Brotherhood, but much of its current rhetoric seems to remain on a primarily symbolic level.

Further, the Brotherhood explicitly accepts that Egypt's constitutional institutions—chiefly the parliament and the Supreme Constitutional Court—ultimately retain the authority to make decisions concerning law, and that this authority derives from popular sovereignty and the text of the Egyptian constitution. Article 2 of the Egyptian constitution—proclaiming the "principles of the Islamic shari'a" to be "the principal source of legislation"—is sufficient for the Brotherhood. Its leaders accept the parliament as having the authority to decide how to translate that general injunction to practical effect, and the Supreme Constitutional Court—despite the secular training of its justices—as the appropriate body to adjudicate challenges to legislation based on Article 2.

Those Brotherhood leaders familiar with the Court's Article 2 jurisprudence cite it approvingly and echo its basic approach.

For the Brotherhood's own purposes, its leaders do feel the need on occasion to solicit guidance on issues that seem to have a shari'a dimension, but their approach is remarkably eclectic. In personal interviews, Brotherhood leaders report consulting with public intellectuals (such as Muhammad Salim al-'Awa and Tariq al-Bishri), Al-Azhar-based scholars, and others. In an internal dispute over a draft party platform, various leaders even attempted to marshal various religious authorities in support of their positions, leading to battle by fatwa within the organization (Brown and Hamzawy 2008).

Indeed, where the Brotherhood's thinking still retains a sharp oppositional edge is in the area of religious authority. And in this regard, the Brotherhood—a movement that arose outside of the state-supported religious establishment and that remains oppositional—has some surprisingly statist elements in its views. This became most apparent in a debate that crested in 2007 and 2008 regarding the movement's call for a body of senior religious scholars to advise the state. That debate is worth a short excursus because it illustrates both the nature and the limitations of Brotherhood thinking about the shari'a and authority.

The idea of forming a body that would express the consensus of credible and qualified religious scholars has circulated in Brotherhood leadership circles in recent years. In one sense, it is a part of the movement's efforts to promote the shari'a through constitutional institutions. But when critics of the Brotherhood hear hints of this proposal, they often charge that what the Brotherhood has in mind is something almost supra-constitutional, akin to Iran's Council of Guardians, a body that has asserted oversight authority over most other constitutional institutions (see Bahman Baktiari's essay in this volume). Indeed, while the Brotherhood's adversaries sometimes use the term "theocratic" to refer to its program, they are more likely to compare it to the Iranian model and assert that the Brotherhood is pursuing its own version of *wilayat al-faqih* (guardianship of the jurist, a concept more fully elaborated in Baktiari's essay). This charge is rejected by Brotherhood leaders, who complain that critics ignore the fact that they wish only to have a body that issues advisory rather than compulsory opinions.

The debate over the Brotherhood's views occurred both within all levels of the organization and outside of its ranks. It was occasioned in part by an attempt by the organization to develop a party platform—in part to answer the criticism that its stand on many public issues was vague and in part to communicate that it could play the role of a responsible opposition party in a democracy if given the opportunity. The platform was drafted by movement leaders and then, in the summer of 2007, circulated to a number of prominent intellectuals for comment. At that point, with the draft platform out in public view, debate exploded, much of it focusing on the "Senior Ulama Council" the Brotherhood draft platform proposed creating.[16] The new body would be elected by religious scholars; it would be consulted by other state bodies, but its opinions would be advisory except where a clear and definitive shari'a-based rule was at stake. Critics immediately charged that the Brotherhood was attempting to slip a new structure into Egypt's political system that would amount to supreme clerical oversight. The charge was exaggerated but not entirely unfounded, at least as the draft platform had it—while the body was to be advisory in most questions, the wording suggested that it would have to be consulted on a wide variety of matters. In addition, it would be politically difficult to ignore a state-sponsored body purporting to speak for the collective wisdom of Egypt's religious scholars. Brotherhood officials argued among themselves before conceding that the platform was poorly drafted and that while they saw the need for such a body, they would not press for its immediate adoption through the platform.

On the surface, the Brotherhood was engaged in a debate over whether its vision of the role of the shari'a was more compatible with liberal constitutionalism or an Iranian-style clerical authoritarianism. But that noisy and sometimes overwrought debate obscured three aspects of the Brotherhood's conception of the shari'a. First, it was highly comfortable with state authority. For the Brotherhood, the Senior Ulama Council was to be an official body speaking with a clear voice. Brotherhood leaders may accept the theory of pluralism in interpreting the shari'a—and indeed, there was to be no requirement that the council's advice be unanimous—but they show vague discomfort with the multiplicity of voices that have emerged as speaking for the Islamic shari'a in contemporary Egypt. Rather than celebrate that cacophony as an intellectual and cultural flowering, they clearly prefer that the Islamic shari'a remain an expert discourse (one in which they portray themselves as far more students than teachers) and that expert opinion inform state policy and legislation.

Second, the call for religious scholars to elect members of this council reflects the Brotherhood's deep concern over opportunism and politicization within some state religious institutions as well as the movement's intervention in disputes among ulama.[17] Differences among Brotherhood leaders did not trump a deep common mistrust of specific religious officials (especially the state mufti and even the shaykh of Al-Azhar) and the feeling that it was possible for the executive to coopt such figures. The Brotherhood has opposed legislation to criminalize the unlicensed issuing of fatwas, clearly fearing that only those scholars close to the government would be allowed to opine on Islamic law. The experience with the Al-Azhar Ulama Front—which Brother-

hood members found both more congenial to its own views and far more independent in its judgments—apparently convinced Brotherhood leaders that
a less craven body of religious scholars is required.

Third, and just as remarkable, is how much trouble the Brotherhood had
articulating its vision of the proper institutional framework for the Islamic
shariʿa in the Egyptian political system. While its general support for policies
and laws informed by a shariʿa spirit is clear, many of its leaders appear to have
given very little thought to particular institutional arrangements and appeared
unprepared when their proposal was closely examined; they were taken aback
by the resulting storm of criticism. The clear lesson from the experience is
not that the Brotherhood favors a specific vision but that it is enmeshed in the
concerns and calculations of the political world, far more focused on practical
realities than on designing structures to implement visions that are not thoroughly accepted by Egyptian society. And its leaders have also not grappled
seriously with a problem that seems likely to arise in any attempts to institutionalize a political role for shariʿa-based institutions: bringing the shariʿa to
politics may also have the contrary effect of politicizing the shariʿa. Electing
a council of ulama might be a short-term and highly specific answer to that
problem in a contemporary Egyptian context, but it is hardly likely to be a
permanent resolution even if it is adopted.

Even more striking than the Brotherhood's move toward greater generality and de-emphasis on specific rules has been the evolution of jihadist
groups. For such groups—emerging out of the most radical interpretations
of Brotherhood-gestated ideas—it was the failure of the Egyptian state to base
itself on the shariʿa that rendered it illegitimate. Such groups often did not
make clear precisely when a state could draw on non-Islamic sources of law,
nor did they generally make clear at what point the Egyptian state had lost its
legitimacy (when it based itself on nationalist and socialist ideologies? When it
adopted a modified version of the Code Napoleon? When it left the Ottoman
Empire? Or at some much earlier point in Egypt's past when the shariʿa ceased
prevailing in social and political relations?) But they were united in a claim that
the Egyptian state had clearly placed itself in a state of war with the faithful.
Specific shariʿa provisions were not at issue; rather, the shariʿa itself was central
to their world-view. And it is perhaps then no accident that one of the first actions taken by one of the radical groups was the kidnapping and assassination
of a senior religious official, the former minister of *awqaf*, in 1977.

If jihadist groups are defined by their insistence that the Egyptian state
has no legitimacy when it comes to religious discourse, the slow road that
many (though hardly all) jihadist leaders took beginning in the late 1990s is
especially striking. In essence, some leaders repudiated their past radicalism
and their repudiations took the form—at least implicitly—of an acceptance

that the Egyptian state had some Islamic credentials and its leaders therefore deserved the deference due to legitimate leaders of the polity. No longer was official deviance from shari'a-based rules regarded as so severe as to justify rebellion—and indeed, the emphasis on a shari'a-based state seems to have receded in the writings of those former jihadists known in Egypt as the "recanters." The most prominent and loquacious of the recantations was written by perhaps the leading jihadist ideologue, Sayyid Imam al-Sharif, known as "Dr. Fadl" (Sharif, 2008). Whether such repudiations arose from a sense that their jihad of the 1990s had been futile, prolonged imprisonment, or simply political and personal maturation, they provoked a wide and bitter debate in radical circles.

THE PIETIST TREND   Observers of Egyptian society—and, of course, Egyptians themselves—have taken note of what is best termed a trend toward greater public piety in Egyptian society. The trend is so diffuse and uncoordinated that it would be misleading to call it a movement (though the term has been used by those who have studied it closely). Pietism takes many forms, from study groups to televangelist programs. But perhaps its two most striking expressions are the widespread popular followings of a wide range of preachers and the formation of small circles of friends who meet regularly to study and discuss religious themes in a group context. The trend is observable at all levels of Egyptian society, but it is so varied as to be resistant to generalizations. The few remarks advanced here should therefore be taken as quite tentative.

At first glance, the piety trend would seem to represent a variety of Islam that is simply not "shari'a-minded," to revive Marshall Hodgson's phrase. Participants would seem to be interested more in an exploration of faith and perhaps in ethical conduct and much less in the legal and political realms. Saba Mahmood, in her ethnographic account of pietist preachers in Cairo, states that "reinstatement of the shari'a remains marginal to the realization of the movement's goals, and few lessons address the issue," though this does not mean that the "movement" maintains a "privatized notion of religion." Instead it advocates a form of piety that brings religious obligations and rituals "to bear upon worldly issues in new ways" (Mahmood 2005, 47)

But while much of the pietist trend may not be oriented around an explicitly political or legal project, this is an overly restrictive way of conceiving of the Islamic shari'a. In fact, the pietist trend might very well be considered to be participating in the consensual themes regarding the shari'a emerging in Egypt today, with their emphasis on general goals and their turn away from a conception of the shari'a as primarily a legal corpus to be applied by the political authorities.

Not only does the pietist trend entail a radical diffusion of interpretive authority—one with deep political ramifications—but it is very much focused on correct social conduct. And its members show signs of drawing heavily—if quite eclectically—from shari'a-based discourses in their quest for answers to practical and ethical questions. Indeed, a large part of the "chaotic fatwa" phenomenon that so frustrates the more tradition- and authority-minded might be attributed to the pietist trend.

In one circle of Alexandria women, for instance, members debated whether they were allowed to travel abroad without a male guardian. Their research techniques would be familiar to a resourceful American undergraduate, though their specific sources differed—they searched some popular Islamic websites, read some sources available online, and consulted Al-Azhar by telephone.[18] In the end, the group member faced with a travel opportunity decided that it was permitted for her to travel alone so long as she did so for a serious purpose, and she received the support of her colleagues. When they moved beyond personal issues to debate broader social and political questions—such as whether the Islamic shari'a prohibits women from serving as a head of state or judge (a discussion occasioned by the appointment of a woman judge in Egypt as well as by Hillary Clinton's candidacy for the American presidency)—they did so in the same freewheeling spirit, one that drew on the various religious authorities available to them but treated none as definitive and reserved final judgment to the individual Muslim.

Religious Authority and Political Authority

The Islamic shari'a seems to have become central to Egyptian politics partly because its content is so flexible. While the stress on it may not please all Egyptians, the implications of its centrality are deflected far more often than they are publicly questioned or resisted. Since the themes that draw consensus support are so plastic, those quietly resentful of their fellow Egyptians' focus on the shari'a have little need to break down an open door.

Yet, however platitudinous, the consensus on the Islamic shari'a does privilege some arguments over others. And it therefore has some political implications that are finally beginning to generate a response, particularly from an Egyptian regime that has shown little tolerance for any organized movement outside of its control. In 2007 the first amendment of the Egyptian constitution was inexplicably amended to introduce the word "citizenship"—inexplicably, that is, unless read in conjunction with another amendment that barred any political parties with a "religious reference." The regime was showing some signs of working to tweak the role of religion in Egyptian politics and respond to the challenge posed by the Muslim Brotherhood. The new stress on Egyptian citizenship was designed not to combat but at least to balance the role of religion in national identity and political discussions; the ban on parties with a religious reference was similarly based on a claim that religion should not be used to divide the country. Clear evidence that these steps constituted an ideological recalibration away from previous formulations was found when embarrassed regime advocates of the amendments were shown documents earlier issued by the governing National Democratic Party that had defined it as having a "religious reference."

As part of the new discourse of citizenship, amendments to the shari'a-based code of personal status were developed; as part of an attempt to counteract the dominance of religious institutions, the cabinet moved to diminish the autonomy given to the Al-Azhar school system and to separate the secular from the religious faculties in Al-Azhar University. The attempt, however modest, to diminish the centrality of religion was based on a sense that the regime was not in complete control of religious discourse.

And indeed, the growing centrality of the shari'a to Egyptian political discourse has led to the participation of more voices in public debates. Some Egyptians—both within the state and outside it—are deeply troubled by this, seeing too much flexibility, the entrance of unorthodox interpretations, the possibility for fatwa shopping, and the collapse of religious authority. But others participate in it and a few are actually encouraged by what they see as an intellectual flowering and an Islamization of public discourse.

Rather than a steady increase in state domination of religion, a more subtle process has been taking place in which political authority shapes religious interpretation but also in which the debates over proper interpretation are replicated within the state apparatus itself.[19] The Egyptian state attempts to organize, regulate, license, and steer this debate. Its efforts are only partly successful. But perhaps more remarkable—if less noticed until now—is the way in which this state effort has led to the emergence of multiple and competing voices within the state itself. The attempt to promote control and uniformity has not completely backfired, but it has brought some of the divergence of interpretation inside official channels. To use a different metaphor, the attempt to subsume the shari'a has resembled a boa constrictor working to digest an elephant: the shape of the serpent dramatically changes as a result of the audacious effort.

Notes

1. For an example of current discussion of *maqasid*, see the report on a discussion led by a leading intellectual, Muhammad Salim al-'Awa (Sayyid 2007).

2. The phrase "changing with the hand" is part of a commonly quoted hadith in

which the Prophet is said to have instructed those witnessing something wrong to change it first with their hands. If they are unable to do so, they should change it with their tongues. And if they are still unable, they should change it with their hearts. For a presentation of some of the interpretive tradition surrounding this hadith, see Cook 2000.

3. Jamal Qutb, personal interview, Cairo, June 22, 2008. For a fascinating ethnographic account of Al-Azhar's role in providing fatwas, see Agrama 2005.

4. While this complaint is voiced increasingly loudly and frequently, it is actually an old one. Skovgaard-Peterson (1997, 101) notes that Egypt's ruler wrote a note to the minister of the interior in 1865 "demanding that measures be taken against people issuing fatwas without permission."

5. Qutb said this to me in a personal interview with me on June 22, 2008.

6. The discussion of textbooks is also based on a survey of secondary school Islamic education textbooks, which are generally titled *Al-tarbiyya al-islamiyya*.

7. These numbers have grown rapidly in recent years. Zeghal (2007, 110) reports an official figure of approximately 1.3 million students in 2000–2001.

8. Professor Muhammad Imam of Alexandria University, personal interview, Alexandria, June 20, 2008.

9. For a very useful study of the pre-1956 shari'a courts, see Shaham 1997.

10. Perhaps the most thorough work on the Court's Article 2 jurisprudence is Lombardi 2006. I have also worked with Lombardi to produce a translation of one of the Court's most interesting rulings on an Article 2 case (Brown and Lombardi 2006).

11. Gamal Hishmat, former Muslim Brotherhood member of parliament, personal interview, Cairo, June 2008.

12. For an analysis of the debate surrounding the 2000 amendment to the personal status code, see Singerman 2005.

13. In personal interviews I have conducted with Muslim Brotherhood leaders since 2004 ('Isam al-'Iryan, 'Abd al-Mun'im Abu al-Futuh, Muhammad Habib, and Jamal Hishmat), all have sought to emphasize the flexibility of the shari'a and indeed referred to flexibility as one of its major virtues. I have written an analysis of the role of the Islamic shari'a in a draft platform issued by the Brotherhood in 2007 (Brown and Hamzawy 2008).

14. Sa'd Al-Katatni, personal interview, Cairo, June 17, 2008.

15. Muhammad Kamal, member of the Shura Council and NDP Political Committee, personal interview, Cairo, June 18, 2008.

16. Actually, the Brotherhood was seeking to re-create and empower a body that had existed earlier in Al-Azhar. Because Brotherhood leaders saw themselves as simply restoring vitality and autonomy to a structure that had existed earlier, the storm of controversy that confronted their proposal took them by surprise.

17. Muhammad Habib, personal interview, Cairo, June 19, 2008; Jamal Hishmat, personal interview, Cairo, June 22, 2008.

18. Meeting with a women's religious issues discussion group, Alexandria, June 20, 2008.

19. Agrama 2005 develops a similar view of religion and state as insinuated into each other's putatively separate domains, though his interpretation emphasizes the domination of the state.

References Cited

Abdo, Geneive. 2000. *No God but God: Egypt and the Triumph of Islam*. Oxford: Oxford University Press.

Agrama, Hussein Ali. 2005. "Law Courts and Fatwa Councils in Modern Egypt: An Ethnography of Islamic Legal Practice." Ph.D. diss., Johns Hopkins University.

Brown, Nathan J. 1997. *The Rule of Law in the Arab World: Courts in Egypt and the Gulf*. Cambridge: Cambridge University Press.

Brown, Nathan J., and Amr Hamzawy. 2008. "The Draft Party Platform of the Egyptian Muslim Brotherhood: Foray into Political Integration or Retreat into Old Positions?" Carnegie Paper, Carnegie Endowment for International Peace, Middle East Series 89, January. http://www.carnegieendowment.org/files/cp89_muslim_brothers_final.pdf (accessed November 10, 2008).

Brown, Nathan J., and Clark Lombardi. 2006. "The Supreme Constitutional Court of Egypt on Islamic Law, Veiling and Civil Rights: An Annotated Translation of Supreme Constitutional Court of Egypt *Case No. 8 of Judicial Year 17* (May 18, 1996)." *American University International Law Review* 21 (3): 437–60.

Cook, Michael. 2000. *Commanding Right and Forbidding Wrong in Islamic Thought*. Cambridge: Cambridge University Press.

Crecelius, Daniel. 1972. "Nonideological Responses of the Egyptian Ulama to Modernization." In *Scholars, Saints, and Sufis: Muslim Religious Institutions since 1500*, ed. Nikki R. Keddie, 167–209. Berkeley: University of California Press.

Dodge, Bayard. 1974. *Al-Azhar: A Millennium of Muslim Learning*. Washington, D.C.: Middle East Institute.

Gaffney, Patrick D. 1994. *The Prophet's Pulpit: Islamic Preaching in Contemporary Egypt*. Berkeley: University of California Press.

Ghobashy, Mona el-. 2006. "Taming Leviathan: Constitutionalist Contention in Contemporary Egypt." Ph.D. diss., Columbia University.

Hallaq, Wael B. 2004. "Can the Shari'a Be Restored?" In *Islamic Law and the Challenge of Modernity*, ed. Yvonne Yazbeck Haddad and Barbara Freyer Stowasser, 21–53. Lanham, Md.: Altamira.

Lombardi, Clark. 2006. *State Law as Islamic Law in Modern Egypt: The Incorporation of the Shari'a into Egyptian Constitutional Law*. Leiden: Brill.

Mahmood, Saba. 2005. *Politics of Piety: The Islamic Revival and the Feminist Subject*. Princeton: Princeton University Press.

Opwis, Felicitas. 2007. "Islamic Law and Legal Change: The Concept of *Maslaha* in Classical and Contemporary Islamic Legal Theory." In *Shari'a: Islamic Law in the Contemporary Context*, ed. Abbas Amanat and Frank Griffel, 62–82. Stanford: Stanford University Press.

Rabiʿ, Majda al-Salih. 1992. *Al-Dawr al-siyasi li-l-Azhar, 1952–1981.* Cairo: Cairo Center for Strategic Studies.

Rheault, Magali, and Dalia Mogahed. 2008. "Iranians, Egyptians, Turks: Contrasting Views on Sharia." *Muslim West Facts Project.* http://www.muslimwestfacts.com/mwf/108739/Iranians-Egyptians-Turks-Contrasting-Views-Sharia.aspx (accessed October 29, 2008).

Rutherford, Bruce K. 2009. *Egypt after Mubarak: Liberalism, Islam, and Democracy in the Arab World.* Princeton: Princeton University Press.

Sayyid, Muhammad. 2007. "The Maqasid of the Shariʿa Are Not Limited . . . Rather It Is Open to Additions of Contemporary Maqasid." In Arabic. *Al-liwaʾ al-islami,* April 26.

Shaham, Ron. 1997. *Family and the Courts in Modern Egypt: A Study Based on the Decisions of the Shariʿa Courts, 1900–1955.* Leiden: Brill.

Sharif, Sayyid Imam al-. 2008. "Guiding Jihadist Work in Egypt and the World." In Arabic. http://www.islamonline.net/servlet/Satellite?c=ArticleA_C&cid=11950323 83037&pagename=Zone-Arabic-Daawa%2FDWALayout (accessed January 2, 2009).

Singerman, Diane. 2005. "Rewriting Divorce in Egypt: Reclaiming Islam, Legal Activism, and Coalition Politics." In *Remaking Muslim Politics: Pluralism, Contestation, Democratization,* ed. Robert W. Hefner, 161–88. Princeton: Princeton University Press.

Skovgaard-Petersen, Jakob. 1997. *Defining Islam for the Egyptian State: Muftis and Fatwas of the Dar al-Ifta.* Leiden: Brill.

———. 2004. "A Typology of State Muftis." In *Islamic Law and the Challenge of Modernity,* ed. Yvonne Yazbeck Haddad and Barbara Freyer Stowasser, 81–97. Lanham, Md.: Altamira.

Starrett, Gregory. 1998. *Putting Islam to Work: Education, Politics, and Religious Transformation in Egypt.* Berkeley: University of California Press.

Toronto, James A., and Muhammad S. Eissa. 2007. "Egypt: Promoting Tolerance, Defending against Islamism." In *Teaching Islam: Textbooks and Religion in the Middle East,* ed. Eleanor Abdella Doumato and Gregory Starrett, 27–52. Boulder, Colo.: Lynne Rienner.

Zaman, Muhammad Qasim. 2002. *The Ulama in Contemporary Islam: Custodians of Change.* Princeton: Princeton University Press.

Zeghal, Malika. 2007. "The 'Recentering' of Religious Knowledge and Discourse: The Case of Al-Azhar in Twentieth-Century Egypt." In *Schooling Islam,* ed. Robert W. Hefner and Muhammad Qasim Zaman, 107–30. Princeton: Princeton University Press.

3. Iran

Shari'a Politics and the Transformation
of Islamic Law

Bahman Baktiari

Iran is the only country in the Muslim world that is directly ruled by the clergy. The regime constantly refers
to Islamic symbols, uses Islamic discourse, and appeals to the public's religious
sentiments to justify the current distribution of power and the structure of
state institutions. The Iranian regime enshrines the principle of *vilayat-i faqih,*
"the rule of the jurist." Ultimate power lies in the hands of the senior *faqih,*
who has veto power over all aspects of the political system. All legislation and
bills have to be in accordance with Islam and are subject to veto by the Council
of Guardians.[1] The council has to approve all bills passed by parliament and
has the power to veto them if it considers them inconsistent with the constitution and Islamic law. The council can also bar candidates from standing for
election to parliament, the presidency, and the Assembly of Experts.

In many Muslim societies, there is a great deal of popular enthusiasm for
strengthening criminal codes by relying on shari'a rulings. According to various polls, some two-thirds of Egyptians, 60 percent of Pakistanis, and more
than half of all Jordanians say that shari'a should be the only source of legislation in their countries (see Robert Hefner's introduction to this volume).
Islamist political parties, like those associated with the transnational Muslim
Brotherhood, make the adoption of shari'a the most prominent plank in their
political platforms (Feldman 2008b).

However, Iran's Islamic experience has led to very different opinions about
shari'a and its suitability for the legal system of a modern Muslim country.
Studying the Iranian case shows how difficult it is to implement laws based on
shari'a. Iran's official Islamization program initially had positive connotations
for many Iranians, who imagined that it would restore the rule of traditional

law; they expected that the application of Islamic law under the auspices of *mujtahids* (distinguished jurists) would ensure perfect justice. However, clerical despotism, corruption, gross mismanagement of a faltering economy, harsh suppression of dissent, and an even harsher version of criminal justice codified as the Islamic Penal Code have provoked increasing disillusionment, alienation, and anti-clericalism. Although Iranian rulers continue to talk of fealty to Islam and Islamic law, they have had a difficult time juggling diverse types of laws within one system, and have created tensions, incongruities, and confusion. Moreover, by assuming powerful public positions in government, clerics have reduced the status of *mujtahids* to that of government officials. Khomeini even went so far as to contend that laws that violate shari'a are binding as long as they serve the interest of the governing elite (Zubaida 2003; Mohammadi 2008). The disillusioning experience of state-sponsored Islamization accounts for the rising popularity of intellectuals who question the absolutist theology of the ruling clerics and utilize indigenous sources of scholarship to oppose clerical hegemony.

One paradoxical and unintended consequence of the introduction and enforcement of shari'a in Iran has been to open up a dialogue about the sources and meaning of Islamic law. This dialogue, in turn, has become a catalyst for the emergence of voices that are changing the terms of reference of Islamic discourses from within. Now women are claiming the right to interpret Islamic sources and to leave behind or go beyond classical formulations to develop new paradigms and reformulate Islamic concepts and law from a feminist perspective (Mir-Hosseini 1996). Other intellectuals have provided shari'a-based arguments for the suspension and abolition of death penalty sentences. It is often argued by traditionalists that shari'a-based laws are unchangeable and irrevocable. However, some thirty years after Iran's Islamic Revolution, we are witnessing a flourishing rereading of sacred texts, a shift some scholars declare to be so radical that it has no counterpart in the rest of the Muslim world.

The Politics of Shari'a in Prerevolutionary Iran

In the nineteenth century, Iran was characterized by a decentralized administration of law, where state-appointed judges, applying both religious and customary law, and a variety of independent *mujtahids* were available for the settlement of disputes. The law of the land was not coextensive with shari'a. Legal disputes or complaints were addressed in a variety of jurisdictions. Government officials, notables, tribal leaders, and ulama acted as judges and arbiters. The ulama confirmed the registrations of contracts, properties, marriages, divorces, and inheritance.[2] They held their own shari'a courts and ruled on penal cases without any government presence (Algar 1969, 11–14). According to one source, the courts were under the authority of senior *mujtahids*. But in Shi'a Islam, *mujtahids* are chosen by people who follow their religious guidance; these leaders are referred to as *marjas*.[3] When a dispute arose, people usually resorted to their *marja* for resolution and settlement, rather than formal court proceedings. Each *mujtahid* could issue his own fatwa, which was binding only on his followers. Armed militias, tribal fighters, and privately contracted police enforced the rulings. However, in important affairs, several *mujtahids* might agree on a fatwa, making it binding on everyone.[4]

The Constitutional Revolution of 1906–11 introduced new ideas and institutions to limit the dictatorial powers of the monarch. Among them were a parliament to pass laws, make the government more representative, and force the king to reign instead of rule, and a written constitution. The idea of such a constitution was immediately challenged by a group of conservative clerics. Shaykh Faz Allah Nuri (1842–1909) objected to it on the ground that it was contrary to shari'a (Ridgeon 2005, 37). He maintained that writing a law separate from the Islamic law, one not contained in shari'a, and forcing subjects to obey it is forbidden. He also found the idea of a constitution unacceptable because it provided for a parliament which would infringe on divinely revealed law. For him, a written constitution fell outside the acceptable Islamic framework (Ridgeon 2005, 52; Baktiari 1996, 10–11).

In response to Nuri, Ayatollah Na'ini attempted to formulate an Islamic justification for constitutionalism. He did so in explicitly Islamic, but highly original, terms:

> Once these three points are clear, there remains no room to doubt the necessity of changing a despotic regime into a constitutional one. This is true, because the former consists of three sets of usurpations and oppressions: 1) It is usurpation of the authority of God and injustice to Him; 2) it is usurpation of the Imam's authority and oppression of the Imam; 3) it also involves oppression of the people. By contrast, a constitutional system is only oppression of the Imam, because his authority is usurped. Thus, a constitutional regime limits three acts of oppressions to one; consequently it is necessary to adopt it. (Moaddel 1986, 538)

The constitutionalists agreed to create a "committee of no fewer than five mujtahids to reject, repudiate, wholly or in part, any proposal that is at variance with the sacred laws of Islam. In such matters, the decision of this committee of ulama shall be followed and obeyed, and this article shall continue unchanged until the appearance of His Holiness the Proof of the Age (i.e., the Hidden Imam)" (Farmanfarmaian 1954). As recently pointed out by Noah Feldman, the Islamic version of judicial review in the constitutions of Afghanistan and Iraq today was borrowed from the Iranian constitution (Feldman 2008a, 127).

Between 1921 and 1979, both Reza Shah and his son, Mohammed Reza, initiated policies that undermined the tacit understanding expressed in the constitution that kings should only reign, and not rule. Both Pahlavi kings introduced Western civil codes into Iranian criminal and commercial laws to an unprecedented degree. The importance of shari'a and Islam was downplayed, while ideologues glorified the pre-Islamic Iranian kingdom and culture. Although the civil code of 1928 was derived from shari'a, officials made sure that everything was administered by the Ministry of Justice in modern court systems. Moreover, the Ministry of Justice opened its own law school to train lawyers, which became the law faculty of Tehran University. A law degree became a requirement for legal practice (Menashri 1992). If clerics wanted to have a role, they were told to get a degree from the law faculty. Only the state courts and the office of the attorney general could approve the referral of a case to a religious tribunal. The latter could take up only matters related to marriage, divorce, and the appointment of trustees and guardians.

Under U.S. pressure, Mohammed Reza Shah embarked on a program of reforms in the 1960s that caused further agitation and conflict with the ulama. His land reform proposals, as well as his initiative to enfranchise women and religious minorities, provoked strong reactions among senior *mujtahids*, including Ayatollah Khomeini. Khomeini harbored strong resentment against Reza Shah and Mohammed Reza Shah for their secularizing measures, which he regarded as humiliating to both Islam and clerics. Mohammad Reza Shah frequently referred to clerics as "black reactionaries" and portrayed them as primitive and narrow-minded.

For centuries, one of the most important symbols of legitimacy in Iran was the respect rulers showed for ulama and the religious institutions. Recognizing the reality of clerical authority and power, rulers rarely tried to impose versions of laws that directly undermined the authority of the ulama—at least not in a way that publicly insulted their status and prestige.[5] However, under Pahlavi rule, government officials, secular intellectuals, and anti-religious elements portrayed Shi'a Islam as the cause of backwardness, superstition, and corruption. These characterizations were accompanied by bitter and persistent attacks on the ulama, who were held responsible for the corruption and moral degeneration of the existing social order (Kasravi 1990). The Pahlavi governments encouraged a nationalist message that increasingly portrayed Islam as an alien faith imposed on Iran by an inferior civilization and a backward ethnic group—that is, the Arabs. In the end, these attacks on the ulama, together with the state's programs of top-down secularization, sowed the seeds for the Islamic Revolution of 1979. Forced into exile in 1963, Ayatollah

Khomeini remained relentless in his opposition to the regime and emerged to overthrow the shah (Mohammadi 2008, 107–108).

The Constitution of the Islamic Republic

After the February 1979 revolution, Ayatollah Khomeini worked on a new constitution and changed the country from a monarchy to a republic: the Islamic Republic of Iran. Reza Khan, who ruled from 1921 to 1941, had isolated the clerical establishment and imposed a dictatorial system on the country, and Khomeini and his allies were determined to avoid repeating the experience. Khomeini also believed that Reza Khan's son, Mohammed Reza Shah, could not have remained in power if the CIA had not supported a coup in 1954 that overthrew a nationalist government.

What finally emerged in December 1979 was an Islamic constitution that is an intellectual and political hybrid of remarkable complexity. The document combines principles of democracy with theocracy, vox populi with vox dei, and modern concepts of representative government with Ayatollah Khomeini's notion of *vilayat i faqih* (guardianship of the jurist). According to this principle, in the absence of the Hidden Imam (the messiah who will return at a time of grave injustice to Muslims), the clergy were the true guardians of the state. Because the ulama are charged with interpreting shari'a and leading the community on the right path, it followed that they should guide the state as well.

The Iranian constitution pays much attention to the question of the compatibility of all legislation with shari'a. "All laws and regulations including civil, criminal, financial, economic, administrative, cultural, military, political or otherwise, shall be based on Islamic principles. This article shall apply generally to all the articles of the Constitution and other laws and regulations" (Article 4). The procedure for implementing this principle is equally clear. It is the duty of the jurisconsults (*fuqaha*) of the Council of Guardians to decide whether or not legislation passed by the parliament (Majles) is in conformity with the precepts of Islam; this is determined by a majority vote of the members of the council (Article 96). The revolutionary authors of these constitutional guidelines borrowed this formulation of shari'a-compatibility from the 1906 constitution, which called for a Committee of Mujtahids to oversee parliamentary legislation (Mohammadi 2008, 115–16).

Although in theory the Islamic Republic is committed to the proposition that Islam is an ideology, it is the only Muslim country to restructure its government in accordance with what purport to be Islamic criteria. According to Articles 5 and 107 of the Iranian constitution, "government from the Islamic perspective" requires placing supreme control over the country's affairs in the hands of a member of the clergy recognized by the majority of the people as their leader. These provisions embody Khomeini's model of Islamic government, *vilayat-i faqih,* in which the leading Islamic jurist (*faqih*) is placed squarely at the apex of political authority (Ramazani 1980, 189). Khomeini first outlined this concept in a series of lectures that were published in 1979 under the title "The Islamic Government." They attracted a large popular audience among both Sunni and Shi'a Muslims, both in their original Persian versions and in an Arabic translation.

According to Article 110 of the constitution, the Islamic republic's senior *faqih* appoints six members of the clergy to the Council of Guardians. These clergy join with the six non-clerical members in deciding whether legislation is in conformity with the constitution; collectively, they have the authority to veto legislation that they find conflicts with Islamic principles (Articles 91–98). The Council of Guardians is also given the authority to supervise presidential and National Assembly elections and referendums (Article 99). The senior *faqih* also appoints the highest judicial authorities, is commander of chief of the armed forces with broad powers of appointment, confirms the election of a president (and may dismiss him after certain initiatives by the Supreme Court or the parliament), and pardons convicts or reduces their sentences upon the recommendation of the Supreme Court (Ramazani 1980, 202).

In addition to the Council of Guardians, the Iranian constitution establishes another unique body called the Expediency Discernment Council of the System. The Expediency Council is required to take into consideration the larger interests of the Islamic system, rather than just shari'a. It meets whenever the Council of Guardians rejects a bill proposed by the Majles as contrary to the principles of shari'a or the constitution, but the Majles then insists on its parliamentary purview and refuses to go along with the Council of Guardians on the grounds that the legislation is in the broader interest of the republic (Article 112). Underlying this arrangement is the doctrine of *zarurat* (necessity), which has a long history in Islamic jurisprudence. In Sunni Islam, the principle of taking the common good (*maslahah*) into account when establishing justice has been accepted since around the ninth century. Among the Shi'a Muslims, in contrast, it appears to be seen as a modern innovation (Opwis 2007). The doctrine of *zarurat* holds that the primary rulings of Islam may be temporarily waived in emergencies or conditions of overriding necessity. Traditionally, it has been applied primarily, not to matters of state, but to extraordinary personal matters and exigencies affecting the individual believer. For example, the prohibition on eating pork might be waived for a Muslim facing starvation. Under the Islamic republic, however, the principle has been extended to apply to a far broader array of political necessities.

As developed and articulated by Khomeini and others since the Iranian Revolution, the doctrine of overriding necessity has been applied to societal issues and broad questions of social justice. It has been argued, for instance, that it may be invoked to suspend the primary rulings of Islam if the existence of the state is threatened or, in Khomeini's words, if inaction would lead to "wickedness and corruption." The first time the doctrine was invoked was in 1981, when the Majles approved a number of social welfare and economic measures (such as nationalization of foreign trade, land distribution, and confiscation of the property of emigrés) that were then vetoed by the Council of Guardians as violating Islamic principles. In October 1981 Khomeini suggested that the Majles could approve such measures on the basis of overriding necessity if it considered them essential for the life of the community. In this instance, however, the Majles and the Council of Guardians were not able to agree on the conditions that justified recourse to the principle of zarurat (Khomeini 1981).

The Iranian constitutional system has thus developed principles for reconciling the Islamic legal system with contemporary requirements, when such reconciliation is deemed necessary. Under this arrangement, the primary norms of shari'a are no longer the exclusive reference for legislation, although in principle all legislation must be compatible with it. The Expediency Council is intended to make it possible to reach a political decision without explicit regard to shari'a criteria. Naturally, decisions were influenced by national interest before the Expediency Council was established, the most obvious example being the ceasefire with Iraq six months prior to Khomeini's decree.

Nothing in the constitution calls for the country's laws and regulations to be compatible with internationally recognized human rights standards, and the members of the Council of Guardians do not concern themselves with other legal or moral criteria when evaluating the acceptability of any particular piece of legislation. The council's official duty is simply to assess the compatibility of legislation with shari'a and the constitution. Still, Chapter 3 of the constitution does guarantee certain human rights. For example, Article 23, entitled "Freedom of Belief," states that "the investigation of individuals' beliefs is forbidden, and no one may be molested or taken to task simply for holding a certain belief" (Schirazi 1998, 12). Article 30 focuses on education, stating that "the government must provide all citizens with free education up to secondary school, and must expand free higher education to the extent required by the country for attaining self-sufficiency." However, it places the judiciary under the exclusive control of clerics chosen by the *faqih* and provides for the extensive revision of the legal codes to render them Islamic. According to Article 67, judges are obliged to examine each case on the basis of the codified laws of the country. In the absence of a relevant law, they are enjoined to deliver their judgment on the basis of authoritative Islamic sources and authentic fatwas. Members of the Council of Guardians and the judiciary are not obliged by law to consider international human rights in such circumstances. Nor does the Iranian legal system direct their attention to a universally recognized conception of justice as it is reflected in internationally accepted standards of fundamental human rights (Ramazani 1980, 202).

There was no consensus among the ulama about Khomeini's principle of government by the jurist. The principle does not exist in the literature of classical Shi'a jurisprudence; indeed, it is found nowhere else than in the writings of Ayatollah Khomeini. The ascendance of a single senior cleric to the summit of state power, and the delegation of extraordinary legislative authority to that cleric, has the ironic effect of placing the autonomy of other *mujtahids* in question. In 1979, many senior religious scholars seemed to be aware of this threat to their traditional authority, and they rejected the validity of *vilayat-i faqih* accordingly. Ayatollah Kazem Shari'atmadari was foremost among those who did so, but other senior clerics quietly concurred in their writing and teaching. Shari'atmadari was a senior *mujtahid* with a wide following; he had been an active participant in the Islamic revolution. In 1982, he was implicated in a "conspiracy to overthrow the regime." He was arrested and then defrocked by state authorities. The measures taken against him were unprecedented in Iranian history. Never before had a senior cleric been defrocked and publicly humiliated by another group of clerics (Gieling 1997, 779).

In 2008, the senior *mujtahid,* Ayatollah Montazeri, in what is probably his most startling attack on the authority of the concept, declared Khomeini's principle a species of *shirk,* or polytheistic "association," a grievous sin in Islam. Montazeri's grounds for condemning it are interesting:

> The views of the faghih have priority over the views of other people only on religious matter and talking about other issues, such as relations with the US or having political relations with other countries, are not the business of the faghih and therefore must be resolved by professional experts . . . Today, every[one] accepts that one cleric cannot be an expert on all the aspects of people's life and for this reason fegh (Islamic jurisprudence) requires expertise and if we accept the expert faghih (cleric ruler) then we must accept the council of clerics. (*Rooz* 2008a)

Shortly before Khomeini died in 1989, the title of the senior *faqih* was changed to *vali amr moslemin,* supreme leader. Khomeini's successor, Ali Khamenei, is a cleric of middle standing with little charisma. Yet the revised constitution gives him great political power. The supreme leader appoints the chief justice and six of the twelve members of the Council of Guardians. In this way, he powerfully influences how the Islamic Republic deals with shari'a, as well as how the "interests of the Islamic Republic" are defined. The evolution of the Islamic Republic's court system is a good reflection of how the regime has tried to balance these interests with shariʻa (Mohammadi 2008).

Family Law

The key characteristic usually cited to identify a state as Islamic is, of course, adherence to and implementation of shariʻa. Shariʻa is held up as the model of legal perfection and the embodiment of the justice of Islam. The call for an Islamic state "is therefore first and foremost a call for law—for a legal state that would be justified by law and govern through it." (Feldman 2008a, 10).

One of the early communiqués issued by Ayatollah Khomeini's office—on February 26, 1979, barely two weeks after the collapse of the Pahlavi regime—announced the dismantling of the Family Protection Law (FPL) and the reinstatement of the shariʻa provisions for marriage and divorce (codified in 1935 as part of the Iranian civil code; Tabari and Nahi 1982, 232). The Family Protection Law of 1967 (and its 1975 amendments) had abolished men's unilateral right to divorce, restricted their right to polygyny, and accorded husbands and wives more or less equal access to divorce and custody rights. At the time, the majority of clerics had not objected to it. However, Khomeini was quite outspoken in his condemnation of the FPL. From exile in Iraq, he issued a sharp rebuke in his book on clarifications of religious questions, *Resaleh towzih al-masael* (The Islamic Epistle). He wrote,

> The law that has recently been passed by the illegal Majles under the name of the Family Protection Law in order to destroy Muslim family life, is against Islam, and both its originators and implementers are guilty before the Shariʻa. Women who are divorced in family courts should consider their divorces as null, and if they remarry they are committing adultery. Whoever marries such women knowingly is also an adulterer, and should be punished according to the Shariʻa by whipping. The children of these men and women are illegitimate and are not entitled to inheritance. (Khomeini 1984, 314)

Not surprisingly, in light of this view, one of Khomeini's first acts after returning to Iran was to suspend the FPL, which he did on February 26, 1979. One of the arguments supporting this suspension was that the courts established by the FPL had no authority to issue verdicts on matters pertaining to divorce because, under Islamic law, men did not need to provide reasons for divorcing their wives. In October of 1979, the Revolutionary Council approved a proposal to replace the family protection courts with special civil courts. The new courts were authorized to preside over disputes between couples. Remarkably, then, although they had once been judged to have no basis in Islamic law, the family protection courts were in essence retained, albeit under a new name, and they continued to function much as they had before the revolution.

Following the traditional conception of shari'a, the postrevolutionary Iranian civil code defines marriage as a contract to which both parties have the right to stipulate conditions. Article 1119 makes this right to contractual conditionality quite clear:

> The parties to a marriage contract may stipulate in it or in another binding contract any condition which is not incompatible with the nature of the marriage contract; for example, it may be stipulated that, if the husband marries another woman or absents himself for a certain period, or fails to continue to provide her with maintenance, or makes an attempt on the life of the wife or maltreats her in a manner that makes their life together intolerable, the wife will have the power of an agent authorized to divorce herself or to appoint another person to obtain her divorce after proving the fulfillment of the stipulated condition in the court and the issuance of final judgment thereon.

The code identifies conditions under which a divorce can be obtained by either party. Husbands can obtain divorce at will. If the divorce is not requested by the wife and she has not failed in any matrimonial duties or behaved immorally, "the husband is required to transfer to the wife up to half of the properties (or any equivalents agreed by the court) earned during the years of marriage" (Mir-Hosseini 1999, 193). In twelve conditions defined by the law, she also has the right to petition a court for a divorce. The twelve conditions are surprisingly far-ranging, and include the husband refusing to pay living expenses, behaving badly, being condemned to imprisonment for five years or more, and taking another wife without the consent of the first.

Iran's shari'a-based family law was presented as intended to "protect the family" and realize women's "high status" in Islam (Mir-Hosseini 1999). It was also intended to reduce the rates of early and arranged marriage, and of divorce. But its consequences have been so strikingly out of line with contemporary social realities, popular notions of justice, and women's aspirations that clergy and laypeople alike have felt compelled to rethink the idea that shari'a is immutable. Ziba Mir-Hosseini, who examined court records and witnessed many proceedings, provided the following account:

> In October 1980, when I first started attending the Tehran branches of the new family courts, now presided over by Islamic judges, women who came to court were astonished to learn that their husbands could now divorce them without first securing their consent. Some remained

incredulous and would ask more than one judge: Can he really divorce me, if I don't agree? Is this what the Shari'a says? In 1985, when I resumed my court attendance, women, although no longer incredulous, were insistent on voicing their discontent; some used every occasion to remind the Islamic judge of his role as custodian of the Shari'a and of the injustice of a system which could afford them no protection. It was common to hear women ask the judge, Is this how Islam honors women? Is this the justice of Islam, that he can dispose of me now that I have lost my youth and replace me with a younger wife? To these questions, the judges had no answer.

The prolongation of divorce hearings forced many women to abandon their cases. Mir-Hosseini found no rulings in which the judge, in deciding what a divorced wife was entitled to, took into account her dowry and other financial compensations the husband had received (Mir-Hosseini 2000, 58).[6]

Another body of research indicates that the change in the civil code did not have the hoped-for effect on marriage rates. In the central city of Yazd, for example, the rates of early and arranged marriages did not change, despite rising levels of education (Tremayne 2006, 70). The national data on the mean age of marriage show that between 1986 and 1996, the mean age of women at marriage increased from 20.1 to 22 in urban areas, reaching 23.4 by 2002, the latest year for which statistics are available (Bahramitash and Kazemipour 2006, 115). If commonly held stereotypes about the implementation of Islamic laws in Iran were true, one would expect not only an increase in the number of early marriages but also a decrease in the number of single women. In fact, however, the general trend in revolutionary Iran has been just the opposite. The Islamization of Iranian family law has also not succeeded in lowering divorce rates. Rates of divorce have increased (table 3.1), as has the percentage of women who have never married or do not remarry after divorce. Among the reasons for these changes are rising literacy rates, increasing urbanization, and improvements in female education. The percentage of girls enrolled in primary schools, for example, has increased considerably, from only 52 percent in 1970 to 91 percent in 2002. In 1970 more than half of all youths aged 7–15 had been illiterate (Bahramitash and Kazemipour 2006, 118).

The 1979 revolution brought women onto the public stage, and the ruling clerics' attempt to impose strict Islamic codes has only marginally reversed this change. The Iranian Nobel Peace Prize laureate, Shirin Ebadi, has described the struggles vividly:

After the 1979 revolution, they [regime authorities] argued that women cannot be judges, and they made us all into peons in the ministry of

justice. But women resisted. We wrote essays, held protests, and organized conferences to insist that women being judges was not incompatible with Islam. In 1999, they finally accepted the argument and said, ok,
women can be judges. So, as you can see, one day they interpret Islam in
such a way that women cannot be judges and the next day they manage
to reverse themselves. (Ebadi 2004)

The imposition of unrealistic Islamic codes has generated a strong response
from those women who want to claim their rights by working within the
system (Mokhrati 2004, 470). The result has been a lively and ongoing debate
over competing visions of male-female relations and the status and rights of
women in Islam; the debate has in turn given rise to new voices supporting the
spiritual, professional, and social equality of men and women. Some proponents of these views have called for more women *mujtahids,* arguing that the
clerical establishment is dominated by males who have little understanding of
women. The shortage of women *mujtahids* has led some to create religious
seminaries for women. In 1996, out of 62,731 students in religious seminaries,
9,995, or 16 percent, were women. Of these, 34 percent were twenty to twenty-
four years old, and 20 percent were between fifteen and nineteen. Almost 90
percent of these women resided in urban areas (Kian-Thiébaut 2002, 65–66).

On August 27, 2006, at a seminar entitled "The Impact of Law's on Wom-
en's Lives," a group of women activists launched a campaign entitled "One
Million Signatures Demanding Changes to Discriminatory Laws." The campaign melded education, consciousness-raising, and peaceful protest. Women
carrying petitions began to go to wherever other women gathered: schools,

Table 3.1. Population Size, Numbers of Divorces, and Divorce Rates in Iran

Year	Population (in thousands)	Population age 15 and older (in thousands)	Divorces	Divorces per thousand people	Divorces per thousand adults
1996	63,273	37,116	37,817	0.598	1.019
1997	64,100	38,524	n/a	n/a	n/a
1998	64,887	40,030	42,391	0.653	1.059
1999	65,661	41,555	51,044	0.777	1.228
2000	66,443	43,042	53,797	0.810	1.250
2001	67,245	44,472	60,559	0.901	1.362
2002	68,070	45,853	67,256	0.988	1.467

Sources: Statistical Centre of Iran 2002, 65; Bahramitash and Kazemipour 2006, 127.

hair salons, doctors' offices, and private homes. Even though the regime arrested several key campaigners, the movement has continued, with women communicating over the internet (Kelly and Etling 2008).[7] The activists are working to connect their campaign to the Convention on the Elimination of All Forms of Discrimination against Women (CEDAW). On several occasions Iran has considered ratifying the convention; in 2003 the sixth parliament, controlled at the time by reformists, agreed to sign it. However, the Council of Guardians rejected it on the grounds that it conflicted with shari'a; the convention has thus remained unratified to this day. Within Iran there are those who defend ratification with reservations for some articles (namely those related to the nationality of women, equality before the law, and family law), as most Islamic countries have done. Others reject ratification because CEDAW bans discrimination on the basis of gender, whereas the shari'a-based Iranian civil code considers the separation of men and women and a distinction between their functions natural and desirable.

In 2002, Iran's reformist parliament (2000–2004) approved a bill that would have given women the same right to divorce as men, which they had lost in 1979. The bill also would have required a man to pay for health care if his wife became ill. (At present, if a man refuses to pay for his wife's care, the case is sent to the courts, and judges have not consistently ruled in favor of the wives.) The Council of Guardians refused to approve the bill, however, ensuring that the reformists were unable to enact this it before they lost power.[8]

Islamic Penal Law

As they had done with family law, Iran's Islamic revolutionaries did not waste any time in abolishing prerevolutionary penal codes, claiming that these drew too heavily from European legal models and were contrary to Islam. In 1982, two criminal acts in accordance with the classical criminal rulings of Shi'a Islam were passed: the Act of Hudud, Qesas, and Other Relevant Provisions, and the Diyat Act. In 1983, the parliament additionally passed the Ta'azirat Acts (Laws of Discretionary Punishments). These acts (the Act of Hudud, Qesas, and Other Relevant Provisions, the Diyat Act, and the Ta'azirat Acts) were experimental, and would be in force for a period of five years.

Legislation on *ta'zir*, or discretionary punishments, raised several important conflicts and debates. Discretionary punishments are defined by Article 16 of the penal code as those "whose form or quantity [e.g., the number of lashes or the size of a fine] has not been determined by *Shari'a*" and is, as a result, left to the discretion of the judge. At the heart of the conflict was the right of the government to institute penal codes which are binding on the decisions of the courts. By doing so, it deprived judges of a right long recognized in classical jurisprudence, namely, the right to use their own discretion in reaching a judgment, as long as they based their rulings on shariʿa. Led by the traditionalists, judges opposed this new principle of shariʿa codification. They argued that, by interfering with a judge's discretion and by fixing penalties which exceeded the hudud (those explicitly set by shariʿa), the legislation violated shariʿa. The disagreement was resolved only in 1996, when the legislation was unified in one act codifying the Islamic Penal Code. The bill stipulated that the judiciary should renew it in 2006, after its impact had been evaluated. However, as of April 2010, the judiciary has not issued its evaluation.

It is important to note that hudud punishments are not of the same character as taʿzir. Punishments for crimes against religion, reason, public order, family, and offspring are exceptionally harsh and often corporal: capital punishment for apostasy, blasphemy against the Prophet, and adultery, and flogging for alcohol consumption. In crimes like these, which typically fall in the domain of hudud, there is not necessarily a private plaintiff. Indeed, even if a crime (such as adultery or sodomy) is committed by consent of all parties, the punishment will be administered; and in the case of rape, of course, the punishment will be even harsher. In such cases, even if the plaintiff waives his or her claim, the punishment is unchanged. Moreover, in cases of apostasy, blasphemy, adultery, and drinking, it is almost invariably administered immediately, in accordance with an Islamic jurisprudential rule which says "no pardon, no mediation and no delay in Hudud" (Rahami 2007, 230).

The reformist government of Mohammad Khatami successfully passed legislation in 2002 that called for the parliament to prepare itself for renewal of the penal code in 2007. However, with the victory of the conservative faction in the parliamentary elections of 2004 and the subsequent election of a conservative president, Mahmoud Ahmadinejad, the renewal has been postponed because of disagreements with the judiciary and demands for a tougher version of the penal code. As a result, the judiciary has been forced to continue operating under the 1996 legislation, and judges frequently interpret the code for themselves. During 2009–10, Iranian courts issued heavy prison sentences to demonstrators and opposition figures on the basis of the penal code.

The Iranian Islamic penal code has been criticized for its harsh punishments and its interference in matters of individual privacy and liberty. According to Article 104 of the code, for instance, the punishment for adultery is death by stoning. The article even specifies that "the size of the stone used in stoning shall not be too large to kill the convict by one or two throws and at the same time shall not be too small to be called a stone." In Iran, serious failings in the justice system have undermined the regime's credibility and its adherence to Islamic principles.

Under Article 24 of the penal code, the supreme leader has the power to grant pardons or to reduce or commute sentences, on the recommendation of the head of the judiciary and "in accordance with Islamic principles." This phrase appears to exclude hudud cases, where the state is not considered to have the right to pardon (and thus contravene God's law). However, in the case of adultery, sodomy, same-sex sexual conduct without penetration, and lesbianism, if the person has confessed to the crime and repented (publicly sought forgiveness from God), then the judge in the case has the power either to seek a pardon from the supreme leader or to insist on the carrying out of the sentence. But for many types of crimes punishable by death, there is no, or only a very limited, possibility of pardon or commutation by the state, particularly for those who have not confessed.

In a study of humanitarian law, the laws of war, and Islam, Hojjatoleslam Muhaqqiq-Damad, an Iranian human rights scholar and theologian, notes the Islamic prohibition on acts of revenge: "The retaliatory act is an illegal act done to retaliate another illegal act" (Muhaqqiq-Damad 2001, 275). He quotes the Qur'an to commend pardon: "The recompense for any evil act is an act identical to it; . . . but whoso pardons and puts things right, his wage falls on God" (274, Qur. 42:40–44).

In cases of alleged adultery, the Islamic penal code gives judges the right to sentence the accused woman to death by stoning even when the crime has not been proved according to the code's own standards and requirements. Article 105 gives the judges—who in Iran are all men—the absolute right to condemn the accused to death by stoning solely on the basis of their own documented "knowledge," which could be their subjective interpretation of the case. Under the Islamic penal code, the death penalty can be applied for spreading corruption on earth (i.e., political offenses), armed robbery, kidnap, rape, adultery, incest, coerced sexual relations of a non-Muslim man with a Muslim woman, and sodomy. Capital punishment can also be applied for apostasy, although this punishment is not specified in the penal code, but is decided on by a judge on the basis of his ijtihad (research in the revealed sources), which is authorized by shari'a.[9]

A number of senior members of the Shi'a clergy have issued statements dissenting from the code's stipulations with regard to death by stoning, insisting that no such punishment should be implemented in modern Iran. Grand Ayatollah Montazeri has stated, for example, that adultery is extremely difficult to prove according to Islamic law, inasmuch as it must be witnessed by four people, a condition that is almost impossible to fulfill. He has also stated that in cases where an individual has confessed to adultery, the penalty should be commuted if the accusation is withdrawn. Equally interesting, he has also stated that, if a sentence of stoning has the potential to damage the reputation of Islam, then it should also not be carried out. Grand Ayatollah Sane'i issued a fatwa in 2007 in which he stated that stonings and amputations should not be carried out during the continuing absence (*ghaybat*) of the Twelfth Imam (Amnesty International 2008b).

On October 1, 2006, a group of Iranian human rights defenders, lawyers, and journalists, led by lawyer Shadi Sadr and journalist Asieh Amini, launched the Stop Stoning Forever campaign to abolish stoning in law and practice. Since the campaign began, five people have been saved from stoning. Others have been granted stays of execution, and some cases are being reviewed or retried. In 2008, nine women and two men were known to be under sentence of execution by stoning (Amnesty International 2008a).

The Rise of Anti-clericalism in Postrevolutionary Iran

One of the most popular Iranian films in recent years, *Marmolak* (Lizard), attracted a wide audience inside the country and did very well at international film festivals. The story revolves around a convicted robber who escapes from prison by dressing up as a cleric. He then travels around the country, simulating prayers and knowledge of the Qur'an. The popularity of the film reflected a growing anti-clericalism caused by, among other things, harsh penalties being justified in the name of Islam and carried out by a clerical regime seen as corrupt, lacking in mercy, and according unelected clerical officials control over the country's electoral process. Demonstrators have used slogans such as "The clerics live like kings while we live in poverty!" One report claims, "Working-class Iranians lamented clerical wealth in the face of their own poverty," and "stories about the Swiss bank accounts of leading clerics circulated on Tehran's rumor mill" (Molavi 2005, 163).

In Western history, the term "anti-clericalism" typically refers to movements that aim to limit or destroy the power exercised, or thought to be exercised, by the Christian clergy. The term is sometimes applied to attitudes and other times to programs intended to reduce that power (Dykema and Oberman 1994; Sanchez 1972). What we are witnessing in Iran today is not an organized movement or program, but rather an amalgamation of precepts and social trends. In its political manifestations, Iranian anti-clericalism represents a blend of precepts drawn from the pre-Islamic past, from Western-influenced thinking about the roles of religion and the clergy in society, and from popular reactions to socio-economic conditions. Consequently, anti-clerical thinking is not unitary, but encompasses divergent attitudes and points of view. However, a common denominator among anti-clericalists is the desire to reduce the influence of the clergy and to secularize the legal and religious affairs of the state. They believe that thirty years of clerical rule in Iran have demonstrated convincingly that classical Islamic precepts cannot be harmonized with the values and needs of modern society.

The intellectual hero of anti-clericalism in Iran today is a figure from the mid-twentieth century, Ahmad Kasravi. Born in 1890 in Tabriz, Kasravi was a prolific writer, and was very critical both of the Shi'a clergy and of the policies of the central government. On March 11, 1946, while being tried on charges of slander against Islam, Kasravi and one of his assistants were knifed and killed in open court in Tehran by followers of a fundamentalist group named Fadayan-e Islam (Devotees of Islam). Today, Kasravi's writings are popular again among young students, journalists, and intellectuals. Although Kasravi authored several books and hundreds of articles, it is his writings on Shi'a Islam, particularly a tract called "The Detrimental Consequences of Islam," that most enraged the clerical establishment. "The question is whether religion is for the sake of the people, or people are for the sake of religion" (Kasravi 1990, 67). He called Shi'a Islam a "perversion whose origin lay neither in ethics nor in theological issues, but in a sordid struggle for dynastic power. It disrupted the country by insisting that its own laws should be enforced on the rest of the population . . . And, worst of all, it preached an anti-democratic political theory, claiming that sovereignty resided in the Imams not in the people" (Abrahamian 1973, 283).

Hashem Aghajari is another, more contemporary intellectual who, although not as hard-line as Kasravi, gained a certain fame for remarks he made in June 2002. A professor with extensive revolutionary credentials thanks to his status as a disabled veteran of the Iran-Iraq war, Aghajari delivered a speech that month entitled "From Monkey to Man: A Call for Islamic Protestantism," in which he argued that Muslims do not need mediators between them and God. Shi'a Islam's clerical hierarchy is not Islamic; rather, it is a model taken from the Catholic Church. This clerical hierarchy must be abolished in an effort to move away from "traditional Islam," which is rigid and doctrinal, toward "core Islam," which is in line with Islamic justice and human dignity. Aghajari faults Shi'a clerics for their selective acceptance of the fruits of modernity. For example, he points out, they are willing to drive luxury cars that the common man cannot afford, but refuse to incorporate human rights into Islamic jurisprudence (Aghajari 2002).

Aghajari's remarks set off such a firestorm that one prominent clergyman compared him to the British author Salman Rushdie, whose book *The Satanic Verses* prompted the Iranian leader Ayatollah Ruhollah Khomeini to issue a fatwa in 1989 calling for his killing. In November 2002, Aghajari was condemned to death for insulting the Prophet and questioning the clergy's interpretation of Islam. The announcement set off the largest and most sustained student protests since 1999. After two weeks, the regime realized that all signals pointed to a major security problem for the regime if Aghajari's sentence were not commuted. Supreme Leader Ayatollah Khamenei ordered a review of Aghajari's case in an apparent effort to defuse the situation. He was released in July 2004.

Aghajari's case demonstrated that the clerics would not tolerate any open advocacy of a reorganization of Islam in a manner that would diminish their role, but intellectuals like AbdolKarim Soroush have used an "Islamic language" to criticize clerical authority. The central theme of Soroush's thought is that the clerics do not have an education adequate for modern times; they are insulated from modern intellectual currents; and, for these reasons, they are not qualified to develop religious thought on faith and ethics in a manner consistent with modern realities. He aims to diminish the authority of the clerics and open up religious knowledge to discussion between lay intellectuals and social scientists. Notwithstanding this, his writings are very popular among young seminary students.

Like Aghajari, Soroush possesses impeccable revolutionary credentials. In the early 1980s, he had held a leading a position in the Cultural Revolution Committee, which was charged with the Islamization of the universities. Starting in the 1990s, Soroush's determined criticism of the clerical establishment contributed significantly to the growth of anti-clericalism in Iran. He has been condemned by the highest members of the clerical establishment and has had his university lectures disrupted by militias who call him a "pseudo-religious intellectual, mercenary pen-pusher" (Fairbanks 1998, 29). Notwithstanding these attacks, Soroush has struck a deep chord with many Iranians who resent clerical domination. He is also popular among those who feel that Islam itself will suffer if the government's misdeeds come to be identified with the clergy and, ultimately, Islam itself (Vakili 1996).

Another person with impeccable revolutionary credentials, Emad Baghi, a former Revolutionary Guard member who fought in Iraq, has also resorted to using Islamic language to undermine clerical authority. The publication of his groundbreaking book *Haqh-e hayat* (Right to Life), which calls for the suspension and abolition of capital punishment in countries following Islamic law, has shaken the clerical establishment. The book has been banned by Iranian authorities, and Baghi has been interrogated and jailed several times for his writings. Baghi's book provides arguments within an Islamic legal framework for suspending or abolishing the death penalty in countries whose laws are based on shari'a. It is often claimed that the laws mandating such penalties are irrevocable. However, Baghi argues that there is no absolute requirement for the death penalty within shari'a or the Qur'anic verses. According to Baghi's research, in cases of murder with the punishment of *qisas*, or retribution, the Qur'an does not mandate capital punishment. In a letter to the head of the Iranian judiciary, Ayatollah Hashemi Shahrudi, Baghi wrote, "The killing of a human being is both the source and propagator of violence and has no relationship to kindheartedness, a caring society, and the benevolence of the Creator. It is hence necessary to stop the spread of crime, felony, as well as executions as soon as possible" (Baghi 2006).

Over the past thirty years, the clerical authorities have constructed an economy designed to operate to their direct and extensive benefit. The popular perception of corruption in these arrangements has greatly undermined the clerics' standing. Critics speak of systemic corruption among a network of clerics determined to remain in power.

In June 2008, Abbas Palizar, a senior member of the Majles Investigative Committee, accused some of the country's most powerful senior clerics of corruption. Palizar was the leading figure of the committee and was charged with drawing up plans to punish those who abused their economic privileges. He was also the advisor to the Majles Economic Committee and the chairman of the Board of Trustees of the House of Industrialists of Iran (Khane Sanatgaran'e Iran). Palizar alleged that a foundation whose membership included several key conservative leaders—including Ali Akbar Nategh-Nouri, a powerful confidante of the supreme leader, and Asqar Owladi, head of Iran's Islamic Coalition Association—had demanded hundreds of cars at 50 percent discounts from the state-owned manufacturer. He also named Ayatollah Imami Kashani (a member of the Council of Guardians and one of the four temporary Friday prayer leaders of Tehran) as the owner of four major mines and a physical therapy center. Another figure Palizar accused of involvement in the scheme was Ayatollah Mohammad Yazdi, an active member of the Council of Guardians and the Experts Assembly, a former head of the judiciary, and the new leader of the Teachers of Qom Theological Center, which is the most important organization of conservative clerics in Iran. Palizar pointed out that Ayatollah Yazdi's son, Hamid Yazdi, "was jobless and requested that arrangements be made so he could export wood from the forests of northern Iran. It is interesting that Hamid Yazdi was a director general at the judiciary" (*Rooz* 2008b). In short, Palizar alleged that criminal corruption was being perpetrated by two senior members of the Council of Guardians, as well as several other high-ranking clerics.[10] Not long after making these allegations public, Palizar was arrested and charged by Tehran prosecutors with "propagating lies" and "confusing public opinion."

Another influence on the growing anti-clericalism has been reports indicating that senior officials in charge of Islamization and enforcement of the Islamic code of behavior have been arrested for violating the very legal principles they oversee. In 2001, the daily newspaper *Hambastegi* reported that a Revolutionary Court judge was arrested in connection with a prostitution ring involving underage girls. In June 2008, Tehran's police chief, who was responsible for a crackdown on "immodestly dressed women," was arrested after being caught in a police raid at an underground brothel with six naked prostitutes. Two years earlier, the chief had been responsible for a campaign for stricter enforcement of Islamic dress regulations. Thousands of young women were detained for violating the Islamic dress code, usually by wearing headscarves that showed too much hair, coats that were tight enough to reveal their figures, or pants that were too short.

Events like these have undermined more than just people's attitude toward the regime. They have reduced overall religiosity. According to one source, Iranian clergy have complained that more than 70 percent of the population do not perform their daily prayers and that fewer than 2 percent attend Friday mosques (*Economist* 2003). A survey of the Tehran population reported that only 16 percent attend Friday prayers at least once a month and nearly 40 percent have never done so. A solid majority of respondents described the political system as either rarely or never responsive to their needs. Some 70 percent believed that they were occasionally mistreated by the state (Azaadarmak and Murat Tezcu 2008, 54).[11] It is not surprising that the cleric most revered by Iranians today is Ayatollah Sistani, who is based in Iraq. He is on record as having stated, "I don't believe that all political ideas should come from within Islam . . . Politics is an experimental, man-made activity and Islam should respect it."

Conclusion

Citizens of states all across the Muslim world today are involved in a growing debate over the relevance of shari'a in contemporary society. Iranian constitutionalists in 1906 viewed the legal tradition of Shi'a Islam not as an alternative to Western democracy, but rather as the only real alternative to despotism and tyranny. However, as our case study of the Islamic Republic of Iran demonstrates, by politicizing shari'a, the clerical regime that rules Iran today has dramatically changed the public's perception of shari'a. Many Iranians have come to see it, not as God's august law, but as a political and legal doctrine used by authorities to amass power.

There are indeed remarkable similarities between the demands of Iranian reformists today and those of the constitutionalists a century ago; the parallels are also striking between the absolute power of the shah in the earlier period and that of the supreme leader today. However, as the demographic data make clear, there are also significant differences between Iran in 1906 and 2009. In 1906, 90 percent of the Iranian population was illiterate, and the country was rural and highly feudal. In 2009, 85 percent of the Iranian population is literate, and seven out of ten Iranians live in cities.

The participation of the clerics in government has led to what Soroush has called "stagnation and ossification of religious thinking and knowledge" (Soroush 2001). Indeed, however much the ruling clerics like to project self-confidence and claim the ability to predict the future, they could not have envisaged an Iran with the characteristics that have developed under the Islamic republic. Their attempts to strike a balance between the republican and Islamic components of governance have become exceedingly complicated, if not confounding. The codification of the Islamic law has actually downgraded the exercise of ijtihad and compromised the authority of judges and the law alike. As one scholar has observed, "Khomeini did revive the position of the scholars. But instead of restoring the balance between the ruler and the scholars, he sought to merge these two separate institutions under a single supreme jurist-ruler—and the failures of the Islamic Republic of Iran are the legacy of this megalomaniacal mistake" (Feldman 2008a, 11).

Three decades after the 1979 revolution, it is apparent that the regime remains committed to the principle of the clergy's uncontested right to rule, on the grounds that clerical rule is synonymous with Islamic rule. But a growing portion of the public starkly disagrees. Clerical rule has undermined support for the clergy and actually diminished the public's confidence in the clergy's understanding of Islam and Islamic law.

Notes

1. The council consists of six theologians appointed by the senior *faqih* (the *vali amr moslemin,* or supreme leader) and six jurists nominated by the judiciary and approved by parliament. Members are appointed for staggered six-year terms, so that half of them may be replaced every three years.

2. After the collapse of the Safavid empire in 1722, political instability and internal dissension strengthened the emerging Usuli school of thought in Iran. The triumphant Usulis were those who claimed a key role for the *mujtahids* in the interpretation of law and doctrine; all believers were supposed to pick a living *mujtahid* to follow, a *marja,* and abide by his judgments. This doctrine gave the *mujtahids* a power beyond anything claimed by the Sunni ulama, and gave to their rulings a sanction beyond anything decreed by the state. The Akhbaris, who claimed that the Sunna provided sufficient guidance and there was no need for rulings by a *mujtahid,* were largely defeated in the course of the eighteenth century (Keddie 1969, 48).

3. As a Shi'a country (and unlike Sunni ones), Iran did not have state-appointed muftis.

4. Brutal treatment of violators of shari'a, particularly thieves, was the principal means the ulama utilized to protect private property against any attack from the urban poor. The best example in the early nineteenth century is Sayyid Mohammad

Baqir Shafti Hujatul-Islam, an extremely wealthy and brutal *mujtahid*, who is reputed to have condemned between eighty and one hundred offenders to death. He often buried them in a graveyard adjoining his house (Algar 1969, 60–61).

5. During the Iranian New Year festivities of March 1928, the first day of the new year coincided with the twenty-seventh of Ramadan, the day on which, according to tradition, the murderer of 'Ali, the first Shi'a imam, was slain. Reza Shah's female relatives decided to celebrate both events at the holy shrine in Qom, and for this observance donned transparent chadors. Some clergymen protested, whereupon Reza Shah drove to Qom from Tehran, entered the shrine with his boots on, and personally manhandled a number of seminarians and clerics, as well as having the cleric who had criticized the queen whipped (Chehabi 1993, 213).

6. The courts were presided over by traditionalist judges who summoned the parties to their chambers, listened to their respective arguments, and then engaged in lengthy discussions and queries. This procedure was consistent with the stipulations and ethos of shari'a courts.

7. Iranian bloggers include members of Hezbollah, teenagers in Tehran, retirees in Los Angeles, religious students in Qom, dissident journalists who left Iran a few years ago, exiles who left thirty years ago, current members of the Majles (parliament), reformist politicians, a multitude of poets, and quite famously the President of Iran, among many others. This has allowed internet-savvy Iranian youth to have access to a wide range of perspectives that criticize the Islamic Republic's policy positions.

8. In the lead-up to the 2004 legislative elections, the Council of Guardians disqualified one-third of the 8,200 individuals who filed papers to stand as candidates. Additionally, a large majority of incumbents were not allowed to stand for the seventh parliament.

9. According to Amnesty International, "the USA and Iran have each executed more child offenders than the other eight countries [in which such executions have occurred] combined and Iran has now exceeded the USA's total since 1990 of 19 child executions" (Amnesty International 2010). "As of May 2009, there were at least 137 known juvenile offenders awaiting execution in Iran, but the total number could be much higher as many death penalty cases in Iran are believed to go unreported. Of the 43 child offenders recorded as having been executed since 1990, 11 were still under the age of 18 at the time of their execution while the others were either kept on death row until they had reached 18 or were convicted and sentenced after reaching that age" (Amnesty International 2009).

10. Both Imami Kashani and Yazdi were appointed to the Council of Guardians in June 1999 by the supreme leader.

11. It can be argued that survey findings must be unreliable in Iran, given the undemocratic nature of the ruling regime. Citizens may falsify their preferences or fear to speak their mind to strangers. Yet, while Iran is not a democracy, it is not a police state either.

References Cited

Abrahamian, Ervand. 1973. "Kasravi: The Integrative Nationalist of Iran." *Middle Eastern Studies* 9 (3): 271–95.

Aghajari, Hashem. 2002. "From Monkey to Man: A Call to Islamic Protestantism." Speech delivered June 19 in Hamedan, Iran.

Algar, Hamid. 1969. *Religion and State in Iran, 1785–1906: The Role of the Ulama in the Qajar Period*. Berkeley: University of California Press.

Amnesty International. 2008a. "Executions of Juveniles since 1990." http://www .amnesty.org/en/death-penalty/executions-of-child-offenders-since-1990 (accessed December 30, 2008).

———. 2008b. *Iran: End Executions by Stoning*. London: Amnesty International. http:// www.amnesty.org/en/library/asset/MDE13/001/2008/en/2b087fb2-c2d2-11dc-ac4a-8d7763206e82/mde130012008eng.pdf (accessed January 5, 2009).

———. 2009. "Child Executions in Iran, 2009." http://www.amnestyusa.org/ all-countries/iran/child-executions-in-iran/page.do?id=1221001 (accessed August 31, 2010).

———. 2010. "Execution of Juveniles since 1990." http://www.amnesty.org/en/ death-penalty/executions-of-child-offenders-since-1990 (accessed August 31, 2010).

Azaadarmak, T., and Gunes Murat Tezcu. 2008. "Religiosity and Islamic Rule in Iran." *Journal for the Scientific Study of Religion* 47 (2): 47–87.

Baghi, Emadeddin. 2006. "Letter to the Iranian Judiciary on the Suspension and Abolition of the Death Penalty." *International Campaign for Human Rights*, April 24. http://www.iranhumanrights.org/2008/08/baghijudiciary/ (accessed July 6, 2010).

Bahramitash, R., and S. Kazemipour. 2006. "Myths and Realities of the Impact of Islam on Women: Changing Marital Status in Iran." *Critique: Critical Middle Eastern Studies* 15 (2): 111–28.

Baktiari, Bahman. 1996. *Parliamentary Politics in Revolutionary Iran: The Institutionalization of Factional Politics*. Gainesville: University Press of Florida.

Chehabi, Houchang E. 1993. "Staging the Emperor's New Clothes: Dress Codes and Nation-Building under Reza Shah." *Iranian Studies* 26 (3–4): 209–29.

Dykema, Peter A., and Heiko A. Oberman. 1994. *Anticlericalism in Late Medieval and Early Modern Europe*. Leiden: Brill.

Ebadi, Shirin. 2004. Interview by Pal Amitabh. *The Progressive* 68 (9): 35–39. http:// www.progressive.org/mag_intv0904 (accessed September 12, 2010).

Economist. 2003. "Survey of Iran: A Secular Democracy-in-Waiting." January 18.

Fairbanks, Stephen. 1998. "Theocracy versus Democracy: Iran Considers Political Parties." *Middle East Journal* 52 (1): 17–31.

Farmanfarmaian, A. 1954. "Constitutional Law of Iran." *American Journal of Comparative Law* 3 (2): 241–47.

Feldman, Noah. 2008a. *The Fall and Rise of the Islamic State*. Princeton: Princeton University Press.

———. 2008b. "Why Shariah?" *New York Times Magazine*. March 16, 46–51.

Gieling, Saskia. 1997. "The 'Marja'iya' in Iran and the Nomination of Khamanei in December 1994." *Middle Eastern Studies* 33 (4): 777–87.

Islamic Penal Code of Iran (IPC). 2001. Translated by the Mission for Establishment of Human Rights in Iran. http://mehr.org/Islamic_Penal_Code_of_Iran.pdf.

Kasravi, Ahmad. 1990. "The Detrimental Consequences of Islam." In *On Islam and Shi'ism,* trans. M. R. Ghanoonparvar, 64–77. Costa Mesa, Calif.: Mazda.

Keddie, Nikkie. 1969. "The Roots of the Ulama's Power in Modern Iran." *Studia Islamica* 29:31–53.

Kelly, John, and Bruce Etling. 2008. "Mapping Iran's Online Public: Politics and Culture in the Persian Blogosphere." Cambridge, Mass.: Berkman Center for Internet & Society, Harvard University. http://cyber.law.harvard.edu/publications/2008/Mapping_Irans_Online_Public.

Khomeini, Ruhollah. 1981. "Letter to Ali Akbar Hashemi-Rafsanjani." *Kayhan,* October 12 (Mehr 20, 1360).

———. 1984. *A Clarification of Questions: An Unabridged Translation of "Resaleh Towzih al-Masael."* Translated by J. Borujerdi. Boulder, Colo.: Westview.

Kian-Thiébaut, Azadeh. 2002. "Women and the Making of Civil Society in Post-Islamist Iran." In *Twenty Years of Islamic Revolution: Political and Social Transition in Iran since 1979,* ed. Eric James Hooglund, 56–73. Syracuse: Syracuse University Press.

Menashri, David. 1992. *Education and the Making of Modern Iran.* Ithaca: Cornell University Press.

Mir-Hosseini, Ziba. 1996. "Stretching the Limits: A Feminist Reading of the Shari'a in Post-Khomeini Iran." In *Feminism and Islam: Legal and Literary Perspectives,* ed. Mai Yamani and Andrew Allen, 285–320. Reading, UK: Ithaca Press.

———. 1999. "Family Law in Modern Persia." In *Encyclopedia Iranica,* ed. Ehsan Yarshater, 9:192–96. Costa Mesa, Calif.: Iranica.

———. 2000. *Islam and Gender: The Religious Debate in Contemporary Iran.* London: I. B. Tauris.

Moaddel, Mansoor. 1986. "The Shi'i Ulama and the State in Iran." *Theory and Society* 15 (4): 519–56.

Mohammadi, Majid. 2008. *Judicial Reform and Reorganization in Twentieth-Century Iran: State-Building, Modernization, and Islamization.* New York: Routledge.

Mokhrati, Shadi. 2004. "The Search for Human Rights within an Islamic Framework in Iran." *Muslim World* 94:469–79.

Molavi, Afshin. 2005. *The Soul of Iran: A Nation's Journey to Freedom.* New York: Norton.

Muhaqqiq-Damad, Sayyid Mustafa. 2001. "International Humanitarian Law in Islam and Contemporary International Law." In *Islamic Views on Human Rights: Viewpoints of Iranian Scholars,* ed. Esmaeil Salami and Jamilih Kukabi, 253–94. Organization for Islamic Culture and Communications, Directorate of Research of Education, Center for Cultural-International Studies. Tehran: Alhoda.

Opwis, Felicitas. 2007. "Islamic Law and Legal Change: The Concept of *Maslaha* in Classical and Contemporary Islamic Legal Theory." In *Shari'a: Islamic Law in the Contemporary Context,* ed. Abbas Amanat and Frank Griffel, 62–82. Stanford: Stanford University Press.

Rahami, Mohsen. 2007. "Islamic Restorative Traditions and Their Reflections in the Post-revolutionary Criminal Justice System of Iran." *European Journal of Crime, Criminal Law and Criminal Justice* 15 (2): 227–48.

Ramazani, Rouhollah K. 1980. "Constitution of the Islamic Republic of Iran." *Middle East Journal* 34 (2): 181–204.

Ridgeon, Lloyd. 2005. "Shaykh Faz Allah Nuri's Refutation of the Idea of Constitutionalism." In *Religion and Politics in Iran: A Reader,* ed. Lloyd Ridgeon, 37–54. London: I. B. Tauris.

Rooz. 2008a. "Ayatollah Montazeri: Velayat Faghih Is 'Shirk', Not Islamic." December 29. http://www.roozonline.com/english/news/newsitem/article/2008/december/29//velayat-faghih-is-shirk-not-islamic.html (accessed September 14, 2010).

———. 2008b. "Unprecedented Revelations against Senior Iranian Clerics." June 10. http://www.roozonline.com/english/news/newsitem/article/2008/june/10//unprecedented-revelations-against-senior-iranian-clerics.html (accessed September 14, 2010).

Sanchez, Jose. 1972. *Anticlericalism: A Brief History.* South Bend, Ind.: University of Notre Dame Press.

Schirazi, Asqar. 1998. *The Constitution of Iran: Politics and the State in the Islamic Republic.* London: I. B. Tauris.

Soroush, AbdolKarim. 2001. "Religion, Thought and Reformation." In Persian. Interview. *Jameh Madani,* March 7.

Statistical Centre of Iran. 2002. "Survey of Socio-economic Characteristics of the Family." Tehran: Statistical Centre of Tehran.

Tabari, Azar, and Yeganeh Nahi. 1982. *In the Shadow of Islam: The Women's Movement in Iran.* London: Zed.

Tremayne, Soraya. 2006. "Modernity and Early Marriage in Iran: A View from Within." *Journal of Middle East Women's Studies* 2 (1): 65–94.

Vakili, Valla. 1996. *Debating Religion and Politics in Iran: The Political Thought of Abdolkarim Soroush.* New York: Council on Foreign Relations.

Zubaida, Sami. 2003. *Law and Power in the Islamic World.* London: I. B. Tauris.

4. Turkey

Islam without Shari'a?

M. Hakan Yavuz

Even though the Turkish state is grounded on secularist principles, the shari'a debate is hardly absent from
contemporary politics, and it has been the main point of contention between
the secularists and Islamic forces. In March 2008, the chief prosecutor of the
Republic of Turkey, Abdurrahman Yalcinkaya, petitioned the Constitutional
Court to ban the governing Adalet ve Kalkinma Partisi (AKP, Justice and Development Party) and bar seventy politicians, including Prime Minister Recep
Tayyip Erdoğan and President Abdullah Gül, from politics, on the grounds
that the AKP was covertly seeking to impose shari'a by dismantling the secular reform of Mustafa Kemal. In order to support the court case and defend
secularism, a number of public demonstrations were organized by several
civil NGOs. The most popular slogan of the Republican demonstrations was
"no shari'a, no coup—democratic Turkey." On July 30, 2008, the court announced its decision not to ban the AKP. Yet it ruled that the party engaged
in anti-secular activities (such as some speeches by the party's leadership, and
lifting the restrictions on university students' wearing the headscarf) and decided to cut by half the party's funding from the treasury. The court defined
shari'a as an alternative religio-political system seeking to replace the secular
democratic structure of Turkey.

Turkey is an interesting case study of a secular system in a predominantly
Muslim society, revealing the ongoing development of the relations between
religion and morality, on one hand, and Islamic politics and democracy, on the
other, within the Muslim world. The Republic of Turkey, implementing the
most rigorous secular project in the Muslim world, used all means available
either to exclude Islamic norms from the public sphere or to ethicalize them

by treating them as voluntary moral principles and stressing their general, universally applicable, nature (Hefner 2000). These moral principles include trust, honesty, self-discipline, charity, justice, solidarity, and peace. According to Sabri Ülgener, a prominent Turkish sociologist, religion in Turkey provides the most effective and flexible shared core values of social unity (Ülgener 2006). The remaining symbols, vocabulary, and tacit assumptions of shari'a offer social integration and a map for action. Religiously informed values provide a shared language in which diverse groups articulate their own visions of Islam and of diverse lifestyles. One could treat Islam as the social grammar of Turkish society; it facilitates public conversation and debate and empowers different groups to form their own political arguments concerning the public good. Conversation, and thus political negotiation, depends on the continued use of familiar terms, yet in Turkey shari'a politics have modified the meanings those terms carry.

In this essay I argue that the meanings of Islam and Islamic law embraced by a significant proportion of the present Turkish population resist the traditional, imposed, constraining features of earlier Muslim society and instead embrace the discursive democratic solidarity of modern Muslim identity. The moral realism at the core of shari'a discourse persists from older into modern Turkey, but many modern Turks no longer find certain cultural accretions, which produce morally arbitrary intolerance, acceptable. Some recognize that certain practices are historically encased, and do not belong to the modern period. Thus radical punishments and archaic legal forms and institutions (which are largely centuries-old solutions to problems that have now been solved in other ways) need not survive in order that Islam survive. The core of Islamic belief can survive without these and other accretions, and modern Turks are proving this by maintaining their identity as Muslims while rejecting a formalistically literal interpretation of shari'a. Where they invoke shari'a or related vocabularies, these are simply emblematic of the core of their belief. This core is bonding, not binding, and militates against the false dichotomy of "sacred" and "secular." Religious expression and practice are mutable and have been changed to stretch secularism around the structure of bonding, democratic core belief. In a society where democracy is fully internalized, religious networks and arguments remain the most effective inner motivating force to shape the rhythm of daily life, and new understandings of Islam are also a product of this life.

Despite theories of secularization, which predict the decline of religion, economic development and the deepening of democracy in Turkey have transformed Islam and brought it into public and political spaces. Old and new social actors are struggling over the meanings of Islamic norms and practices and are constantly competing to reconfigure Islam in new forms to meet emerging challenges. Charles Taylor argues that "modern developments destabilize early forms of religion and . . . religion has to be recomposed, reformed" (Taylor 2008). In the case of Turkey, one sees these new configurations of Islam being formulated by the believers themselves. Islam in Turkey is undergoing major transformations as a result of the expansion of political-economic spaces and the public sphere (Göle and Ammann 2006). Islamic activism in Turkey stresses ethicalized Islam instead of Islamic law enforced by the state. Many conscious Muslims believe that ethicalized Islam is more effective in shaping interpersonal relations than state-imposed Islamic law.

In this chapter, then, I argue that the contemporary understandings of Islam in Turkey are largely free from shari'a discourses as a result of certain socio-historical transformations and the existence of a powerful anti-shari'a legacy. Indeed, the meaning and role of shari'a also vary among the four main groupings active within what we can call the Islamic sector. Each grouping has its own mode of understanding Islam and shari'a. These four configurations are the state-centric "enlightened" Islam of the Directorate of Religious Affairs (DRA); "societal Islam," as formulated and defended by Alevi and Sunni Nurcu groups; "political Islam," the movement whose primary aim is to mobilize voters and win control of the government; and the radical yet very effective Islam as an ideology of resistance to the nation-building secular project of Mustafa Kemal.

Before explaining Turkey's overall departure from formalist understandings of shari'a, I submit here a few definitions upon which my conceptions of Turkish history, sociology, theology, and legal tradition rely. First, the departures from shari'a witnessed in Turkey suggest the country's embrace of an "ethicalized" understanding of Islam. This is to suggest not that formal constructions of shari'a are lacking in ethical content, but that shari'a and ethics represent particular and general kinds of morality, respectively. To the extent that shari'a is derived from the Qur'an and Arabic custom, it represents a fraction of humans' collective normative experience—a significant fraction, but a fraction nonetheless; whereas the term "ethics" more naturally represents a broader category containing all such fractions. Whether the prescriptions of shari'a are more righteous than those of other systems is not in question here. Rather, what matters is the particular, authoritative character more typical of the first, and the general, consensual character more typical of the latter.

In order to better understand the contested nature of shari'a and the gradual efflorescence of ethical Islam in Turkey, this chapter seeks to answer the following four questions. First, what does shari'a mean in the Turkish context? Why have significant numbers of Turks developed a new conceptual framework to discuss ethical, not legal, aspects of Islam? Second, what are the socio-intellectual origins of the diverse and even conflicting meanings of shari'a?

Third, what accounts for these diverse understandings of the role of Islam in the public and private spheres? Finally, who has authority to speak on matters of shari'a?

In order to answer these questions, I will start with a discussion of recent surveys on understandings of shari'a, and will seek to understand public discourse on shari'a through a focus group I formed during field research in 2008. In the second section, I will provide socio-historical background by laying out historical and political parameters within which Islamic actors and movements debate shari'a. In this section, after introducing the dual nature of the Ottoman legal system and bureaucracy, I will summarize how the decline of the state led to two diametrically different solutions: a more public and political understanding of shari'a and a secularized state system. This section of the chapter will also examine 1) the secular reforms of the Tanzimat period (1839–78), and the ulama's reaction to them; 2) Mustafa Kemal's Jacobin secularization, intended to cleanse Islam from public spaces; and 3) the socio-political impact of recent neo-liberal economic policies (1980–present). The last part of the chapter will examine the four Islamic perspectives on shari'a. As a result of the socio-historical parameters of Turkey, there is a growing emphasis on bonding (identity-based and moral) rather than binding (legal and mandatory) aspects of Islam. In Turkey, the majority of the population tend to define those Islamic practices and rules that are enforced by the power of the state as shari'a and do not support such enforcement. Thus, neither a theory of the personalization of Islam nor one of the desacralization of Islamic practices captures the dynamic process of Islamic bonding. Such bonding redirects the religious vision toward structures of solidarity and identity rather than a binding legal system to be enforced by the state.

The Turkish Puzzle: "We Are More Muslim but without Shari'a"

In a major public survey in 1999, 36 percent of those interviewed in Turkey declared themselves "Muslim first," while 21 percent said they were "Turkish first." A 2006 survey found a major shift in these percentages, with those who said they were Muslim first having increased to 45 percent, while the latter remained at around 19 percent (Çarkoğlu and Toprak, 2000, 2006). Some observers might assume that the increase in the proportion declaring themselves "Muslim first" would lead to calls for the implementation of shari'a law. However, this is simply not the case. Recent polls have shown that the proportion of citizens demanding a shari'a-based religious state has dropped dramatically, from 21 percent in 1996 to 9 percent in 2006 (Toprak and Çarkoğlu 2006).[1] Yet this change has occurred at precisely the same time that Turks have come to identify less as Turkish and more as Muslim. This raises the obvious question of why more people identify Islam as their primary identity, yet fewer demand implementation of shari'a? In order to answer these questions, during the summer of 2008 I organized two focus groups in Istanbul to understand how ordinary Turks understand Islam and shari'a.

I arranged the focus groups in two different Istanbul neighborhoods. One of the groups met three times in a coffee shop in Istanbul's Maltepe district.[2] The customers of this coffee shop vary widely in age, which is not common in Turkey and which made this an interesting, if not scientifically representative, sample. I decided to ask questions of some of the coffee shop's patrons as a way of understanding what ordinary Turkish citizens think about Islam and shari'a. Since I know some people in this shop, they were comfortable discussing both their official and private views with me.

This group consisted of nine people, including both secular and pious Muslims, and some ordinary Turks who worked in Saudi Arabia. Almost all participants differentiated Islam from shari'a. It included two males in their early twenties and seven between 34 and 64 years old, five of whom were high school graduates and two of whom were college graduates. In the last general election, in 2007, four of them had voted for the pro-Islamic AKP, one for the Republican People's Party, and one for the Felicity Party; one had not voted. When I asked participants in the focus group, "What is shari'a?" their responses varied widely. They included "punishing criminals in inhumane ways," "giving too much power to ulama to make rules about Islam," "a system necessary in the past because people were less educated," "a legal system practiced in many Arab countries and Iran," and "a way of maintaining Islamic life by the power of the law." Despite this great variation, all respondents viewed religion as central to their morality and social orientation. One person put it thus:

> Look! Islam is the religion of God with the purpose of creating a good moral society. Not religious [dindar] but moral [ahlakli] society. In other words, people have to respect each other, be just, and not harm one another. A religious society means a society where people perform their religious rituals. In other words, a religious society is not necessarily a moral society. Islamic rituals are instruments to create this moral society. The purpose is morality. Now, shari'a, on the other hand, means laws that are based on the Qur'an and hadith but made by ulama. Many years ago it was the only way, but now we have parliaments to make the laws. You don't need shari'a in this age, but rather a good parliament. Look at Saudi Arabia or Iran: They are both governed by shari'a. How many people want to live in these countries? They all want to get out. They

both have shari'a without Islam. Mustafa Kemal did the right thing by updating Islam and freeing Islam from shari'a.

In these and other comments, respondents make a clear distinction between religion and morality and regard shari'a as a legal system made by ulama. The focus-group participants all agreed that lawmakers should come from the ranks of elected politicians, not the ulama. Indeed, when I asked what the problem with ulama was, one of the participants responded,

> Shari'a is a set of Islamic rules that are interpreted by the ulama in the cases of Saudi Arabia or Iran. The sources and making of these rules are very deep and require a long-term education and smart people. The main problem in many Muslim countries, including Turkey, is the poor educa tion of ulama. In Turkey, students who graduate from high schools prefer to study medicine, engineering, or law. If their [university entrance exam] score is not enough to enter their first five choices, some of them enter the divinity faculties. Thus, [most] students who study Islam at the divinity faculties are not the best minds. So why do you want them to make the rules? Look at the imams in our mosques . . . They are not always properly educated. There are very few imams that I would feel comfortable with. The laws must be made by parliament because people over there are much better educated. So the best minds should make the law.

The ulama's lack of education emerged as a major concern in these conversations, as did the experiences of Iran and Saudi Arabia, which were seen in largely negative terms. Some participants rejected an understanding of Islam such as is seen in those countries. One respondent put it this way:

> Islam is not an authoritarian political system as one sees in Saudi Arabia or Iran. Their religious leaders are not properly educated to understand Islam. Islam, as the last message of God, wants man to be good and use his reason. Islam is thus a religion of reason. If it is not reasonable, it cannot be Islam. Stoning or hanging people to death are not reasonable actions anymore, for example. Look at Iran, a group of mullahs are ruling the country in the name of Islam. They are using Islam for their own interests.

Another participant agreed with this and argued that democracy is the best system through which to further the goodness and justice of Islam.

> There is no model of government in the Qur'an but rather a set of principles, such as consultation, justice, and distributing political posi-

tions on the basis of merit, not piety or solidarity. So as long as these principles are respected, [political systems] can take different forms. In 2008, the best Islamic system is democracy because these principles are best served by democracy. This means that the law must be debated and made by the elected representatives of the people, not by a group of half-educated ulama.

All respondents regard Islamic ideas of morality and justice as pillars of Muslim identity. When I asked participants to provide an example of good Islamic practices, they all referred to the classical period of the Ottoman empire. They believe that the Ottoman state survived more than five hundred years because of its proper understanding and implementation of Islam. One participant who had worked in Jeddah put it this way:

> We Turks should not accept Arab or Persian understandings of Islam as the true Islam but rather develop our own Turkish understanding of religion, since we are much freer than they are. Islam cannot be understood in an oppressive political system. Thus, what is presented as shari'a is also mostly Arab *adeti* [Turk. *gelenek,* traditions] and not revelations of God.

Indeed, all respondents had strongly internalized a sense of Turkish nationalism or ethnicity that defines itself against Arab or Iranian understandings of Islam. The conversations revealed two tacit assumptions: that shari'a is a legal system implemented by Muslims who are not "Turks," and that it was implemented in the past or in traditional societies. When I asked about the corruption and widening economic polarization in a Turkish society that is secular and democratic, the respondents all agreed that the current malaise is an outcome of society's weakening moral fabric. They explained it not in terms of weakening religiosity, but rather as the result of a poor understanding of the moral core of Islam. When I asked them to elaborate about this "moral core" (*ahlaki çekirdek*), they defined it in terms of "human dignity," "not taking or giving bribes, treating people equally," "being kind to the needy and weak," and disciplining one's desires and emotions to become a better person. Participants stressed the importance of inculcating Islamic values of trust, honesty, and charity in everyday interactions. They argued that Islam requires morality and if one lacks proper morality, rituals by themselves are "empty practices."

In sum, on the basis of the focus-group interviews, what we see in the case of Turkey is the separation of Islam as an ethical system from shari'a as a binding and enforceable legal system. Unlike Egyptians, the Turkish Muslims narrowed the definition of shari'a to "a set of enforceable laws" and preferred to stress Islamic ethics and economic development (see also Nathan Brown's and Robert Hefner's chapters in this volume). During the 1970s and 1980s, many pious Turks pushed for the expansion of opportunity spaces through Islamic solidarity and bonding, seeking a voice in the parliament and the coalition governments. A consensus emerged that redefined Islam without shariʿa. Islam became a network of bonding and solidarity, couched in the grammar of public debate. Shariʿa is not a focal political concern for most ordinary Turkish Muslims. Nor is it for the major moderately Islamist groups, like the AKP. The AKP has controlled the government since 2002 without framing its agenda with reference to shariʿa. Turkish Islamic movements in the 1970s and 1980s were not confrontational, as they were in Egypt, and most never questioned the legitimacy of the Turkish state, since the state provided a relatively successful legal system, along with some political opportunities via representation in the parliament.

The forms and meanings of Islam within Turkey have multiplied and gained new significance in the past few decades. Actors and currents in the Islamic sector share three tendencies. A new class of Islamist intellectuals, separate from the traditional ulama, have made Islam more visible in public debates; Islam has been reconfigured as an identity, a form of morality, and a web of social solidarity and mobilization that increases the influence of Islamic actors while reducing that of secular intellectuals; and a "shariʿa-free" Islam has developed, focused on bonding solidarity rather than binding legal norms. As a result of Ottoman use of the terms *kanun* and *yasa* (Sultanic law) for shariʿa, which is usually understood as Islamic law, and of socio-political developments in modern Turkey, the understanding of shariʿa went through a major transmutation. Accordingly, in Turkey today, shariʿa is very much identified with fiqh (Islamic jurisprudence) and its implementation in other Muslim countries. In other words, although shariʿa means "the totality of God's commandment," or the divinely ordained way to decide what is required, forbidden, recommended, disapproved, or merely permitted in human actions, in Turkey it is generally understood as a set of binding rules of conduct (*amaliyyat*) that exclude matters of belief (*iʿtiqadiyyat*) and of ethics (*akhlaqiyyat*). In the following section, I examine the socio-historical background to these contemporary views of shariʿa.

The Socio-historical Matrix

As the Umayyad and Abbasid empires started to concentrate power in the hands of rulers, Muslim jurists utilized shariʿa to check state power (Yılmaz 2007). Thus, shariʿa protected the community against the will of the rulers. In contrast, shariʿa, in the sense of enforceable rules, has also been used by the rulers, especially by the Ottoman sultans, as a homogenizing and often oppressive instrument against diverse heterodox Muslim communities. In Ottoman times, some non-Sunni or heterodox communities sought to create a shared vocabulary of dissent through an anti- or alternative-shari'a discourse. These groups utilized Islam and shari'a to create a space in opposition to a state they deemed oppressive. There was no elaborate civil society ranged against traditional religious institutions, as there was in Europe, but rather a powerful discourse of justice that was utilized to check arbitrary and authoritarian forces of the state. As a result of this historical legacy, dissenters against the power of the state in the name of shari'a had (and today have) two characteristics: they were (and are) teachers of grand narratives of justice based on ideals of a just Muslim society; and they interpreted (and still interpret) Islamic norms as instruments of political mobilization against oppressive rulers.

Ottoman Islam was marked by deep tensions between ulama and bureaucracy; between shari'a and *kanun;* and between diverse heterodox and orthodox Muslim groups (Karamustafa 2005). The state always worried about this fragmented religious landscape and the possibility of millenarian challenges from heterodox Muslim movements. To counteract this fragmentation, the state tried to regulate and control Islam in two ways: it deported or removed heterodox Muslim communities like the Alevis to geographically isolated places; and it promoted orthodox (Sunni-Hanafi) Islam by sponsoring the formation of a class of religious scholars who were to operate within the state bureaucracy. The state controlled the ulama's education, provided their salaries, and appointed them to positions in a religious hierarchy (Feldman 2008, 52). Indeed, Şerif Mardin argues that "in the Ottoman empire, ulama were more clearly integrated with the apparatus of the state" (Mardin 2006, 350). The ulama acted as the agents of the Ottoman state in making and implementing policies intended to ensure the state's survival and the peaceful coexistence of different communities. Thus the Ottoman state was not only Islamic, as Noah Feldman has claimed (Feldman 2008, 21), but also secular. It was Islamic in that the sultan was the head of Sunni Islam, ulama were fully integrated into the state bureaucracy, and shari'a was fully operational, along with *kanun.* But it was secular in that it had a well-disciplined bureaucracy freed from ethnic or religious loyalties and with primary allegiance to the Ottoman state. The bureaucracy also used *kanun* to expand its influence. The Ottoman bureaucracy and *kanun* laws apart from shari'a played a central role in the state's projects of centralization and modernization during the nineteenth century (Davison 1990).

The affairs of the Ottoman state were carried out according to the sovereign's laws, known as *kanun,* which were seen as separate from Islamic law (see İnalcık 2000, 39–46). Since Ottoman social life was regulated as much by the sultan's laws as by Islamic legal injunctions, some historians have hesitated to describe the Ottoman Empire as an "Islamic state" (Cin 1992). *Kanun* governed state and public affairs. In this way, the Ottoman empire developed an independent and quasi-secular legal system, complementing shari'a and its vision of a virtuous and just society.

The Ottoman state also used religious law to control and counteract heterodox Muslim communities, and to combat separatist tendencies that were apparent on its frontiers and were often associated with heterodox Islamic movements. These heterodox groups always remained suspicious of shari'a and regarded it as a tool used by the state to undermine their communal and intellectual autonomy (Ocak 2007). For instance, Kızılbaş communities, now known as Alevi, always rejected the Sunni-Hanafi understanding of shari'a and developed their own version of shari'a which stressed inner aspects of Islam, as well as distinctive communitarian rules. As the Ottoman state expanded, religious diversity of this sort came to be seen as a potential threat, and thus religion was used to destroy alternative sources of solidarity (İnalcık 1993, 81, 100). Later, in the early twentieth century, the marginalized heterodox Muslim communities would become the main supporters of the secularizing reforms of Mustafa Kemal.

As the Ottoman system began to decline in the late eighteenth century, the ulama called on the state to become more Islamic and fulfill its religious functions. However, the civilian and military bureaucracy had a different opinion on the causes of the decline. They saw it as the result of, among other things, the promotion of incompetent people to positions of authority, thereby weakening the bureaucracy, encouraging pervasive corruption, and stifling scientific and technological innovation. A small number of high-ranking ulama supported the elite bureaucracy's position. To reverse the decline of the Ottoman state, the secular bureaucracy started to implement reforms, reorganizing the army, opening new schools to teach European ideas of science and technology, and improving taxation policies. Even though the higher ulama supported these reforms under Selim III (1789–1807) and Mahmud II (1807–39), they gradually came to take exception to their speed and breadth, especially of those involving education and the adoption of European practices.

The Tanzimat reforms (1839) gradually undermined the power of ulama by introducing a new set of regulations that widened the gap between statute law and shari'a. Additionally, there was a growing belief in government circles that shari'a in its classical form was ineffective by comparison with Western law. In response to this belief, the state codified commercial and criminal law. With the establishment of the School of Administration (Mülkiye) in 1859, the Ottomans adopted a new administrative legal system based on the French model.

Efforts to codify shari'a culminated in the promulgation of the Ottoman Majalla, or Mecelle, in 1877. This reform relied heavily on the Hanafi jurists and was the first application of the technique of *tahhayyur,* or choosing the most appropriate principles from diverse Islamic legal schools. This Islamically influenced civil law was in force until it was repealed and replaced by the Turkish Civil Code in 1926. The establishment of a universal educational system in the 1850s and 1860s, and of high schools in the 1880s and 1890s, freed education from the hands of the ulama and eventually opened the way for a new elite animated with a spirit of scientific positivism and vulgar materialism. The ulama could not compete with the new school system, but they used shari'a as a mobilizing force with which to resist these Westernizing (and secularizing) reforms.[3] But their efforts did not enjoy broad support among the empire's Muslim population.

In countries like India, Malaysia, and Egypt, Muslim communities came to emphasize shari'a as a means of maintaining a religious and communal identity apart from that of the colonial power. But since Turkey has never been colonized by outside powers, shari'a did not become a tool for building an anticolonial Turkish identity, or a way of marking a significant boundary against the colonizing Western countries. European ideas on politics and secularism were not introduced via military occupation, but rather by Ottoman intellectuals. Discourse on shari'a did not come to involve, then, a struggle between European and Turkish forces, but rather a heated public debate among Turkish intellectuals, politicians, and religious figures.

Reforms and the Ulama

In analyzing the historical development of the discourse on shari'a within Turkey, it is important to remember that these interpretations comprise a complex set of narratives which reflect the interactions of interested secular and religious groups. These interpretations influence the configuration of political institutions and the state's attitude toward Islamic activism. Of key importance were the ulama, represented in the political system by the institution of the *şeyhülislam,* the mufti of Istanbul; the Ottoman state, increasingly influenced by secular ideals; and the Young Turks, intellectuals who embraced secularism and liberalism and were the driving force behind political reform in the twilight of the nineteenth century and the early twentieth (Cihan 1994).

The Ottoman state had long recognized the power and utility of the ulama as a way of legitimizing state authority. Thus the Ottomans organized the ulama into a formal institution under the authority of the sultan or caliph (Repp 1986). At the top of this religious hierarchy stood the *şeyhülislam.* He was the highest authority to issue *fetvas* (fatwas), and he oversaw the implementation of shari'a. Thus the *şeyhülislam* was a powerful political, as well as religious, figure. However, as a political institution, the Office of the Şeyhülislam (Bab-ı Meşihat) did not develop as much as other ministries. In 1839, the Ottoman state established the Council of State (şura-yı Devlet) to weaken the domestic influence of the şeyhülislam.

As the Ottoman state became more influenced by European concepts of political statecraft and secularism, the role of the şeyhülislam and, by association, the role of shari'a as a meaningful legal code, diminished further. For example, with the establishment of the Ministry of Education (1857) and the Ministry of Justice (1870), most of the functions of the şeyhülislam were marginalized, as new, secular institutions performed the same duties. With the establishment of criminal courts under the Ministry of Justice, his legal power was further eroded. In 1916, the government placed all mehakim-i şer'iye (courts) under the administration of the Ministry of Justice and all madrasas under that of the Ministry of Education; all of these were formerly under the authority of the şeyhülislam.

This weakening of the şeyhülislam and the ulama was taken further by the actions of the Young Turks. The Young Turks were organized under the Committee of Union and Progress (CUP); they were responsible for the 1908 revolution which introduced constitutional monarchy and limitations on the power of the sultan. The CUP aimed to redefine state-society relations by introducing the ideals of nationalism and citizenship. The Young Turks also aspired to introduce new identities, economic systems, and institutions in place of traditional (religious) institutions. They stressed the importance of reason and European positivism for restructuring state and society. Some groups within the CUP were opposed to allowing any role to religion. One member of the Young Turks in particular, Ziya Gökalp, who is considered the intellectual father of Turkish nationalism, was instrumental in weakening one of the key religious state institutions—the Office of the Şeyhülislam.

In 1917, Gökalp issued a report at the party convention of the CUP in which he revealed his opinion of that office. He distinguished religious (diyanet) from public, social matters (kazai) (Berkes 1998, 451). The first sphere, he said, included belief, rituals, and morality; the second included social, economic, and political issues. He proposed that the Ministry of Justice deal with all legal matters and courts and asked the Office of the Şeyhülislam to deal with only religious beliefs, rituals, and moral concerns. He also called for the administration of madrasas, mosques, and Sufi lodges to be placed under the jurisdiction of the Ministry of Justice. This report was accepted by the CUP convention and put into practice. The şeyhülislam was removed from the cabinet; religious courts were placed under the authority of the Ministry of Justice; the administration of religious endowments (waqf) was removed from the Office of the Şeyhülislam and given to different ministries; and madrasas were placed under the administration of the Ministry of Education. All of these actions drastically reduced the role of Islam within the state. Thus, one could argue that secularism originated during the Ottoman Empire and under the conditions of the First World War, under the influence of the Young Turks and their political organ, the CUP. During the post-Tanzimat period (1878–1913), rather than eliminating shari'a-oriented institutions, the state sought to marginalize them. Mustafa Kemal would go further, replacing these remaining religious institutions with secular ones.

"Othering" Shari'a

In the aftermath of World War I, one particular member of the CUP, Mustafa Kemal, played the central role in establishing secularism as the foundation for the new Republic of Turkey. Republican reforms included abolishing the caliphate and establishing the Directorate of Religious Affairs in 1924; closing madrasas and replacing them with a unified educational system in 1924; banning Sufi orders in 1925; prohibiting the fez and the veil in 1925; adopting the Swiss Civil Code and severing the link with shari'a in 1926; replacing Arabic script with the Latin alphabet in 1928; abrogating the constitutional provision that made Islam the state religion in 1928; granting full political rights to women in 1934; introducing secularism as a constitutional principle in 1937; and, in 1938, prohibiting the establishment of a society or party based on religion or sect. These radical measures were defended as the "requirements of contemporary civilization" and aimed to create a secular society in which religion would be under the direct control of the state. The Kemalist state justified its coercive secularism by portraying Islam as the main reason for Turkey's economic underdevelopment and social malaise.

A series of popular regional rebellions against Kemal's reforms soon broke out, many in the name of protecting and restoring shari'a. The first such major rebellion was the 1924 Shaykh Said Rebellion (Gologlu 2006, 113–44). In 1930, the republic confronted a second major rebellion by another Naksibendi shaykh, who called on people to rebel against Kemal's Westernizing reforms and restore shari'a (Gologlu 2006, 331–38). Faced with this opposition, Kemalist officials came to characterize even reasonable dissent as the "rebellion of shari'a"; in this manner, the concept of shari'a was redefined as fanaticism and religious resistance to the secular nation-building project of Mustafa Kemal.

It is as a result of these long-established official discourses that today there are such different understandings of shari'a. Some Turks and Kurds want to see Islam play a bonding role in the public sphere, but there is almost no support for the implementation of Islamic law. Those who do call for the establishment of an Islamic state and the "restoration of shari'a" (şeriat isteriz) use these calls to express their opposition to the existing Kemalist system and authoritarian governments. By contrast, the opponents of Islamism reject any role for Islam in the public sphere, and frame their opposition in the words "Damn shari'a!" (*Kahrolsun şeriat*). This group defines shari'a in opposition to the secular system, and their banner is "Turkey is a secular country and it will always remain secular!" (*Türkiye laiktir; laik kalacak!*). Those who chant "Damn shari'a" are Muslim, but they distinguish Islam from shari'a. Finally, to Turkey's sizable Alevi community, shari'a means their persecution and marginalization. Alevis thus reject any form of shari'a and defend the secular nature of the republic.

With the advent of a multi-party system, some Islamic groups reactivated shari'a as a way of enhancing bonding among the Sunni-Hanafi population and also mobilizing the electorate against the secularist political parties. They argue that Kemalist reforms have undermined the country's religious fabric and normative order. Indeed, under the influence of the translated works of Sayyid Qutb and Sayyid A. A. Mawdudi, a few Islamist intellectuals have sought to overcome secular legacies and treat shari'a as a bulwark against Westernization.

Today, then, discussions of shari'a and Islamic ethics have come to center on two interrelated concepts: the moral rejuvenation of society via the construction of Islamic identity, and the undertaking of political projects to reform existing institutions, policies, and laws. The understanding of shari'a has evolved to consider religio-secular debates and concerns. If a crowd of people chant "We want shari'a" or "Shari'a is the solution," they mean that shari'a law provides a way of defining and living the "good life" and a set of religious principles guiding believers toward the ideal society. Calls for shari'a represent a desire for tangible social and political change and for religious revival. Shari'a is not viewed merely as a means of returning to a previous era of religiosity, then, but as a means of instituting substantive political policy for the betterment of society.

Securitization of Shari'a: Şeriatçı

In 1950, under the multi-party system, both the establishment and the Republican People's Party of Mustafa Kemal framed shari'a as an attempt to stop the modernization process; they also portrayed resistance to reforms as shari'a rebellions (*şeriatçı ayaklanması*) that should be criminalized. After the 1960 military coup, secularist intellectuals portrayed shari'a in similar terms as backward fanaticism, a manifestation of the ideology of the *umma*, the community of Muslim believers, against the "modern notion of nation" (Aygün 1992). This secularist version of shari'a has guided the rulings of the Turkish

Constitutional Court on the headscarves issue and on the banning of pro-Islamic parties. The court has always had a very negative understanding of shari'a. For example, in 1997 it declared that

> "secularism" is a civilized way of life which tears down the dogmatism of the Middle Ages and constitutes the cornerstone of rationalism, science, improving the concept of freedom and of democracy, becoming one nation, independence, national sovereignty and the ideal of humanity. In a secular order, however, religion is depoliticized and no longer serves as a tool of government. It is restored to its original and respectable place and left to the conscience of individuals. Application of secular law to civil affairs and religious rules to religious affairs is one of the principles upon which contemporary democracies are built. Public affairs cannot be regulated according to religious rules (Shari'a) which cannot be the basis for regulations. (Turkish Constitutional Court 1998)

In short, judicial discourse in Turkey has been shaped by a rationalist and modernist understanding of religion. The Constitutional Court has consistently declined to differentiate Islam as a faith from Islam as an ideology, and has portrayed Islamic activism as opposed to the republic's modernization.

This aggressively secularist ideology is built on the distinction that "religion controls the inner aspect of the individual, while secularism controls the outward aspect of the individual" (Yavuz 2003, 102). Kemalist "secularism" was meant to represent "progress" and "civilization" against Islamic "backwardness," which it framed in terms of shari'a and used as an accusation against those who resisted reforms, called şeriatçı.[4] Kemalist ideology has long been obsessed with "the security of secularism," and this obsession is expressed in its fierce opposition to any public manifestation of shari'a. Resistance to or even mild questioning of secular objectives has been viewed as tantamount to high treason against the state. However, rather then rejecting Islam itself, the Kemalist establishment created its own secularism-friendly Islam, which it referred to as "enlightened Islam" (çağdaş İslam).

Mustafa Kemal was not opposed to religion per se, but he wanted to construct a progressive Islam that would be in the service of nation-building and economic development. In keeping with this principle, a Directorate of Religious Affairs (DRA), under the office of the prime minister, was established in 1924. The function of the DRA was to "administer the Islamic affairs of faith, rituals, moral principles, and to enlighten the society about religion and govern the places of worship."[5] Turkish secularization therefore has not recognized the autonomy of religion, but tried to control it and use it for the state's nationalizing and secularizing goals. The state integrated religious institutions and functionaries into the governmental structure to create a Turkish version

of   mogenous and nation-
ali: rse varieties of Islam,
su   ; of Islam in what was
in   ιadvertently stimulated
th   ιred a struggle between
th   . To this day, the secular
e   :presentation within the
s   ment which seeks to re-

                                                  ιd political life generated
                                                  ɔlican reforms remained
securely ιιι μ.ι.--   lation of the multi-party
system and the introduction of neo-liberal rι ω.ω.nic policies in the 1980s,
however, the state's power retreated somewhat. Conservative Muslim groups
saw Islam as an oppositional identity they could use to challenge the Kemalist
establishment.

Opportunity Spaces and the "Shari'a-Free" Islam

Somewhat ironically, there is a close relationship between the successes of
Mustafa Kemal and the growth of Islamic reformation. The urbanization of
Anatolia coincided with the development of the multi-party system in the
1950s. A second socio-economic transformation of Turkey took place as a result of the neo-liberal economic policies of Turgut Özal in 1980, whose election to power was made possible by the implementation of the multi-party
system. The emergence of a new class of "conscious" Muslims was thus in
some ways the consequence of the appearance of new opportunity spaces created by the 1980s' liberal economic reforms (Yavuz 2009). During this period,
many groups in society tried to create their own public language to discuss
political and social issues. This new public language was largely derived from
Islamic idioms and moral frames.

Islam came to be the moral language most accessible to these diverse urban
groups. Even though Kemalist secularism controlled the public spaces in urban centers, it had a very limited presence in large rural areas until the 1960s.
Most importantly, Kemalism as a secular nation-building ideology had little
influence on people's private moral judgment. This privatized and suppressed
Islamic identity was brought out in part by the socio-economic transformation that started with Özal's neo-liberalism in the 1980s (Yavuz 2003). Islamic
movements benefited from the democratization of the country. The governing Justice and Development Party (AKP) is itself a beneficiary of these ongoing transformations.

At the same time, however, new fault lines have emerged within the Islamic sector. The old division between the secular state and the Islamic political parties is less active, and the tensions are now more within the secular and Islamic sectors of Turkish society. The Islamic sector has divided over the issue of who holds the religious authority to define contemporary Islamic principles. Turkey is experimenting with a new version of Islam that focuses on identity and life-style, with limited legal or binding force. This experiment is perhaps exemplified by the AKP's ability to both extol secularism and also claim to defend Islam. The two aims are no longer seen as mutually exclusive. In the following section, I seek to map out the actors and movements within the Islamic sectors and their understandings of Islam, shari'a, and religious authority generally.

Turkey's Islamic Landscape

The main characteristics of the Islamic sector are its diversity, its distinctive gender norms, and its greater focus on bonding (social solidarity) than binding aspects of Islam. In Turkey, the religious sector is cross-cut by four primary currents: the political Islam of pro-Islamic parties, state Islam, the social Islam of the Sufi and Nurcu groups, and the radical Islam of other groups.

Political Islam

One figure more than any other has dominated Turkey's political Islamic current: Necmettin Erbakan. Erbakan has played a leading role in the establishment of four parties: the National Order Party, the National Salvation Party, the Welfare Party, and the Virtue Party (Toprak 1981; Yavuz 2003; Yesilada 2002). All of these parties were eventually banned by the Constitutional Court on the grounds that they were "seeking to implement Shari'a" (Yavuz 2003, 247). Today's ruling AKP evolved out of the Virtue Party, which was banned in 2001.

In 1998, the Turkish Constitutional Court banned and dissolved Turkey's Welfare Party on the grounds that it sought to introduce "rules of Shari'a" which were "incompatible with the democratic regime." At the time of dissolution, the party held 158 seats out of 450, and it had secured more than 21 percent of the popular vote in the 1995 election. Moreover, before the decision of the court, Erbakan served as prime minister of the coalition government. In its long ruling the court presented legal arguments to the effect that "democracy is the antithesis of Shari'a" (Turkish Constitutional Court 1998). In the aftermath of the ruling, the Welfare Party appealed to the European Court of Human Rights (ECHR). In 2001, the ECHR upheld the dissolution

of the Welfare Party, concluding that "shari'a is incompatible with the fundamental principles of democracy" (ECHR 2003). On the request of the Welfare
Party, the case was referred to a Grand Chamber of the ECHR. In 2003, the
seventeen judges of the Grand Chamber unanimously upheld the decision,
arguing,

> Like the Constitutional Court, the Court considers that Shari'a, which
> faithfully reflects the dogmas and divine rules laid down by religion, is
> stable and invariable. Principles such as pluralism in the political sphere
> or the constant evolution of public freedoms have no place in it . . . It is
> difficult to declare one's respect for democracy and human rights while
> at the same time supporting a regime based on Shari'a, which clearly di-
> verges from the Convention values, particularly with regard to its crimi
> nal law and criminal procedure, its rules on the legal status of women,
> and the way it intervenes in all spheres of private and public life in ac-
> cordance with religious precepts . . . In the Court's view, a political party
> whose actions seem to be aimed at introducing Shari'a in a State party
> to the Convention can hardly be regarded as an association complying
> with the democratic ideal that underlies the whole of the Convention.
> (ECHR 2003)

The ECHR also referred negatively to shari'a's treatment of women and sexual minorities and to hudud punishments like hanging and stoning.

As this ruling illustrates, both the Turkish and European courts mislead-
ingly 1) translated shari'a as "Islamic law," making it synonymous with penal
law; 2) stripped shari'a of its broader moral dimensions and fluidity; 3) treated
religion and secularism as opposed entities; and 4) categorically rejected the
idea that Islamic values could be compatible with human rights. The court
treated "the principles of secularism . . . [as] one of the fundamental principles
of the State which are in harmony with the rule of law and respect for human
rights and democracy" (ECHR 2003). The legal reasoning of the ECHR has
transformed secularism into a sine qua non condition for democracy and human rights. Faced with these and other rulings, the current pro-Islamic AKP
has been careful not to take policy initiatives that might be considered anti-
secular. Turkey's application for membership in the European Union is enhancing secularism and the rights and liberties of religious people at the same
time (Kösebalaban 2007).

State Islam

By state Islam, I mean the representation of Sunni-Hanafi Islam formulated by
the Department of Religious Affairs (DRA) and the divinity faculties under the

control of the public university system. There are many private universities in Turkey, but no single private divinity faculty.[7] With the establishment of the DRA, the founding fathers of the republic wanted to address the question of "who speaks for Islam and who is the legitimate speaker" (Tarhanlı 1993). The state strictly controls religious services, education, and the production of official religious knowledge. The DRA's charge is to interpret and explain Islam, and the DRA has the exclusive right to answer citizens' questions about the interpretation and application of religious rules. The DRA's Council of Higher Religious Affairs (Din işleri Yüksek Kurulu), which consists of fifteen scholars of Islam from the divinity faculties (some elected and some appointed), offers written answers to the actual questions arising out of new social interactions and changing contexts (Hacıoğlu 1992, 14–34). However, the DRA's conclusions on these matters are not legally binding. The DRA issues "answers" (fatwas), which are non-binding religious opinions. It is left to believers to decide whether they want to implement them. Thus, in Turkey shari'a, as the operationalization of Qur'anic principles, takes the form of fatwas rather than binding law. It touches on matters of marriage, divorce, dietary rules, the use of musical instruments, and interest rates.

The DRA shies away from any debate about shari'a. When I asked Professor Ali Bardakoğlu, the head of the DRA, to define shari'a, he responded,

> The perception of shari'a in Turkey is very complex. Two diametrically conflicting views exist. One group regards shari'a as the source of economic and political problems and the sign of underdevelopment and traditionalism. In short, shari'a, for them, is the legal system of a fanatic society. The other group regards it as the perfect system, a cure-all, for a secular state. For this group, their shared motto is "Shari'a is the solution." One wonders how shari'a would address questions of unemployment, healthcare, and the relations between the military and civilian politicians. This group is much weaker. Today very few groups would demand shari'a as an enforceable legal system in Turkey. These two opposing views shape each other, and their political conflict is very much framed in terms of "for" or "against" shari'a. Our understanding of Islam is very much shaped by the Ottoman legacy, and also there is very heavy Sufi influence. Thus the debate is about identity and morality and very little about shari'a itself.[8]

Indeed, a recent publication by the DRA on Islam provides broad coverage of myriad issues—with the notable exception of shari'a, which receives not one entry.[9] In 2006, the DRA changed the name of the room in which experts met and responded to questions from ordinary citizens on Islam from the Fatwa

Room (Fetva Odası) to the Center for Answering Religious Questions (Dini Soruları Cevaplama Merkezi), dropping the term *fetva* (fatwa) altogether. When I asked Professor Ilhan Yıldız, who works for the DRA, about the reasons for dropping shari'a from the lexicon of the DRA, he answered, "Shari'a, for the DRA, is Islam and it is about worship, faith, and morality. Yet, since the meanings of shari'a are the sources of tension and even conflict in the public debate, the DRA does not use it." Yıldız also told me that "the DRA also hesitates to answer any question about politics. It defines its mission in terms of informing people about Islam, maintaining religious mosques, supporting national integration, and preventing the radicalization of Islam. In short, shari'a is not the concern and people stay away from the word itself."[10]

From 1930 to 2000, the Council of Higher Religious Affairs issued 20,260 written answers to questions from the people. These responses have been classified under a broad array of headings, including ritual, economics and finance, family law, medicine, sectarian concerns, and other religions (Bıçakçı 1994).[11] They have been guided by several key aims, including maintaining religious unity and tradition, preserving the social and political peace of the society ("no compulsion in Islam"), and affirming the principle that there is "no hardship in Islam." In formulating these responses, the council mostly utilized Hanafi sources, along with some Shafi'i and Maliki legal rulings as well. The responses are fully committed to the principles of *aqidah* (creed) and *ibadat* (worship) but consistently adopt relatively liberal positions on social affairs (*mu'amalat*). The questions about social affairs are usually answered from the perspective of the public interest and common good (*maslahah*).

Rather than shari'a, many bureaucrats of the DRA call for an "Islamic way of life" that is guided by general moral principles. Indeed, some might argue that the current position of the DRA is in fact in accordance with the original message of Islam, which stressed the moral aspect of life more than the legal one. Since the Qur'an, according to the eminent Pakistani scholar Fazlur Rahman, is primarily concerned with general ethical concerns and principles, one has to grasp its holistic ethical system before formulating concrete legal rulings.[12] Wilfred Cantwell Smith has argued that shari'a concerned the "moral" more than it did the "legal" (Smith 1965, 593).

Since Kemalist reforms mean that justice in Turkey cannot be dispensed by *qadis* (Islamic judges), the religious scholars who issue these judgments are more akin to spiritual advisors than authoritarian directors. The DRA is the main official force for upholding the Hanafi-Sunni interpretation of Islam, in accordance with the needs of the state. Since the state itself is critical of shari'a, the DRA has developed a largely secularized language to discuss religious issues.

Divinity Faculties

In Turkey, the divinity faculties play an important role not only in producing and reproducing religious knowledge, but also in containing radical ideas.[13] The divinity schools used to be dominated by Fazlur Rahman's understanding of fiqh and Islam. In recent decades a variety of new ideas have been introduced, including radical ones like those of Sayyid Qutb and Maulana Mawdudi (1903–79). The "traditionalization" of Islamic thought undertaken by Syyed Hussein Nasr (b. 1933) has also become popular, including among the Islamicly rooted political elite, such as Ahmet Davutoğlu, the foreign minister. The understanding of shari'a among the Islamic political elite has been deeply shaped, if not determined, by these three Muslim scholars.

Among the divinity faculties, there are two main approaches to the issue of shari'a: traditional approaches, such as those of Hayrettin Karaman, and modernist ones, such as those of Yaşar Nuri Öztürk. In their writings and public discussions of normative questions, these two professors offer very divergent perspectives on shari'a and base their arguments on different modes of religious reasoning. Karaman always begins with traditional and specific authoritative sources and seeks to develop an Islamic answer with direct reference to these sources. By contrast, Öztürk grounds his reasoning on general principles of human rights and the Qur'an. Öztürk rejects the classical commentaries on shari'a as time-bound and contextual. Both men have large followings in society. They represent polar opposites in Turkey and, for this reason, merit analysis.

Traditionalists: Hayrettin Karaman

By "traditionalists," I mean those who equate the historically given shari'a and its associated commentaries to Islam as a whole, and who consider the interpretation of Islam's sacred texts as more or less fixed. In this view, reason is subordinated to revelation and expected to accommodate itself to the traditional categories of revealed knowledge. Professor Karaman, who recently retired from the divinity faculty of Marmara University, has worked closely with the Fethullah Gülen movement and also has his own column in the pro-AKP government daily, *Yeni Şafak*. He is well respected in conservative circles and never hesitates to air his views. In some scholarly circles, he is regarded as Turkey's Yusuf Qaradawi, although it is recognized that he lacks Qaradawi's international stature.

Since Karaman equates Islam with the historical shari'a, he considers those Muslims who reject the historical shari'a to be *kufr*, unbelievers. Karaman rejects interpretations which claim to show that shari'a is compatible with modern ideas of human rights, and sees those who attempt to reform shari'a in accordance with such ideas as undermining or destroying Islam. In his view, shari'a is comprehensive and fixed, and an Islamic state is necessary in order for people to live as Muslims (Karaman 1994).

Karaman also points out that "shari'a has two meanings: it means the totality of religion [Islam], and it also means the rules of worship and *mu'amalat* [social affairs], including politics, economics, and social order" (Karaman 2002, 212). In keeping with his understanding of shari'a as comprehensive and political, he takes strong exception to those who promote pluralist understandings of it. When asked by a journalist why shari'a has a negative connotation in Turkey, Karaman responded,

> We are responsible for this by ignoring the education and teaching of shari'a along with its implementation. We fail to teach our understanding of shari'a as a whole. Different individuals, groups, and political movements picked and chose certain aspects of shari'a and never provided the totality of it . . . Many people perceived the meaning of shari'a by looking at these individuals, groups or movements in society. (Karaman 2006, 212–13)

In 2003, there was an interesting exchange between Karaman and Professor Murat Çizakça, who studies Islamic charity networks, over the definitions of "being Muslim" and Islam in relation to shari'a. In response to Karaman's statement that "without believing that shari'a is the highest and most truthful legal system, there will not be Islam," Professor Çizakça argued that "according to Çarkoğlu and Toprak's survey, between 78–85 percent of those surveyed responded negatively on the implementation of shari'a rules with regard to marriage, divorce, and especially inheritance. Should we thus consider 78–85 percent of Muslims of Turkey as non-Muslim since they do not accept the basic shari'a rules?" Karaman responded by arguing that "it is not logical to be a Muslim and not to accept shari'a rules. . . . Those who do not live by shari'a are considered 'fasiq Muslims'" (those who are sinful and disobedient to God; Karaman 2003, 25, 30). Karaman and many other scholars of divinity faculties argue that when a person becomes a Muslim, he or she accepts the full legal system of Islam.

Karaman's writings thus make clear that, in his view, shari'a is not voluntary, but so urgent and mandatory that the state must force believers to live according to its stipulations. For less traditionalist scholars, like İlhami Güler, a prominent divinity professor at Ankara University, Islam is one, but shari'a varies in changing contexts (Güler 1999). Thus, shari'a, for Güler, is not a specific body of laws but a set of general principles that articulate the duties of Muslims to God and to others in the human community.

Modernist Intellectuals: Yaşar Nuri Öztürk

The modernist approach to shari'a is exemplified in the writings of Professor Yaşar Nuri Öztürk.[14] Öztürk seeks to accommodate religion to the scientific mode of thinking by updating religious terminology in accordance with the sensibilities of modern peoples and societies (White 2005, 98). In order to create a new understanding of Islam, Öztürk goes directly to the Qur'an; indeed, he refers to his approach as "Qur'anic Islam" (Kuran İslamı). He also argues that each period in history requires its own shari'a. Öztürk does not equate Islam to the historical shari'a and he rejects the notion that shari'a is unchanging. He insists that shari'a is the totality of time- and space-bound human understandings of Islam. It is useful, as long as we do not use it to repeat mistakes, but it cannot serve as a comprehensive guide to modern reasoning and solving modern problems.

Öztürk argues that the norms we derive from the Qur'an should represent the spirit of the age we live in. He and other modernist Muslim intellectuals reject the idea that shari'a should be treated as fixed and sacred rules. Öztürk argues that "those who demand shari'a" are not demanding Islam, since "shari'a is not the name of the religion brought by the Qur'an" (Öztürk 2008, 98). Indeed, he argues that shari'a is "the way of yesterday." He attacks Karaman, arguing that "those who claim that shari'a equals Islam are wrong. This is not the case. Their claim is an approach unscholarly and un-Islamic." For Öztürk, shari'a is best conceived as "a set of attitudes, ways of doing things, and norms that vary from believer to believer and from society to society . . . Thus, shari'a is the collection of interpretations, that is context-bound . . . Those who claim that shari'a is Islam seek to turn tradition into a religion." (Öztürk 2008, 98–99). Öztürk appears regularly on television, promoting his view that shari'a and Islam are not the same. For him, the main sources of crisis in the Muslim world are variable, but include the hegemony of the fiqh of the Umayyad period, which evolved under the circumstances of tribal and desert life, and the reduction of Islam to shari'a. He proposes a new understanding of Islam, responsive to modern socio-political sensibilities and freed from prefigured notions of the historical shari'a.

By differentiating Islam from shari'a in this manner, Öztürk accuses those who call for the implementation of shari'a of misunderstanding the dynamic nature of Islam. He rejects any role for the historical shari'a in public life, viewing it as dangerously authoritarian and inimical to democratic understandings of Islam. In order to get believers to read the Qur'an and make their own decisions, and to free the Qur'an from the ulama, Öztürk supports the use of Turkish translations of the Qur'an and the saying of everyday prayers in Turkish (Öztürk 2002).

As these examples show, shari'a is a point of bitter contention in public Islamic discourse in modern Turkey. Some see it as a heritage of the past that is obsolete and must be discarded; Islam should not be understood from the perspective of shari'a debate. Indeed, for Öztürk, the historical shari'a stands in the way of the proper profession of Islam. In contrast, Karaman sees shari'a as a legal and normative vision for all times. Traditionalists like him hold that a fixed and finished understanding of shari'a has already been achieved, and consider themselves duty-bound to perpetuate it. The great majority of Turkish Muslims fall between these two positions, holding to the conviction that shari'a must be rediscovered in ways suited to modern times and needs.

Social Islam: The Textual Community of Said Nursi

Sociologically speaking, there are two major Muslim communities in Turkey: the Sunni majority, and the Alevi minority. I will examine first the Alevi conception of shari'a and then will move on to that of the larger and more influential (Sunni) Nurcu movement. In the interest of brevity, I will not examine the Naksibendi (Naqshabandiyya) Sufi orders.

Shari'a as the Ideology of the "Other Muslims": The Alevi Perspective

The Alevis are the second-largest religious community in Turkey, after the Sunnis. They are a multi-ethnic religious group that includes Turks and Kurds and that constitutes between 15 and 20 percent of Turkey's total population. They speak various languages, although most speak either Turkish or Kurdish dialects (Kurmanji, Dimili, and Zaza). The Alevis are a syncretic religious community in that their belief system combines elements of Shi'ism, Turkish shamanism, and some Christian religious elements. Because their religious ceremonies take place in *cemevi* (meeting places) and include music and the mixing of the sexes, they have always been seen as deviating from orthodox Islam and have been persecuted (Yaman 2007, 154). The Alevi belief system was passed down through lineages of *dede,* or holy men; to this day it has remained a largely oral tradition with few fundamental documents. As a result of this lineage and the lack of a standardized textual tradition, the Alevi belief system varies from region to region. Yet Alevis differentiate themselves from Sunni Muslims by, among other things, not abiding by the Sunni-Hanafi conception of shari'a. Alevis do not perform the five daily prayers, fast during Ramadan, or make a pilgrimage to Mecca; they also reject the authority of the ulama.

Intracommunal conflict in the Alevi community is resolved by the mediation of *dede.* Individuals found guilty of misdeeds are deemed *düşkün,* transgressors, and ostracized from the community (Yıldırım 2001). At the time of Mustafa Kemal's reforms, the Alevi community quickly became one of the main supporters of efforts to remove Sunni-Hanafi Islam from the public sphere. Alevis have also been central to the development of anti-shari'a discourses in Turkey, characterizing shari'a as partisan and as a reflection of the desert conditions of early Islam.

David Shankland, a leading authority on Alevi ritual and identity, observes that to Alevis shari'a means "praying in the mosque, interpreting the Koran literally, and following the 'five pillars,' that is, the daily round of religious life as they understand it to be in a Sunni village" (Shankland 2003, 84). In other words, for Alevis, shari'a encompasses not only things they do not do, but things that they refuse to recognize as inherent to Islam. Shari'a is also the main boundary marker between Sunni and Alevi communities (Erüreten 2006). Ali Yaman, a scholar of religious history who studies Alevi ritual and belief, notes that the "Alevi faith defines itself very much in opposition to shari'a and frames Sunni Islamic revival as an attempt to roll back the reforms of Mustafa Kemal."[15] In fact, many Alevi intellectuals warn of the "siege of the Alevi community" by the shari'a-centered Islamist movements (Şener and İlknur 1995; Aslan 2002). Most Hanafi-Sunni Muslims, especially religious scholars, do indeed have a decidedly negative view of Alevis, not least because of the Alevi rejection of shari'a.

The Nurcu Movement

The second major Muslim community in Turkey consists of the followers of Said Nursi (1877–1960). Nursi authored several volumes of Qur'anic exegesis known as the *Risale-i nur külliyatı* (The Epistle of Light). He went on to establish modern Turkey's most powerful faith movement (Vahide 2005).[16] This text-based faith movement is known today as the Nurcu (or Nur) movement.

Nursi was born in the eastern Anatolian province of Bitlis. In his work, he developed new ways of understanding Islam and society that oppose the expanding influence of positivist epistemology in the Muslim world. In contrast to the modern positivist current, Nursi emphasized 1) the synthesis of Islam and science; 2) the acceptance of democracy as the best form of governance within the rule of law; 3) the raising of Islamic consciousness by indicating the connection between reason and revelation; and 4) the achievement of salvation, in both this world and the next, through education and freedom. Nursi invited his followers to come together in reading circles to discuss his writings. These reading circles are also known as *dershanes,* or what I have called textual communities (Yavuz 2003).

Nursi's writing also places great emphasis on the social, political, and cultural implications of living in a faithful society rather than a faithless one.

He defined faith as the understanding of human life, from birth to death, in terms of Qur'anic concepts. He argued that by replacing faith through imitation (taklidi iman) with faith by inquiry (tahkiki iman), Muslims would be able to resist the forces of modern positivism, especially materialism and atheism. A Muslim, Nursi explained, must inquire as to why he or she is created. As they become conscious of these questions, Muslims can construct a community organized around this religious consciousness. Faith, therefore, is the basis of a moral community and the source of knowledge concerning the phenomenal world. Nursi expressed his beliefs in terms of the concepts of faith (iman) and life (hayat), emphasizing that everyday practices and the social order should be shaped by Islamic principles (shari'a; see Nursi 1996, 1606).

Nursi developed two separate but integrated notions of shari'a, viewing each as complementary to the other. The first shari'a, in his view, is that which guides the voluntary actions of human beings; the second is the şeriat-ı fitriye, or body of natural laws. Both forms of shari'a proceed from the same source— the Creator. Thus, from his perspective, shari'a as a social order results from a community of conscious believers. Its realization is possible only if people live faithfully by Islamic principles. Nursi argued that faith is formed through connections between the heart, the brain, and the spirit, and is expressed in life by behaving according to Islamic morality.

Nursi imagined a gradual transformation of Turkish society, beginning with raising the consciousness of individual Muslims. He sought to equip individual Muslims with the necessary tools to guide their lives in accordance with Islamic precepts. This would lead to implementing faith in everyday life, from which a shari'a-governed society would naturally evolve. By a shari'a-governed society, Nursi meant a law-governed, just society. His understanding of the state differed from that of the Young Turks and the later Kemalists, for he treated the state as the servant of the people. He also argued for a Muslim state that respects the basic rights of the people and integrates shari'a rules into state legislation. Since the state is a servant of the people, its employees need not even be Muslims, he holds, because their duty is to serve the people in accordance with the law.

Nurcu Understanding of Shari'a

In June and July 2008, I organized three focus-group sessions with Nursi's followers at the historic Rüstempaşa Madrasasi in Cağaloğlu, Istanbul. Since the Nurcu movement is divided into different groups along class, ideological, and ethnic lines, I tried to include Nurcus from different social and ethnic backgrounds. The group had twenty-four participants, and conversation focused on their understanding of shari'a and on interpreting the results of the surveys of anti-shariʻa feeling among ordinary Turks. During the first meeting, I discussed the survey indicating that most Turks identify themselves as Muslims but only 7 percent want shariʻa implemented. I asked participants whether we could read the survey's findings as a sign that there is an Islam without shariʻa. On hearing my question, the participants all turned to look at the most senior man in the group, who said,

> I think the survey reports what it hears from the people. Islam should not be reduced to shariʻa as it is practiced in some Muslim countries. Look at Ustad [Said Nursi]: he provided us with a new "Islamic window" [*Islami bir pencere*] to look at the outside universe, society, and especially ourselves from the perspective of faith [*iman*]. What he did was an ijtihad [reaching a decision by investigating the Islamic sources], and he focused first on faith and then expected us to live by shariʻa. In short, from the perspective of the Ustad, *iman* is the necessary condition of shariʻa. You need to build your Islamic consciousness on the basis of *iman*, then you can live by Islamic norms of shariʻa. No *iman*, no shariʻa.

Another participant argued that

> Islam is about faith [*iman*] and morality [*ahlak*], not about government or the legal system. As Nursi argues in his writings, some Christian countries are governed by Islamic principles that respect human rights, freedom, and justice. They have Islamic characteristics, even though their population is not Muslim, in terms of the rule of law and respect for human dignity; thus one might say they are governed by shariʻa. Where Muslim countries deny basic rights and implement cruel punishments in the name of Islam, we cannot say this is shariʻa.

In the discussion that followed, several different understandings of shariʻa were evident. One of the participants rejected the survey findings, saying,

> I tend to disagree with this survey result. Did they tell the people what shariʻa is? No. I am sure there must be questions about Saudi Arabia or Iran before they asked, "Do you want shariʻa?" Why do we let other people define shariʻa for us? We must understand shariʻa not as a fixed set of rules but rather as a source of general moral principles that are derived from the Qur'an and hadith. I would argue that there is no contradiction between a secular state, like the U.S. or Germany, and shariʻa—a set of general moral principles that help us to define what is right or wrong. A conscious Muslim can live without any problem in a secular state and live his own shariʻa as well.

When I asked about the conflict between the secular law and shari'a rules, the participants all agreed that those rules require reinterpretation on the basis of contemporary sensibilities. One man observed,

> What Said Nursi says is the following: 99 percent of shari'a consists of morality, worship, and virtue and only 1 percent deals with political issues. This statement indicates that shari'a is about morality, worship, and virtue. Only 1 percent of shari'a deals with what we might consider as being political. So even though in our discussions shari'a is hardly used, we know that it is a way to sacred truth.

When I asked respondents about Muslims in Egypt or Jordan mobilizing to restore shari'a, one of Nursi's followers responded in the following manner:

> Shari'a is the flag that believers are mobilized under to struggle against despotic systems and colonial powers. Thus, shari'a should always be in the hands of society, not the state. When it becomes a state system it will become despotic, such as in the cases of Iran and Saudi Arabia.

The participants focused on the necessity of faith (*iman*) as the ground for Islamic ways of life. By referring to the writings of Nursi, they sharply differentiated faith from shari'a. For all of them, shari'a is an outcome of faith-based community. They all agreed that positive law must be made by the parliament, and had a sense that Islamic law is not fully compatible with democracy. Indeed, Nursi argues that there must be first faith (*iman*), then living one's life according to that faith, and then shari'a. Without the first two, the last—shari'a—will become oppressive. In other words, shari'a is an outcome of faith and virtue (*fazilet*).

From these respondents' perspective, it is not the state, but believers and the community of the faithful (*umma*) who are most important for the development and observance of shari'a. In this view, shari'a must be founded in the sphere of personal faith and practice. This foundation effectively distributes legal interpretive authority among all the faithful. In other words, for these followers, Nursi's message is that we should not put undue emphasis on shari'a but instead ground our observance on faith.

Because of the strong influence of Sufism on the movement, the followers of Nursi tend to emphasize the inner aspect of Islam, speaking of building good character through Islamic morality and practices. One of the leaders of the Nurcu community said, "The problems we confront as Muslims do not stem from the lack of shari'a but rather from weak or fragile faith." The participants all had a positive view of shari'a, yet they were hesitant to see it reduced to codified and enforceable law. One of the participants in the discussion expressed the matter this way: "In some Muslim countries you have shari'a without Islam, since they do not truly understand the purpose of Islam—and what is worse, their faith is weak." The followers of Nursi argue that reflective faith is the first important condition for a just and moral society, and it is in this context that shariʻa is most likely to flourish.

Conclusion

In the course of conducting fieldwork for this project, I came to the conclusion that there is no clarity about what "shariʻa" means in contemporary Turkish discourses. Today, the term's classical meaning seems to be rarely invoked. Some believers seek to embrace shariʻa, but they do so on the grounds that shariʻa is a corpus of moral principles, not fixed rules or punishments. Others want to dispense entirely with shariʻa, since they understand it not as a body of hallowed moral principles but as a collection of antiquated rules. The claim that Islam and shariʻa are two different things and the claim that Islam and shariʻa are one and the same can both be defended on the basis of the history of Islam and theology.

"Shariʻa" has a long history, but it has never been as central to Muslim discourses as it has become in the past generation. Both the concept and the debate it inspires, however, are drastically different in the Turkish context than they are in Arab countries. In Turkey, Islamic movements tend to frame their agenda in terms of Islamic identity, morality, and justice, and they hesitate to call for a shariʻa-based system. Secularism and secular state institutions are enshrined in and protected by the constitution. Since the Turkish constitution recognizes only the parliament as having the authority to craft legislation, it criminalizes any attempt to Islamize the legal system or even propose a law on the basis of the Qurʼan. The constitution identifies the state as secular and aggressively defends its secularism as the founding principle of the republic. The same constitution which criminalizes any attempts to Islamize the legal system also empowers the state to shape public religious discourse through the Directorate of Religious Affairs.

Because making any political demand on the basis of Islam or shariʻa is a criminal act, a new discourse of Islamic normativity has developed to escape secularist persecution. Yet Turkey is one of the most democratic Muslim societies, with vibrant Muslim social and political activism, along with extensive Islamic networks in civil society. This socio-political diversity is at the core of competing understandings of shariʻa in Turkey, and will likely remain there for some time to come.

Notes

This research is based on my fieldwork in Turkey, which included interviews and two focus groups during the summer of 2008. I wish to acknowledge Professor Faris Kaya, who helped me organize the Nurcu focus group. I am indebted to the participants in both groups, especially Cüneyt Mehmet Simşek of Uludağ University, who gave a presentation on Said Nursi's understanding of shari'a. I am greatly indebted to Bernard Weiss, Ali Tekkoyun, Fatih Yaman, Ergun Yıldırım, Kenan Camurcu, and Etga Uğur, who translated a number of documents. Finally, I would like to thank Robert Hefner, Muhammad Qasim Zaman, and the participants in the Shari'a Politics project who provided helpful comments.

1. This survey is based on interviews with 1,492 individuals from around Turkey. A 2008 Gallup survey of Muslim countries indicates that "most Egyptians (64%) polled say Sharia must be the *only* source of legislation, but few Turks (7%) say the same" (Rheault and Mogahed 2008).

2. This coffee shop also has a small prayer room on its second floor. People gather here to play cards, drink tea or Turkish coffee, and especially to chat about political issues. Customers are usually from the Bayburt and Erzurum regions of Turkey.

3. A number of nineteenth-century rebellions were carried out in the name of "enforcing shari'a." The most important ones were the Kuleli incident of 1859 and the March 31 Rebellion of 1908 (see Berkes 1998, 203, 341).

4. The Kemalist conception of secularism was derived from Auguste Comte's positivism, a doctrine that seeks to replace religion with science and create a new society by using technology.

5. Article 1 of the 1965 Law recognized the duties and functions of the DRA. As of 2001, the DRA owned 75,002 mosques, and 64,157 of its 88,506 civil-service personnel worked within mosques; see *Diyanet İşleri Başkanlığı 2000 Yılı İstatistikleri* (Ankara: Diyanet İşleri Başkanlığı, 2001).

6. See, for example, the statement of the public prosecutor against the AKP, which claims that the AKP "is seeking to restore a Shari'a state" (AK 2008, 20).

7. Neither the DRA nor the divinity faculties recognize the Alevi form of Islam, which is professed by 15 to 20 percent of the population. Moreover, although the majority of Turkey's Kurds adhere to the Shafi'i legal school, they have limited representation. The established doctrine of the DRA is Sunni-Hanafi, as it was in Ottoman times.

8. I met with Ali Bardakoğlu, the head of the DRA, in July 2008 and had a long conversation with him about the meaning of shari'a and the role of his institution in the representation of Islam. His *Religion and Society: New Perspectives from Turkey* (2006) does not mention shari'a even once.

9. *İslam'a giriş: Ana konulara yeni yaklaşımlar* (Ankara: Diyanet İşleri Başkanlığı, 2007). This 409-page book contains sections on the sources of Islam (*kaynaklar*), faith (*iman*), morality (*ahlak*), worship and rituals (*ibadetler*), and everyday life (*gündelik hayat*).

10. Interview with İlhan Yıldız, July 2008.

11. There are very few studies of these fatwas. The two master's theses I have consulted, Bıçakçı 1994 and Eren 1994, are descriptive, not analytical attempts to examine religious change through these questions and answers.

12. It must be emphasized that Rahman's interpretation does not mean dismissing the legal principles contained in the Qur'an.

13. There are twenty-two divinity faculties in Turkey, with 2,034 academic personnel.

14. Öztürk has written dozens of books on theological questions. He is also a frequent contributor to daily newspaper columns. He says that secularism, understood as the separation of religion and state, was Atatürk's crowning achievement when he founded the Turkish republic: "Secularism means that the government is legitimized not by God or divine right, but by the will of the people. I don't think it's possible for Islamic societies to embrace democracy without a truly secular constitution" (Erzeren 2006).

15. E-mail interview with Ali Yaman, June 19, 2008.

16. Most Kurds in Turkey belong to the Shafi'i school of Sunni Islam, whereas most Turks belong to the Hanafi school. Some Hanafi Turkish Nurcus follow the Shafi'i rites during their daily prayers because of their loyalty to Said Nursi. Said Nursi was consciously Kurdish, yet he always rejected Kurdish nationalism and considered Turkey the common homeland of the Ottoman nation. As a result of the political situation that has prevailed since the establishment of the Kurdistan Workers Party (PKK), many Turkish Nurcus react strongly to any mention of Nursi's ethnic origin. By contrast, some Kurdish nationalists seek to nationalize the personality and writings of Said Nursi as "Kurdish."

References Cited

AK Party. 2008. *AK Party's Response to the Indictment*. Ankara: Elips.

Aslan, Hıdır. 2002. *Şeriat Kıskacında Alevilik*. Istanbul: Günizi Yayıncılık.

Aygün, Hakan. 1992. *Şeriatin Ayak Sesleri*. Ankara: Ekin.

Bardakoğlu, Ali. 2006. *Religion and Society: New Perspectives from Turkey*. Ankara: Diyanet İşleri Başkanlığı.

Berkes, Niyazi. 1998. *The Development of Secularism in Turkey*. New York: Routledge.

Bıçakçı, Ahmet. 1994. "T. C. D. İ. Başkanlığı D. İ. Y. Kurulu Kararlarının Din Sosyolojisi Açısından İncelenmesi (1946–1965)." MA thesis, Ankara University.

Çarkoğlu, Ali. 2004. "Religiosity, Support for Şeriat and Evaluations of Secularist Public Policies in Turkey." *Middle Eastern Studies* 40(2): 111–36.

Çarkoğlu, Ali, and Binnaz Toprak. 2000. *Türkiye'de Din, Toplum ve Siyaset*. Istanbul: Turkish Economic and Social Studies Foundation.

———. 2006. *Türkiye'de Din, Toplum ve Siyaset*. Istanbul: Turkish Economic and Social Studies Foundation.

Cihan, Ahmet. 1994. "Modernleşme Döneminde Osmanlı Ulaması (1770–1876)." Ph.D. diss., Istanbul University.

Cin, Halil. 1992. "Tanzimat Döneminde Osmanlı Hukuku ve Yargılama Usulleri." In *150. Yılında Tanzimat*, ed. Hakkı D. Yıldız, 11–32. Ankara: Türk Tarih Kurumu.

Davison, Roderic H. 1990. *Essays in Ottoman and Turkish History, 1774–1923: The Impact of the West*. Austin: University of Texas Press.

ECHR (European Court of Human Rights). 2003. *Case of Refah Partisi (The Welfare*

Party) and Others v. Turkey: Judgment. February 13. http://www.iilj.org/courses/documents/RefahPartisivTurkey.pdf (accessed September 12, 2010).

Eren, Selim. 1994. "T. C. D. İ. Başkanlığı D. İ. Y. Kurulu'na 1966–1985 Yılları Arasında Vatandaşlarımız Tarafından Sorulan Sorular ve Cevapların Din Sosyolojisi Açısından İncelenmesi." MA thesis, Ankara University.

Erüreten, Bahir Mazhar. 2006. Laiklik ve Şeriat Çatışması: Türkiye'de Siyasal Dinci Bağnazlık. Istanbul: Toplumsal Dönüşüm Yayınları.

Erzeren, Ömer. 2006. "Religion and Politics in Turkey: Portrait; Yasar Nuri Öztürk." Translated by Paul Cohen. Qantara: Dialogue with the Muslim World. http://www.qantara.de/webcom/show_article.php/_c-476/_nr-669/i.html (accessed January 16, 2009).

Feldman, Noah. 2008. The Fall and Rise of the Islamic State. Princeton: Princeton University Press.

Göle, Nilüfer, and Ludwing Ammann, eds. 2006. Islam in Public: Turkey, Iran, and Europe. Istanbul: Bilgi Universitesi.

Goloğlu, Mahmut. 2006. Türkiye Cumhuriyeti Tarihi (1924–1930): Devrimler ve Tepkileri. Istanbul: İş Bankası Yayınları.

Güler, İlhami. 1999. Sabit Din Dinamik Şeriat. Ankara: Ankara Okulu Yayınları.

Hacıoğlu, Ramazan. 1992. "Hilafetten Diyanet İşleri Başkanlığına Geçiş" Ph.D. diss., Ankara University.

Hefner, Robert W. 2000. Civil Islam: Muslims and Democratization in Indonesia. Princeton: Princeton University Press.

İnalcık, Halil. 1993. The Middle East and the Balkans under the Ottoman Empire. Bloomington: Indiana University Press.

———. 2000. Osmanli'da Devlet, Hukuk ve Adalet. Istanbul: Eren.

Karaman, Hayrettin. 1994. Türkiye'de İslamlaşma ve Önündeki Engeller. Istanbul: Ensar.

———. 2002. "Şeriat Düzeni," Laik Düzende Dini Yaşamak. 2nd ed. Vol. 3. Istanbul: Iz Yayıncılık.

———. 2003. İslâmın ışığında günün meseleleri. Istanbul: İz Yayıncılık.

———. 2006. "Din, Millet ve Şeriat Aynı Şeydir," Laik Düzende Dini Yaşamak. 5th ed. Vol. 2. Istanbul: İz Yayıncılık.

Karamustafa, Ahmet. 2005. "Origins of Anatolian Sufism." In Sufism and Sufis in Ottoman Society, ed. Ahmet Yaşar Ocak, 67–95. Ankara: Turk Tarih Kurumu.

Kösebalaban, Hasan. 2007. "Turkey and the Question of European Identity." Mediterranean Quarterly 18 (1): 88–111.

Mardin, Şerif. 2006. Religion, Society, and Modernity in Turkey. Syracuse: Syracuse University Press.

Nursi, Said. 1996. Risale-i nur külliyatı. 2 vols. Istanbul: Nesil.

Ocak, Ahmet Yaşar. 2007. "Sufi Milieux and Political Authority in Turkish History: A General Overview (Thirteenth–Seventeenth Centuries)." In Sufism and Politics: The Power of Spirituality, ed. Paul L. Heck, 165–95. Princeton: Markus Wiener.

Öztürk, Yaşar Nuri. 2002. Ana Dilde Ibadet Meselesi. Istanbul: Yeni Boyut Yayınları.

———. 2008. Allah ile Aldatmak. Istanbul: Yeni Boyut Yayınları.

Repp, R. C. 1986. *The Müfti of Istanbul: A Study in the Development of the Ottoman Learned Hierarchy.* London: Ithaca.

Rheault, Magali, and Dalia Mogahed. 2008. "Many Turks, Iranians, Egyptians Link Sharia and Justice." Analysis of a Gallup poll. July 25. http://www.gallup.com/poll/109072/Many-Turks-Iranians-Egyptians-Link-Sharia-Justice.aspx (accessed January 17, 2009).

Şener, Cemal, and Miyase İlknur. 1995. *Şeriat ve Alevilik.* Istanbul: Ant Yayınları.

Shankland, David. 2003. *The Alevis in Turkey: The Emergence of a Secular Islamic Tradition.* London: Routledge.

Smith, Wilfred Cantwell. 1965. "The Concept of Shari'a among Some Mutakallimun." In *Arabic and Islamic Studies in Honor of Hamilton A. R. Gibb,* ed. George Makdisi, 581–602. Leiden: Brill.

Tarhanlı, İstar B. 1993. *Müslüman Toplum, "laik" Devlet: Türkiye'de Diyanet İşleri Başkanlığı.* Istanbul: AFA.

Taylor, Charles. 2008. "Akbar Ganji in Conversation with Charles Taylor." *The Immanent Frame: Secularism, Religion, and the Public Sphere,* a blog of the Social Science Research Council. http://blogs.ssrc.org/tif/2008/12/23/akbar-ganji-in-conversation-with-charles-taylor/ (accessed July 9, 2010).

Toprak, Binnaz. 1981. *Islam and Political Development in Turkey.* Leiden: Brill.

Toprak, Binnaz, and Ali Çarkoğlu. 2006. *Religion, Society and Politics in the Changing Turkey.* Istanbul: Turkish Economic and Social Studies Foundation.

Turkish Constitutional Court. 1998. "Anayasa Mahkemesi kararı." http://www.anayasa.gov.tr/index.php?l=manage_karar&ref=show&action=karar&id=2165&content=Refah Partisi (accessed September 12, 2010).

Ülgener, Sabri. 2006. *Zihniyet ve Din: İslam, Tasavvuf ve Çözülme Devri İktisat Ahlakı.* Istanbul: Derin.

Vahide, Şükran. 2005. *Islam in Modern Turkey: An Intellectual Biography of Bediüzzaman Said Nursi.* New York: State University of New York Press.

White, Jenny. 2005. "The End of Islamism? Turkey's Muslimhood Model." In *Remaking Muslim Politics: Pluralism, Contestation, Democratization,* ed. Robert W. Hefner, 87–111. Princeton: Princeton University Press.

Yaman, Ali. 2007. *Alevilik ve Kızılbaşlık Tarihi.* Istanbul: Nokta Kitap.

Yavuz, M. Hakan. 2003. *Islamic Political Identity in Turkey.* New York: Oxford University Press.

———. 2009. *Secularism and Muslim Democracy in Turkey.* Cambridge: Cambridge University Press.

Yesilada, Birol. 2002. "The Virtue Party." *Turkish Politics* 3 (1): 62–81.

Yıldırım, Ali. 2001. "Alevilikte Hukuk Sistemi." In *Aleviler,* ed. Ismail Engin, 37–50. Hamburg: Deutsches Orient Institute.

Yılmaz, Hakan. 2007. "Islam, Sovereignty, and Democracy: A Turkish View." *Middle East Journal* 61 (3): 477–93.

5. Afghanistan

The Local and the Global in
the Practice of Shari'a

T. Barfield

Local Definitions of the Law

Shari'a is defined in two different ways in Afghanistan. A narrow interpretation, common among clerics, describes shari'a as a set of laws and regulations based on fixed sources such as the Qur'an, Sunna, and hadith. Such a code is universal and fixed, and its legitimate interpretation rests exclusively in the hands of well-trained Muslim scholars. A second and more populist view holds that shari'a is a set of rules and practices that also reflect national traditions and mores; this view mixes orthodox Islamic laws with local customs. It is this interpretation of shari'a that is most widespread in Afghanistan. Afghans readily assert that because they themselves are good Muslims, their customs must naturally be in accord with Islamic principles as well. So strong is this belief that shari'a principles are the foundation of government and social life that few secular modernists have been willing to challenge it outright. Rather than seeking to disestablish religion, as was done in Turkey, their strategy has been to praise shari'a's principles while creating a system that allows secular state laws to override it.

Localizing Shari'a Supporters and Opponents

The development of Afghanistan's legal system reflects the country's multiple positions on the role shari'a should play in society. The country's three distinct but overlapping legal systems (shari'a, state, and customary) each have opposing views on which principles take priority.

The Shari'a System

The officially recognized shari'a law system in Afghanistan is based on the Hanafi legal tradition (Kamali 1985, 19–74). It was implemented by trained religious judges (*qazi;* Ar. *qadi*) who were part of a larger class of professional clerics (*'ulama*) who issued opinions (*fetwa;* Ar. *fatawa,* pl; *fatwa,* sing.) on religious issues. The clerics still see themselves as protectors of a divinely inspired and universally applicable tradition in which religion and government are inextricably melded. Until the formation of the modern Afghan state in the late nineteenth century the ulama ran the legal system independently, providing both the system of laws and the judges to interpret it. This autonomy was progressively restricted by secularizing modernist rulers who demanded that the clergy recognize the state's right to promulgate laws on its own and control the appointment of judges. The Taliban's rejection of this secularized state model was the high-water mark of Islamic clerical influence. After taking control of the Afghan state in the late 1990s, the Taliban abolished the national legal codes on the grounds that the existing shari'a system already met all of an Islamic society's needs.

The shari'a system is not uniform, however. Shi'a Muslims long chafed under the rule of the majority Sunnis, whose use of the Hanafi legal tradition was at odds with their own Jafari interpretation.[1] They did not receive relief until the new 2004 Afghan constitution finally authorized the use of the Jafari tradition within the Shi'a community.[2] More significant is the enormous gap between rural and urban clerics. The latter are more open to innovations and more sophisticated in their interpretations of shari'a law. The former have a hard time differentiating between Afghan custom and shari'a law. As one university-based expert on shari'a explained,

> We can divide the understanding of Islam in Afghanistan into two categories. One is the rural or traditional or primitive interpretation of Islam, which is based almost entirely on our customs and traditions. Second is the urban, which tries to find a more modern interpretation of Islam. Because of the stronger influence and dominance of the primitive interpretation of Islam, we are not able to open our doors to the science and technology of the modern world. You can find a lot of ulama in Afghan villages who have not even heard of computers and the internet, or books that are published by Islam's major academic institutions. Those who know or have access to new technology are very few and almost totally marginalized. (Samim interview)

Even supporters of the shari'a system in Afghanistan have pointed to a number of weaknesses that hinder its application. Because the Sunni Hanafi tradition has no authoritative hierarchy, even minor clerics can set their own opinion against others, leading to widely differing judgments in cases that present the same facts. (For example, there is a wide range of opinions on *riba*, interest payments on loans or bank deposits.) Nor has Hanafi fiqh (jurisprudence) been codified in Afghanistan.[3] Jurists use a wide variety of sources to justify their opinions, and each madrasa has its own interpretation of them. As a result, both practices and interpretations vary by region and ethnic group. Clerics in Kabul and Herat who were trained in more liberal centers of Islamic leaning have been open to ijtihad (the right to derive new rulings or interpretations), while clerics in Kandahar who studied in more conservative Pakistani madrasas reject such innovations.

Such differences over the interpretation of Islamic law are products of Afghanistan's history as a cultural crossroads and explain why a single "Afghan" shari'a tradition never developed. Before 1978 the Afghan government controlled the training of those who wished to qualify for government positions, through either state shari'a law schools or secular law faculties. Madrasas trained local mullahs, but at a low level. Those who wanted higher religious education went abroad, because Afghanistan had no outstanding educational institutions of its own. Delhi was the most popular destination, after the Soviets ended religious teaching in Bukhara, but other students studied in Egypt and Saudi Arabia, where they were exposed to new ideas. By contrast, those trained in Pakistan, where the influence of Deobandi madrasas was strong, were limited to a highly conservative curriculum that discouraged or prohibited innovation. These institutions became particularly strong because they served the large Afghan refugee community in Pakistan during the Soviet occupation and later supported the Taliban's policies. Shi'as from Afghanistan had historically sought training in Iraq's Karbala but in the 1980s shifted their studies to the Iranian city of Qom, where more activist schools of thought prevailed.

During most of the twentieth century central governments in Kabul attempted to reduce the influence of madrasas by insisting that state judicial officials obtain degrees from universities, either secular law schools or faculties of shari'a law. Both were state-sponsored and offered a wider range of topics than madrasas, although the quality of the faculty was uneven. This is still the case today, as a member of the shari'a faculty in Herat explained.

Most of the subjects we study in our law schools are taken from Islamic laws. For instance, our criminal law is almost entirely based on shari'a. The only problem is the lack of deep and objective understanding of Islamic jurisprudence among professors and lecturers in our universities. Fortunately, we have currently managed to include Islamic jurisprudence studies in the shariʿa schools. Also, I believe the studies and research which are done in Western and non-Islamic universities on Islamic law are a very important source of information. I think if we manage to have access to those studies, it will greatly improve our capacity.

Of course, there are fundamental differences between the methods and teachings of religious madrasas and shariʿa schools, though this does not mean we deny their similarities. Shariʿa schools are more open to non-religious subjects and focus on religion from a more academic point of view. Madrasa teachings have nothing to do with academic methods and teachings. Regarding madrasas outside Afghanistan (as a large number of Afghans studied abroad), we have two kinds of madrasas. Madrasas in Iran and Egypt offer teachings that are mostly academic and focus on an analytical approach to religious topics. In South Asia most of the studies are purely subjective and traditional. In Egypt the approach to religious studies is not based on one school of jurisprudence, while in traditional madrasas, only one school of jurisprudence—in this case, Hanafi—is considered the basis for all studies and analysis. Sometimes it is even considered blasphemy to look at or base your researches on other schools. I heard that in certain cases it is punishable by eighty lashes. Regarding madrasas in Pakistan, I think that Pakistan's military and intelligence services are playing an important role in influencing the teachings and even fatwas. That is why we have all these suicide bombers coming to Afghanistan. (Samim interview)

Attitudes in the Pashtun east have always been more sympathetic to the madrasa system, in which most of the lower ranks of mullahs have been trained. A report by the International Crisis Group estimated that the more than ten thousand madrasas in Pakistan enrolled a half-million students, many from poor families attracted by the offer of free food and lodging. It warned that their graduates were particularly "susceptible to romantic notions of sectarian and international jihads, which promise instant salvation," because of their narrow worldview and poor economic prospects (ICG 2002, 1).

These Pakistani madrasas have had a profound impact on eastern and southern Afghanistan, because their graduates dominate the clerical establishment in these regions. According to one cleric in Nangrahar, their poor education is offset by their piety and sincerity: "To be honest, the madrasa is more attractive, as it only trains those who want to serve people and Islam, while a university only produces those who believe in getting higher posts, getting into government, and who prefer worldly things to real salvation" (Naʾaimy interview).

The State System

State legal codes were first introduced into Afghanistan in the early twentieth century. The foundation for this change was laid by Amir Abdur Rahman (r. 1880–1901), who took control of the country's judicial institutions as a way to increase his own control over both the government and Afghan society. Arguing that as the amir of Afghanistan he had the right to determine the state's implementation of religious law, Abdur Rahman made his own wishes quite clear and found clerics willing to support him even over the objections of other ulama.[4] Over the course of his reign the number of dissenters declined dramatically, especially after he put the *qazis* on the state payroll, making them part of the government. He then went on to create his own examinations that prospective *qazis* needed to pass before they could be employed (Kakar 1975, 50–53, 152–63) Under the modernizing King Amanullah (r. 1919–29), Afghanistan first instituted state law codes designed to supersede the shari'a system, although shari'a was to remain in force in the absence of any state regulation. He also began appointing non-clerics as judges to staff the courts and decide cases according to these national codes (Nawid 1999).

Afghan modernists of the 1920s saw conservative Islamic values as a barrier to social and economic change in the country. Excited by the ferment of social change in Turkey, Iran, and the newly established Soviet Union, they strongly backed King Amanullah's reforms. However, even they were shocked when Atatürk abolished the caliphate in 1924 and imposed a thoroughly secular state in Turkey. They were also repelled by the Soviet Union's policy of atheism and its persecution of Muslims in Central Asia, which led a wave of refugees to seek sanctuary in northern Afghanistan. As a result, though Amanullah modeled his codes after similar reforms in Turkey and Iran, he took great care to stress that his laws were in accordance with Islamic principles (although he insisted that state regulations superseded any interpretation of shari'a law where the two conflicted). Amanullah won grudging approval of these new codes from various *loya jirgas* (national assemblies) that included many urban ulama. The lower-ranking clerics in the countryside, however, argued vehemently that such man made laws were illegitimate. They particularly objected to those concerning family law and women's rights. These laws, although never extensively enforced, became (along with increased levels of taxation and conscription) the focus of the rural opposition that led to the overthrow of Amanullah's government in 1929 (Nawid 1999, 43–71, 218–21).

The Musahiban dynasty came to power after a brief civil war and gained the support of the conservative clergy by abandoning Amanullah's law codes and putting members of the ulama in charge of the state judiciary for the next two decades (Olesen 1995, 172–96). The new regime also persecuted secular supporters of Amanullah, less because of their beliefs than because they were deemed politically unreliable (Gregorian 1969, 293–321, 342–71). It was not until 1964 that King Zahir Shah (r. 1933–73) felt secure enough to create a new constitution that once again made explicit the primacy of state law over shariʿa where the two were in conflict, but even this was only stated after another clause asserted that all laws must be in accord with shariʿa principles (Dupree 1980, 547–87). This compromise worked very well, because the existing Hanafi legal system stressed a peaceful Islam and the ulama and other prominent religious figures were already tied into the Musahiban government. Conservative clerics who complained about the social and legal reforms made during the 1970s had little influence within the religious establishment, in part because the government focused on implementing reforms first in Kabul, where they had considerable support, and allowing the countryside to change at its own pace (Barfield 1984).

In the 1960s and 1970s the expansion of educational and employment opportunities that came in the wake of new development projects funded by both the United States and the Soviet Union produced a new political opposition. Two small leftist parties arose, one popular among the Persian-speaking bureaucracy (Parcham) and the other among Pashtu speakers in the military (Khalq); both held that the pace of change was too slow, because the country needed radical change. Although small in number and Kabul-based, the parties' leadership saw themselves as an elite vanguard that would use the existing state structure to promote a state-sponsored revolution. The leaders got the chance for which they had hoped when they seized power in a bloody coup in 1978 under the banner of the People's Democratic Party of Afghanistan (PDPA) (Arnold 1983).

The PDPA immediately announced that Afghanistan was a secular socialist state, and quickly removed religious figures and symbolism from government. Because successive Afghan governments had maintained that they were working within shariʿa principles, the role of shariʿa in government had previously provoked little public discussion. Now not just the role of shariʿa but Islam itself moved squarely into the foreground. Resistance to the PDPA's policies became so widespread that within eighteen months the regime was on the verge of collapse. It was saved only by the invasion of the Soviet Union in December 1979. In the hope of winning broader support, the new regime reverted to the compromise of "conformity with Islam" employed by previous governments. It also reintroduced public displays of religiosity, such as reading prayers on public occasions, restoring mosques, and paying stipends to mullahs who supported the regime (Giustozzi 2000, 20–32, 57–64). But the damage had already been done and opponents of the regime framed their opposition in religious terms.

Using a religious ideology to justify opposition to Afghan central governments had a long tradition, but the post-1979 resistance to the Soviet occupation was organized quite differently from earlier efforts. Traditional tribal leaders, rural clerics, and established Sufi networks were sidelined by Islamist political parties whose leaders emerged from the same hotbed (and hothouse) of political radicalism that produced the PDPA: the state universities. Based in the shari'a law faculty of Kabul University, the Islamists founded a party in 1973 that later became known as Jamiat-i-Islami (Islamic Society). Its leaders included such faculty members as Burhanuddin Rabbani and Ghulam Rasul Sayyaf and a former student at a technical university, Gulbuddin Hekmatyar. Drawing inspiration from the Muslim Brotherhood in Egypt, they sought to establish an Islamic state based on shari'a law. Although there were fewer of them than of the leftists (perhaps only a few thousand), their membership was multi-ethnic and drawn from the state educational system rather than the traditional madrasas that produced the ulama. After Mohammad Daud took power from King Zahir Shah in 1973, he attempted to wipe out the Islamists, particularly after they mounted a series of very small-scale insurrections against him in 1975. None of these risings, including one by Ahmad Shah Masood in the Panjshir Valley, generated any local support and they were quickly crushed by the army, forcing the surviving Islamist leadership into exile in Pakistan (Roy 1990, 54–83).

Although the Islamists never had a mass base of political support within Afghanistan, Pakistan's insistence that they lead the resistance against the PDPA and the Soviet occupation catapulted them into political prominence (Roy 1990, 110–38). Their parties politicized shari'a, giving it a prominence it had not previously held in Afghanistan. In this process they were influenced by Islamist parties in Pakistan such as the Jamiat Ulama Islami (JUI), for which shari'a had always had more political significance than it had in Afghanistan (see Muhammad Zaman's chapter in this volume). As Afghan refugees poured into Pakistan, their reliance on the expanding network of Deobandi madrasa schools for educating mullahs also began to have an influence, which increased over the years. These schools were much more Salafi than the schools that had produced the old Afghan ulama, not only in their stress on the centrality of shari'a principles in government but in their conservative interpretation of them (Matinuddin 1999, 12–20). In particular, the Islamists viewed shari'a as a political blueprint for building a new state, whereas ordinary Afghans assumed that shari'a was a reflection of existing society, whose values the state should respect (Roy 1995, 41–60).

The fall of the PDPA in 1992 brought the mujahedeen parties to power, but they soon fell out with one another and began a civil war that led to the rise of the Taliban. The Taliban took power in 1996 and held it until ousted by the American invasion of 2001. Because the national state structure collapsed as the Taliban took power, there was no meaningful state policy during this period that can be examined. The Taliban proclaimed they were running a religious government that needed no law codes because shari'a was all that was needed. The state system was revived in a series of national *loya jirgas* that ratified the creation of the Karzai administration in 2002 and approved a constitution in 2004. While much international aid has been devoted to restoring the formal state system of justice by training judges, building courthouses, and distributing law codes, the state system remains quite weak. It did not replace the customary system of law that had long existed in rural Afghanistan.

The Customary Law System

Local communities that resolve disputes in the absence of (or in opposition to) state or religious authority use what may be described as a customary system. It is based on a common cultural and ethical code that generates rules binding on its members. Communities use this code to resolve disputes, evaluate actions for praise or blame, and impose sanctions on violators of local norms. The most elaborate of these systems is the Pashtunwali, the code of conduct for Pashtuns. While such systems of customary law are found universally throughout rural Afghanistan, their specifics vary widely and often idiosyncratically. In addition, far from being timeless and unchanging, they were always subject to a great deal of manipulation and contestation within the community. Although rural people often insist that customary law and shari'a were the same, the ulama hold customary law systems in contempt, arguing that they violate orthodox Islamic practices in areas such as inheritance, marriage payments, and blood feud practices. On the basis of their training in a literate and urban tradition of orthodox Islam, the ulama are quick to condemn such local systems as not in accord with shari'a and have often used their influence to demand that they be replaced with standard shari'a interpretations.

As a Mecca-trained member of the shari'a law faculty in Herat explained,

> Afghanistan is very closed and to some extent "primitive" in certain parts of the country. Most of what we call shari'a laws and regulations are actually our own traditions and customs that are based on tribal laws. They have nothing to do with Islam and with shari'a law or our civil laws. The problem is that each tribe has its own traditions that contradict Islam in almost all fields, especially women. In shari'a law, women have the right to work, education, and [participation in] almost every social, economic, and cultural field. The rigid and meaningless tribal codes reject these

rights and oppose women's participation in social life. Unfortunately our people are following these tribal regulations and even force them on those who oppose them. It is very sad. For instance, on the issue of women's inheritance, both Islamic laws and our civil laws clearly state the right of women to inherit. But these rigid tribal laws deny women their basic rights. It is against shari'a and I believe it is a crime that should be punished. We should never attach these tribal traditions to shari'a law. (Samim interview)

Rural clerics are generally more sympathetic to these tribal codes, in part because they live within the tribal milieu and have only limited power to change established practices. They also view their urban clerical rivals as too prone to compromise with the elites who run the state and too liberal in their attitudes. In this respect they find the rural population useful allies in opposing state law codes to which both groups object (Barfield 2008).

Government officials have also taken a dual approach to the customary system. While high-level officials in Kabul reject it outright, their subordinates in rural areas find it expedient to refer many cases to community councils (*shuras*) or tribal assemblies (*Pashtun jirgas*) for judgment even though they employ customary law. As an official in the northern rural province of Takhar explained,

> In every case, the priority is always with the civil law, but when we cannot find a resolution, we refer to shari'a and at the end to the tradition and customs of the people. In most cases, we encourage people to solve their disputes through local *shuras* and councils. They have the right to choose their arbitrators. We never interfere in this process, but at the end we stamp the arbitration paper as the representative of the court, which gives it legal value. (Faisal interview)

A deputy district attorney in Mazar-i-Sharif, the largest city in northern Afghanistan, took a similar view:

> According to Islam, using *shuras* and consulting is always encouraged as the best way to settle disputes. *Shuras* have been a part of social life in Afghanistan from ancient times. They can work on social, family, and criminal cases. Most of these cases used to be solved by *shuras*. (Wafa interview)

Another example of how custom trumps ideology among Afghans is the fact that *muta* (temporary marriage) was rejected by Afghan Shi'as who moved to Iran, even though it was religiously permitted and practiced in Iran.

Social and Intellectual Currents as Regards the Law

Afghans have long viewed shari'a as the natural foundation of both state and society and thus rarely felt the need to question its role. When Afghanistan was declared an Islamic republic in the Bonn Accord of 2001, the label was descriptive rather than prescriptive and hence empowered no particular ideology. As a result, Afghanistan is a place where the concept of Islamic politics is little debated, because its people assume there can be no other type. In addition, intellectuals have played almost no role in framing ideological debates about shari'a. With the exception of Sayyid Jamal-al-din al-Afghani in the mid-nineteenth century, one is hard-pressed to name any Afghan intellectuals who have published integrated and comprehensive theories of the role of religion in society and government. Instead, factions (pro and con) employed easily repeated shibboleths, the intellectual foundations of which were rarely well known. This does not mean that debates about shari'a do not emerge. They do, but they tend to focus on specific hot-button issues, particularly family law, women's rights, or freedom of religion, around which factions can mobilize their supporters and discomfit their opponents politically. Issues that are not emotionally charged (shari'a views on economic issues such as interest payments, for example) rarely inspire significant opposition even when state laws are in obvious disagreement with shari'a principles.

As noted above, all political groups in Afghanistan take for granted the pervasiveness of Islam, regardless of whether they consider it positive or negative. The conflict over the past century has been between those who wished to see Afghanistan transformed and those who opposed the process. While this has often been portrayed as a battle between secular modernists and Islamists, the division is more complex. It has had as much to do with conflict over the limits of the central government's power, the cultural gap between elites in Kabul and the inhabitants of the countryside, and questions of taxation and conscription as it did with religion (Barfield 2010, 164–73). It is this very set of cross-cutting issues that has prevented Islam from becoming a distinct ideology. Factions that would raise the Islamic banner in one context would ignore it in another. For example, changes in the legal status of women imposed by King Amanullah in the 1920s and by the PDPA after it took power in 1978 were decried as un-Islamic and used to justify rebellions in rural areas. But these same rebels had long ignored complaints by orthodox clergy that their own tribal customs concerning women's inheritance rights and marriage procedures also violated shari'a law. Similarly, since 2001 the most successful secular advocates for international human rights in Afghanistan have been those who have taken the time to ground them in Islamic history and philosophy. By contrast the Taliban, though declaring themselves the purest champions of shari'a, lost credibility when they used force to impose their views of Islam on everyone in the country without tailoring them to Afghan tradition.

Afghanistan has never been a land of mass political movements based on ideology. The bulk of the population has been rural, with low levels of literacy and political structures grounded on the *qawm*, nested affinity groups based on kinship, ethnicity, religious sect, and locality. Political mobilization of these groups tended to be interest-based rather than ideological. They were rarely swayed by abstract arguments of any type. Ideologies had a much greater impact on urban elites, who viewed control of the state as the best way to make changes of any type. It was these elites who set the course of Afghan history, despite their small numbers. Regardless of ideology, all of these groups looked to the state as the agent of change that could transform society from the top down, by force if necessary. During the 1960–70s, when both the communists and the radical Islamists first formed distinct parties, their membership was small and confined primarily to Kabul. For example, the PDPA probably had only six thousand active members when it came to power in 1978, and its Islamist rivals perhaps half that number (Giustozzi 2000, 4; Roy 1990, 71–74). Neither the Islamists nor the communists attempted to create countrywide networks or built up a rural political base at this time. Nor did the Islamists have much success in selling their more radical vision of an Islamic state to the existing clerical establishment, which numbered in the hundreds of thousands.

One reason the Islamist parties could not count on the automatic support of the ulama was that most of their leaders were non-clerics recruited from state-sponsored universities. They therefore lacked the classical seminary training the ulama demanded of their higher-ranking members. The ulama also had a long tradition of working with the state and had been largely coopted by it. It was only after the PDPA came to power that the Islamist parties and their leaders created a mass following, and these parties were based less on ideology than on coercion and the patronage derived from their exclusive access to foreign aid and weapons funneled to them by Pakistan. In this sense the radical Islamists were as dependent as the PDPA on foreign support to maintain their dominance. It was a pattern that continued after the PDPA collapsed in 1992 and the Taliban rose to power with the financial and military support of Pakistan.

This helps explain why Afghanistan fell victim to both radical communists and radical Islamists over the course of twenty years: both the PDPA and the Taliban announced their plans to radically transform, with the help of foreign allies, a society that had no desire to be transformed. The two had something else in common as well: a weak understanding of the philosophical basis of the ideologies they were imposing. The Soviets excoriated the leadership of the PDPA for their poor knowledge of Marxist dialectics (Giustozzi 2000,

34–35). Clerics from Al-Azhar University in Cairo, among many others, took an equally dim view of the Taliban's knowledge of Islamic jurisprudence and philosophy. Egypt sent a mission to Kandahar in March 2001, which failed to convince Mullah Omar that the destruction of the Bamiyan Buddhas was not justified by Islamic law, and the delegation blasted the Taliban government for its ignorance. Rather than seeing Afghanistan as a model Islamic state, the delegation accused the Taliban of what might be termed "shari'a malpractice":

> Because of their circumstances and their incomplete knowledge of jurisprudence they were not able to formulate rulings backed by theological evidence. The issue is a cultural issue. We detected that their knowledge of religion and jurisprudence is lacking because they have no knowledge of the Arabic language, linguistics, and literature and hence they did not learn the true Islam. (Khalil 2001)

Since the establishment of the Karzai government in the wake of the American expulsion of the Taliban in 2001, divisions in society have appeared over a new issue: how to balance international norms against both Afghan traditions and shari'a principles. As in the past, the split has highlighted existing conflicts in Afghanistan between urban modernists and rural conservatives. In this respect it is as much a cultural as a legal issue, particularly in areas where shari'a values clash with individual liberty. In the context of a democratic Afghanistan that remains dependent on international aid for its survival, such issues (while relevant to only a limited number of legal cases) highlight fundamentally different worldviews.

Features of Shari'a Highlighted in Public Discussions

International Law vs. Shari'a Law

The issues of shari'a that are most commonly discussed today are those that are generally agreed on in Afghanistan but disputed by the outside world. Afghanistan has signed almost every international human rights convention.[5] Although such conventions require signatories to bring their national laws into accord with the conventions, Afghan regimes never bothered to do so, and indeed most Afghans were unaware the country had signed them. After 2001 the UN and various international NGOs began to assert that Afghanistan had an obligation to meet the requirements of the conventions it signed and enforce their protections internally.

These circumstances have generated a number of conflicts between the international community and Afghans. For example, Afghans interpreted freedom of religion exclusively within an Islamic context: the right of all Muslim sects to be treated equally and without prejudice. And in this regard, the post-2001 acceptance of non-Sunni religious practices and legal systems marks considerable progress in Afghan social policy, since earlier governments actively discriminated against Shi'as and Ismailis. On the other hand, Afghans rejected any notion that other faiths were in any way equal to Islam, or that non-Muslims had a right to proselytize, or that freedom of expression meant tolerating criticism of Islam or the Prophet.

Although it is a right explicitly recognized by the international conventions Afghanistan signed, no political figure in Afghanistan has ever been willing to defend the right of a Muslim to leave his faith for another, an act of apostasy that carries the death penalty in Afghanistan. Indeed, Afghans find it impossible to believe that such a thing can even occur, and such converts (if they exist) maintain their invisibility by never publicly admitting to their new faith. As a result, public debate about the rare cases that have emerged sets Afghan values against international ones. A notorious example occurred in March 2006 when Abdul Rahman, an Afghan who converted to Christianity in Europe, was jailed on the charge of apostasy and sentenced to death. The Afghan public fully supported the charge and thought capital punishment appropriate unless Rahman chose to recant and return to Islam. The international community demanded his release on the grounds that Afghanistan was a party to the Universal Declaration of Human Rights, which guarantees freedom of religion, including the right of individuals to choose and leave faiths as they wish. The Karzai regime found itself in a difficult position, since the constitution declared that Afghan laws were to be in accord with shari'a principles and the Afghan court system was keen to hand down a conviction and a death sentence. In the face of a blizzard of editorial condemnations in their own countries, representatives of the international community threatened to cut off their support of the government if the death penalty was carried out. But Afghan religious affairs adviser Moulawi Balooch told the *New York Times,* "Our Constitution says that the judiciary power is independent, and the president has signed the Constitution . . . We cannot intervene in this case, and it is up to the judges and the court what to do with it" (Munadi 2006). While it was possible to offer an Islamic defense using the Qur'anic injunction "Let there be no compulsion in religion," no one in Afghanistan was interested in doing so. In the end Karzai finessed the problem by spiriting Abdul Rahman out of the country to asylum in Italy and asserting that his conversion was evidence of a mental disorder for which he could not be held accountable (Morarjee and Murphy 2006).

While the question of apostasy tends to unite Afghans in defense of Islam, the use of shari'a by conservative clerics to punish those who disagree with them is more divisive. An example of this use is a case that arose in northern Afghanistan in early 2008 when a journalism student, Sayed Perwiz Kambakhsh, was sentenced to death (later reduced to twenty years' imprisonment) for distributing a controversial article taken from the internet that questioned the interpretation of certain Qur'anic verses about women. Hafizullah Khaliqyar, the attorney general of Balkh Province, defended both the sentence and the trial, arguing that

> this was not a violation of human rights or press freedom, nor a violation of rights of a journalist . . . [Kambakhsh] violated the values of Islam. He did not make a journalistic mistake; he insulted our religion. He misinterpreted the verses of the Koran and distributed this paper to others. All ulama [Islamic clerics] have condemned his act. (Radio Free Europe 2008; interpolations in original)

Defenders of Kambakhsh attacked this argument in two ways. The first was by claiming that the court had ignored the clauses in the Afghan constitution that guaranteed freedom of speech, of which this judgment was an obvious abridgment. Second, and more discomfiting to defenders of shari'a in Afghanistan, was by asserting that the verdict did not appear to be in line with Islamic law. As Abdullah Attaei, an expert in shari'a who had studied at Al-Azhar University in Egypt, explained,

> If the convicted person doesn't accept that he wrote the article, and if he denies being quoted, then no court can judge his faith . . . When he denies that he wrote the article, then no one has the right to arrest or investigate him or even to try to prove him guilty. (Ibid.)

In this and other cases, judges who seek to apply shari'a law in Afghanistan often employ common cultural standards rather than legal reasoning. In this sense the formal legal system, although purporting to uphold shari'a standards, is often really just another form of customary law in which popular opinion substitutes for legal analysis. The dean of Herat University's law school argued that one part of the problem was the failure of successive Afghan governments to seriously consider the agreements they were signing, when some of their provisions were so at odds with local practices.

> In our society the interpretation of shari'a is deeply influenced by local traditions and superstitions. The Afghan government has accepted the human rights declaration. Because concepts such as freedom of speech and the marriage of a Muslim woman to a non-Muslim man contradict Afghan traditions and our interpretation of shari'a law, it would have been better if our government considered this before signing it. (Soroush interview)

How Much Shari'a Is Enough?

Despite these debates about specific issues, there is far less controversy over whether the system as a whole meets a specific standard. Afghans recognize that regions and ethnic groups have different traditions of shari'a interpretation, and one positive aspect of political development since 2001 has been a greater willingness to accept the validly of such differences. The influence of Sufi orders (Naqshbandiya, Qadiriya, and Chistiya) among Sunni Muslims in Afghanistan also helps maintain such tolerance. Historically Afghanistan has not witnessed hostility between the ulama and the Sufi orders, because Sufi leaders have not been excluded from the ulama and many ulama are themselves members of Sufi brotherhoods. Kandahar, the home of the Taliban, has a long tradition of Sufi practices, and many ordinary Taliban members observed them in spite of the movement's overt disapproval of them.

Almost all public debates therefore focus on government laws and actions, but many of those who see shari'a as taking priority over state laws also recognize that Afghan society itself has never been truly shari'a-compliant, because of its adherence to customary practices. A faculty member at Nangrahar University explained it this way:

> Islamic principles are solid and unchangeable, though their interpretations may vary according to each society. For instance, marriage is an Islamic obligation but the way it is performed and conducted varies in each part of Afghanistan. Some believe in a long period of engagement, up to one year, before marriage, while, according to Islamic laws, it is not necessary to wait that long. On the other hand, according to our tradition, a *wakil,* a representative, should ask a woman's approval before marriage and convey it to the mullah, while Islam insists on direct discussion with the woman and her direct approval. (Na'aimy interview)

One of his colleagues specializing in Arabic further argued that the details of shari'a practices were of little interest to most people.

> Every Islamic society must base its laws on shari'a. In Afghanistan, most of our laws are based on shari'a, though there are certain regulations that are based on individual decisions. As an example, a Muslim woman should not travel abroad without her *mahram* [a close male blood relation], which I heard they do. I do not think there is any serious discussion about it in Afghanistan. (Hamid interview)

However, a more legally and politically absolutist approach to shari'a denies the right of governments to make any laws on a topic where the shari'a has taken a position; this view was expressed by the vice-chancellor of the same shariʿa faculty at Nangrahar.

> In the past all the laws of Afghanistan were based on shariʿa. Today some current laws contradict shariʿa law . . . The majority cannot change shariʿa law. It is the word of God and no one is allowed to change it. (Munib interview)

By way of contrast, a female attorney, head of the attorney general's office in the western province of Herat, argued that state law codes and shariʿa were intertwined and not in conflict.

> Legitimacy of laws in Afghanistan comes from two sources: God's laws and the laws written by men. The punishments that are mentioned in shariʿa are unchangeable: for instance, *hudud Allah* [Islamic laws ordained by God]. If we cannot find a clear reference in shariʿa, then it is allowed to refer to civil or criminal laws. I believe there is no contradiction between these laws and democracy in its modern interpretation. If by democracy we mean freedom of belief, freedom of speech, the right to work, the right to live, the right to have a house, the right to marry, and the right to establish a family, Islam defined and explained them 1,400 years ago. In shariʿa, the concept of *shura,* or consultation, is considered one of the pillars of social life in a society. The members of these *shuras* come from the best-known and best-educated members of a society. We call it also *shura ahl hal wa aqd.* Their decisions are based on God's laws and people's need. I do not see any contradiction between shariʿa and democracy. (Bashir 2008)

Strong defenders of legalist shariʿa principles are idealists. They assert that the law's implementation would lay the foundation for a government free of corruption and oppression.

> All social and economic initiatives and activities should be understood according to shariʿa teachings. For instance, trade is highly recommended in Islam, as it benefits humanity, but when it comes to interest and trading in narcotics, these are forbidden, as they damage communities. In terms of social life, shariʿa guarantees a sound and safe social life. When shariʿa is properly implemented, it eradicates all the roots of corruption and mismanagement. A good example of this is the period of the righteous caliphs, in which almost all aspects of social life were based on shariʿa. (Hamid interview)

> Shariʿa regulates social and economic life in society. When shariʿa law is fully implemented, it is possible to control problems such as adultery,

murder, theft, and poverty. To look at it from an economic perspective, shari'a brings economic prosperity to a society. For example, shari'a rejects adultery and emphasizes marriage, as adultery destroys the social basis of a society and also damages its economic foundation. (Saeedi interview)

The more common view of shari'a is less sanguine. People see it as a model for how individuals should act, not how life really is or could be. They are less concerned about whether the national government gives precedence to state or shari'a laws than with their belief that government courts and judges are corrupt and biased, regardless of whether they employ state law codes or shari'a. In addition, the vision of creating such an ideal world through shari'a as a political project lost much of its luster under the Taliban. The implementation of what they proclaimed to be a pure shari'a system imposed so much misery on Afghanistan that they discredited the notion that shari'a was a simple cure for all of society's ills. In addition, the enthusiasm with which the Taliban imposed punishments such as amputation for theft, stoning for adultery, and the execution of homosexuals by collapsing mud walls over them was not matched by an adherence to rules of evidence or legal procedure that Islamic jurisprudence normally demanded in such cases. More significantly, the Taliban attempted to radically transform Afghan cultural and social life in the name of a shari'a system. These efforts included but were not limited to prohibitions of music, films, television, dance, and other entertainment; a demand that barbers cease shaving their customers' faces and that men's beards be of a minimum length; and prohibiting women from working or even leaving their houses without being escorted by a male relative. Defenders of shari'a could with some justice say that this was not "true shari'a" but rural Pashtun cultural values masquerading as such. But just as more moderate secular modernists find it difficult to escape the legacy of the radical Marxist policies implemented by the PDPA, which have been roundly rejected, Islamists find it difficult to shake the legacy of the Taliban.

The experience of decades of warfare in Afghanistan has meant that the question of using violence to achieve political aims is not a theoretical one. While a small minority feel that it is permissible under shari'a to commit acts of violence in jihad for the sake of Islam, a broader majority have been keen to declare that it is not. In the words of Mohammad Faridoun Soroush (interview), dean of the School of Law and Political Sciences at Herat University,

Violence is illegal and against the teachings of shari'a. All our laws strictly forbade physical as well as psychological violence. Islam strictly forbade violence whether for Islam or against it. It is unacceptable.

The Status of Women as a Zone of Contestation

The most contentious public debates on shari'a take place on issues over which Afghan society itself has long been divided, such as the rights of women. Conservatives attack Western conventions of gender equality as un-Islamic and play to rural fears that Kabul elites are once again attempting to impose an alien ideology on the countryside. This warning has become a standard element of Friday mosque sermons that rail against democracy and human rights in general on the grounds that they contradict Afghan culture and the Muslim religion. In rural areas, particularly, it is easy to link human rights and democracy with life-style changes associated with urban elites such as the adoption of Western dress, the mingling of men and women in public places, and tolerance of alcohol consumption, all of which are seen as destructive to tradition and social order.

While defenders of women's rights are mostly associated with secular modernist viewpoints in contemporary Afghanistan, liberals today often attempt to turn the tables on their opponents by accusing them of supporting traditional customary systems that violate shari'a principles. In this they follow a long line of ulama who, for more than a century, have condemned Pashtun tribal traditions that deny women their inheritance rights and allow them to be exchanged in marriage to end blood feuds. One professor of shari'a law expressed the problem this way:

> Most of our social, economic, political, and cultural practices are alien to shari'a laws. This causes shari'a to be marginalized in favor of rituals, beliefs, and traditions. Shari'a law almost lost its practical aspect in Afghan society. I should say this is not a new phenomenon. It begins in the Umayyad and Abbasid periods, where shari'a laws and practices were put aside in favor of traditions and the ruling class's wishes. If you look at Afghans, our practices, whether social or economic, sometimes contradict basic shari'a principles. For instance . . . in the social sphere of life, our behavior and practices are against shari'a. Look, when we treat a woman as property, inherit a woman as a thing, we violate the basic Qur'anic and Islamic principles. I know that in several Afghan tribes in the south and east, they inherit the woman as a commodity, and when her husband dies, she has not the right to decide for herself, and the relatives of her husband choose her another husband. They call it protection of *namus* [women's honor], only to justify this barbaric action. In terms of marriage, shari'a states that the man can see the woman before the marriage, but in our society, it is considered impossible. (Samim interview)

Educated women have also been quick to argue that conservatives who seek to restrict their freedom in the name of Islam do so in error, arguing that in fact shari'a is inherently supportive of women's rights.

> Islamic shari'a is the first law that discusses women's rights in detail among all other religions. Islam praises women and orders men to treat women with respect. God says that heaven is beneath the mother's feet. On the issue of inheritance, Islam says that women can inherit half of what a man will. It makes sense, as God made men responsible for the livelihood of women and children. I do not think it contradicts interna tional conventions. Let us think of an example. When God created the universe, it put a distance between the sun and Earth at around 150 mil- lion kilometers. Think what will happen to life on Earth if this distance increases or decreases even one kilometer. Then how can you compare the One who made such a perfect system with those who make earthly laws? No comparison at all. (Bashir interview)

Unlike neighboring countries, Afghanistan has never attempted to codify sets of laws that govern women's dress or behavior. Instead it is cultural at- titudes that define what is possible in terms of *hijab* (modest dress for women, often associated with veiling) and other women's issues.[6] For this reason many professional women, such as Mariza Basil, a former judge who now works on legal reform, argue that reforming the legal system should take a back seat to changing cultural attitudes. Even if better laws were passed, they point out, women would have little access to the court system and less faith in the judges. Basil also notes that because the issue of family law is so contentious, Afghans would rather avoid discussing it. For this reason the parliament has simply tabled proposed reforms and refused to vote on them either positively or nega- tively (Basil interview).

The Applicability of Western Models

Notwithstanding conflicts over issues surrounding the specific application of international norms to shari'a or Afghan traditions, the public discourse about the applicability of Western models in Afghanistan is generally positive. The most common position is that "if Western models respect our culture, tradi- tions, and religion, then there is no problem with their adoption and imple- mentation in Afghan society. Islam praises knowledge but opposes anarchy and corruption" (Bashir interview). This is sometimes phased more confron- tationally as "We are open to learning knowledge and science from everyone, but no one is allowed to teach us whom or what to believe in. The Western models that conform to Islamic teachings are acceptable" (Munib interview).

A still more conservative view inverts the statement: "Western models are not applicable to Islamic societies as long as they are not reformed according to Islamic traditions and shari'a" (Hamid interview).

These Afghan attitudes are shaped by the country's unique history, having avoided colonial rule and the dislocations of modernization. As a result, disputes arise over the concrete, rather than theoretical, application of Western models. This is not the case in Afghanistan's neighbors. In the former Soviet republics of Central Asia, the legacy of Russian models in language, culture, and politics remains strong. The politics of national identity there cannot be disentangled from them, and Islam is only one of many identities that compete for influence in those societies. The legacy of British colonial rule in Pakistan is strongest in its legal system and governmental organization, and Pakistani debates about the role of shari'a law run up against this inherited infrastructure. Pakistan also justified its separation from India on the grounds that South Asian Muslims needed their own state, making the role of religion there a central political issue. Iran, although not colonized by the British or Russians, developed its modern national identity in opposition to their interference in Iranian affairs. Since the revolution of 1978, Iran has also self-consciously portrayed itself as a model Islamic country in which shari'a and its implementation remain a central preoccupation. By contrast, Afghanistan's national, cultural, and religious identities are far less self-conscious. Having turned away both British and Soviet attempts to occupy the country, Afghanistan has a much more positive sense of itself as victor rather than victim. Afghans are also more secure in their religious identity: unlike Pakistan, Afghanistan never felt the political need to prove its bona fides as a Muslim society, since it could be nothing else.

Associations, Parties, and Movements

Political parties in Afghanistan today are not well developed and have been associated with their leaders rather than party platforms. President Karzai prohibited candidates for parliament in 2006 and 2010 from running as representatives of parties or political associations or from creating party slates that might have presented distinct points of view. (Karzai has repeatedly opposed the formations of political parties as "divisive" and refused to found one to support his government in parliament.) For this reason they play a relatively small role in Afghan politics.

The parties that do exist are largely products of the period of resistance to the Soviets in the 1980s. Their leaders continue, in different guises, to dominate politics today. While they often identify themselves generically as "mujahedeen" and protectors of Afghanistan's independence and Islamic values, their misrule after taking power from the PDPA in 1992 is well remembered and undermines their popular appeal. Three parties are most associated with insistence on using shari'a law in government:

> The Jamiat-i-Islami (Islamic Society) consists of moderate Islamists led by Burhanuddin Rabbani. It is mainly Tajik by ethnicity, although it has Pashtun members as well. Regionally the party dominates the northeast and west. Rabbani was president of the mujahedeen government in Kabul until he was expelled by the Taliban in 1996. After 2001 the party gained additional regional factions led by the followers of the late Ahmad Shah Masood. These included Yunus Qanuni, who formed the Afghanistan e Naween (New Afghanistan Party) and became speaker of the House of Representatives (the lower house of parliament) in 2006; Ismail Khan, the former governor of Herat; and Atta Mohammed Nur, the governor of Mazar-i-Sharif.
>
> The Islami Barai Azadi Afghanistan (Islamic Union for the Liberation of Afghanistan) is a radical Salafi party led by Abdul Rasul Sayyaf. During the Soviet war it had little broad political support, but considerable financial support from Saudi Arabia. Sayyaf became an ally of Karzai after 2001.
>
> The Hizb-i-Islami (Islamic Party), led by Gulbuddin Hekmatyar, is a radical Islamist party, mainly Pashtun and strongest in eastern Afghanistan. Although Hekmatyar has remained in armed opposition to the Karzai regime since 2001, the party has sympathizers and former members in the current government.

Two additional, more traditional parties, led by established ulama and Sufi leaders, are less politically Islamist. The Jabha-i-Najat-i-Milli Afghanistan (Afghanistan National Liberation Front) is a secular party with a Pashtun tribal base and monarchist support. It is led by Sibghatullah Mojaddedi, whose family has long led the Naqshbandiya Sufi order in Kabul. The Mahaz-i-Milli-Islami (National Islamic Front) is a royalist party led by Sayed Ahmad Gailani, whose family is descended from the leaders of the Qadiriya Sufi order. It is supported particularly by the Durrani Pashtuns in the south. Neither of these parties was strongly centralized, and much of their support fell to Karzai after 2001.

Other parties owe their strength to protecting the interests of an ethnic group or region, rather than to ideology. The two most important of these are the Wahdat-e-Mardum (People's Islamic Unity Party) and the Junbesh-i-Milli Islami (National Islamic Movement). The Wahdat-e-Mardum is a Shi'a Hazara resistance party originally founded (as the Hizb-i-Wahdat, or Islamic Unity Party) by Abdul Ali Mazari, who was killed by the Taliban in 1995. It is currently led by Haji Mohammad Mohaqiq under its new name. The Junbesh-i-Milli Islami is led by Abdul Rashid Dostum, an ethnic Uzbek whose power base is in northwestern Afghanistan. A former PDPA general and unabashed secularist, he owes his popularity among the Uzbek to having made them a force to be reckoned with in national politics. Expelled by the Taliban, he returned to northern Afghanistan as a supporter of the United States and the Karzai government.

Additionally, there are those who support (or at least sympathize with) the PDPA vision of a more secular Afghanistan, and those who support the Taliban, who envision the opposite.

While the leftist parties have largely disappeared from public view, the secular modernists have had a much higher public profile because of the aid they have received from international organizations. Civil organizations that focus on democracy, human rights, civil liberties, and women's rights are now very influential. In some ways they resemble the PDPA without its socialism. Secular candidates did surprisingly well as individuals in the 2006 parliamentary elections, playing off the resentment, in Kabul and other cities, of attempts by mujahedeen factions in government to censor the press, films, and television. Certainly the concerns they address have a long history in Afghanistan and the values they espouse are well received in urban areas, particularly Kabul. The resources and international connections that these groups access through foreign NGOs enhance their reach but at the same time make them vulnerable to critics who claim they are advocates of alien and un-Islamic cultural values. For this reason many of these groups have been keen to root concepts of international human rights in an Afghan and Islamic context. They also appeal to a new generation—the majority of Afghans were born after the Soviets left the country in 1989. This younger generation has grown tired of the same old faces and of debating issues that emerged in the 1970s.

The Taliban are the polar opposites of the secular modernists. While they do not form a party in government, their former members have little trouble fitting in with the conservative factions in parliament. They are strongest in the rural Pashtun regions of the country, where the Karzai government has either failed to establish itself or has misgoverned the local population. Those now in armed rebellion against the Karzai government would like to restore an Islamic emirate and return to the strict shari'a standards imposed a decade ago. However, the Taliban's version of shari'a mixes popular interpretations of Islam with Pashtun culture. They have dropped their unpopular prohibition of television and music that made their stern vision of pure Islamic society so unpopular when they ruled Afghanistan.

Shari'a and the State since 2001

The collapse of the PDPA government in 1992 created a political vacuum that was initially filled by the Islamist party leaders who had been based in Pakistan. But rather than creating a new Afghan state, they quickly fell into a civil war that destroyed what was left of the state structure. Political power devolved to the regions. Some, like Ismail Khan's Herat and Dostum's Mazar, became mini-states. Politics in other areas, particularly in the Pashtun east and south, verged on anarchy. And Kabul, the historical center of state power, became a battleground, much of it reduced to rubble and government institutions mere shells. The Taliban arose as a response. They drove the old mujahedeen parties from Kabul in 1996 and over the next four years took control of nine-tenths of the country. Although they pronounced shari'a to be the supreme law of land, they did nothing to codify it or institutionalize its use. Poorly educated clerics, Mullah Omar and his companions appeared to think that shari'a was self-evident: they knew it when they saw it.

In the wake of the U.S. intervention in 2001 that toppled the Taliban from power in only ten weeks, many former resistance leaders who had allied themselves with the Americans returned to the public sphere as part of the Karzai administration. They played a particularly significant role in insisting that religion take center stage in the first articles of the 2004 constitution (Islamic Republic of Afghanistan 2004).

> Article 1
> Afghanistan shall be an Islamic Republic, independent, unitary and indivisible state.
> Article 2
> The sacred religion of Islam is the religion of the Islamic Republic of Afghanistan. Followers of other faiths shall be free within the bounds of law in the exercise and performance of their religious rituals.
> Article 3
> No law shall contravene the tenets and provisions of the holy religion of Islam in Afghanistan.

These articles have not, however, given the Karzai regime a theocratic character or placed the interpretation of state laws in the hands of clerics. Like such provisions in earlier constitutions, they were understood to justify shari'a only in the absence of state laws. The constitution is also vague about who has the legal standing to challenge state laws or the standards that would be used by the court to determine their validity.

Article 130

> In cases under consideration, the courts shall apply provisions of this Constitution as well as other laws.
>
> If there is no provision in the Constitution or other laws about a case, the courts shall, in pursuance of Hanafi jurisprudence, and, within the limits set by this Constitution, rule in a way that attains justice in the best manner.

Article 121

> At the request of the Government, or courts, the Supreme Court shall review the laws, legislative decrees, international treaties as well as international covenants for their compliance with the Constitution and their interpretation in accordance with the law.

The 2004 constitution was therefore less ideological in character than it might seem. There is no constitutional court of review that gives clerics automatic veto power over legislation, as there is in Iran. And in the years since the constitution's ratification, the Afghan Supreme Court has never taken up (or even been presented with) a constitutional challenge to a law or government regulation, even though some (like that permitting interest charges on loans) would seem easy targets. Nor has the Karzai government come under any serious criticism for this lapse. The explanation for this lack of concern lies in the Afghan perspective on what role Islam should play in government.

Afghans have historically assumed that an Islamic government is a government composed of good Muslims, not one that takes a particular ideological stance. Since Afghans also believe that good Muslims will naturally do the right thing, they have focused on the overall tone of the state laws rather than their jurisprudential specifics. Abdul Majid Samim, a professor of shari'a law at Herat University, explained it this way:

> Regarding the legitimacy of laws in Afghanistan, I should say that in our laws we tried to keep a delicate balance between shari'a laws and principles of democracy. The lawyers and ulama who wrote our present constitution and laws managed to model them on the Egyptian system, which is based on shari'a but must be approved through a democratic process in the parliament. The entire process, from drafting the constitution, through discussion in parliament, to ratification by the president, indicates a democratic process. Although I cannot say it is perfect, it is very encouraging. If you look at our civil laws, 80 percent of them are based on shari'a and Islamic jurisprudence. Only 20 percent are copied from non-Islamic sources. When a law is discussed in the parliament, if it is a law that does not contradict the basics of Islam and shari'a, then we cannot call it un-Islamic. The Prophet says, "When the Muslim com-

munity considers an issue acceptable, God accepts it too." I believe a Muslim community never accepts a law that contradicts the principles of Islam. (Samim interview)

Conflict has arisen not over principles but over the application of the laws. After 2001 the judiciary remained composed of Taliban holdovers and so represented a conservative shari'a stronghold where Sayyaf's faction, in particular, had considerable power. Rather than fight over constitutional issues in principle, conservatives instead simply attempted to maintain their existing stranglehold on the judicial branch of government through their members. The struggle over principles was double-edged: many of the existing judges lacked formal training in shari'a law and would be hard put to justify their decisions using it. Rather than move against the existing structure, Karzai instead attempted to appease Sayyaf and other conservatives by keeping them on in powerful positions. This provided an opening for Karzai's opponents in the parliament to use their power of confirmation to challenge both him and Sayyaf. In March 2006 parliament refused to confirm the serving chief justice of the Supreme Court, Fazel Hadi Shinwari, because he was seen as too conservative and had no higher education, which the constitution set as a requirement. He was replaced by the US.-educated Abdul Salam Azimi, a technocrat more sympathetic to state law codes than shari'a. While his appointment did not immediately change the overall composition of the judiciary, it made it more difficult for conservatives to use the courts to veto laws as un-Islamic, because the new chief justice was far less likely to entertain such challenges than his predecessor even if they did arise.

Conclusion

It has often been said that fish take the water they swim in for granted. Analyzing shari'a in the context of Afghanistan presents similar difficulties. If one asks rural Afghans, in particular, how they solve problems or organize their affairs, the answer they provide invariably refers to shari'a. But as many of the urban commentators quoted above, particularly those well trained in shari'a law, have noted, what these rural Afghans are really referencing is their own customary understanding of Islamic values. Such understandings are often highly idiosyncratic and have little grounding in the sophisticated urban traditions that gave rise to Islamic jurisprudence. On the other hand, the belief that shari'a is a way of acting that leads to greater equity, social justice, and general harmony, that it substitutes reason for violence, and that it protects Muslims from tyranny when properly employed produces a powerful ethical system. Proponents of international human rights are correct in believing that the way to instill respect for what appear to be alien concepts is to root them in an existing Islamic tradition.

Over the past thirty years Afghans have suffered at the hands of those who believe they have the right to impose absolute values upon others. For this reason, totalizing ideologies—whether of Islamic or non-Islamic origin—are met with suspicion. Because Islam in Afghanistan is still considered an all-encompassing way of life, it cannot be reduced to a form of ideology. Issues that spark debate in other Islamic countries, and that originated in those countries' experiences with colonialism, nationalism, rapid economic change, and mass urbanization, have only pale echoes in Afghanistan. Afghans see themselves as Muslims living in a land of Muslims. They have been invaded by outsiders but have always outlasted them. This has left them secure in their cultural identities and given them a belief in themselves. In Afghanistan shari'a remains just another part of life, to be integrated into a larger mosaic.

Notes

1. Shi'ism became dominant in Iran under the Safavids in the sixteenth century, and the Jafari legal school took root there at that time. By contrast, Muslims in Afghanistan, central Asia, and South Asia remained predominantly Sunni. Rulers there gave primacy to the long-existing Hanafi legal school as a way to highlight their own orthodoxy and to set themselves off from Iran.

2. Article 131 of the Afghan constitution provides that "the courts shall apply the Shia jurisprudence in cases involving personal matters of followers of the Shia sect in accordance with the provisions of the law. In other cases, if no clarification in this Constitution and other laws exist, the courts shall rule according to laws of this sect."

3. Ironically, the People's Democratic Party of Afghanistan attempted to create such a codification and teach it in Kabul. Although it was viewed as intellectually sound, it lacked legitimacy because a communist government had sponsored it.

4. For example, the amir once demanded that a mullah be put to death because he had preached that Muslims must regard Christians as brothers since they were "people of the book." The first council of clerics who heard the case refused, finding the mullah innocent of any charge of heresy. A second panel called to try the case again could muster only two clerics willing to uphold the death penalty even after the amir made his wishes clear. One would have probably sufficed, since the amir immediately used this minority opinion to have the offending cleric stoned to death (Kakar 1979, 178–79).

5. Afghanistan has ratified and is accordingly bound by the following relevant instruments: the Geneva Conventions of 1949 (acceded 1956); the Genocide Convention of 1948 (acceded 1956); the Convention on Non-applicability of Statutory Limitations to War Crimes and Crimes against Humanity of 1968 (acceded 1983); the Convention on the Elimination of All Forms of Discrimination against Women of 1979 (acceded 1980); the International Covenant on Civil and Political Rights of 1966 (acceded 1983,

but not to the optional protocol); the Convention on the Elimination of All Forms of Racial Discrimination of 1966 (acceded 1983); the Convention against Torture and Other Cruel, Inhuman, Degrading Treatment or Punishment of 1984 (ratified 1987); and the Convention on the Rights of the Child of 1989 (ratified 1994).

6. For example, it has been widely noted that President Karzai refuses to let his wife make public appearances, although as a physician she could serve as an important role model.

Interviews

Bashir, Maria. Head of the attorney general's office, Province of Herat. Interview by Salahudine Aryapur. August 2008.

Basil, Mariza. Former judge. Interview by Thomas Barfield. August 2008.

Faisal, Qazi Abdul Qadir. Judge in the Secondary Court of Takhar. Interview by Thomas Barfield. April 2006.

Hamid, Mir Hamad. Dean of the Arabic Department, Shari'a Faculty, Nangrahar University. Interview by Sapad. August 2006.

Munib, Asrar ul Hai. Vice-chancellor of the Shari'a Faculty, Nangrahar University. Interview by Sapad. August 2008.

Na'aimy, Ataullah. Lecturer, Nangrahar University. Interview by Abdul Jabar Sapand. August 2006.

Saeedi, Mowlavi Saeed Ul Rahman. Department of Hajj and Religious Affairs. Interview by Abdul Jabar Sapand. August 2006.

Samim, Abdul Mjid. Head of the Islamic Studies Department, Shari'a Faculty, Herat University. Interview by Salahudine Aryapur. August 2008.

Soroush, Mohammad Faridoun. Dean of the School of Law and Political Sciences, Herat University. Interview by Salahudine Aryapur. August 2008.

Wafa, Nik Mohammad. Deputy district attorney, Mazar-i-Sharif. Interview by Thomas Barfield. April 2006.

References Cited

Arnold, Anthony. 1983. *Afghanistan's Two-Party Communism: Parcham and Khalq.* Stanford: Hoover Institution Press, Stanford University.

Barfield, Thomas. 1984. "Weak Links on a Rusty Chain." In *Revolutions and Rebellions in Afghanistan*, ed. Nasif Sharani and Robert Canfield, 139–69. Berkeley: Institute of International Studies.

———. 2008. "Culture and Custom in Nation-Building: Law in Afghanistan." *Maine Law Review* 60 (2): 347–73.

———. 2010. *Afghanistan: A Cultural and Political History.* Princeton: Princeton University Press.

Dupree, Louis. 1980. *Afghanistan.* Princeton: Princeton University Press.

Giustozzi, Antonio. 2000. *War, Politics and Society in Afghanistan.* Washington, D.C.: Georgetown University Press.

Gregorian, Vartan. 1969. *The Emergence of Modern Afghanistan*. Stanford: Stanford University Press.

ICG (International Crisis Group). 2002. *Pakistan: Madrasas, Extremism and the Military*. ICG Asia Report no. 36, July 29.

Islamic Republic of Afghanistan. 2004. *Constitution of Afghanistan*. Adopted by the Constitutional Loya Jirga on January 4. Unofficial translation. http://www.supremecourt.gov.af/PDFiles/constitution2004_english.pdf.

Kakar, Hasan. 1979. *Government and Society in Afghanistan: The Reign of Amir Abd al-Rahman Khan*. Austin: University of Texas Press.

Kamali, Mohammad Hashim. 1985. *Law in Afghanistan*. Leiden: Brill.

Khalil, Muhammad. 2001. "Egypt's Mufti Wasil Interviewed on Recent Visit to Afghanistan." *Al-Sharq al-Awsat*, London, March 20. In Arabic. http://www.lexis-nexis.com/.

Matinuddin, Kamal. 1999. *The Taliban Phenomenon*. Oxford: Oxford University Press.

Morarjee, Rachel, and Dan Murphy. 2006. "Conversion a Thorny Issue in Muslim World." *Christian Science Monitor*, March 27.

Munadi, Sultan M. 2006. "Mental Health Evaluation May Derail Case against Afghan Convert to Christianity." *New York Times*, March 27.

Nawid, Senzil. 1999. *Religious Response to Social Change in Afghanistan, 1919–29*. Costa Mesa, Calif.: Mazda.

Olesen, Asta. 1995. *Islam and Politics in Afghanistan*. Richmond, Surrey: Curzon.

Radio Free Europe. 2008. "Afghanistan: Journalist Given Death Sentence for 'Blasphemy.'" *Radio Free Europe/Radio Liberty*, January 23. http://www.rferl.org/content/article/1079389.html (accessed July 15, 2010).

Roy, Olivier. 1990. *Islam and Resistance in Afghanistan*. 2nd ed. Cambridge: Cambridge University Press.

———. 1995. *Afghanistan from Holy War to Civil War*. Princeton, N.J.: Darwin.

6. Pakistan

Shariʿa and the State

Muhammad Qasim Zaman

In the aftermath of the terrorist attacks of September 11, 2001, Pakistan received a great deal of international attention. The Pakistani government and military had close relations with the Taliban of Afghanistan, but were forced to abruptly change course after 9/11 as they became part of the U.S.-led War on Terror. The social, religious, and political impact of this shift (and questions about the degree to which such a shift has, indeed, been effected), continuing political and economic instability, the government's inability to regulate the activities of the country's twenty thousand or so madrasas, and the rise of a deadly insurgency with its strident conceptions of the shariʿa in parts of Pakistan's Khyber Pakhtunkhwa province—these and other changes have all brought Pakistan very much to the center of international attention in journalistic, scholarly, and policy circles.[1]

This essay is not primarily concerned with these broad-stroke political developments, however, but rather with evolving debates on the shariʿa among Pakistani Muslims of varied intellectual and religio-political orientations. Such debates make up a crucial part of the larger context in which contemporary contestations on Islam and politics in Pakistan ought to be understood. Who are the major contributors to these debates? How have the particular orientations to which they belong evolved in modern South Asia? What are some key themes in discourses on the shariʿa in Pakistan? How have questions relating to the reform of particular shariʿa norms been addressed in the Pakistani context? And why have modernist approaches to the shariʿa been considerably less successful, as this chapter suggests, than conceptions endorsed by Islamists and the ulama? These are among the questions this essay seeks to address.[2]

The Shari'a in British India

From the late eighteenth to the mid-twentieth century, conceptions and practices related to the shari'a were shaped in highly significant ways by the British
presence in South Asia. With the passing of the rich and populous province
of Bengal, in eastern India, into the control of the East India Company in the
mid-eighteenth century, the British were confronted with the need to devise
a system of judicial administration for the local inhabitants. Regulation 2 of
1772 provided that "in all suits regarding Inheritance, Marriage, Caste and all
other religious Usages or Institutions, the Laws of the Koran with respect to
Mahometans, and those of the Shaster with respect to the Gentoos [Hindus]
shall be invariably adhered to" (quoted in Travers 2007, 118). English judges'
ignorance of Islamic and Hindu law had initially necessitated that they be assisted by Hindu and Muslim scholars and jurists, a practice that continued until 1864. The British, however, had a low opinion of these native officers of the
court and, as the colonial judicial administration evolved, the judges came to
base their rulings not on the advice of indigenous legal assistants but rather on
a small body of what colonial officials saw as the uniquely authoritative com-
pendia of religious law. The result of this marriage of Islamic legal texts and
English common law, as administered by mostly non-Muslim judges, was the
Anglo-Muhammadan Law, which still serves as the basis of the legal system of
Pakistan and, so far as Muslims are concerned, of India as well. Though limited to matters of personal status (in particular, marriage, divorce, and inheritance), this was the "shariat" (Ar. *shari'a*) as the British in India understood it.

This highly circumscribed and, in many ways, novel shari'a did not, however, extend to all parts of India. The princely states, whose autonomy the
British had recognized when the rest of the Indian subcontinent had come
under formal British rule, had their own legal norms—including, in some
cases where the ruler of the principality was a Muslim, ones derived from
the shari'a. And regions like the Muslim-majority province of the Punjab—
now the most populous of Pakistan's four provinces—would long continue
to be subject to local customary norms rather than to the prescriptions of the
shari'a.

British colonial conceptions of the shari'a came to be broadly shared by
Muslim modernists, a new and growing segment of the colonial Muslim
population, many of whom were educated in newly established institutions
of Western learning in India or, in some cases, in England. But there were important differences. Unlike the British, Muslim modernists tended to believe
that the "spirit" of Islam, properly understood, could be shown to be compatible with Western liberal values and that particular Muslim norms and institutions ought to be reinterpreted in the interest of such compatibility. They

also believed that, in essence, Islamic law was dynamic rather than static and, consequently, that it was capable of responding to changing times. It needed, however, to be reformed in order to regain its true spirit, its dynamism (see, for example, C. Ali 1883; M. Iqbal 1934, 139–70).

Though many Muslim modernists were trained in the English common law tradition, this view of the dynamism of Islam was in obvious tension with the premises of the colonial legal system. For all the changes in conception and practice that the shari'a underwent in colonial India, British officials liked to think that the shari'a, as administered by colonial courts, was true to how the great medieval authorities had conceived of it. This meant that new constructions of the law, which diverged from the views enumerated in the Islamic legal handbooks recognized in colonial courts, were often inadmissible (Fyzee 2003, 82). Such colonial conceptions of the law were in partial and unintended accord with, and tended to strengthen, the views of the traditionally educated Muslim religious scholars, the ulama, who had long been committed to affirming the authority of their juristic forbears. Muslim modernists, on the other hand, wanted to rethink particular norms, to demonstrate the compatibility of Islam with modern liberal values, to reform their communities, and, not least, to improve Western opinions of Islam. None of this could be achieved by allowing the shari'a to be practiced "unchanged."[3]

But if the modernists and the ulama disagreed with each other in their views of the legal tradition, they did agree on the need to extend the reach of the shari'a in colonial India. This did not usually mean putting into effect elements of Islamic law no longer recognized in British courts, for instance, criminal law. Rather, it meant extending the shari'a—as understood by colonial officials—to communities that had previously not been governed by it. Among the most important of such regions was the Punjab in northern India. Here the British had recognized the practices of the province's "agricultural tribes" as the basis of the law, which meant that the transfer of property outside these tribes was severely restricted and, in stark conflict with the detailed provisions of the Qur'an, women did not have a share in inheritance. Though the Punjab's rural magnates were often opposed to being subjected to shari'a norms on matters of inheritance—which would have meant endless fragmentation of their holdings—Muslims in urban Punjab as well as elsewhere in India were keen to see un-Islamic customary norms give way to the shari'a. This was a popular and symbolically powerful cause and, under the leadership of Muhammad 'Ali Jinnah (d. 1948), who would soon emerge as the leader of the movement for a separate Muslim homeland, it led to the enactment of the Shariat Application Act of 1937.

Significantly, in shepherding the bill through the Central Legislative Assembly, Jinnah had no great qualms about excluding inheritance to lands defined as "agricultural" from its purview. This meant that, while the Punjab formally came to be governed by the norms of the shariʿa, customary practices continued to be in effect in the rural areas of this predominantly rural province (Gilmartin 1988, 169–74). Jinnah was guided by his pragmatic recognition that this strategic concession would garner the support of the landholding elite for the bill, as well as that of the colonial government, whose interests in the Punjab were tied to this elite. Yet, as David Gilmartin has argued, it also illustrates a key difference in how the modernists and the ulama—who had both wanted to see Islamic law extended to the Punjab—have tended to view the shariʿa. "The key to Jinnah's ultimate success in leading the bill through the assembly was his realization that . . . the details of the bill . . . were less important than the symbolic value of the bill as an expression of the common 'communal' identity of all of India's Muslims" (Gilmartin 1988, 172). The ulama, for their part, were scarcely indifferent to matters of religious symbolism, yet the substantive content of the shariʿa was at least as important to them as its symbolic appeal; and to tailor the shariʿa to considerations of political expediency was, in their view, to make a mockery of it.

The ulama represented a rich tradition of scholarship on Islamic law, which they continued into colonial times and beyond (Zaman 2002). In British India, they had come to be divided into a number of rival doctrinal orientations, among the most influential of which was the Deobandi, centered on a loose network of madrasas, the first of which was founded in 1867 in the north Indian town of Deoband.[4] Irrespective of doctrinal orientation, however, and while significantly influenced by colonial conceptions of the law, the ulama were deeply perturbed by how Islamic law had fared in British India. As Muhammad Anwarshah Kashmiri, a leading Deobandi scholar, put it in 1927, "The Muhammadan Law [sic] . . . that is practiced under the British government is so defective that calling it Muhammadan shariʿa law [qanun-i sharʿ-i Muhammadi] is tantamount to insulting the shariʿa. This is because, in observing its defects, an uninformed person might come to believe that the shariʿa itself is inadequate and defective" (Kashmiri 1980, 1:430–31).

The ulama's misgivings about the colonial shariʿa sprang, inter alia, from its mode of implementation in British India. Unlike the modernists, the ulama tended to believe that Islamic law could be implemented only by a shariʿa-based judge (qadi) or, at least, by a judge who was Muslim. For instance, it was only a Muslim judge who could validly dissolve the marriage of a woman whose husband had gone missing. In the 1920s and 1930s, many ulama gradually came to recognize that informally constituted local committees of righteous Muslims could, in certain cases, stand in for the qadi. This could help address some of the problems resulting from the absence of Muslim judges and, to them, it was clearly preferable to resorting to colonial non-Muslim judges. In contemporary India, many Deobandi and other ulama have had a similar view.

It was not just a question of who, Muslim judges or non-Muslims, implemented shari'a norms, however. As noted, the ulama were also profoundly distrustful of how Muslim modernists viewed the shari'a. Since the late nineteenth century, a chorus of modernist voices had been calling for reform of various aspects of Islam and Islamic law, from polygyny and female seclusion to the "blind imitation" (taqlid) of past authorities. Yet polygyny was sanctioned by the foundational texts themselves. And taqlid—which, to many ulama, carries no pejorative connotations but signifies, rather, a principled adherence to the agreed-upon methods and doctrines of their school—was a defense against precisely the sort of capricious interpretations of the sacred law that the modernists were thought to indulge in. Jinnah's willingness to compromise on who would or would not be governed by his shari'a bill had again confirmed the ulama in some of their worst fears. An important segment of the Deobandi ulama was allied with the Indian National Congress, a Hindu-dominated but secular political party that claimed to represent the people of India as a whole. This might seem odd, but these ulama saw—and their successors have continued to see—secularism not only as compatible with Islam but, in the Indian context, as necessary for the preservation of Muslim identity and culture. They were especially distrustful of Jinnah and his Muslim League. But even among those who supported rather than opposed the demand for a separate Muslim homeland under Jinnah's leadership, there was some apprehension that the modernists might be rather less constrained than colonial officials in subverting Islamic norms in the new Muslim homeland (Zaman 2008a, 121, 35–56).

Such worries perturbed Islamists such as Sayyid Abu'l A'la Mawdudi (d. 1979), who had founded his Jama'at-i Islami in 1941, even more than they did the ulama. After all, the ulama had learnt centuries ago to make their peace with iniquitous governments as long as the latter allowed them sufficient space in which to provide religious guidance to the community. The ulama, too, sought a ruler who would uphold and implement shari'a norms, of course, but many among them believed that they could manage in the absence of such a ruler. It was on this basis that they had accommodated themselves to British colonial rule in India, and a similar conviction guided those who decided to live in a Hindu-majority secular India rather than move to Pakistan at the time of the partition of the Indian subcontinent in 1947. Mawdudi, however, had a very different view. To him, it was political leadership that defined the fundamental orientation of the people it governed, and it was impossible to imagine a virtuous society, living according to God's law, if "the reins of State are in the hands of agnostic and evil men" (Maududi 1976, 3; cf. Maududi 1960, 67).

Loci of Shari'a Discourse in Pakistan

The Modernists

Contrary to Mawdudi's strictures, Muslim modernists have never seen themselves as being unfaithful to Islamic norms. Nor, for that matter, have they necessarily advocated secularism in the sense of a clear separation of the religious and the political. For all the ambiguities of Jinnah's numerous invocations of Islam in the course of the movement for a separate Muslim homeland, he left little doubt among his audiences that Islam would play an important public role in the new state. This view has been repeatedly affirmed by the modernist elite since the earliest days of independence. The Objectives Resolution, adopted by the Constituent Assembly of Pakistan in 1949, laid down, for instance, that "sovereignty over the entire universe belongs to God Almighty alone" and that "Muslims shall be enabled to order their lives in the individual and collective spheres in accord with the teaching and requirements of Islam as set out in the Holy Quran and the Sunna" (for the text of this document, see Binder 1963, 142–43). Successive Pakistani constitutions have made similar pronouncements, and many judges of Pakistan's higher courts, especially from the late 1960s, have frequently invoked Islam in ruling on various laws and executive measures (Lau 2006, 9).

In Pakistan as elsewhere, the modernist governing elite have sought to reform particular institutions and practices in accordance with what they take to be the spirit of the Qur'an and how it ought to be adapted to changing needs. A major example of this is the Muslim Family Laws Ordinance of 1961, enacted under the military regime of General Ayub Khan, which placed severe restrictions on polygyny besides introducing some changes in the Islamic laws of inheritance. The reasoning underlying these measures was that, properly understood, the ethical teachings of Islam not merely justified but necessitated them. Thus, while Qur'an 4:3 allows a man to be concurrently married to up to four women, it also stipulates that the husband ought to be equitable toward his wives; later in the same chapter, the Qur'an notes that it is not possible to treat one's wives with "equal fairness." The standard modernist argument on this matter has been that the Qur'an, while recognizing the need for polygyny in extreme circumstances, essentially points toward its abolition, so that legislation in that direction cannot be deemed un-Islamic.

Modernist initiatives have emerged from the executive branch of the government, as did the 1961 Muslim Family Laws Ordinance, more often than they have from the parliament. That the country has long been governed by military or quasi-military regimes goes a long way toward accounting for this. More recently, much of the initiative and backing for the Protection of Women

(Criminal Laws Amendment) Act 2006 came from the military regime of General Pervez Musharraf (1999–2008), though it was a pro-Musharraf majority in the parliament that formally enacted this law. More will be said on this legislation and the controversies surrounding it later in this chapter.

Both the executive and the legislature have been assisted in their deliberations on Islamic law by the Council of Islamic Ideology. Since its establishment in 1962, the Council has addressed queries from the government on whether particular laws are in conformity with the Qur'an and the normative example (Sunna) of the Prophet Muhammad. Since the late 1970s, when the Islamizing regime of General Muhammad Zia al-Haqq came to power (1977–88), it has also concerned itself with comprehensively reviewing all existing legislation to ascertain its accord with Islamic norms. Members of the council have been drawn from the higher judiciary, religious intellectuals, and the ranks of the ulama, though the latter have always been outnumbered by others. The council was clearly envisaged by Pakistan's multiple constitutions as a modernist site on which matters relating to Islam would be debated with a view to guiding public policy. It has frequently lived up to this intention, providing advice to the government as well as a veneer of legitimacy, by way of Islamic reasoning, for particular modernizing initiatives. The very name of its recently launched journal, Ijtihad (2007–), bespeaks its modernist stance in seeking to rethink Islamic legal norms and arrive at new legal rulings. Its close identification with, and dependence on, the government has allowed it to express modernist views despite the opposition of many Islamists and ulama. By the same token, such dependence has also had an adverse effect on its standing in some religious circles.

The Pakistani higher courts represent another site for the articulation of modernist discourse. Pakistani judges have not enjoyed the same security of tenure that judges in many other countries take for granted, however, as illustrated, for instance, by the dismissal of the chief justice of the Supreme Court of Pakistan by President Musharraf in March 2007.[5] Given their Westernized legal training, lawyers and judges have often also been reluctant, as one retired judge of the Supreme Court put it, to learn the intricacies of Islamic law late in their careers (K. Khan 2007, 36). They have not been averse to asserting what the Qur'an and the Sunna "really" mean on particular issues and invoking their right to ijtihad in doing so. Yet, lacking any credible grounding in the Islamic legal tradition, they have often been vulnerable to severe challenges by the Islamists and the ulama on this score. More often than not, they have looked to the executive branch of the government for guidance on how to rule on matters relating to Islamic law. This has been the case not only with the Pakistani higher courts in general but also with the Federal Shari'at Court and the Shari'at Appellate Bench of the Supreme Court, both comprising judges

from the higher courts alongside some ulama and both established as part of
General Zia al-Haqq's effort to Islamize the country's legal system.

Institutions of higher learning might have been expected to provide fertile
ground for modernist thought as well, but they have seldom done so. In part,
this is attributable to the persistent weakness of the public education system
in Pakistan. But it also has to do, in no small measure, with two other factors.
First, much as in the case of the higher judiciary, those in the humanities and
the social sciences have often lacked the opportunity for any sustained exposure to the Islamic intellectual and religious tradition, with the result that their
ability to engage with this tradition remains limited (Qureshi 1975, 114–21). Second, and despite the prominence of Islam in official discourse, the study of
Islam remains a highly contentious matter and those concerned with devising
the country's educational policies have often preferred to limit themselves to
fostering a broad if superficial consensus on what they take to be fundamental
Islamic norms (cf. Nelson 2009). In a pattern familiar in other Muslim societies as well, many modernist and Islamist intellectuals have had little formal
training in Islamic studies, that is, little instruction in the Islamic sciences, at
the institutions at which they were educated. Javed Ahmad Ghamidi (b. 1951),
a prominent religious intellectual in contemporary Pakistan, is one example.
Though he is best known for his extensive writings on the Qur'an, Ghamidi's
formal education consists only of a B.A. Honors in English from Government
College, Lahore, a colonial-era institution of Western learning. Ghamidi is,
indeed, a serious scholar of the Arabic language and the Qur'an, but his Islamic learning derives entirely from informal study with Amin Ahsan Islahi
(d. 1997), a leading Qur'an exegete who was once associated with Mawdudi
and his Jama'at-i Islami (Masud 2007, 357–58). Many modernists have followed
an educational path not dissimilar to Ghamidi's, without, however, the benefit
of the sort of further studies with which he has supplemented it.

While opponents of Muslim modernists frequently paint them in dark,
broad-brush strokes, it is worth reminding ourselves both that the differences
between the modernists, the Islamists, and the ulama are not always very precise and that the modernists frequently differ considerably among themselves.
Like the Islamists, the modernists seek to derive their norms directly from
the Islamic foundational texts, largely unmediated by centuries of scholarly
discourse on these texts and norms. Yet some modernists, such as the noted
scholar Fazlur Rahman (d. 1988), were able, when necessary, to demonstrate
considerable grounding in the scholarly tradition.[6] On the Islamist side, the
same was largely true of Mawdudi, which, in turn, underlay his considerable success in making common cause with the ulama on questions relating to the place of Islam in Pakistan. That Ghamidi himself was associated
with ulama like Amin Ahsan Islahi, and at least some of Ghamidi's associates

combine a madrasa education with Western learning, again suggests the lack of sharp boundaries between various orientations. Nor are Ghamidi's own positions necessarily "modernist" in all instances (Masud 2007). Like Rahman, Ghamidi has sought to considerably restrict the authority of the hadith as a source of legal and religious norms, thereby facilitating the revaluation of legal norms. He has argued against capital punishment for apostasy (Masud 2007, 370), and he has also been at the forefront of those calling for amending the much-criticized Hudood Ordinances promulgated by General Zia al-Haqq in 1979. Yet Ghamidi is far more interested in explicating the teachings of the Qur'an than he is in making a case for their compatibility with the modern world. While he is keen to limit the scope of Qur'anic punishments, he does not rule out their application in particular instances (Ghamidi 2008, 609–30). Unlike Rahman, who, in the 1960s, offered detailed arguments showing that modern forms of financial interest were not the usury (*riba*) forbidden by the Qur'an, Ghamidi takes all forms of financial interest to be forbidden (Rahman 1964; Ghamidi 2008, 508–12). To the extent that Ghamidi might be seen as a modernist, he is an uncertain member of that fragmented camp. His work also illustrates, perhaps, the considerable distance Pakistani modernism has traveled in a conservative direction since the days of intellectuals like Fazlur Rahman.

The Ulama and the Islamists

It would not be an exaggeration to say that intramodernist disagreements pale in comparison with contestations within the ranks of the ulama. There is a long history of polemic and conflict between the Sunnis and the Shi'a, of course, but the divisions between the Deobandis, the Barelawis, and the Ahl-i Hadith—all of whom emerged as distinct doctrinal orientations within the Sunni community in colonial India—have been no less intense. In late colonial India, the Deobandis themselves were bitterly divided on the question of whether or not to support the demand for a separate Muslim homeland, as has been seen. Islamists such as Mawdudi and his followers have also had difficult relations with the ulama, and not just with the Deobandis. Despite their many disagreements, however, most ulama—at least among the Sunnis—as well as the Islamists profess to agree that the public implementation of Islamic norms provides much of the rationale for the establishment of Pakistan. To the extent that they have been able to submerge their differences under a veneer of unity, it is this rhetorical position that has provided that veneer. And they have exercised considerable influence on the modernist elite from this vantage.

This influence is reflected, for instance, in the aforementioned Objectives Resolution as well as in the Islamic provisions of Pakistan's successive constitutions (1956, 1962, 1973). The head of the state must be a Muslim, the government must "enable" people to live according to Islamic norms, and no laws should be "repugnant" to the teachings of the Qur'an and the Sunna. In 1974, the government of Zulfiqar 'Ali Bhutto (1972–77) bowed to pressure from the ulama and the Islamists in declaring the Ahmadis to be non-Muslims. Though the Ahmadis view themselves as Muslims, they see the founder of their community, Mirza Ghulam Ahmad (d. 1908), as a prophet, thereby contravening the Muslim consensus that Muhammad was the last of God's prophets. Though hardly known for personal piety, Bhutto's government shepherded through the parliament a constitutional amendment which defined a "Muslim" in such a way that the Ahmadis were unambiguously excluded.

General Zia al-Haqq went further than any previous head of the government in his promises to publicly implement Islamic law. In 1979, he promulgated a series of hudud (or "hudood") laws, purporting to impose Qur'anic penalties for drinking, theft, brigandage, fornication and adultery (zina), and the false accusation of adultery. He took measures to "Islamize" public education and the economy, and he established the aforementioned Federal Shari'at Court and the Shari'at Appellate Bench of the Supreme Court. Nor was this the end of state initiatives toward Islamizing what had long professed to be an Islamic Republic. In 1991, Prime Minister Muhammad Nawaz Sharif oversaw, with much fanfare, the passage of the Enforcement of Shari'ah Act to further underscore his government's commitment to the implementation of Islamic norms (for the text, see Mehdi 1994).

Even as measures such as those of Zulfiqar 'Ali Bhutto, Zia al-Haqq, and Nawaz Sharif have been influenced by the ulama and the Islamists, they represent a serious dilemma for many in the latter camps. After he became prime minister a second time in 1997, Nawaz Sharif campaigned vigorously for a constitutional amendment that would make it possible to approve future constitutional amendments not through the cautious procedure laid down in the 1973 constitution, but rather through a simple majority in each house of the parliament or, failing that, a simple majority in a joint session of the parliament. This new procedure was ostensibly meant to finally remove "any impediment in the enforcement of any matter relating to the Shariah" (Dawn 1998). That such measures served to enhance the power and reach of the executive more than they Islamized the country is seldom lost on the ulama, however. For their part, the latter have been fiercely jealous of the autonomy of their institutions, and they have resisted government regulation, e.g., of their madrasas, even by regimes toward which they have been generally well disposed. Furthermore, as the ulama and the Islamists clearly recognize, the interpretation and implementation of "Islamic" norms has typically been the preserve of the modernist judges, bureaucrats, and politicians, which means that when these modernists are not seen as resisting the implementation of Islamic norms, they are viewed as putting them into effect according to their own whims and in pursuit of their own goals.

Many among Pakistan's leading ulama and Islamists have nonetheless been frequently willing to cooperate with the governing elite in matters relating to the implementation of Islamic norms. And they have made some surprising concessions in this regard. The draft of Pakistan's first constitution had entrusted the country's highest court with the function of ruling on whether particular laws were repugnant to the teachings of the Qur'an and the Sunna. The ulama and the Islamists had accepted that the court should have the final say on the matter, in spite of the fact that modernist judges of the court were not known for being sympathetic to them (Binder 1963, esp. 336–38). For all their Islamic provisions, moreover, Pakistani constitutions have been remarkably vague on precisely how Islamic norms would be implemented in the country. The ulama and the Islamists have nonetheless been generally willing to see these constitutions as Islamic, and they have usually focused their energies not on contesting this constitutional and political framework but rather on having successive Pakistani governments live up to their constitutional obligations.

Many among the ulama and the Islamists have often also been cautious in resisting what they see as the government's un-Islamic measures. They have denounced such measures in no uncertain terms, yet they have usually, though not invariably, sought to avoid a direct confrontation with the government. Such caution may be taken to suggest a recognition of the limits on their political influence and—in marked contrast with the stance of militant groups in contemporary Pakistan—their distaste for radical challenges to constituted political authority. It also reflects considerable pragmatism in their approach toward politics: working, despite reservations, with the governing elite to further Islamic causes; and, when there are limited avenues to this end, striving to foster public opinion against the "un-Islamic" positions of the government as a way of pressuring it. The latter strategy has not necessarily strengthened the electoral prospects of the ulama and the Islamists, which suggests that ordinary voters have often failed to be persuaded by any simple equation between the implementation of the shari'a and a vote for the religious groups. It also suggests that many people have misgivings about the implementation of the shari'a as either the ulama or the Islamists understand it. At the same time, however, the ulama and the Islamists have often succeeded in putting the governing elite on the defensive in matters relating to Islam, and this even when they have been unable to dislodge particular modernist legal enactments.

Dominant Themes in Shariʿa Discourse

What precisely are the issues that have figured prominently in the discourses on the shariʿa, so far as the ulama and the Islamists are concerned? Foremost among these is the idea that, since it is God's law, Muslims have no choice in whether or not to submit to the shariʿa. The question of whether the shariʿa should be implemented is therefore illegitimate in a Muslim society (Maududi 1960, 67; M. T. ʿUthmani 1993, 8 and passim), the more so in what professes to be an Islamic republic. The real question then becomes how the shariʿa ought to be put into effect. Here the ulama have insisted that they, as scholars of Islamic law, ought to have oversight over the processes whereby shariʿa norms are enacted into law and codified. Significantly, however, they have seldom disputed the idea that the shariʿa can or should be codified—a remarkable adaptation to evolving conceptions of the law given that, for much of its history, the shariʿa is best viewed not as a "code" in the European continental sense but rather as an ongoing, multi-faceted discourse on how to discern, interpret, and live according to Islamic legal and ethical norms (see Robert Hefner's introduction to this volume). They insist that God is the ultimate lawmaker, but they also recognize that it is through human legislation that this law can be implemented. The ulama have been rather more willing than the Islamists to allow a role for human understanding in the articulation of divine law (Zahid al-Rashidi et al. 2007, 61–63). But even Islamist ideologues like Mawdudi granted that there are parts of Islamic law that are "subject to modification according to the needs and requirements of the changing times and [that] it is this part . . . which endows it with wide possibilities of growth and advancement" (Maududi 1960, 61–62). On the other hand, there are the "unalterable" laws, viz., those "laid down in explicit and unambiguous terms in the Qurʾan or the authentic Tradition of the Prophet, like the prohibition of alcoholic drinks, interest and gambling, the punishments prescribed for adultery and theft and the rules of inheritance etc." (Maududi 1960, 60). In this respect, there is not much difference between the views of the Islamists and those of the ulama and, for that matter, little dispute among the ulama themselves.

The views the ulama and Islamists hold on particular aspects of Islamic law often follow from these positions. As Mawdudi's statement suggests, rules relating to the rights of women, for instance, would fall into the category of immutable laws, so that any effort to prohibit or severely restrict polygyny—as the Muslim Family Laws Ordinance did—when the Qurʾan allows it would be illegitimate. Dealings in financial interest, which Islamists and most ulama see as categorically prohibited by the Qurʾan, would likewise jeopardize a regime's Islamic credentials. Similarly, setting aside the punishments mandated in the Qur'an, the hudud, would be a violation of divine law (on this, see the following section).

One might well expect that ideas of social and economic justice would figure prominently in the Islamists' and the ulama's discourses on the shari'a. To a certain extent, they certainly do, both because there is good Qur'anic warrant for these ideas and because the grinding poverty that afflicts large sectors of society in South Asia makes these subjects unavoidable. Such ideas were, in fact, prominent in the work of some Deobandi ulama of the first half of the twentieth century, notably 'Ubayd Allah Sindhi (d. 1944) and 'Abd al-Rahim Popalzai (d. 1944). In general, however, the ulama and Islamists have often remained reticent in fully embracing this theme. A good part of the explanation has to do with its prominence in modernist discourse. In a famous letter to Jinnah, the influential modernist poet and philosopher Muhammad Iqbal of Lahore (d. 1938) observed that if Islamic law "is properly understood and applied, at least the right to subsistence is secured to everybody" (M. Iqbal n.d., 16). Though he did not expound on it in this context, Iqbal's view of what the "proper" understanding and application of Islamic law entailed was quite different from that usually held by the ulama and the Islamists. In the late 1960s and 1970s, the idea of "Islamic socialism" was also much in vogue in some sectors of Pakistani society, as it was in many other Muslim societies; it was especially prominent in the populist rhetoric of Prime Minister Zulfiqar 'Ali Bhutto. For their part, though with some notable exceptions, the ulama and the Islamists have been hostile to such trends and have therefore had to rate social and economic justice relatively lower among their priorities.

But it is not just against Muslim modernists and their socialist subset that the ulama and the Islamists have sought to guard the community. In recent years, vigilante groups have arisen in different parts of the country to enforce the shari'a and their conceptions of shari'a-based social justice. In the tribal areas of Khyber Pakhtunkhwa, where such groups have emerged in the form of a neo-Taliban insurgency in the years following the collapse of the Taliban regime in Afghanistan, appeals to socio-economic justice have featured prominently in the pronouncements of the vigilante leaders (Filkins 2008, 61).[7] Mangal Bagh, the leader of one of the most violent of such groups, was paraphrased as saying in August 2008 that "he would not allow anti-social or anti-Islamic activities in the Khyber Agency [part of the province's tribal areas] and would do whatever it takes to achieve this goal." His group, he said, "had taken the responsibility for ensuring social justice of the area, which should have been the prime concern of the political authorities in the tribal territory" (*News* 2008). As will be observed later, some leading ulama in contemporary Pakistan have not been altogether unsympathetic to some of the activities of these militant groups. At the same time, however, these groups also threaten to undermine the ulama's own authority, and the ulama have looked upon them, and their vigilante conceptions of social justice, with considerable misgiving.

Debates on matters relating to Islamic law in contemporary Islam have frequently invoked the idea of the overarching "purposes" or "goals" of the shariʿa (*maqasid al-shariʿa*), and it is worth asking whether this idea has had any significant place in discourses on the shariʿa in Pakistan. Since the time of the great jurist al-Ghazali (d. 1111), many Sunni scholars have argued that the shariʿa is guided by certain fundamental concerns—viz., safeguarding the interests of human beings in matters relating to life, religion, intellect, progeny, and property (Hallaq 1997, 112–13, 168–74). A key implication of this idea is that particular legal norms can be rethought in light of the overall purposes the sacred law is supposed to serve. A *maqasid*-based approach to the law has created new possibilities for legal and social reform, which explains its popularity in many modernist and reformist-Salafi circles (see Hefner's introduction). But it has had a mixed reception among the ulama.

Despite their desire to be guided as far as possible by the norms of their Hanafi school of law, many Deobandi ulama in contemporary India have come to favor reevaluating particular rulings with reference to the shariʿa's larger goals (Islamic Fiqh Academy 2004). Pakistani Hanafis are notably less enthusiastic on this score, however. It is true that they have not necessarily been constrained by their school tradition; and state legislation, for all the criticism directed against it by the ulama and the Islamists, has helped weaken school boundaries. Even so, these boundaries have remained stronger in South Asia than in many other parts of the Muslim world and, it seems, somewhat stronger in Pakistan than in contemporary India. Consequently, Pakistani ulama and Islamists have been more resistant to initiatives toward rethinking particular norms in light of the shariʿa's general principles, its "spirit," than have Islamists and ulama in many other Muslim societies. For their part, and as a corollary to this, the modernizing governing elite have challenged the ulama's views only in the most gingerly manner. Nor have they been particularly successful in finding effective allies among the ulama, as illustrated by the controversy over the Protection of Women Act of 2006.

The Problem of Legal Reform:
Transgressing God's Limits?

In February 1979, four Hudood Ordinances were promulgated by the government of General Zia al-Haqq. Among the highlights of Zia al-Haqq's Islamization, these measures sought to base Pakistan's criminal laws on a firm Islamic and, indeed, Qur'anic footing. Unlike certain other countries where the hudud laws have been in operation—notably Saudi Arabia, Sudan in the last years of General Ja'far al-Nimeiri, Iran after the 1979 revolution, and Afghanistan under the Taliban—Pakistan has never put these laws into full effect. No thieves have had their hands cut off and no one convicted of adultery has been stoned to death by the authority of the state. Many people were publicly flogged during Zia al-Haqq's early years in power, though not, strictly speaking, in accordance with hudud laws (Peters 2005, 155–60). Many more people, men and women, were, however, charged with hudud offenses, especially in matters relating to fornication, adultery, and rape. Indeed, much of the attention that Zia al-Haqq's Hudood Ordinances have received has to do with sexual crimes; and it is on this aspect that I will also focus here.

Critics of the Hudood Ordinances have frequently pointed out that these laws are unsuited to a modern state, that they have caused great hardship to women, and, indeed, that they misconstrue Islamic criminal law itself. For instance, the ordinance relating to *zina* did not make a clear distinction between the legal consequences of consensual sexual intercourse and those of rape, with the result that a woman alleging sexual assault could find herself charged with sexual impropriety if she failed to produce the requisite witnesses to testify to the assault. The fact that women (and men) have been acquitted in court, especially on appeal to the Federal Shari'at Court and the Shari'at Appellate Bench of the Supreme Court, has not prevented people from being brought to court on *zina*-related charges. Though shari'a norms and those upholding them have long stood in a tense relationship with local customary norms (see the following section), the hudud laws promulgated by the Zia al-Haqq regime tended to become an instrument of social control. As political scientist Charles Kennedy observed in 1988, there was "seemingly widespread use of the Zina Ordinance to file nuisance or harassment suits against disobedient daughters or estranged wives" (Kennedy 1996a, 64; also see Jahangir 2006, 9; Cheema and Mustafa 2009, 15–16).

Benazir Bhutto, who became prime minister shortly after the death of General Zia al-Haqq in 1988, was well known for her opposition to the Hudood Ordinances. Yet, during her two terms in office (1988–90, 1993–96)—both of which came to a premature end with the dismissal of her government on charges of corruption—she remained under intense pressure from the religious parties as well as the center-right Pakistan Muslim League to demonstrate her Islamic commitment. This obviously meant that any effort to amend, let alone to repeal, the Hudood Ordinances was deemed impolitic. Nawaz Sharif, who twice succeeded Benazir Bhutto as prime minister (1990–93, 1997–99), was much given to the rhetoric of Islamization, as has been seen. Although the Hudood Ordinances were not implemented under him any more than they had been under his predecessors, the laws themselves firmly remained part of the criminal justice system. It was only in the final years of General Pervez Musharraf that the laws relating to sexual crimes were amended through parliamentary legislation.

In marked contrast with the Islamizing orientation of General Zia al-Haqq, General Musharraf wanted to guide the country on the path to "enlightened moderation." In particular, in the aftermath of the terrorist attacks of September 11, 2001, the Musharraf regime sought to distance itself from ties with radical religio-political groups, ranging from the Taliban in Afghanistan to those engaged in a militant insurgency in Kashmir, India's sole Muslim-majority province. Musharraf also challenged the ulama and Islamists on a variety of issues. He launched an ambitious effort to regulate the madrasas, promising the establishment of new, government-sponsored "model madrasas," requiring all institutions of religious education to subject themselves to government oversight as the condition for their continued functioning, and expelling non-Pakistani students from these institutions. Another major initiative of the government was its overturning the previous judgments of the Federal Shari'at Court and the Shari'at Appellate Bench of the Supreme Court on the matter of financial interest. Rather than continually seeking extensions of the deadline by which the Pakistani economy was to become "interest-free"—as previous governments had done—Musharraf reconstituted the membership of the Shari'at Appellate Bench and soon obtained a new judgment on financial interest (Zaman 2008b). Over the years, Musharraf also repeatedly stated that the Hudood Ordinances needed to be revised. In November 2006, substantial revisions were finally made in the ordinances relating to *zina* and false accusations of *zina* in the form of the Protection of Women Act.

Yet if Musharraf intended to confront the ulama and the Islamists, he was scarcely oblivious to the many constraints on his ability to do so. The drastic change in Pakistani policies following September 11, from a close relationship with the Taliban to a new, if tense and often ambiguous, alliance with the United States in the War on Terror, has led to severe—and continuing—tensions in Pakistani society and much unrest in the Khyber Pakhtunkhwa province, which borders Afghanistan. The ulama and the Islamists vociferously condemned this volte-face and they have often interpreted all governmental efforts to regulate madrasas as motivated by American pressure. In some instances, at least, they have had considerable success. The 2002 general elections led to unprecedented gains by the alliance of the religious parties, the Muttahida Majlis-i 'Amal (MMA). Though still a relatively small group in the lower house, the National Assembly, the MMA became an important presence there, and Mawlana Fazlur Rahman, the general secretary of this alliance, became the leader of the opposition in the lower house. The MMA also won a majority in what was then the North-West Frontier Province, where it was able to form a government (Weiss 2008). For all its rhetoric, the Musharraf regime was not notably successful in regulating the madrasas; and its ambitious early initiatives were quietly shelved in the face of opposition not just from the MMA but also from the ulama at large.[8]

President Musharraf was, however, determined not to allow the ulama to block amendments to the Hudood Ordinances, just as he had not allowed the ulama and the Islamists to obstruct his effort to obtain a favorable judicial verdict on the question of financial interest. In the latter instance, two individuals with tenuous claims to being "ulama" had been appointed to the Shari'at Appellate Bench on seats reserved for ulama in order to secure a favorable verdict (Zaman 2008b, 65–66). In the case of the hudud laws, too, the Musharraf regime sought to find allies among the ulama. The ulama, however, were generally hostile to any change in these laws. And the MMA, whose members of parliament included many ulama, repeatedly threatened that it would resign en masse if the government moved any legislation that could be construed as contravening the Qur'an and the normative example of the Prophet. Representatives of the government offered frequent public assurances that "nothing would be done contrary to the Holy Quran and Sunnah" (Hassan 2006c; cf. Hassan 2006a); they also repeatedly sought to persuade the ulama and, in particular, the MMA to support the proposed legislation.

At one point, the government requested a team of prominent ulama, including Muhammad Taqi 'Uthmani, the vice-president of a leading Deobandi madrasa in Karachi and believed by some to have been among the architects of Zia al-Haqq's Hudood Ordinances (Dawn 2006), to help negotiate with the MMA. Members of the "government's ulama team"—as they were often characterized in the national media (e.g., Dawn 2006)—themselves had many misgivings about the proposed bill, however. While the Hudood Ordinances mandated the punishment of stoning to death for those convicted of rape, the proposed bill made this crime punishable only under the somewhat less stringent provisions of the Pakistan Penal Code. The ulama on the government team were strongly opposed to moving rape out of the list of hudud crimes. These ulama also insisted that, in case the requisite four witnesses were not available to testify to an act of adultery or fornication, the act in question should still be subject to some form of "discretionary" punishment (ta'zir), i.e., something less than the hadd punishment but sufficiently severe to deter such acts. For its part, the proposed bill made it difficult to punish anyone for consensual premarital or extramarital sex. The ulama invited by the government to help with the negotiations on the proposed legislation seem to have been given the impression that their demands for modifications in the bill were acceptable to the government. Taqi 'Uthmani was quoted as saying at one point that "all issues had been settled unanimously and there was delay in preparing the revised draft [only] because every clause was considered in light of Quran and Sunnah" (Wasim 2006). Leaders of the MMA had had considerable misgivings about the proposed bill, but the endorsement of the government-appointed ulama seems to have eased many of their concerns, too.

The governing elite were not of one mind on this issue, however. Chaudhry Shuja'at Husain, the leader of the Muslim League faction that controlled the parliament in close alliance with General Musharraf, was the key person negotiating with the religious groups in and outside parliament. He was considerably more receptive to the ulama's views than many others in the government, including President Musharraf himself. In any case, the bill that was actually passed by the National Assembly and the Senate and ratified by President Musharraf in late 2006 was significantly different from the version the government-appointed ulama had apparently consented to. Rape was no longer a *hadd* crime, i.e., not subject to the penalty of stoning to death. Consensual sex remained a punishable offense, but accusations now had to be lodged in the relevant court rather than with the police, making them more difficult to file, and it was left to the court's discretion whether or not to admit the complaint. Perhaps the most important achievement of this new law was to ensure that women victims of sexual assault could not themselves be accused of sexual misconduct and punished for it (Jahangir 2006, 5–6).[9] The ulama did not object much to this last-mentioned aspect of the new legislation. They did, however, vociferously denounce other key provisions of the Protection of Women Act. As Mawlana Fazlur Rahman, the leader of the opposition in the National Assembly and the head of a party which had had close ties with the Taliban of Afghanistan, dramatically put it, this law was intended to turn "Pakistan into a free sex zone" (Asghar 2006). And President Musharraf's appeal to the nation, in the wake of the National Assembly's passage of the bill, to support the "progressive elements" against the "extremists" (I. A. Khan 2006) was interpreted by the MMA leadership as "a declaration of war against Islamic culture and civilization" (Hassan 2006b).

Ironically, it was Taqi 'Uthmani, a key member of the team of ulama the government had appointed to help win over the MMA leadership, who emerged as by far the most articulate critic of the Protection of Women Act. He had been writing on the proposed legislation in leading Pakistani newspapers while the bill was being considered by parliament, and he continued his scathing criticism after it became law (M. T. 'Uthmani 2006a, b, c, d, e, f). Offering a detailed, point-by-point analysis of the bill, Taqi 'Uthmani argued that it clearly contravened the teachings of the Qur'an and the hadith, and he cited many examples of the relevant Qur'anic passages and of hadith to illustrate this point. But he also built his case against this legislation on other grounds:

I myself have been directly hearing cases registered under Hudood Ordinance, first as a Judge of Federal Shariah Court and then for 17 years
as a member of Shariah Appellate Bench of the Supreme Court. In this
long tenure, not once did I come across a case in which a rape victim was
awarded punishment because she was unable to present four witnesses.
(M. T. 'Uthmani 2006f)

That criminal charges *could* be filed, and often were, against women under
these laws is largely ignored here, except by way of a brief acknowledgment
of the laws' abuse at the hands of the police. If men could misuse the Hudood Ordinances against hapless women, as has frequently been argued, Taqi
'Uthmani claimed that women, too, had used them in their own interest. In
a move calculated to address the English-educated members of his audience,
Taqi 'Uthmani cited the work of the aforementioned Charles Kennedy—who
has written extensively on Islamic laws in Pakistan—to suggest that some
women charged with adultery had alleged in court that they had been raped
by their lover; in such instances, the courts had tended to convict the man
but to exonerate the woman (M. T. 'Uthmani 2006f, citing Kennedy 1996b,
74). Adducing this testimony from "an unbiased non-Muslim scholar who has
got no sympathies toward the Hudood Ordinance" helped demonstrate Taqi
'Uthmani's own familiarity with Western scholarship. It also sought to show
that women's oppression under the Hudood Ordinances was largely a matter
of malicious propaganda. But Taqi 'Uthmani's point here was also that if some
women could already use the Hudood Ordinances to avoid being punished
for consensual extramarital sex, the new law would provide both men and
women greater opportunity to do so. At the same time, he argued, the protections that the Hudood Ordinances had provided to women, for example by
prescribing a draconian punishment for rape, had now been weakened. As
the title of one of his articles on the subject had it, the new law amounted to
"making Pakistan safe for rapists" (M. T. 'Uthmani 2006d).[10]

The language some of the ulama have used to denounce the Protection
of Women Act of 2006—turning Pakistan into a "free sex zone"; making the
country "safe for rapists"—plainly illustrates the degree of their hostility to
this measure and, more broadly, to what they see as the Westernizing policies
of the ruling elite. Yet even such stridency has not necessarily translated into
a complete break with the government pursuing such policies. As has been
observed, the MMA had repeatedly threatened to resign en masse from the
National Assembly in the event the Hudood Ordinances were amended along
the lines they eventually were. Its members did not resign, however, when
the bill became law. There was a serious rift in the MMA on this issue: the
Islamist Jama'at-i Islami, the party that Mawdudi had once led, was in favor

of resigning while Mawlana Fazlur Rahman, the MMA general secretary and the leader of the ulama-led Jam'iyyat al-'Ulama-i Islam, was opposed to this. Fazlur Rahman seems to have believed that staying in the National Assembly gave the religious parties greater influence than leaving it, though the elected ulama have often also been insecure about whether they would be reelected. By the time of the next general elections, in early 2008, there was no longer an alliance of the religious parties. The Jama'at-i Islami boycotted the elections, and the other religious parties won few seats in the National Assembly. It was the mainstream political parties—the Pakistan Peoples Party of the recently assassinated Benazir Bhutto (d. 2007) and the Pakistan Muslim League faction led by Nawaz Sharif—that were the big winners in these elections.

Yet if, in practice, the ulama and the religious parties have often been considerably more pragmatic than their rhetoric would suggest, the effects of their rhetoric can scarcely be discounted. This rhetoric has arguably contributed toward delegitimizing Pakistani governments on Islamic grounds. Taqi 'Uthmani did not mince words in asserting that the bill which later became the Protection of Women Act "blatantly violate[d] the injunctions of the Quran and Sunnah" (M. T. 'Uthmani 2006d; cf. Cheema and Mustafa 2009, 41–44). This would be a serious charge in any Muslim society, but it is especially grave in the Islamic Republic of Pakistan, where the government is constitutionally mandated to ensure that no legislation is repugnant to the Islamic foundational texts. The ulama's arguments have not gone unchallenged. Religious intellectuals like Javed Ahmad Ghamidi have tried to educate the public about the many inadequacies of Zia al-Haqq's Hudood Ordinances, and the Council of Islamic Ideology—of which Ghamidi was a member—did the same in a detailed report on these laws (Council of Islamic Ideology 2007; cf. Hashimi 2004). But Ghamidi's own views on hudud are not devoid of equivocation, as observed earlier; and his appeal in some circles scarcely matches the national and international standing that Taqi 'Uthmani has come to enjoy as an authority on Islamic law. Not unlike Mawdudi in an earlier generation, Taqi 'Uthmani is by far the most articulate religious intellectual in contemporary Pakistan, a fact that has made him something of an unofficial spokesman for the ulama *and* the Islamists. Ironically, in calling upon a team of ulama to help make the case for reforming the Hudood Ordinances, the government itself lent further credibility to those who soon emerged as the severest critics of this initiative.[11]

Not long after the passage of the 2006 Act, a new confrontation between the Deobandi ulama and the government further weakened the latter's legitimacy on religious grounds. (This came, it is worth noting, on the heels of the widely condemned dismissal of the chief justice of the Supreme Court, who was fired by General Pervez Musharraf in March 2007 and whose cause

became the focal point of a powerful non-religious, civil society–based challenge to the military regime.) In early 2007, in the very heart of the nation's
capital, Islamabad, two brothers in charge of the Lal Masjid (Red Mosque) and
a madrasa for girls attached to it began engaging in vigilante action to uphold
what they regarded as the demands of the shariʿa. Madrasa students took over
a public children's library to protest against the demolition of mosques built
on public property without government authorization; the city's video and
DVD stores were threatened with dire consequences if they did not remove
"objectionable" items; massage parlors, alleged to be brothels, were raided
and, in one instance, several Chinese men and women working there were
kidnapped, causing serious embarrassment to the Pakistani government; a local shariʿa court was established in the city; and there were incessant demands
that the government commit itself to implementing the shariʿa throughout
the country and, not least, that it repeal the Protection of Women Act. The
Lal Masjid was said to have large amounts of ammunition and, on one occasion, the mosque's imam went so far as to threaten that "our youth will commit suicide attacks if the government impedes the enforcement of the Sharia
and attacks Lal Masjid and its sister seminaries" (Raza 2007). The government
tried to negotiate with the two brothers and, once again, a team of prominent
religious scholars was mustered to help with these negotiations. In the end,
the government decided to storm the mosque, killing nearly a hundred people
inside, including the younger of the two brothers.

Among the ulama the government had summoned to negotiate with the
Lal Masjid brothers was Mufti Muhammad Rafiʿ ʿUthmani, the president of
the Dar al-ʿUlum madrasa of Karachi and the elder brother of Taqi ʿUthmani.
Like his brother's public commentary on the Protection of Women Act, Rafiʿ
ʿUthmani's verdict on the government's handling of the Lal Masjid affair was
harsh. He was critical of the Lal Masjid brothers for their vigilantism: "To establish a state within a state is to take the law into one's own hands. The shariʿa
does not consider this permissible" (M. R. ʿUthmani 2007, 5). But he reserved
the most unsparing criticism for Musharraf's military regime, and not just
with reference to the Lal Masjid operation:

The people of Pakistan have nurtured the military with their taxes and
with great financial sacrifice. [The military] is our trust, our savings, our
power, the guardian of our borders—and we are proud of it. But you
are misusing it in cowardly, unjust, and foolish campaigns . . . You are
using this military according to the dictates of [our] enemies . . . Your
courage no longer works in Kashmir. You have withdrawn your troops
from Kargil. Nor does your courage help defend the western borders
in preventing NATO forces from violating Pakistan's sacred frontiers.

Your "courage" is now directed instead against the madrasa in Bajaur [in the tribal areas of Khyber Pakhtunkhwa] and in killing its wronged students. Your bravery is now focused on the boys and girls of the Hafsa Madrasa [attached to the Lal Masjid in Islamabad]. Such are your cowardly, unjust, brutal acts. Yet you say that peace and security should be established. You do everything to destroy peace and security, and then you tell us that the ulama should play their part in restoring peace. (M. R. ʿUthmani 2007, 9)

The Lal Masjid episode was followed by a spate of suicide bombings, especially in the Khyber Pakhtunkhwa province. This was not the beginning of the phenomenon of suicide bombings in Pakistan but, in many instances, those perpetrating these acts now sought to present them as vengeance for the desecration of the mosque and the destruction of the madrasa in Islamabad. More generally, the Lal Masjid episode added fuel to the neo-Taliban insurgency (see the following section). Leading Pakistani ulama have had to tread a difficult path in the face of such militancy. On the one hand, they have distanced themselves from vigilante activism, and they have condemned suicide bombings in Pakistan (al-Faruq 2008). On the other hand, as Rafiʿ ʿUthmani's censure shows, they have been harsher in denouncing the un-Islamic ways of the government.[12] Such denunciations have helped undermine the government's claims of commitment to Islamic norms. They have also served to indirectly facilitate precisely the sort of vigilantism typified by the Lal Masjid brothers: for if the shariʿa norms are there to be implemented and the government will not do so, then, the implicit argument goes, *someone* must stand up for their defense and implementation.

Customary Norms, the Shariʿa, and the State

If successive Pakistani governments have had great difficulty negotiating the place of the shariʿa in the state, they have not always fared much better in regulating local customary norms. Throughout the history of Islam, both the shariʿa and the state have had a complex relationship with local custom. While Muslim jurists did not recognize custom as a formal source of shariʿa norms, it often played a significant role in their thought. Yet local customs also contravened shariʿa norms, for instance in the realms of marriage, divorce, inheritance, and sexual mores. And even as the ulama have recognized that they will need to make their peace with particular customs, they—and other representatives of state authority—have long sought to curb the excesses of customary practice in their locales.

In British India, as observed earlier, customary practices had come to be recognized by the colonial state in certain parts of the subcontinent. Though the Shari'at Application Act of 1937 had brought Islamic laws of personal status to the Punjab, agricultural holdings in rural Punjab had been exempted from following the Islamic rules of inheritance. These rules eventually came to be extended to all of the Punjab. Yet, as Matthew Nelson has argued, customary norms have continued to have a strong hold on local practice. Few people would publicly contest the principle that the shari'a ought to have effect, but this formal recognition does not necessarily translate into actual adherence to the shari'a (Nelson 2010). The effects of customary norms extend well beyond denying women their rights of inheritance, and they are scarcely limited to the Punjab. In recent years, the Pakistani media have frequently reported in considerable detail on instances from different parts of the country in which women have been brutally murdered—sometimes by their fathers, brothers, and husbands—after being accused of sexual impropriety. Young girls have, on occasion, been given away to forestall or settle tribal vendettas. The Criminal Law (Amendment) Act of 2004 imposed severe penalties for many of these custom-based offenses (Lau 2008, 451–52), but they have continued to take place throughout the country (Hussain 2009; *Dawn* 2009b; Kiani 2010).

As in colonial Punjab, a Shari'at Application Act had been enacted in 1935 for the non-tribal regions of the then North-West Frontier Province. Here, too, the local notables (usually referred to as *maliks* and *khans*) had opposed it, without, however, explicitly challenging the authority of the shari'a. In a question sent to Mufti Kifayat Allah, a leading Delhi-based Deobandi jurisconsult and the president of the Jam'iyyat al-'Ulama-i Hind, some of these local notables had expressed their reservations as follows:

If it is the intention of the exalted government to give the shari'a to us, the Muslims of the Frontier, then we request that the entirety of our spiritual and worldly life be in accord with the Qur'an and the hadith. That is, the establishment of the institutes of religion, their renewal and reform, hudud and discretionary punishments, the collection of taxes, and judicial administration [should all be in accordance with Islamic law] . . . If all this is granted to us, we will be grateful to the exalted government. If, on the other hand, some Muslim members of the legislative and constituent assembly seek to implement a so-called Shari'at Bill in pursuit of particular political considerations, then we would like to be excused [from any such legislation]. For this amounts to a degradation of our religion. Even under the present customary law [*qanun-e riwaj*], there is no legal impediment to a Muslim giving out shares to women according to the Islamic law of inheritance. If the exalted government cannot grant us the entire shari'a, as stated above, then [it should recognize that] we have our own customary law, [which is] different from the Muslim personal law. (Kifayat Allah 1971–77, 9:274–75)

The Deobandi mufti was not impressed by these arguments. In his response, he argued that Muslims might well be excused from following the shari'a if the government *prevented* them from doing so, but they had no excuse in matters where they did have the opportunity to freely practice it; and to neglect some shari'a norms on grounds that certain others could not be practiced was "sheer ignorance . . . a way of avoiding the shari'a and of clinging to custom" (Kifayat Allah 1971–77, 9:276).

While the above exchange concerned the non-tribal areas of the province, customary norms were, and remain, much stronger in the tribal areas, whose autonomy the British had recognized; these regions, the Federally Administered Tribal Areas, have long continued to be autonomous in Pakistan as well. Those inhabiting these regions have been governed by a combination of customary tribal norms, often shared on both sides of the Pakistan-Afghanistan border, the shari'a as understood by the local religious functionaries, and some colonial-era regulations, overseen by representatives of the government and intended to keep the tribesmen from posing serious threats to the authority of the otherwise distant government.

Yet, even as the state largely left the tribesmen to their own devices, they have scarcely been insulated from political and religious developments in and outside the country. For instance, during the 1970s, the socialist rhetoric of the government of Zulfiqar 'Ali Bhutto contributed its share to undermining the authority of the local *maliks*, traditionally the largest landowners, and to creating a new sense of economic exploitation among the landless and impoverished tribesmen (cf. Lindholm 1996, 89). The Soviet occupation of Afghanistan, the arrival of large numbers of Afghan refugees in the tribal areas, and the participation of Pakistani tribesmen in the Afghan war also brought major changes to the tribal areas. As Sana Haroon observes, "demographically, economically and socially, everything had changed" by the time the Soviet Union withdrew from Afghanistan in 1989 (Haroon 2007, 207). These regions have continued to bear the brunt of a growing instability along the Pakistan-Afghanistan border. Many Arab Islamists participating in the Afghan war passed through the tribal areas; and since the fall of the Taliban in Afghanistan, many of these Arab Islamists have resided in these regions (Haroon 2007, 197–216). In recent years, these Islamists, together with disaffected and hitherto disenfranchised local tribesmen, have contributed to the formation of the neo-Taliban insurgency which has challenged the authority of the Pakistani government but also, significantly, traditional structures of social, political, and religious authority in the tribal areas. Large numbers of local *maliks* and *khans,* and many religious functionaries allied with them, have been targeted by the neo-Taliban in an effort to reshape the local landscape in a stringent Islamist form. According to one 2008 estimate, "in South Waziristan [one of the principal centers of the insurgency], the Taliban and Al Qaeda [had] killed more than 150 *maliks* since 2005, all but destroying the tribal system" (Filkins 2008, 61). According to another estimate, more than five hundred tribal leaders had been killed between 2004 and 2008 in the tribal areas, and others have continued to fall prey to the neo-Taliban elsewhere in the province (Perlez and Shah 2008).

In areas under their control, the Pakistani Taliban have dispensed what they see as shari'a justice. In many cases, this has been in line with tribal norms, for example on matters of "honor," though it is the symbolism of the shari'a that has often characterized it (for some examples, see Shinwari 2007; *Dawn* 2007, 2008a, 2008b, 2009c). As with the Lal Masjid brothers, the implicit reasoning here is that people ought to take the initiative in implementing the shari'a if the state fails to fulfill this function. It was in taking such initiative that Baitullah Mehsud (d. 2009), the founding head of an umbrella organization of the neo-Taliban, had likewise announced, in summer 2008, that he was establishing a new Islamic judicial system in South Waziristan (Bhittani 2008).

The Movement for the Implementation of Muhammad's Shari'a (TNSM), which gained a significant following in the Swat District of Khyber Pakhtunkhwa's Malakand Division in the mid-1990s, offers another illustration of how demands for the shari'a are intertwined with the actual or perceived failures of the state as well as its unfulfilled promises. A princely state like many others in South Asia, Swat and its adjoining regions were formally brought under Pakistani jurisdiction in 1969 and designated as the Provincially Administered Tribal Areas (Sultan-i-Rome 2008). These regions were governed by a mix of bureaucratic fiat, colonial-era laws, and tribal custom, a combination as notable for its harshness as it was for its judicial inefficiency. In 1994, the Supreme Court of Pakistan ruled that these laws were unconstitutional, which led to a legal vacuum in this region. It was in this context that the TNSM, led by one Mawlana Sufi Muhammad, challenged governmental authority in the name of the implementation of the shari'a (R. Yusufzai 1994). The government announced measures in 1994 and then again in 1999 toward implementing the shari'a, but these were widely viewed as cosmetic and did little to satisfy supporters of the TNSM.

The TNSM was banned in early 2002 in the aftermath of Sufi Muhammad's decision to send thousands of volunteers to fight alongside the Taliban against U.S. forces in Afghanistan. Sufi Muhammad himself was incarcerated for several years. In the meanwhile, many of his followers came to attach themselves to the neo-Taliban insurgency which, in Swat and adjoining areas, was led by Mawlana Fazlullah, Sufi Muhammad's son-in-law (I. Khan 2009). Under Fazlullah's leadership, the insurgents attacked government installations, carried out targeted assassinations, and systematically destroyed government schools—especially those for girls.[13] They also imposed various penalties, including flogging and gruesome executions, on those deemed guilty of particular offenses. Ironically, it was Sufi Muhammad who eventually came to be seen by the government as representing the side of moderation in helping tame the challenge that Mawlana Fazlullah posed to state authority. In early 2009, the government agreed yet a third time to implement the shari'a throughout Malakand Division. This agreement proved short-lived, however, in the face of the neo-Taliban's unrelenting efforts to extend their sphere of influence into other areas.[14] Since late spring 2009, the Pakistani military has prosecuted its operations against neo-Taliban and allied groups—in Swat and subsequently in South Waziristan—with considerably greater determination than had been the case earlier. But the neo-Taliban, too, have been unsparing in their response, and not just against the military or, for that matter, in areas where they have been strongest. One estimate puts terrorism-related deaths in Pakistan in 2009 at about 3,300, of whom more than a thousand were due to no fewer than seventy-six suicide attacks that year (Wasim 2009).

Many Deobandi ulama have continued to waver between the neo-Taliban and the government. As they did in regard to the Lal Masjid brothers, the ulama have repeatedly argued that resorting to violence against the government in pursuit of shari'a norms is inappropriate, and they have lamented the loss of life and property that such actions have entailed. At the same time, however, the ulama have continued to castigate successive Pakistani governments for their failure to implement shari'a norms. Implicit here is, once again, the idea not only that such implementation is mandated by God and, indeed, by the constitution, but also that the failure to implement the shari'a leads precisely to the sort of challenges to governmental authority as are represented by the neo-Taliban and the TNSM.[15] Significantly, even as the ulama have long argued against custom-based practices, some among them have attributed the persistence of such practices to the state's failure to implement the shari'a (Hassan 2008; cf. Zahid al-Rashidi 2007, 50–51). From this vantage, people would not need to resort to custom-based ways of protecting their honor and punishing moral infractions if the state had given them the opportunity to have recourse to shari'a norms. The argument against customary norms becomes, once again, a lament over the state's failure to implement the shari'a.

Conclusions

Many of the difficulties successive Pakistani governments have faced in regard to contestations on the shari'a and the ambiguities of Islam in the public sphere are not of their own making. For instance, the colonial administration's view that the inhabitants of India should be thought of in terms of distinct religious communities and that these communities ought to be governed by their own religious laws—at least on matters of personal status—created considerable and ongoing contestation on who had the authority to safeguard, interpret, and administer these laws. It also paved the way for demands that the shari'a ought to govern all facets of life and that the legitimacy of a state established as a homeland for Muslims depended on its ability to do so. The rhetoric of an Islamic homeland had, furthermore, played an important role in late colonial India in mobilizing Muslim support for the demand for Pakistan; and while the country's ruling elite have continued in various ways to contribute to this rhetoric, they have also found themselves constrained by the need to pay at least lip service to it as a way of legitimizing their often tenuous claims to authority. The neo-Taliban insurgency in the tribal areas of Khyber Pakhtunkhwa would, for its part, seem to be very much a product of the policies Pakistani governments and the military have pursued in relation to Afghanistan over several decades. Yet, even here, recent militant challenges to the state have arisen in the aftermath of Pakistan's realignment with the U.S.-led War on Terror in the post–September 11 world. This, again, is a context which obviously goes far beyond anything wrought by the particular policies of the Pakistani governing elite.

My point here is not, of course, to try to exonerate the Pakistani ruling elite for the many conflicts that have centered on Islam and the shari'a throughout the country's history. It is simply to remind ourselves that these conflicts have complex roots, and that they cannot be reduced to any single, overarching explanation. At the same time, there can be little doubt that the weak political legitimacy of the military regimes and the notorious corruption and incompetence of many a civilian and military government have, together with the ruling elite's own Islamic rhetoric, continued to strengthen those who insist that "sincere" efforts to implement the shari'a would cure the country's ills. The chronic failure of these governments to provide for even the most basic needs of large numbers of people has, in turn, further delegitimized them in the name of a shari'a-based socio-economic justice.

Even as Pakistani governments have been repeatedly challenged under the banner of the shari'a, they have not exactly been helpless in the face of such challenges. Important modernist laws have been enacted throughout the history of the country, from the Muslim Family Laws Ordinance to the Protection of Women Act of 2006. They have been upheld by the Pakistani higher courts and, despite vociferous opposition from the ulama and the Islamists, they have largely withstood efforts to revoke them (Lau 2004, 375; cf. Hallaq 2009, 485–86). At the same time, as we have observed, particular modernist initiatives have continued to erode the legitimacy of successive Pakistani governments. One of the most remarkable aspects of the controversy surrounding the Protection of Women Act was the failure of the Musharraf government to muster the support of any influential voices within the ranks of the ulama. Those the government had called upon to help make its case for the bill, like Taqi ʿUthmani, were already highly critical of the measure; and Taqi ʿUthmani soon emerged as the severest critic of the 2006 Act. In the case of the Lal Masjid episode, likewise, some of the ulama brought to negotiate on the government's behalf with those holed up in the mosque were openly sympathetic to the Lal Masjid brothers; and they later emerged, once again, as some of the government's severest critics for its handling of this episode.

In general, the Pakistani governing elite have done little to cultivate any substantial constituency among the ulama. Governments have repeatedly sought to reform madrasas, but these efforts have been widely viewed in Pakistani religious circles as attempts to subject their institutions to bureaucratic regulation and ultimately to destroy these "bastions of Islam" in the country. Besides bureaucratic oversight, government efforts at madrasa reform have usually focused on simply adding some modern sciences to the curriculum of the madrasas. Many ulama are increasingly open to this juxtaposition of the "traditional" and the "modern," for it helps them broaden the reach of their institutions (Zaman 2007, 77–82; cf. Ghumman 2009). But it has yet to lead to any significantly non-traditional approaches to the study of Islam. The governing elite have continued to call upon the ulama at particular moments of crisis, but, while this has enhanced the stature and influence of the ulama and sometimes bolstered the legitimacy of particular governments, it has seldom contributed very much toward effective collaboration between the government and the ulama on furthering particular reformist causes. What it has done instead is create a perception of the governing elite's opportunism in appealing to the ulama and the Islamists.[16] Meanwhile, modernist intellectuals have continued to articulate their own positions. Yet the combination of political opportunism in appealing to the ulama and the constraints that changing government interests have often placed on sites of modernist discourse have continued to enervate reformist thought in Pakistan.

It is worth asking why, if Pakistani governments have been unwilling or unable to cultivate reformist and modernizing trends among the ulama, the latter themselves have often been at best unsympathetic to particular initiatives toward social and legal reform. This is surely not for any lack of intellectual engagement on the part of leading ulama with issues of pressing importance. For instance, the controversy over the Protection of Women Act 2006 generated a spate of writings by them. Indeed, the ulama appear to have written more extensively *in opposition to* this legislative measure than its supporters have in its favor. Nor have the ulama failed to adapt to particular challenges at various times throughout their long history. Yet the fact remains that they have expressed themselves considerably more forcefully in opposing government-initiated legal reform on the grounds that it infringes on the shari'a than they have in calling for, say, the outlawing of particular customary practices which *also* contravene shari'a norms. It is tempting to suggest that this reticence has to do, in part at least, with the ulama's perception that to endorse governmental ventures in Islamic legal reform is to embolden the governing elite in undertaking more radical measures toward marginalizing the place of Islam in public life and further "Westernizing" the country.

Deobandi ulama have likewise been hesitant to unambiguously condemn the excesses of the Taliban. The Taliban are broadly recognizable as Deobandi, which partly accounts for this hesitation. There surely is also the fear of retribution—a fate some prominent critics of the Taliban have suffered.[17] Nor do the ulama wish to come across, in denouncing the Taliban, as endorsing the Pakistani and U.S. military operations on both sides of the Pakistan-Afghanistan border. But there is also the concern, as Zahid al-Rashidi, the head of a prominent Deobandi madrasa in the Punjab, observes, that an unqualified endorsement by the ulama of efforts to combat terrorism would be seen by the government as an expression of support for *all* its policies, including a condoning of the government's failure to implement Islamic law (Zahid al-Rashidi 2009a).

This chronic lack of trust in the government is not unique to Pakistan any more than it is peculiar to the ulama. In contemporary India, to take just one example here, much of the Muslim religious leadership has continued to profess faith in secularism as the guarantee of continued Muslim survival, but it has also been deeply suspicious of what it sees as efforts to trespass on a separate Muslim identity in the guise of fostering uniform secular commitments. There is an instructive contrast to be observed between the Deobandi ulama of India and Pakistan, however. As noted earlier in this essay, some Deobandi ulama in contemporary India have sought to rethink Islamic legal norms in light of the overarching "purposes of the shari'a" and in the interest of adapting these norms to the conditions of Muslim India. For all its contradictions and failures, Indian secularism provides the space in which these new discourses have come to be articulated (cf. Ahmad 2009). But the enormous pressures Muslims of contemporary India have faced, as an economically disenfranchised minority viewed with grave suspicion by an overwhelming

Hindu majority, have also necessitated efforts to articulate "moderate" Islamic positions and to adapt at least some Islamic norms to evolving needs. The Pakistani ulama have not experienced similar pressures. Yet, as we have seen, the sort of Islamist radicalism that now confronts Pakistan threatens not only the government and civil society but also, in the name of increasingly strident constructions of the shari'a, the religious scholars themselves. Such unprecedented challenges may well be an impetus for new kinds of cooperation between the ulama, moderate Islamists, and the state, anchored in new ways of thinking about the shari'a and its place in public life.

Notes

Earlier versions of this paper were presented at the Lahore University of Management Sciences, Lahore, Pakistan, in January 2009, and the Institute of Islamic Studies, McGill University, Montreal, Quebec, in September 2009. I am grateful to both institutions for the opportunity to share my work and to their faculty and students for insightful questions and comments. I wish as well to express my gratitude to Dr. Muhammad Khalid Masud of the Council of Islamic Ideology, Islamabad, for an illuminating discussion. I would also like to thank Robert W. Hefner for very helpful comments on an earlier draft.

1. Khyber Pakhtunkhwa is the new name of the province previously known as the North-West Frontier Province. The name was changed as part of wide-ranging constitutional amendments in 2010.

2. My usage of some key terms merits a brief comment at the outset. By "ulama," I mean those educated in institutions of traditional Islamic learning and basing their claims to religious authority on a sustained engagement with the historically articulated Islamic scholarly tradition. Those I refer to, for lack of a better term, as "modernists" are characterized above all by the desire to rethink and adapt Muslim practices, institutions, and norms in light of the imperatives of modernity, as they understand them. The "Islamists" share much with the modernists in, inter alia, their intellectual backgrounds and their critique of the ulama and their scholarly tradition, but it is their single-minded concern with the public implementation of Islamic norms that sets them apart from the modernists. While it is analytically useful to distinguish these competing strands, they should not be seen as internally cohesive camps nor, by the same token, as necessarily irreconcilable on all issues with groups that otherwise oppose them.

3. For a modernist critique of the assumptions underlying the colonial legal system, see Tyabji 1940, 84–88; cf. Kugle 2001, 304–307.

4. Other doctrinal streams within Sunni Islam in modern South Asia include the Barelawis and the Ahl-i Hadith. Both the Deobandis and the Barelawis belong to the Hanafi school of law, but their beliefs and practices set them apart from one another. Whereas the Deobandis seek to self-consciously anchor their legal norms and even their Sufi practices in the Qur'an and the hadith, Barelawi piety centers on highly ritu-

alized forms of devotion to the Prophet Muhammad and various Muslim saints and their shrines, as well as on seeking the intervention of these holy personages in daily life. The Ahl-i Hadith espouse a more austere form of text-based belief and practice than the Deobandis, let alone the Barelawis. The key difference between the Deobandis and the Ahl-i Hadith relates not to theology, however, but rather to law. In marked contrast with the staunchly Hanafi Deobandis, the Ahl-i Hadith reject the authority of the medieval schools and—like Salafis elsewhere—seek to base their belief and practice directly on the Islamic foundational texts. Given their shared opposition to the devotional piety of the Barelawis, there is, from the latter's viewpoint, not much to differentiate between the Deobandis and the Ahl-i Hadith (or, as the Barelawis often characterize them, the Wahhabis/Najdis, with reference to Muhammad ibn 'Abd al-Wahhab [d. 1791] of Najd in Arabia).

5. The chief justice, Iftikhar Muhammad Chaudhry, was later reinstated by the full bench of the Supreme Court, only to be dismissed once again by President Musharraf when he declared a state of emergency in Pakistan in November 2007. Justice Chaudhry was eventually restored to office in March 2009, in the wake of countrywide protests spearheaded by lawyers.

6. The son of a Deoband-educated religious scholar, Rahman studied at the University of the Punjab and received his Ph.D. in Islamic philosophy from Oxford University. He later taught at the University of Durham, McGill University in Montreal, and the University of Chicago. During the 1960s, he was the director of the Islamic Research Institute, a constitutionally mandated body established—like the Council of Islamic Ideology—to advise the government on matters relating to Islam. For his reflections on his experiences in Pakistan during this decade, see Rahman 1976.

7. I follow Giustozzi (2008) in characterizing this insurgency as "neo-Taliban" or, occasionally, as the Pakistani Taliban.

8. In the meantime, according to the estimates of the Ittihad-i Tanzimat-i Madaris-i Pakistan, a non-governmental coalition that oversees madrasas belonging to various doctrinal orientations, the madrasa population has continued to grow markedly. In October 2009, this organization put the number of madrasas registered with it at "over 20,000," with a student body of nearly 2.8 million. An overwhelming majority of these madrasas (about 12,000) belong to the Deobandi orientation. Government figures, it is worth noting, put the *total* number of madrasas in the country at around 12,000 and the number of those studying at these institutions at 1.5 million. There continues to be much uncertainty not only about the number of madrasas in the country but also about the range of institutions encompassed by this term. That only a fraction of the existing madrasas are registered with the government is not in dispute, however. For these figures, see Ghumman 2009.

9. For the full text of the act, see "Protection of Women (Criminal Laws Amendment) Act, 2006," http://www.pakistani.org/pakistan/legislation/2006/wpb.html (accessed April 21, 2010).

10. This article draws on an essay by Taqi 'Uthmani in the Urdu language as well as on the text of an interview with him. It is not clear if he chose its title himself. But given that it appears on a website associated with his madrasa and in view of his

knowledge of the English language, it seems reasonable to assume, at the very least, his approval of how the article has been titled.

11. Ghamidi saw the government's overtures toward the ulama as a slight to the Council of Islamic Ideology, whose *raison d'être*, after all, was to advise the government on precisely such issues. In protest, he tendered his resignation from the council (N. Iqbal 2006), though President Musharraf did not accept it.

12. The Barelawis have been notably less ambivalent than the Deobandis in condemning vigilante activism of the sort represented by the Lal Masjid brothers, which they blamed on a militant nexus of the Deobandis and the Wahhabis (Qadiri 2007). At the same time, the Barelawis have been at pains to argue that their condemnation of such vigilantism does not amount to their condoning of particular governmental initiatives "in opposition to the Qur'an and the Sunna" (Qadiri 2007, 6–7).

13. As one estimate, citing government figures, put it in August 2008, "there are 566 girls' schools in Swat . . . Of these, 131 have either been set alight or closed, rendering 17,200 girls school-less" (Ansari 2008, 68).

14. An early 2009 video showing a young girl being publicly flogged in Swat for alleged moral infractions also did much to turn public opinion in favor of a sustained military operation in Swat. See *Dawn* 2009a.

15. Deobandi ulama of Pakistan have sometimes tried to make a distinction between the post-9/11 Taliban of Afghanistan, whose actions against the U.S.- and NATO-led troops in Afghanistan they largely support, and the Pakistani Taliban, whom they view with considerable misgivings though not in altogether unambiguous terms (see, for instance, Zahid al-Rashidi 2009b, 17–18; cf. Zahid al-Rashidi 2009a). They have also made a distinction between the "moderate" (*mu'tadil*) ulama and notables of the tribal areas, on the one hand, and those, on the other, who are "ablaze" (*mushta'il*) at the anti-Islamic policies of the government. According to this view, the policies in question have tended to divest the moderates of the moral authority with which to argue against the radicals. See *al-Faruq* 2008, 8.

16. This is not to say that the relationship between the government and the ulama has necessarily been adversarial. The ulama have long had a strong interest in political stability and many among them—as well as among the Islamists—have benefited from government patronage. The fact that some leading religious figures have responded to government appeals for intervention suggests, moreover, that they have not been averse to being called upon on such occasions. The point here is, rather, that the governing elite have never seriously cultivated reformist views among the ulama, with the result that appeals to the ulama have tended to be based on short-term interests, which themselves have frequently remained unfulfilled. In the long run, such appeals have undermined rather than bolstered the government's Islamic credentials.

17. The most notable instance is the June 2009 assassination of the Barelawi scholar Mufti Sarfaraz Na'imi, the head of a prominent madrasa in Lahore and a vocal critic of the Taliban (M. Ali 2009). For a Deobandi instance (the assassination of Mawlana Hasan Jan, a scholar from Peshawar who "had condemned suicide bombings as un-Islamic"), see A. Yusufzai 2007.

References Cited

Ahmad, Irfan. 2009. *Islamism and Democracy in India: The Transformation of Jamaat-e-Islami*. Princeton: Princeton University Press.

Ali, Cheragh. 1883. *The Proposed Political, Legal, and Social Reforms in the Ottoman Empire and Other Mohammadan States*. Bombay: Education Society's Press.

Ali, Muhammad Faisal. 2009. "Suicide Bomber Kills Anti-Taliban Cleric Allama Naeemi." *Dawn* (Karachi), June 13.

Ansari, Massoud. 2008. "The Ticking Bomb." *Herald* (Karachi), August, 67–70.

Asghar, Raja. 2006. "Some Respite for Women, At Last: Protection of Rights Bill Gets Through NA." *Dawn* (Karachi), November 16.

Bhittani, Alamgir. 2008. "Parallel Judicial System Set Up on Baitullah's 'Decrees.' " *Dawn* (Karachi), August 17.

Binder, Leonard. 1963. *Religion and Politics in Pakistan*. Berkeley: University of California Press.

Cheema, Moeen H., and Abdul-Rahman Mustafa. 2009. "From the Hudood Ordinances to the Protection of Women Act: Islamic Critiques of the Hudood Laws of Pakistan." *UCLA Journal of Islamic and Near Eastern Law* 8:1–48.

Council of Islamic Ideology. 2007. *Hudood Ordinance 1979: A Critical Report*. Islamabad: Council of Islamic Ideology.

Dawn (Karachi). 1998. "Text of the Fifteenth Constitutional Amendment Bill." August 29.

———. 2006. "Govt's Ulema Team Seeks Time to Review Bill." September 10.

———. 2007. "Woman, Two Men Stoned, Publicly Executed." March 15.

———. 2008a. "Couple Stoned to Death in FATA." April 2.

———. 2008b. "Three Brothers Executed in Wana." September 25.

———. 2009a. "Flogging in Swat Outrages Nation: Video Captures Girl's Agony." April 4.

———. 2009b. "Over 7700 Cases of Violence against Women in 2008." February 18.

———. 2009c. "Video Shows Killing of Man and Woman." April 18.

al-Faruq (Karachi). 2008. "Mawjuda buhran—asbab awr 'ilaj: Mulki surat-i hal par mulk ke mumtaz 'ulama-yi kiram ka mushtaraka mawqif." 24 (4) (May): 5–10.

Filkins, Dexter. 2008. "Talibanistan: A Journey into Pakistan's Tribal Areas." *New York Times Magazine*, September 7, 54–61, 114–16.

Fyzee, Asaf A. A. 2003. *Outlines of Muhammadan Law*. 5th ed. Delhi: Oxford University Press.

Ghamidi, Javed Ahmad. 2008. *Mizan*. Lahore: al-Mawrid.

Ghumman, Khawar. 2009. "Enrolment in Seminaries Rises by 40pc." *Dawn* (Karachi), October 28.

Gilmartin, David. 1988. *Empire and Islam: Punjab and the Making of Pakistan*. Berkeley: University of California Press.

Giustozzi, Antonio. 2008. *Koran, Kalashnikov, and Laptop: The Neo-Taliban Insurgency in Afghanistan*. New York: Columbia University Press.

Hallaq, Wael B. 1997. *A History of Islamic Legal Theories: An Introduction to Sunni usul al-fiqh.* Cambridge: Cambridge University Press.

———. 2009. *Shari'a: Theory, Practice, Transformations.* Cambridge: Cambridge University Press.

Haroon, Sana. 2007. *Frontier of Faith: Islam in the Indo-Afghan Borderland.* London: Hurst.

Hashimi, Muhammad Tufayl. 2004. *Hudud Ordinance: Kitab wa sunnat ki rawshani main.* N.p.: 'Awrat Foundation.

Hassan, Ahmed. 2006a. "Govt Yields to MMA on Hudood Laws." *Dawn* (Karachi), September 12.

———. 2006b. "MMA to 'Resign' in December." *Dawn* (Karachi), November 17.

———. 2006c. "NA Committee to Review Amended Draft: Hudood Law Standoff." *Dawn* (Karachi), September 16.

———. 2008. "Uproar in Senate over Burying of Women Alive." *Dawn* (Karachi), September 2.

Hussain, Imtiaz. 2009. "Karo-kari, Sexual Abuse Major Offences in Sindh: Watchdog." *News* (Islamabad), January 3.

Iqbal, Mohammad. N.d. *Letters of Iqbal to Jinnah.* Lahore: Shaikh Muhammad Ashraf.

———. 1934. *The Reconstruction of Religious Thought in Islam.* Oxford: Oxford University Press.

Iqbal, Nasir. 2006. "CII Objects to Having Been Sidelined on Hudood Laws." *Dawn* (Karachi), September 22.

Islamic Fiqh Academy. 2004. *Maqasid-i shari'at: Ta'aruf awr tatbiq.* Delhi: Islamic Fiqh Academy Publications.

Jahangir, Asma. 2006. "What the Protection of Women Act Does and What Is Left Undone." In *State of Human Rights in 2006,* by the Human Rights Commission of Pakistan, 5–15. Lahore: Human Rights Commission of Pakistan. http://www.hrcp-web.org/hrcpDetail_pub3.cfm?proID=374 (accessed September 28, 2008)

Kashmiri, Muhammad Anwarshah. 1980. "Khutba-i sadarat." In *Jam'iyyat al-'Ulama-i Hind: Dastawizat-i markazi ijlasha-yi 'am 1919–1945,* ed. Parvin Rozina, 1:386–451. Islamabad: Qawmi idara bara-yi tahqiq-i tas'rikh wa thaqafat.

Kennedy, Charles. 1996a. "Implementation of the Hudood Ordinances." In *Islamization of Laws and Economy: Case Studies on Pakistan,* 55–67. Islamabad: Institute of Policy Studies.

———. 1996b. "The Status of Women in Pakistan." In *Islamization of Laws and Economy: Case Studies on Pakistan,* 69–82. Islamabad: Institute of Policy Studies.

Khan, Iftikhar A. 2006. "Musharraf Finds Kind Words for PPP." *Dawn* (Karachi), November 16.

Khan, Ismail. 2009. "From Son-in-Law to Father-in-Law." *Dawn* (Karachi), February 18.

Khan, Khalilur Rehman. 2007. "Sadarati khutba." In *Pakistan main hudud qawanin,* ed. Shahzad Iqbal Sham, 35–40. Islamabad: Shari'a Academy, International Islamic University.

Kiani, Marium. 2010. "Violence against Women Increased 13pc in '09." *Dawn* (Karachi), February 2.

Kifayat Allah. 1971–77. *Kifayat al-mufti*. Edited by Hafiz al-Rahman Wasif. 9 vols. Delhi: Hafiz al-Rahman Wasif.

Kugle, Scott Alan. 2001. "Framed, Blamed and Renamed: The Recasting of Islamic Jurisprudence in Colonial South Asia." *Modern Asian Studies* 35:257–313.

Lau, Martin. 2004. "Pakistan." *Yearbook of Islamic and Middle Eastern Law* 9 (2002–2003): 372–78. Leiden: Brill.

———. 2006. *The Role of Islam in the Legal System of Pakistan*. Leiden: Martinus Nijhoff.

———. 2008. "Pakistan." *Yearbook of Islamic and Middle Eastern Law* 12 (2005–2006): 443–72. Leiden: Brill.

Lindholm, Charles. 1996 "Contemporary Politics in a Tribal Society: Swat District, NWFP, Pakistan." In *Frontier Perspectives: Essays in Comparative Anthropology*, 73–105. Karachi: Oxford University Press.

Masud, Muhammad Khalid. 2007. "Rethinking Shari'a: Javed Ahmad Ghamidi on Hudud." *Die Welt des Islams* 47:356–75.

Maududi, Sayyid Abul A'la. 1960. *The Islamic Law and Constitution*. Translated and edited by Khurshid Ahmad. Lahore: Islamic Publications Limited.

———. 1976. *The Moral Foundations of the Islamic Movement*. Lahore: Islamic Publications Limited.

Mehdi, Rubya. 1994. *The Islamization of the Law in Pakistan*. Richmond: Curzon Press.

Nelson, Matthew. 2009. "Dealing with Difference: Religious Education and the Challenge of Democracy in Pakistan." *Modern Asian Studies* 43:591–618.

———. 2010. *In the Shadow of Shari'ah: Islam, Islamic Law, and Democracy in Pakistan*. London: Hurst.

News (Islamabad). 2008. "Mangal Bagh Extends 'Controls' to Landikotal." August 29.

Perlez, Jane, and Pir Zubair Shah. 2008. "Pakistan Uses Tribal Militias in Tribal War." *New York Times*, October 24.

Peters, Rudolph. 2005. *Crime and Punishment in Islamic Law*. Cambridge: Cambridge University Press.

"Protection of Women (Criminal Laws Amendment) Act, 2006." http://www.pakistani.org/pakistan/legislation/2006/wpb.html (accessed April 21, 2010).

Qadiri, Sayyid Wajahat Rasul. 2007. "Lal qal'a se lal masjid tak." *Ma'arif-i Rida* 27 (12): 5–27.

Qureshi, Ishtiaq Husain. 1975. *Education in Pakistan: An Inquiry into Objectives and Achievements*. Karachi: Ma'aref.

Rahman, Fazlur. 1964. "Riba and Interest." *Islamic Studies* 3:1–43.

———. 1976. "Some Islamic Issues in the Ayyub Khan Era." In *Essays on Islamic Civilization*, ed. Donald P. Little, 284–302. Leiden: Brill.

Raza, Syed Irfan. 2007. "Lal Masjid Threatens Suicide Attacks." *Dawn* (Karachi), April 7.

Shinwari, Ibrahim. 2007. "Woman and Three Men Publicly Executed." *Dawn* (Karachi), June 5.

Sultan-i-Rome. 2008. *Swat State (1915–1969) from Genesis to Merger: An Analysis of Political, Administrative, Socio-political, and Economic Development.* Karachi: Oxford University Press.

Travers, Robert. 2007. *Ideology and Empire in Eighteenth-Century India: The British in Bengal.* Cambridge: Cambridge University Press.

Tyabji, Faiz Badruddin. 1940. *Muhammadan Law: The Personal Law of Muslims.* 3rd ed. Bombay: N. M. Tripathi.

'Uthmani, Muhammad Rafi'. 2007. "Lal masjid intizamiyya awr hukumat ke darmiyan mudhakarat kiyun nakam huwe?" *al-Balagh* (Karachi) 42 (7): 3–14.

'Uthmani, Muhammad Taqi. 1993. *Nifaz-i shari'at awr us-ke masa'il.* Karachi: Maktaba-i Dar al-'Ulum.

———. 2006a. *Amendments in Hudood Laws: The Protection of Women's Rights Bill; An Appraisal.* Islamabad: Institute of Policy Studies.

———. 2006b. *Hudud qawanin: Mawjuda bahth awr a'inda la'iha-yi 'amal.* Islamabad: Institute of Policy Studies.

———. 2006c. *Hudud qawanin main tarmim: Tahaffuz-i huquq-i niswan bill kiya hai? Aik mutala'a.* Islamabad: Institute of Policy Studies.

———. 2006d. "Making Pakistan Safe for Rapists." http://www.albalagh.net/women/0096.shtml (accessed on October 29, 2007).

———. 2006e. "The Real Contents." *Dawn* (Karachi), December 24.

———. 2006f. "The Reality of 'Women Protection Bills.'" http://www.hudoodordinance.com (accessed on October 29, 2007; the site is no longer available).

Wasim, Amir. 2006. "MMA Rejects 'Agreed' Draft: Impasse on Hudood Bill Persists." *Dawn* (Karachi), September 15.

———. 2009. "Terror Incidents Claimed 3,300 Lives This Year." *News* (Islamabad), December 31.

Weiss, Anita M. 2008. "A Provincial Islamist Victory in Pakistan: The Social Reform Agenda of the Muttahida Majlis-i-Amal." In *Asian Islam in the Twenty-first Century,* ed. John L. Esposito et al., 145–73. Oxford: Oxford University Press.

Yusufzai, Ashfaq. 2007. "Wafaqul Madaris VP Shot Dead." *Dawn* (Karachi), September 16.

Yusufzai, Rahimullah. 1994. "Malakand: Armed Insurrection and Political Inadequacies." *News* (Islamabad), November 11.

Zahid al-Rashidi, Abu 'Ammar. 2007. *Hudud ordinance awr tahaffuz-i niswan bill.* Gujranwala: al-Shari'a Academy.

———. 2009a. "Dahshat-gardi ke khilaf fatwe ki shar'i ahmiyyat." *Roznama Pakistan* (Lahore), December 22.

———. 2009b. "Madhhabi tabaqat, dahshat-gardi awr Taliban: Aik sawal-name ke jawabat." *Al-Shari'a* (Gujranwala), November–December, 2–21.

Zahid al-Rashidi, Abu 'Ammar, Mu'izz Amjad, Khurshid Nadim, and Faruq Khan. 2007. *Aik 'ilmi wa fikri mukalama.* Gujranwala: al-Shari'a Academy.

Zaman, Muhammad Qasim. 2002. *The Ulama in Contemporary Islam: Custodians of Change.* Princeton: Princeton University Press.

————. 2007. "Tradition and Authority in Deobandi Madrasas of South Asia." In *Schooling Islam: The Culture and Politics of Modern Muslim Education,* ed. Robert W. Hefner and Muhammad Qasim Zaman, 61–86. Princeton: Princeton University Press.

————. 2008a. *Ashraf ʿAli Thanawi: Islam in Modern South Asia.* Oxford: Oneworld Publications.

————. 2008b. "Religious Discourse and the Public Sphere in Contemporary Pakistan." *Revue des mondes musulmans et de la Méditerranée* 123:55–73.

7. Nigeria

Mapping a Shariʻa Restorationist
Movement

Paul M. Lubeck

The year 1999 will be remembered as a pivotal moment in Nigerian history. A transition to civilian democracy ended sixteen years of corrupt and increasingly brutal rule by authoritarian generals from the Muslim north (e.g., Ibrahim Babangida and Sani Abacha). In their place, Olusegun Obasanjo, a born-again Christian and former general from the Yoruba-speaking southwest, was sworn in as the democratically elected president of Nigeria's Fourth Republic. The highly popular transition to civilian rule not only ended years of egregious human rights abuses, but civil society and trade union resistance augured well for the revitalization of Nigerian democracy. It was a time of renewal, hope, and relative optimism for Nigerians.

To be sure, most Nigerians in 1999 held the northern generals and their civilian advisors responsible for destroying the prosperity, public institutions, and international reputation of the nation. Nigeria had fallen to pariah status within the international community. General Babangida's annulment of the June 12, 1993 electoral victory of M. K. O. Abiola deeply enraged the Yoruba people of the southwest as well as other democrats. In time, these offenses provoked a popular movement demanding a sovereign national conference to consider transforming Nigeria into a decentralized confederation. Subsequently, General Abacha's unprecedented personal corruption and brutally repressive policies not only caused the death of the northern populist leader Shehu ʻYar Adua but resulted in Nigeria's expulsion from the Commonwealth. Finally, by hanging Ken Sara-Wiwa for demanding that the indigenes of the Niger Delta be allowed to control the natural resources of their area, Abacha succeeded in mobilizing the global human rights community to demand sanctions against Nigeria and provoking waves of rebellion in the oil-rich Niger Delta.

Fortuitously, however, the sudden death of General Abacha in 1998 opened the door to a transition to democracy. Faced with widespread international and national hostility and many internal divisions, northern Muslim elites reluctantly recognized that the continuation of the federation depended upon agreeing to support a "power shift" from the Muslim north to the Christian south in the impending 1999 presidential election. A brokered agreement among Nigeria's elites produced two Christian presidential candidates from the Yoruba-speaking southwest, and the "power shift" to the southwest became inevitable.

Obasanjo's victory disrupted and terminated the long-standing political arrangements that gave the Muslim north political control over the federal government apparatus. Historically, Muslim political elites had specialized in constructing delicate multi-ethnic coalitions that enabled them to hold political control over the federal center, a solution which compensated them for their inability to control their share of the technical positions in the federal bureaucracy. Because of the north's comparative educational and economic backwardness, technical positions in the federal bureaucracy were controlled by southern groups. Accordingly, for the northern Muslims, the "power shift" to Obasanjo provoked insecurity, soul-searching, and a generalized feeling of being pushed to the margins of political and economic power.

Although his supporters claim he campaigned overtly on the issue, political observers in the federation were initially surprised when, in October 1999, Sani Ahmed, the governor of Zamfara State, signed two bills reintroducing shari'a criminal law (hudud) into this small, mostly rural state in northwest Nigeria. Ironically, in the historical memory of the northern states, Zamfara was a renegade community, for its rulers had rejected the iconic Islamic eighteenth-century reform movement of Usman dan Fodio. For a number of reasons, "playing the shari'a card," according to informed observers whom I interviewed, was a radical departure from the long-standing preferences of more established northern politicians, who specialized in constructing multiethnic coalitions to hold federal political power and control the distribution of petro-rents.

Nonetheless, in spite of the material and political costs of playing the shari'a card, within months of Zamfara's decision a broad-based popular movement for the implementation of shari'a spread like a raging wildfire across the northern states. It was spearheaded by committees of the pious, ulama, professionals, students, and Islamic civil society groups who used demonstrations, public marches, zealous vigilantes, and numerous petitions to demand that states immediately implement shari'a criminal law without compromise or delay.

Regardless of the preferences of the elites who feared the consequences of doing so, once the shariʿa card had been played by Sani Ahmed the shariʿa movement was unstoppable until the twelve most northerly state legislatures had implemented shariʿa criminal law, which they did within two years. In the following sections I argue that the shariʿa movement was driven by a new generation of Islamic reformers who, while drawing upon eclectic sources, are largely inspired by neo-Salafi legal models and discourses originating in the Gulf states and Saudi Arabia. The latter should be distinguished from the Salafi reformers of the late nineteenth century, like Mohammed Abduh and Rashid Rida. Neo-Salafi doctrines privilege the Qurʾan and the Sunna of the Prophet, respect the companions of the Prophet, and reject subsequent innovations such as Sufism and Muslim modernist reasoning (ijtihad) for the public good (*maslahah*). While neo-Salafi legal reasoning relies heavily on Hanbali doctrines, it is important to emphasize that when scriptural legal movements travel through global networks and are applied by reformers living in large, complex societies, like those of northern Nigeria, they become intermingled with each other. Therefore, while shariʿa reform was powered by neo-Salafists, Nigeria's legal system remained largely Maliki because the existing shariʿa judges adjudicating personal and family law were trained in the Maliki, not the Hanbali, tradition.

What exactly were the consequences of the hudud legislation? Hauwa Ibrahim, a counsel who defended northern Muslim women accused of adultery, summarizes them:

> The Shariʿa courts in these states have jurisdiction over several new offences beyond personal law, including theft, unlawful sexual intercourse, robbery, defamation, and drinking alcohol. The Shariʿa courts may impose punishments, pursuant to the provisions of the Shariʿa Penal Code Law (SPCL), that include death; forfeiture and destruction of property; imprisonment; detention in a reformatory; fines; caning (flogging); amputation; retaliation; blood money; restitution; reprimand; public disclosure; boycott; exhortation; compensation; closure of premises; and warning, among others. (Ibrahim and Lyman 2004, 3–4)

To explicate the political sociology of the shariʿa movement in northern Nigeria, this essay will review the political economy of Nigeria, the debate over the relationship of shariʿa to Nigerian federalism, the history of shariʿa law in northern Nigeria, sectarian disputes over Islamic reform, and the challenges posed to northern Muslim interests. After reviewing these issues I will analyze the implementation of shariʿa and the different interpretations of shariʿa voiced by northern Muslims.

Understanding the Political Economy of Nigeria

To understand the politics of the shari'a movement and why it was so popular in the northern Muslim states requires understanding how decades of political and economic mismanagement by military and civilian rulers have rendered shari'a an attractive political alternative for Nigeria's northern Muslims. At the heart of Nigeria's crisis of governance lies the resource curse, or the "paradox of riches." Nigeria's extraordinary natural resources stand in sharp contrast to its abysmal failure to realize even a tiny portion of its obvious potential. All informed accounts juxtapose Nigeria's dazzling promise to its miserable performance: chaotic governance, endemic corruption, criminal indifference to public good on the part of elites, cyclical communal conflict, and an overall failure to mobilize its rich natural endowments for the public good. Most of all, Nigeria represents a catastrophic failure on the part of elites to construct a hegemonic consensus on how to organize, develop, and regulate a national society.

The promise arises from its formidable material resources: Nigeria possesses vast petroleum and gas reserves, climatic variation supporting large-scale and variegated agricultural production, a citizenry with a deeply embedded entrepreneurial ethic, and—by African standards—a gigantic internal market of 150 million consumers. In fact, one of every five sub-Saharan Africans lives in Nigeria. Compared to all other African states, Nigeria's unusual scale means that it is in a unique position to develop a large-scale manufacturing sector that could easily be supplied by regionally specialized commercial agricultural enterprises. Alas, scale also produces diversity, insularity, fragmentation, and gridlock. Practically, Nigeria is a highly inchoate polity of at least four hundred ethno-linguistic groups residing in thirty-six different states, all of whom are aggressively competing for access to oil and natural gas rents. Roughly equally divided between Christian and Muslim believers, Nigeria can in practice be governed only in a federal constitutional system.

Nevertheless, structural, cultural, and strategic forces conspire to make Nigeria the poster child of a dependent petro-state governed by an oligarchic network of rent-seeking and criminally negligent politicians. The "oil resource curse" weighs heavily on the head of the Nigerian polity. Once a regionally diversified exporter of agricultural commodities (e.g., cocoa, palm products, peanuts, timber), with a substantial industrial manufacturing base poised for deep import substitution in various regions, Nigeria has seen its petroleum and natural gas production overwhelm and marginalize all other economic sectors since the mid-seventies. Unfortunately, strategic shifts in the global politics of energy security since September 11, 2001, have decisively inflated the significance of Nigeria's energy sector. The United States has defined the Gulf of Guinea as a new energy security zone, one expected to supply 25 percent of American imports by 2025, with Nigeria destined to provide 60–70 percent of oil imports. Nigerian crude oil's light weight, low sulfur content, lower transport costs, and security advantage over that of the Persian Gulf mean that it fetches a premium price from U.S. refiners. In 2007, Nigeria supplied 11 percent of American oil imports, nearly 46 percent of Nigerian production, and total United States–Nigeria trade reached $29 billion (U.S. Department of State 2009). Today, oil and natural gas represent at least 37–40 percent of Nigeria's GDP, 95 percent of its foreign exchange earnings, and 83 percent of federal government revenue, with an estimated annual export value of $90 billion in 2008 (U.S. Department of Energy 2009). Sadly, since the energy sector is an enclave without significant linkages to the "real" economy, the petro-rents generate a vicious cycle—the Nigerian syndrome—which has reproduced poverty, inequality, and industrial stagnation.

The easy wealth flowing from the distribution of petro-rents has created a system of oligarchic rule in Nigeria, now institutionalized as a pathological social structure of accumulation, one that creates disincentives and barriers to transformative and dynamic investments which could raise the productivity of the agricultural and manufacturing economy. What this means is that Nigeria is ruled by a multi-layered, institutionalized oligarchy, composed of self-serving politicians, businesspeople, political fixers, "godfathers," former military officers, and elite bureaucrats who share a common interest in gaining access to the clientelistic networks responsible for the redistribution of petro-rents. Even though fractions of the oligarchy occasionally do represent the interests of their ethnic, regional, and religious communities, they have much more in common with members of the oligarchy than with the increasingly impoverished constituencies they claim to represent. Again, because political parties are owned by major oligarchs (godfathers), they not only strangle democratic reform movements but, in effect, block developmental gains because they lack any recognizable ideology, active membership, programmatic platform, or desire to transform Nigerian living standards.

Hence, while energy revenues have skyrocketed in the last decade, access to electricity and water has declined significantly not only among the urban population but also among the labor-absorbing manufacturing sector. Actual standards of living have declined sharply, especially in the northern states, and are now below those at independence, especially in the areas of maternal mortality, life expectancy, and educational standards. The World Bank estimates that 70 percent of the petro-rents have been expatriated and that 80 percent of the hundreds of billions of petro-dollars earned by Nigeria are controlled by 1 percent of the population (Lubeck, Watts, and Lipschutz 2007). Thus the UNDP Human Development Index shows Nigeria's ranking declining from

151st to 159th between 2004 and 2006, despite rising petroleum prices. These figures explain why the proportion of the population living in poverty doubled to 70 percent between 1981 and 2004 (Spinoza and Vallée 2008). Not surprisingly, oligarchic rule created a polarized income structure, shameless elite consumption, criminality at all levels of governance, and high youth unemployment, which, in due course, fueled rising levels of communal violence when shari'a was implemented in the northern states.

The Politics of Shari'a within a Contested Federal Polity

The bedrock structural condition upon which Nigerian federalism rests is the stark fact that no single identity group—lineage group, ethnic group, nation, religious group, or geographical region—constitutes a numeric majority large enough to exercise hegemony over its rivals. Even if class, regional, or sectarian differences did not divide them, there is no demographic majority group. Indeed, the "big three" communal groups—Yoruba, Igbo, and Hausa-Fulani—are estimated to constitute, in total, only two-thirds of the population. Since the end of the Nigerian civil war, minorities residing in the territories of these groups have had to be accommodated for an electoral alliance or legislative program to succeed. Moreover, the constitutional requirement (Section 134, Article 2b) that the president win "not less than one-quarter of the votes cast at the election in each of at least two-thirds of all the States in the Federation and the Federal Capital Territory" requires the formation of cross-regional alliances to win the all-powerful post of president.

Inadvertently, perhaps, Nigeria's high level of political fragmentation produces a perverse form of pluralism, one in which the required consensus among elite bargainers becomes powerful enough to block any single group from holding uncontested hegemonic power over the state apparatus. Historically, the boundaries of identity groups have shifted as new identities, such as religious or ethnic affiliation, have been reinvented according to changes in the opportunity structure, in access to global networks, or in the capacity of political entrepreneurs to invent new discourses of mobilization (such as "indigenous" people). Alliances, therefore, are fluid and constantly shifting. All of these factors—fragmentation, elite bargaining, and federal rights—mean that centralized federalism must be accepted—if reluctantly by some—for Nigeria to continue to exist as a polity, but such federalism has proved ineffective for raising living standards or institutionalizing legitimate democratic representation. Instead, it privileges the talents of culturally sensitive and seasoned elite bargainers from different groups who have always negotiated backroom agreements and electoral alliances. In the case of shari'a, the elite bargainers failed to restrain genuine popular movements spearheaded by a new generation of religious politicians calling for the restoration of full shari'a.

Ethno-national identities nurture political fragmentation. Hence, for a wide variety of reasons—including the desire to secure larger shares of petro-rent, protect minority rights, punish rivals, prevent marginalization, and resolve internal ethno-national conflicts—Nigeria, like India, has continually created new subnational units (e.g., states). There were 3 relatively autonomous such regions at independence in 1960; 4 regions in 1963; 12 states in 1967; 19 states in 1976; 21 states in 1987; 30 states in 1991; and 36 states and a federal capital territory at Abuja in 1996. Currently, Nigeria has 774 local government authorities (LGAs). While their creation is rationalized by the rhetoric of autonomy and identity politics, it is obvious that the resulting fragmentation, administrative weakness, and fiscal dependence of the state system have actually strengthened the powers of the federal government while, at the same time, limiting its ability to implement change. The weakness of the states has encouraged the informal concept of six geographically defined zones, each comprising six states, which are used for forging compromises, organizing associational life, and defining distribution networks. While it was never written into constitutional law, the negotiations among the regional elites about the power shift of 1999 also produced an informal agreement to share power by rotating the presidency among the different zones of Nigeria approximately every eight years. Like the explicitly undemocratic compromises embedded within the American electoral system, zoning has traditional legitimacy in West African politics. Rotation of the presidency rewards elites who wait their turn to hold power. My interviews confirm that zoning has wide (though not universal) support among Nigerian political actors.

Implementing shari'a criminal law was premised upon reconstructing an already existing shari'a court system, limited to personal and family law, in the northern states. Again, ironically, the advocates for the implementation of shari'a criminal law based their claim on the liberal constitution's protection of religious freedom. They argued that powers allocated to the states empowered them to introduce shari'a criminal law solely for Muslims, and further that its limitation to Muslims would protect the rights of non-Muslims. Accordingly, they claimed, to forbid states to implement full shari'a would be unconstitutional, because it would violate Muslims' constitutionally protected religious freedom. The advocates of shari'a law thus grounded their position on several arguments: a clever interpretation of the states' rights provisions, which was initiated by southern Christian Nigerian agitation for regional cultural autonomy; the claim that the constitution guaranteed Muslims full religious freedom and thus a right to be ruled by shari'a criminal law; and finally, with regard to the provision that limited the application of shari'a criminal law to Muslims alone, the claim that this arrangement reflected moderation, compromise, and respect for federalism because it stopped short of imposing a full shari'a regime (by imposing punishments for apostasy, blasphemy, and other such acts).

To be sure, the 1999 constitution poses many barriers to full shari'a implementation in the northern states. For one thing, although it permits customary law and shari'a law in the areas of personal and family affairs, it also states that "the Government of the Federation or of a State shall not adopt any religion as State Religion." Another barrier concerns the judiciary. Regardless of decisions made in local shari'a courts or by the state shari'a court of appeal, the secular federal court system has the authority to overrule earlier decisions and hand down an unappealable judgment. Notwithstanding several efforts to amend the constitution so as to establish a separate shari'a court of appeal at the federal level from the 1970s to today, there is no federal shari'a court of appeal in Nigeria. Finally, even at the state level, the state's chief justice administers all the shari'a courts and all judgeships in the twelve states that have implemented shari'a criminal law and may overrule their decisions at any time.

An additional constraint on shari'a criminal law is due to the federal government's constitutional monopoly over security and the centralization of policing authority at the federal level. According to Rotimi Suberu, an expert on Nigerian federalism, this means "that the sharia-implementing states have been forced to rely on [the] secular, ineffective, corrupt, understrength, and allegedly partisan unitary Nigerian Police Force for the enforcement of their Islamic codes" (Suberu 2008, 67).

Several states—including Kano and Zamfara—responded to their lack of policing and prosecutorial authority by creating religious police, the *hisba*, who were authorized to enforce shari'a law, create an Islamic moral order, and contain the actions of independent Islamist vigilantes. In 2006, the struggle between shari'a states and the federal government came to a head when the inspector general of police arrested two *hisba* leaders and proscribed Kano's *hisba* organization. The clash was apparently precipitated by the *hisba's* efforts to enforce gender segregation in public transport by harassing women sharing motorcycles (*achaba*) and other public vehicles with men. When Kano State sued the federal government to release the *hisba* officials, the Federal Supreme Court in March 2007 ruled that Kano did not have jurisdiction, describing the conflict as an administrative dispute. This ruling not only let stand the federal government's monopoly of police powers under the authority of the inspector general of police, it avoided making a formal statement on the legality of shari'a criminal law in Nigeria. In practice, the national police's assertion of a monopoly over police functions reduced the public activities of the *hisba*, even though they continue to operate in Kano (Suberu 2008). What this means is that the Nigerian police and the public prosecutors are the only organized legal body that can arrest people and require them to appear before a shari'a court. Hence, in the absence of an organized criminal justice system, enforcement of shari'a criminal law depends on the rather capricious decisions of the Nigerian police—who, like the army, have the right to import alcohol and consume it in their barracks.

The Appeal of Islamic Reform under Political and Economic Crisis

Over the thousand years since Islam was first introduced into the northeastern state of Borno, the uneven process of Islamization has transformed the region's political and economic life, created a public religious culture, and, to a significant degree, Islamized northern societies' cultural practices. The debate over the role of shari'a in the northern Muslim states in one form or another has been pivotal to this process across ethnic groups, precolonial polities, social classes, and genders for the past millennium.

More generally, several long-term patterns underlying what Hodgson (1974) calls the long-term process of shari'aization are observable in the predominantly Muslim northern states. Muslim revitalization movements seeking reform (*tajdid*) almost always originate in the pilgrimage centers of Mecca and Medina, and constantly inspire local Nigerian sects to imitate a specific reform practice. Understanding the shari'a movement in northern Nigeria, however, requires acknowledging the fact that the different waves of Islamic reform are not simply regional expressions of a desire for *tajdid*. Instead, each wave is an extension of a parallel process of Muslim globalization, one that was consolidated as a networked proto-globalization system by the end of the first millennium.

Historically, charismatic preachers, Muslim jurists, Sufi mystics, or groups of Islamic scholars (who were often also traders) pursued *tajdid* in the northern states. Typically, self-conscious communities pursuing *tajdid* withdrew from the surrounding corrupt society; some launched reformist or even revolutionary jihadi movements to subordinate non-believers or to purify backsliders; and still others practiced *tajdid* in their hearts and by their acts, expressing their protest as pious, observant Muslims. Because the discourse of *tajdid* is inscribed so deeply in the northern Muslim public's understanding of Islamic reform, *tajdid*-inspired movements are inevitable during moral, economic, or political crises. In turn, cycles of enthusiastic *tajdid* are, predictably, followed by deep disillusionment when these movements fail to institutionalize the imagined "community of virtue."

Today, all of the demographic dice are loaded in favor of militant Islamist youth movements in northern Nigeria. High fertility rates, youthful marriage, near-universal female marriage, conspiratorial hostility to "Western" family planning programs, and improved infant survival rates since the 1960s have created a population bubble which, in due time, has given rise to a gigantic youth cohort that has overwhelmed already constricted labor markets. Nigerian tertiary educational institutions, for example, have grown exponentially since independence, from two in 1960 to more than a hundred today, with an estimated enrollment reaching 182,000 in 1990 (Fourchard 2005, 342). One example of the regional educational imbalances and the uneven breadth of subsequent growth is that, of the 2,290 students enrolled in the two Nigerian universities in 1960, only three hundred (13 percent) were from the Northern Region, which represented half of the population (Sanusi 2007, 181). Murray Last notes that metropolitan Kano has increased at least tenfold in the last forty-five years, that villages registering 1,500 taxpayers in 1955 now have populations exceeding 75,000, and that these changes have provoked a widespread feeling of "vulnerability" as well as "physical and spiritual insecurity" (Last 2008, 42ff.).

Accordingly, the shari'a reform movement was founded upon three interconnected bases: first, several large cohorts of secondary and tertiary school leavers entering saturated labor markets after 1983; second, a shared sense of declining social and economic opportunity as a result of economic crises associated with the boom-and-bust cycle of the petro-markets; and third, widespread disillusionment with the insatiable greed and incompetence of secular politicians, both civilian and military.

In any event, for the cohorts entering young adulthood in the eighties, the catastrophic failure of Nigeria's postcolonial development project was read through the cultural lens of *tajdid* rather than a secular nationalist or radical framework. There is no doubt that for the youths participating in the Muslim public sphere in the eighties, the spectacular failure of Nigerian oligarchic rule confirmed what their cultural nationalist and anti-imperialist instincts told them was true. For these cohorts, the obvious failure of Western-imposed institutions to meet their material and spiritual needs confirmed that they should recommit themselves to *tajdid* in order to implement shari'a as an alternative path to realizing Muslim self-determination. Viewed from this understandable yet utopian perspective, the triumph of the shari'a movement in the northern Muslim states was predictable, if not overdetermined, by the convergence of demographic, structural, institutional, and cultural forces. Given the decline of secular alternatives and the embeddedness of *tajdid* in the Muslim public discourse, joining one or more Muslim reform movements was an entirely rational option for northern Muslim youth.

Kane's analysis of the neo-Salafi group 'Yan Izala brilliantly illustrates how religious entrepreneurs effectively linked their spiritual capital with the material capital of local businessmen and wealthy military officers so as to promote religious reform against established Sufi brotherhoods (*turuq*) (Kane 2003). Here one must recognize how the spiritual and material economy articulate with each other. Not only did the collapse of employment opportunities in the modern sector flood the spiritual economy with a pool of reform-minded recruits, the resulting material and spiritual insecurity increased both the demand for, and the opportunity for religious entrepreneurs to deliver, spiritual and educational services to a new clientele.

To be sure, there are some barriers to entry into religious entrepreneurship. Religious entrepreneurs must practice "innovative authenticity" in order to convince members of the Muslim public sphere that the discourse or ritual practice they are advocating is authentically Islamic, superior to existing choices, and not yet available locally. This discursive practice is truly challenging. Indeed, to avoid the charge of un-Islamic innovation (*bidah*), the spiritual entrepreneur must legitimate his practice by linking it to the Prophet or his companions (*ahl al-Salaf*). In order to compete in the spiritual marketplace, therefore, a purveyor of innovative authenticity must provide an appealing religious practice or spiritual experience that is not currently available, yet one that is defendable against the charge of *bidah*. In the case of the shari'a movement, flourishing links to globally networked Islamic centers in the Middle East provided the prestigious discursive content for creating innovative authenticity, while wealthy local patrons provided the material resources for successful entrepreneurs to implement a *tajdid* program. Of course, the absence of an effective hierarchy of authority, low barriers to entry, and the easy opportunity for discursive innovation resulted in the formation of a plethora of splinter groups rapidly dividing from the original reformist movement, such as Boko Haram, which rose from the 'Yan Izala.

Shari'a in the Northern States: A Historical Overview

After Islam was introduced into northern Nigeria at Borno during the first millennium, several waves of *tajdid* gradually extended the influence of shari'a in the northern states. The documentary record confirms that shari'a was established in Kano as early as the fifteenth century, under the Hausa king Rumfa (1463–99). Rumfa was assisted by al-Maghili, a North African scholar, who wrote a treatise for him on Islamic government entitled *The Obligations of Princes* (Naniya 2002). By the latter half of the eighteenth century, a charismatic legal scholar and Sufi from a clerical Fulani clan, Usman dan Fodio (1754–1817), inspired a jihad against backsliding rulers who refused his call for

Islamic reform and the enforcement of shari'a. Dan Fodio's movement established the Sokoto Caliphate, one of the largest, most complexly organized, and ethnically diverse political and economic units ever recorded in precolonial African history. Today the restoration of shari'a criminal law reimagines itself in the caliphate's shari'aization policies.

While several northern states—Borno, Yobe, Zamfara, and Kebbi—remained outside the caliphate, dan Fodio's reform movement has become the exemplary model for aspiring *mutajdids* to emulate today. Note that while dan Fodio was primarily a charismatic preacher, a jurist, and a shari'a-minded legal reformer, he was also a practicing Sufi who used Qadiriyya networks to publicize and promote his reform movement. Umar, for example, asserts that "the Qadiriyya was adopted as a kind of official Sufi order" and Loimeier cites documents suggesting that membership in the Qadiriyya was required among the jihadi elite (Umar 1993, 154; Loimeier 1997). Nonetheless, while there is abundant evidence that shari'a increasingly defined the perspective of ruling groups, urban dwellers, and ulama networks, the degree to which shari'a practices actually regulated the lives of rural commoners and servile groups is more difficult to assess. Accordingly, the key points here are not only that the promotion of shari'a reform became the legitimating discourse for the caliphate's Muslim elites, but also that the now venerated leaders of the Sokoto Caliphate institutionalized membership in a mystical Sufi order, the Qadiriyya, and some may have even converted to a rival brotherhood, the Tijaniyya (Last 1973).

The British conquest was completed by 1903, after a millenarian resistance movement (Mahdism) was suppressed by a joint Muslim-British force. Drawing upon their experiments with indirect rule and "Anglo-Muhammadan" law on the Indian subcontinent (see Muhammad Zaman's chapter in this volume), the British amalgamated the Muslim polities of Borno, Sokoto, and other states with those of non-Muslim groups in order to form the Protectorate of the Northern Provinces of Nigeria. The British agreed to "rule along native lines" by appointing Muslim emirs, not interfering with the Muslim religion, enforcing a modified version of Islamic law, and prohibiting Christian missionaries from proselytizing among Muslims. Realistically, of course, with less than a hundred men and a small number of officers to govern the vast Protectorate of the Northern Provinces (a vast territory of 276,034 square miles and "a population estimated at 8.7 million" [Umar 2006, 24]), the British had little choice but to pursue "colonialism on the cheap" by governing indirectly through Muslim rulers and shari'a. This required centralizing and rationalizing the already existing Muslim administration in order to collect taxes and maintain law and order through shari'a courts.

Indirect rule had many paradoxical effects. With so few officers serving, without cultural support from evangelical Christian missionaries, and with widespread Muslim cultural and political resistance, the impact of the British on northern societies was very limited. While colonialism extended the technical domination of the British and Muslim rulers, mostly through improvements like rail and road transport, radio and telegraph communications, and superior weaponry, the same improvements also centralized the power of emirs over their subjects by eliminating traditional checks on arbitrary rule. Within the Northern Provinces, where at least a third of the population were non-Muslims, the British not only extended the territorial range of Muslim rule over non-Muslims but also introduced a colonialized version of shari'a law (e.g., Anglo-Muhammadan) into the non-Muslim areas, which were increasingly Christian.

Sani Umar seeks to undermine the consensus position that British rule strengthened and expanded the position of Islam in colonial Africa and in Northern Nigeria in particular. Anderson, for example, argues for the uniqueness of shari'a criminal law in colonial Northern Nigeria:

> The case of Northern Nigeria was, indeed, almost unique, for up till [1960] this was the only place outside the Arabian Peninsula in which the Islamic law, both substantive and procedural, was applied in criminal litigation—sometimes even in regard to capital offences. (Anderson 1976, 27–28)

Umar (2006), however, will accept none of this. Instead, he rejects Anderson's generalizations by using Arabic texts that give voice to a counternarrative that shows how emirs, judges, and the ulama resisted British efforts to gradually "modernize" (read "colonize") shari'a. For him, British efforts to modernize shari'a only distorted and subverted the integrity and true practice of shari'a law in the eyes of Muslims.

Umar shows that the British subverted shari'a law in several ways: canonical punishments like stoning, amputation, and penance were eliminated (although he notes that these sentences had never been commonly carried out); rules of evidence and legal procedures were subverted; British-appointed emirs, unqualified in shari'a law, were appointed as appellate judges over truly qualified Muslim judges to support the centralization of the colonial state; alien legal scholars introduced "Anglo-Mohammedan" law from the British empire; and, with the judicial reforms of 1933, shari'a courts became completely subordinate to British courts of appeal. Notwithstanding these restrictions, the Native Authority courts, both Muslim and customary, were widely used by colonial subjects. For example, in 1947, the northern provinces recorded 197,586 civil cases and 72,214 criminal cases, of which the overwhelming majority were heard in shari'a courts (Christelow 2002, 191).

Since the Northern and Southern protectorates were never integrated before World War II, during the transition to national independence the status of shari'a law became a contentious issue between the British and Muslim northern elites. In constitutional terms, the negotiations produced a decentralized federal state in which the British allowed the northern Muslims to control the largest region in exchange for eliminating shari'a criminal law. For the Muslim public, the bargain was double-edged. On one hand, it created a Muslim-dominated and relatively autonomous northern region which protected northern Muslim interests within the federation, including those of the northern civil service, who faced competition from better-educated southerners. On the other, it forced the northern regional legislature to accept the shari'a compromise of 1960 which effectively eliminated shari'a criminal law. Modeled after the penal code of the Sudan, the new Northern Nigerian Penal Code eliminated the shari'a criminal legal system in favor of a code that drew upon "Islamic penal jurisprudence and English common law tradition" in a compromise designed to protect the rights of Christian and traditional religious communities within the Northern Region, who accounted for a third of the population (Mahmoud 2002). The system of shari'a courts and judges, however, was not abolished; instead, its jurisdiction until 1999–2000 was limited to civil and personal law. Understandably, northern Muslim agitation for a return to shari'a surfaced during the constitutional conference of 1977–78 and again in 1987–88, when Muslims unsuccessfully demanded a Federal Shari'a Court of Appeal.

To summarize this snapshot of shari'a in the northern states: first, some version of shari'a law has been in force within many northern Muslim communities for at least five hundred years. Second, a version of shari'a criminal law has been enforced for hundreds of years—under the Hausa kings, the Sokoto Caliphate, the sultanate of Borno, the British protectorate, and now the northern governors—except for a comparatively brief thirty-nine-year interlude between 1960 and 1999. And finally, given the demonstrable persistence of shari'aization as a long-term historical process implemented under so many different political regimes, the question is not whether Muslims regard shari'a criminal law as legitimate, but how that law is to be interpreted and enforced.

Shari'a and Sectarian Conflict:
The Politics of Transnational Linkages

Earlier I described how Sufi networks practicing *tajdid* extended the frontier of Muslim power in precolonial northern Nigeria. In general, Sufi influence in West Africa increased significantly under colonial rule. The most dramatic change in northern Nigeria was that Sufism extended beyond the ulama and ruling groups to thoroughly penetrate the commoner trading groups and their associated ulama. If colonialism brought greater freedom and financial power to the Muslim merchant class, Sufism provided the spiritual solidarity and social networks for their consolidation as a powerful new social group. The reasons for this growth of the merchant class are well documented: Not only did the colonial order bring peace, end slave raiding, increase commodity production, require the production of export crops to pay higher taxes, and support the extension of Islamic education and law, it vastly improved commercial, transportation, and communications infrastructures, which bolstered the trading and financial opportunities of Muslim mercantile capitalists.

All of the latter material changes vastly increased opportunities for Sufi leaders (*moquaddams*) to recruit followers into wider networks that reached from West Africa to the Hijaz. Since Islamic scholars were often traders, an expanding network of Sufi lodges (*zawiyas*) also offered invaluable services like credit, brokerage, and market information to members of their brotherhood. Equally important, Sufi networks integrated Muslim traders, scholars, and students from different ethnic groups and regions into a new trans-ethnic identity: northern Muslim. In sociological terms, the Sufis' daily rituals provided disciplinary practices that intensified trans-ethnic social solidarity, making members feel safer as they engaged in negotiating complex credit arrangements within patron-client networks situated in an expanding colonial market economy. Thus, for burgeoning trading groups who were suddenly vulnerable to new financial risks and who feared the uncertainties of expensive colonial courts for dispute resolution, Sufi lodges, collective rituals, and charismatic leadership met the growing social need for an institutionalized network to support their spiritual and material interests.

During the colonial era of northern Nigeria, no Sufi brotherhood thrived more than the Tijaniyya; no Tijani leader claimed more followers than the Senegalese *moquaddam* Shaykh Ibrahim Niass; and, unfortunately, no Sufi brotherhood's claims enraged neo-Salafi reformers more than those of the Tijaniyya-Niassiyya. A number of factors contributed to the rise of the Tijaniyya in northern Nigeria. Politically, from the 1830s, when Alhaji Umar Tall introduced the Tijani initiation (*wirdi*) from Mecca into the Sokoto elite, the Tijaniyya represented an enduring challenge to the monopoly on authority enjoyed by the Qadiri-affiliated rulers of the Sokoto Caliphate. Similarly, during the nationalist period, the Tijaniyya challenged the authority of the conservative nationalist leader Ahmadu Bello, who was not only the leader of the dominant northern party, the Northern Peoples Congress (NPC), but also a direct descendant of Usman dan Fodio. In the nineteenth century, the emir of Zaria was deposed for his Tijani affiliation; in 1963, Bello deposed the Tijani-affiliated emir of Kano, Mohammed Sanusi (Loimeier 2005b, 350; Loimeier 1997).

On the other hand, many Muslims found the exclusionary and pretentious doctrines propagated by the Tijaniyya highly objectionable. The Tijaniyya's Algerian founder, Ahmad al-Tijani (1737–1815), claimed to have experienced a direct link with the Prophet through a vision in which the Prophet affirmed that "he was the 'seal of wilaya' [the final mediating saint] in the same way that the Prophet Mohammad was the seal of prophethood" (Vikør 2000, 450). In addition to offering members salvation and prosperity through a direct link to the Prophet, the Tijaniyya forbade members to affiliate with rival Sufi orders. Similarly, the brotherhood reduced the number, complexity, and ascetic rigor of esoteric spiritual exercises. Thus the Tijaniyya not only guaranteed salvation but granted Tijanis additional time and incentives to become engaged in the world as successful traders. Of course, these practices attracted the enthusiastic support of Muslim mercantile capitalists, so that their client and credit networks became increasingly intertwined with those of the brotherhood.

Nonetheless, until the rise of the Senegalese shaykh Ibrahim Niass (1900–75), Sufism was largely limited to a literate and prosperous elite: the ulama, the scholar-traders, and their advanced students. Previously, Sufism "impacted only a small group of scholars and students" because *tasawwuf* (Sufism) "was considered the 'final step' of a scholar" who had already completed study of the Qur'an, the hadith, and other Islamic sciences (Loimeier 2005b, 353). Niass's singular achievement was to transform the Sufi spiritual experience into a mass movement accessible to uneducated commoners, thereby integrating different Muslim communities in Nigeria and West Africa. To accomplish this feat, Niass first declared that he was the expected "Reformer of the Age"; second, he renewed his initiations into all Tijani spiritual lineages in order to obtain the most direct link possible to the founder; and third, he introduced a popularized version of the initiation and educational rite, *tarbiyya,* which was accessible not only to the learned and ascetic, but also to the illiterate and uneducated (Paden 1973).

Consequently, although he originated from a low-caste blacksmithing group in Senegal, Niass's charisma and ambition empowered him to become a transformative leader even among Nigeria's elites. In 1937, he successfully initiated the emir of Kano into the Tijaniyya-Niassiyya lineage (Paden 1973). Niass's success derived from his ability to promote his mystical concept of *tarbiyya* (e.g., esoteric spiritual education) among a largely uneducated mass audience. Elsewhere, in the frontier regions of the Middle Belt, the Tijaniyya-Niassiyya brotherhood had similar effects: it recruited illiterates via *tarbiyya,* integrated members of competing clans, promised followers spiritual and economic success, and extended the commercial networks of the trading groups (Mohammed 1993).

Nationalism, Reformism, and the Modern Muslim Public Sphere

As influential opinion makers, the leaders of Sufi brotherhoods were lavishly patronized by wealthy merchants and courted by aspiring politicians during the nationalist era following World War II. However, while they could influence electorates, Sufi leaders lacked the credentials, vision, and linguistic skills to become directly involved in the intense political negotiations regarding the constitutional form of the new Nigerian state. Understandably, Sufi attention was directed inward, toward realizing an esoteric communal experience, and not toward constructing a new Muslim public sphere in the Northern Region. Responsibility for the construction of the Muslim public sphere fell instead upon the shoulders of the northern nationalist leaders and their advisors. These men had been educated in elite English-language schools like Katsina College, hybrid but essentially modern institutions, which had been established by the colonial state to rationalize indirect rule and create an educated administrative class.

Educated in Western as well as Islamic learning, the Muslim nationalist leaders struggled among themselves, as well as with the British and southern nationalists, over the questions of how to balance national and regional powers, the position of non-Muslims in the Northern Region's government, and the role that shari'a would play in the embryonic Nigerian polity. Thus, even though eminent nationalist leaders—including the progressive Mallam Aminu Kano (Northern Elements Progressive Union) and the conservative Ahmadu Bello (Northern Peoples Congress)—may have sought the support of Sufi brotherhood leaders, their objectives during these negotiations were quintessentially modern, bureaucratic, and nationalist. They sought to limit the autonomous patrimonial powers of the emirs, their courts, and the police; build effective political party organizations; and use the autonomous powers of the Northern Region's government to develop and modernize educational, economic, social, and political institutions in their comparatively backward region. In order for Bello to carry out his conservative modernization project, in the face of resistance to the northern regional government from the emirs and their Sufi allies, Bello required a new source of religious legitimacy, a new Islamic discourse, and a new national religious organization to advance his conservative yet modernizing Muslim project. His strategy involved reaching out to allies in the wider Muslim world, especially Saudi Arabia, creating a new Islamic reform organization, the Jama'at Nasr al-Islam in 1962, and recruiting a religious advisor from a Sokoto-based judicial family named Abubakar Gumi (1922–92).

Gumi was destined to be the person most responsible for the restoration of shari'a criminal law in Nigeria. He was a legal scholar known for prodigious scholarship, indefatigable polemical energy, and a practical commitment to promoting the interests of the northern Muslim political elite. Under the patronage of Bello and subsequent northern heads of state, such as President Shagari (1979–83) and General Babangida (1985–93), Gumi spearheaded neo-Salafi Islamic reform for nearly forty years, challenging what he believed were the brotherhoods' un-Islamic innovations (*bidah*), sponsoring the upgrading of modern Islamic education, and insisting on the need to fully implement shari'a law at all levels in Nigeria. Whatever Shaykh Ibrahim Niass accomplished in making the Tijaniyya a mass movement in the colonial era, Gumi surpassed him in advancing neo-Salafi reform and shari'a law in the postcolonial era.

Unlike the modernizing national elites whom he often advised on Islamic affairs, Gumi chose to pursue a modern Arabic and Islamic education by attending and teaching at the School of Arabic Studies (SAS) at Kano. Subsequently, when the British refused to send him to Al-Azhar in Cairo for fear that he would fall under the influence of the Muslim Brotherhood, he studied law at Bakht ar-Ruda College in Khartoum in 1954–55 (Loimeier 1997). His fluency in Arabic and his courage in challenging the authoritarian sultan of Sokoto for having accepted British imperial titles endeared him to Ahmadu Bello, who appointed him as his translator when they were on hajj together in Saudi Arabia. Fortuitously, when the Saudis broke diplomatic relations with Britain over the Israeli, British, and French invasion of Egypt in the 1956 war, thus leaving Nigerian pilgrims subject to deportation from the Hijaz without diplomatic representation, Bello appointed Gumi as the first Nigerian Pilgrims' Officer in Saudi Arabia and later as his personal representative to the World Muslim League (Rabitat al-Alam al-Islami), a Saudi-controlled, neo-Salafi reform group.

All of these appointments were critical for Gumi's ascendance as a political power broker as well as the preeminent voice for the restoration of shari'a in Nigeria. Since the hajj is so important for the approximately one hundred thousand Nigerians who undertake the pilgrimage each year, Gumi's integration into the scholarly networks in the pilgrimage cities gave him unprecedented prestige and great leverage for legitimating a neo-Salafi movement for *tajdid* in Nigeria. His appointments not only provided him with opportunities to assume roles in Saudi universities and prestigious Rabitat-linked agencies, they also enabled him to become a trusted broker for the distribution of Saudi patronage in Nigeria. When the petro-boom of 1973–74 swelled Saudi and Gulf state coffers, Gumi was ideally positioned to distribute Saudi patronage to neo-Salafi reformers.

It is also important to emphasize the impact that exposure to neo-Salafi groups like the Muslim Brotherhood had on Gumi's intellectual formation. Loimeier (1997, 180ff.) argues persuasively that Gumi's networking and appointments in Saudi Arabia and Egypt brought him under the influence of Muslim Brotherhood thinkers as well as South Asian neo-Salafis like Maududi. Gumi absorbed the methods and doctrines propagated by Sayyid Qutb, including the latter's methods of Qur'anic commentary (*tafsir*) and his willingness to condemn practicing Muslims as unbelievers (*takfir*). Similarly, after translating anti-Ahmadiyya works by South Asian scholars, Gumi supported Maududi's request that the Rabitat declare the Ahmadiyya heretics and thus unacceptable as pilgrims (Loimeier 1997, 160). In 1974, Gumi also convinced Nigerian Islamic authorities to require prospective pilgrims to certify that they were not Ahmadiyya members before arranging for their visas for the hajj. In effect, Gumi had leveraged his influence as a member of the governing council of the Rabitat to empower him to define who was an orthodox Muslim in Nigeria.

Equally important, in opposition to conservative scholars of fiqh (law), Gumi not only supported the reopening of the gates of ijtihad but "adopted a position which is generally identified with the ideals of the Salafiyya and the Ikhwan al-muslimin [Muslim Brotherhood] " (Loimeier 1997, 181). Interestingly, unlike his patrons in Saudi Arabia, Gumi was a strong advocate for increasing Muslim women's access to education and their participation in electoral politics as well as in the Muslim public sphere. He translated the Qur'an into Hausa and used Saudi largesse to distribute hundreds of thousands of copies. He was among the first preachers to use radio (in 1966) to broadcast his sermons and Qur'anic exegeses; he also recorded his sermons on inexpensive cassettes for distribution to his followers.

The Discursive Shift to Reformism:
'Yan Boko and the 'Yan Izala

Gumi's intellectual and political career was devoted to an unrestrained frontal assault on the intellectual and doctrinal legitimacy of Sufism. Methodologically, after subjecting Sufi beliefs, rituals, and writings to rigorous scriptural analysis, Gumi concluded that Sufism is filled with un-Islamic innovations not found in the Qur'an or Sunna, and therefore constitutes un-Islamic belief. Indeed, he asserted that Sufism is a post-Islamic religion, whose praise songs to the Prophet make it impossible to see either God or the Prophet (Loimeier 1997, 230).

At first, these claims provoked a firestorm of denunciations, violent confrontations, and even threats against his life. In response to the damage inflicted to their prestige as well as their membership, rival Sufi groups joined forces to form organizations like the Fityan al-Islam to defend the orthodoxy of their practices. By 1978, Gumi's authority over the Jama'at Nasr al-Islam was challenged by Sufis at the northern regional level, and his effort to insert shari'a law into the federal constitution of the Second Republic failed. At this point Gumi and his followers made a strategic decision to create a modern, populist, mass-based organization to spearhead a neo-Salafi reform movement and to transform Nigeria's Muslim public sphere.

The organization's name, Jama'at Izalat al-Bidaa wa-Iqamat as Sunna or 'Yan Izala, presages the contemporary movement to restore shari'a criminal law in northern Nigeria. Meaning "Society for the Removal of Innovation and the Restoration of the Tradition," it was taken from a work by Usman dan Fodio, *In Favor of the Sunna and Against Innovation* (Paden 2002). To counter the Sufi accusation that it was a foreign, Wahhabi sect, the 'Yan Izala demonstrated its modernity by registering as a legal entity with the Federal Ministry of Internal Affairs in 1985 (Umar 1993). While today it constitutes a powerful network like the Sufis, the 'Yan Izala is organized as a modern civil society group with membership lists, a constitution, statutes, appointed offices, branches, and an extensive network of modern Islamic schools. The organization has affiliates in several neighboring countries, especially Niger.

The Muslim Students' Society (MSS) also came to play a key role in mobilizing popular support for the restoration of shari'a. Founded in Lagos in 1954 by Yoruba Muslims who felt isolated at Methodist Boys' Secondary School, and named after a Burmese organization of the same name, the MSS eventually became one of the largest voluntary organizations in Nigeria. Its organizational power derives from its unified national structure and its extensive network of branches in secondary and tertiary institutions. In 1970, the MSS had more than seven hundred branches (Paden 2008, 30); most of the leadership of the shari'a movement was associated with it at some time in their student careers. By organizing Muslim students at all levels from secondary school through university, the MSS incubated a wide variety of Islamic political and social movements, including those with radical tendencies, like Nigerian Shi'ism, and reformist tendencies, like the Council of Ulama. It is no exaggeration to say that the shari'a movement embodies the political project of a generation whose worldview was defined during their time as students in secondary and tertiary institutions while participating in MSS campaigns for the recognition of Muslim rights, the Islamization of politics, and the implementation of shari'a law in Nigeria.

Against this historical backdrop, it is easy to see how Gumi's combination of polemical assaults on Sufism and the introduction of globally sourced neo-Salafi doctrines appeared so compelling to a newly educated audience. Once the economic crisis of the eighties dashed their hope for secure employment as teachers or ulama in the state sector, Muslim university graduates were readily available for mobilization into populist, neo-Salafi reform movements like the 'Yan Izala and the shari'a movement. While opposed to magic and all Sufi forms of *bidah,* the 'Yan Izala targeted the beliefs and practices of the Tijaniyya for especially vitriolic excoriation. Indeed, for the 'Yan Izala, the list of Tijani *bidah* is extensive: bodily rocking, breathing, and chanting during prayer to induce trances; claims that *tarbiyya* achieves a mystical state of ecstasy, without rational explanations or scriptural referents to support them; the claim that the Prophet and the four rightly guided caliphs participate in Tijani prayers (*dhikr*); and the mystical veneration of Sufi saints' tombs (Loimeier 1997, 194ff.). 'Yan Izala leaders also heaped ridicule on the belief that the Tijani litany *salat al-fatih* (said to be equally powerful whether the initiate understood the words or not) was transmitted by the Prophet to Ahmad al-Tijani. Alas, when this litany was shown to have originated centuries earlier with Shaykh Muhammad al Bakri (1492–1545), the Tijaniyya suffered serious defections and a loss of prestige among the educated just as they had earlier in North Africa (Kane 2003, 127ff., 133).

Turning to explanations for the social basis of recruitment, Kane argues persuasively that the (alternative) modernity of 'Yan Izala practices and doctrines clearly appealed to youthful, urbanized, educated, and reform-minded Muslims in the northern states. Beliefs and practices stressed individual, unmediated examination of the Sunna, and the obligation of literate believers to exercise individual reason in interpreting Muslim beliefs and practices. Fueled by the surplus of unemployed graduates who were bolstered by the certainty of their *tajdid,* the Izala movement inspired peripatetic preachers to reach out to smaller towns and even villages, where they proselytized among youths, women, and partially educated groups. Their preachers emphasized simple, scriptural forms of worship, unencumbered by time-consuming rituals, chants, or supplementary prayers. The movement's commitment to building and staffing free or subsidized Islamic schools not only attracted many new members but also created opportunities for gainful employment in the spiritual economy during the economic crisis of the 1980s.

Above all else, the 'Yan Izala's open egalitarianism appealed to youthful recruits. Traditionally, northern Hausa-speaking Muslim groups inculcate a deep sense of shame (*kunya*) into primary social relationships. *Kunya,* therefore, serves to consciously and subconsciously construct a social subject that must defer to a hierarchal, patriarchal, and rigidly scripted cultural authority. For example, to avoid the embarrassing accusation that they lack *kunya* (*rashin kunya*), people avoid stating the names of first-born children, certain in-laws, and spouses. Youths and women are required to defer to patriarchs. Most importantly for newly educated youths, expensive gifts must be made to ulama, family members, and future in-laws at every stage of a life cycle: birth and naming ceremonies, marriages, funerals, and religious holidays. Marriage payments are especially onerous, and are deeply resented by youths desiring to start families (Kane 2003).

In opposition to these customs, the more individualistic and egalitarian 'Yan Izala offered an alternative modernity, a life-style that recognized both individual reason and dignified piety. It renounced deferential genuflections traditionally required of youths to elders and eliminated costly bride wealth and dowry payments; this reform relieved youths wishing to form families of excessive debt, as well as control by their extended families. Youths, of course, found these reforms liberating, for they allowed them to become more individualized within a new community of believers. Thus, while neo-Salafi reform demanded that youths renounce customary practices like dancing, wrestling, music, and spirit possession rites (bori), its accompanying egalitarianism also contributed to individual emancipation from patriarchal control.

In a movement critics denounce as neo-Wahhabi, nothing is more paradoxical than the 'Yan Izala's support for the rights of women. Traditionally, under the hegemony of Sufism, Hausa-speaking women in most northern Muslim cities did not have access to Islamic education; married women in cities were in purdah if their husbands could afford it; and women were expected to express shame (kunya) by remaining in the household and were certainly not to be active in the Muslim public sphere. Practically, orthodox Islam was what husbands and senior male relatives said it was. In opposition, the 'Yan Izala mobilized its preachers to encourage Muslim women to attend its Islamic schools in the evenings or on Saturdays and Sundays. This meant they could participate more in the Muslim public sphere, provided they dressed modestly by wearing the hijab. In addition to educating girls in its Islamiyya schools, the 'Yan Izala initiated a program of mass Islamic education for married women by providing gender-segregated classes, thus avoiding the charge of gender mixing (ikhtilat). Consequently, the Izala movement provided Muslim women new opportunities to share their "separate but equal" experience of Islamic education as well as to learn more about their rights under shari'a. Kane (2003, 140) has no doubt about the rising number of women enrolled in 'Yan Izala schools, estimating that they "run into the thousands if not hundreds of thousands."

Transitioning to Shari'a: Conflicts, Crises, and Fragmentation

During the decade before the implementation of shari'a criminal law, the northern Muslim community was divided by sectarian conflicts and challenged by the rise of militant Pentecostal Christianity. Many independent Muslims denounced the 'Yan Izala radicals for dividing the community (*fitna*) with their allegations that traditional Muslims and Sufis are not Muslims. In addition, after the death of Gumi in 1992, splinter groups spun off from the 'Yan Izala and a new breed of independent intellectuals emerged in the northern universities who were not affiliated with any particular sect.

Even more fragmentation and divisions appeared when a Shi'a movement broke off from the MSS in Zaria with the funding and support of Iran, a rival to Saudi and Sunni global influence. Led by Ibrahim el-Zakzaky, a social science student at Ahmadu Bello University, and calling themselves the Islamic Movement of Nigeria or 'Yan Brothers, the Shi'as confronted both the Sunni authorities and the military government. Inspired by the Iranian revolution to demand an Islamic state in Nigeria, the Shi'as recruited among the most radical elements of the Islamist community, calling for campaigns against the West, Christians, the 'Yan Izala, and the military governments. El-Zakzaky was imprisoned and later released by the military. The Shi'a movement itself soon splintered, allegedly over El-Zakzaky's affiliation with Iran and the heretical content of Shi'a beliefs, creating a new, radical Sunni movement in 1994 called Jama'at Tajdid Islam. All of these divisions heighted insecurity among Muslims in the north, and thereby encouraged observant believers to view shari'a as a strategy for restoring Muslim unity.

However disconcerting the intra-Muslim conflicts were, the rise of Pentecostal Christianity in Middle Belt states represented an even greater threat to northern Muslim interests. Pentecostal Christians offered fierce opposition to efforts to implement shari'a criminal law in these border states. From the 1980s until today, the borderland region, with its mix of Christians and Muslims, has been the site of bloody intercommunal violence. Ironically, paralleling the Islamization processes, the process of Christianization has served to unify smaller ethnic groups in this region and facilitated the formation of a common Christian identity in opposition to long-dominant Muslim rulers.

Christian memories of exploitation by Muslim slave raiders in the precolonial era and discrimination since independence stoked grievances that found an effective voice in militant Pentecostal Christianity. Historically, communal violence in Nigeria was based upon ethno-national (e.g., tribal) identities, but as religious identities became increasingly politicized and nurtured by militant global networks, religion gradually displaced ethnicity as an identity marker. Religion often became the preferred discourse with which to "other" one's neighboring competitors. The specific disputes provoking these violent conflicts arose over many issues: conversions, land rights, migrant rights, political representations, control over schools, accusations of blasphemy, political patronage, Nigerian membership in the Organization of the Islamic Conference, state subsidies for the hajj, and, of course, the place of shari'a in the 1987–88 constitution. In a classic example of mirror-image victimization, each side accused the other of seeking to dominate, marginalize, and convert its opponents.

Shari'a, of course, confirms the Christians' worst fears. Conversely, in 1990, Muslim fears of marginalization were confirmed when leaders of a failed coup led by a Christian Tiv, Major Gideon Orkar, made a radio announcement stating that discrimination against the Middle Belt must end and, most importantly, that five of the far northern states were to be excised from the federation. In fact, the evangelical and Pentecostal strategy was demonstrably similar to the Muslims'. Both mobilized resources and doctrines from global networks; both stoked the fears of militant believers, discouraging tolerance and dialogue; and neither hesitated to stage large public spectacles in volatile communities.

The local elections of December 1987 marked the tipping point for northern Muslim political fortunes. Muslims were justifiably alarmed because Christians, who were now politically unified and skillfully organized by the Christian Association of Nigeria (CAN), made significant electoral gains throughout the Middle Belt. Gains were registered even in Kaduna, a city that had formerly been an unquestioned stronghold for northern Muslims as well as home of the northern political elite known as the "Kaduna Mafia."

What, then, had changed in the Middle Belt since Ahmadu Bello eliminated shari'a criminal law in the compromise of 1960 in order to mollify northern Christians? The answer lies in the politicization of religious identities among Christians and Muslims and, specifically, the rising organizational power of CAN and the militancy of an evangelical and Pentecostal Christianity fueled by global networks. In 1970, "pentecostals and charismatics *combined* represented less than 5% of Africans," but by 2006 Pentecostals alone represented 12% (about 107 million [Pew Forum 2006a]). In Nigeria, where Pentecostal growth is rapid and their voice increasingly assertive, they represent 18% of the population and 48% of all Protestants, roughly equal to Nigerian Catholics and Anglicans combined. Political consciousness has also increased. According to the Pew survey, 75% of Nigerian Pentecostals believe religious groups should express views on social and political questions (Pew Forum 2006b).

Organizationally, the northern branch of the Christian Association of Nigeria provided the agency required to transform this demographic potential into a militant, grass-roots movement. CAN played a key role in weaving evangelicals and Pentecostals into a new alliance with like-minded Christians from southern Nigeria, thus rupturing the previous northern-based alliance. This new alliance, of course, was opposed to Muslim hegemony in the borderlands as well as to the domination of corrupt northern military regimes.

Ruth Marshall-Fratani, an expert on Nigerian Pentecostalism, stresses the role of new global technologies in which "images, ideas and forms are locally appropriated and used in the creation of new subjectivities and collectivities" (Marshall-Fratani 1998, 311). She argues that these global images are rearticulated within certain strains of Pentecostalism in ways that sharpen the divide between Muslims and Christians:

> Central to [the Pentecostal] strategy of winning Nigeria is the demonisation of Islam. The competition that Islamic movements represent, not only in terms of the religious field, but also in terms of the appropriation of the state-dominated public sphere, results in the linking in Pentecostal discourse of the evil spiritual forces at work behind Islam to the current state of economic and political decline, capitalising on the resentment felt widely among southern Christians about the northern (read Muslim) domination of national politics since independence, and growing fears about the "Islamisation" of the nation-state. (Ibid., 309)

Restorationism: The Politics of Implementing Shari'a

The divisions among northern Muslims, coupled with the challenge represented by militant Pentecostalism, contributed to a heightened sense of insecurity among northern Muslims after the power shift of 1999 carried Obasanjo to power. Subsequently, northern Muslim industrial and commercial groups also felt severely disadvantaged by the way Obasanjo liberalized the Nigerian economy, privatized state industries, and restructured the banking industry. And for obvious reasons, the Bush administration's launching of the "global war on terror" increased the northern Muslim sense of defensiveness. Taken together, these experiences provoked disillusionment with the possibility or perhaps the appropriateness of achieving modern development and the likelihood of achieving higher living standards. Social energy was redirected more exclusively toward bolstering communal boundaries between groups within the northern states. Rather than pursuing realistic economic development projects, Islamic redistribution projects were emphasized. Subscribing to the shari'a movement in the broadest possible sense—as a way of life—became an important instrument for refashioning northern Muslim identity.

The discourses articulated by the architects of the shari'a project provide an excellent window into the ways a new generation of independent public intellectuals are reconstructing northern Muslim identity. In April 2001, more than four hundred delegates met in London at a conference sponsored by the Nigeria Muslim Forum (UK) entitled "The Restoration of Shariah in Nigeria: Challenges and Benefits." Accompanied by emirs and governors from the shari'a states of Nigeria, delegates heard several learned scholars present papers advocating the restoration of shari'a criminal law. Interestingly, the presenters did not represent the harsher, Wahhabi-oriented neo-Salafists, who are more active in promoting shari'a law at the grass roots. Instead, they were Western-educated Muslim intellectuals respected for their moderation, independence, and sympathy for women's rights. Speakers included Professor Ali Mazrui, Professor Auwalu Yadudu, Dr. Muhammed Tabiu, and Malam Ibraheem Sulaiman.

Several papers at the conference referred directly to the degradation of shari'a courts during colonialism and the need to defend the restoration of shari'a criminal law as a cultural right protected by the Nigerian constitution. Just as Mohammed Sani Umar argued above, Tabiu (2001) pointed out that under colonialism the administration of the shari'a was corrupted to such a degree by the British that many learned and respectable scholars avoided appointment as judges. Yadudu (2001) emphasized that shari'a arose from the democratic dispensation and was an assertion of group identity protected by the constitution. Sulaiman (2001) challenged the Nigerian umma to abolish illiteracy, affirm democracy, and improve livelihoods by employing scientific knowledge acquired over the ages. He argued that science must be a source of Islamic law.

To be sure, popular support for implementing shari'a is driven by many different motivations. The new Muslim intellectual elites represent shari'a as a restorationist political project, one intended to assuage the wound inflicted on the umma by colonial rule. The boundaries of the umma, too, are reimagined by restorationism, for it now includes communities that rejected the Sokoto Caliphate, such as Borno, Zamfara, and Kebbi. Serving on one of the many state commissions—on shari'a, zakat, or hisba—empowers observant elite and professional Muslims to expunge the pollution inserted by colonial subjugation and appeal to believers to invest in creating a postcolonial Muslim identity. Writing on identity within Islamist movements elsewhere, Burgat insightfully conceptualizes these emotions as a stage following those of political and economic decolonization, by referring to "the reaction to the cultural impact of the colonial irruption that today has ignited the Islamist 'third stage' of the 'rocket of de-colonisation'" (Burgat 2003, 49).

As noted above, once the governor of Zamfara introduced shari'a criminal legislation, popular demand for the implementation of shari'a spread like a wildfire across the northern states. The nature of shari'a implementation, however, varied significantly, according to the zeal of the local shari'a movement, the strength of traditional rulers who encouraged moderation, and the proportion of non-Muslims within a state. With a large Christian population, Kaduna State registered high levels of religious conflict over the implantation of shari'a in 2000, leading to at least 1,500 deaths, the displacement of some 30,000 people, and increased residential segregation of Christians and Muslims in the city of Kaduna. In 2003, a riot occurred over the Miss World contest. Subsequently, the Muslim governor of Kaduna negotiated the limited application of shari'a in the state. Niger State also has a mixed population and has licensed liquor sales as a result. Zamfara, on the other hand, has implemented the harshest and most intolerant regime of any Nigerian state, and Kano ranks close behind, with greater communal conflict and very active *hisba* groups. States like Katsina, Borno, and Sokoto, although more homogeneously Muslim, are known for implementing shari'a with moderation. A member of the Katsina shari'a commission whom I interviewed spoke of shari'a as a voluntary educational project, a way of life, and not a license to inflict cruel punishments. Readers must bear in mind not only that the shari'a criminal laws are uncodified but that their interpretation and enforcement vary widely according to the decisions of local judges.

The poor members of the popular classes rallied around shari'a because they hoped that the *zakat* tax on the affluent (2.5 percent of liable assets) would result in the redistribution of wealth. Indeed, a supporter of shari'a, Murray Last, describes its implementation in Zamfara as having a millenarian quality, especially for the poor, who expected it to lead to economic justice and redistribution of wealth (Last 2000). In Kano, for example, approximately a million people turned out to celebrate the passing of shari'a in 2000. The banning of alcohol, prostitution, gambling, and immodest dress also appears to enjoy popular support even among evangelical Christians, according to interviews with local researchers. Aside from the intellectual project of Muslim public intellectuals, a major source of support for shari'a came from Muslim commoners (*talakawa*) who were disillusioned with the performance of the secular state's legal and criminal justice systems. Complaints against secular law included rising criminality, increased armed violence, endless delays and appeals, the cost of legal counsel, lack of access to dispute resolution, and corruption. The advantage of shari'a, advocates argued, was that judgments would be swift, access improved, and citizen participation increased because Muslims already spoke the language of shari'a and understood its principles of justice, which was not true of Nigerian common law.

The actual implementation of shari'a by popular groups was, of course, marked by arbitrary imprisonment, vigilantism by self-appointed religious police (*hisba*), intimidation of Christians, and the infliction of punishments without trial. Human Rights Watch published an exhaustive report (2004) documenting the human rights abuses associated with the implementation of shari'a law. This and other reports have led critics to complain that shari'a is applied only to the poor, the weak, and women, while the powerful and wealthy avoid coming before a shari'a judge. (Indeed, Muslim critics challenged me to disprove this generalization.)

Implementation did succeed in raising the level of popular participation in legal and other forms of shari'a-minded governance. Each state absorbed educated Muslim males by appointing many advisors on Islamic legal issues, impaneling commissions to advise on all issues, and, in general, creating a link between Islamic civil society groups, informal *hisba* community groups, and salaried state officials. Kano State, for example, has commissions for shari'a, *hisba, zakat,* censorship of the media, and societal reorientation (*Adai dai ta sahu*). Today, quotations from the Qur'an, in English and Arabic, are posted on road signs throughout Kano City, and billboards exhort the *umma* to realize a "republic of virtue" by fulfilling the ideals of *dar al Islam.* One can agree with Murray Last's observation that the shari'a movement has introduced a new form of citizenship, that of the *umma,* one which is both regional and global, to complement Nigerian citizenship (Last 2008).

The high levels of participation in shari'a implementation raise questions about demographic cohorts and the generational politics of the activists and scholars. Sanusi describes the core activists as "from poor backgrounds," having "little Western education," "settlers in their host communities," using "Wahhabism as a vehicle for social mobility and as a challenge to the establishment" (Sanusi 2007, 184). Thus it is easy to see how competition among the activists for access to power, status, and resources drives the implementers to purer and more extreme stances. At the same time, despite the chaos and abuse of human rights, the implementation of shari'a has incorporated large numbers of men (although not women, to be sure) into a disciplined social project, that of restoring the northern shari'a-minded *umma.* In contrast to the Egyptian situation described by Carrie Wickham (2002), where an ossified political system and a centralized state prevented a new generation of Islamistic reformers from attaining political power, Nigeria's federal system and the open, participatory structures in the shari'a states have created many opportunities for a new generation of MSS graduates to hold office and advisory posts. It is entirely likely that these offices have incorporated groups whose grievances have the potential to threaten security and the positive features of democratic rule.

Assessing Gender Issues under the Restoration of Shari'a

Several conflicting trends must be recognized when evaluating how the restoration of shari'a affected gender relations and the condition of women. It is irrefutable that the shari'a movement is intensely focused on controlling the public behavior and opportunities of girls and women. Indeed, the shari'a movement's organizational apparatus—commissions, the *hisba* patrols, and generalized control over public morality—has increased the power of extremely conservative and narrowly trained ulama to regulate women, especially those who are poor, uneducated, and powerless. Nevertheless, women's education has increased significantly during this period and, equally important, civil society groups have raised the profile of women's issues involving health, education, and access to justice. These two trends constitute a dialectic which is working itself out in the communities of Muslim northern Nigeria.

As indicated above, the Sufi brotherhoods were associated with the seclusion of women and the reduction of traditional (pre-Islamic) rights enjoyed by northern women, but not with restricting their religious education. Elite women, typically the bright daughters of ulama, have traditionally had access to Islamic learning since the jihad (Mack and Boyd 2000). One major trend that has continued is the increase in the number of girls and young women who are enrolled in the state-sponsored and private Islamic educational systems. Umar's research on female ulama not only presents two superb ethnographic profiles of ulama (*mallama*) with contrasting interpretations of Islamism but also provides some estimates of female enrollment in Izala-sponsored schools. He estimates that from a third to as many as one-half of the graduates of such schools are women, and that up to a quarter of the women graduates have completed university degrees in Islamic studies (2004, 109). The increasing Islamic education of women in Western and Islamic studies is, arguably, the most powerful change occurring in the Muslim world and it is affecting the rights of women living under shari'a law in northern Nigeria.

Interviews with female ulama, educated women, and health providers confirm that the number of female Islamic teachers is increasing, the number of educated women participating in Islamic civil society groups is growing, and these women are participating in the debates within the public sphere regarding the meaning and application of shari'a. To be sure, this is a middle- and professional-class phenomenon, but, nonetheless, this is a radical change within the conservative Muslim societies of northern Nigeria. Interviews with female judges indicate that women are engaging with and debating personal status law, divorce rights, and other issues related to shari'a law. Gwarzo's field work on Islamic civil society organizations in Kano found virtually no female participation in Islamic community organizations, with the exception of one that evolved out of an adult literacy program (Gwarzo 2003, 2006). Among professional women, the trace influence of MSS is represented by former students who formed the Muslim Sisters Organization to support Islamic and health education. It is an elite organization, led by the wives of officials, and has avoided controversy. The Federation of Muslim Women's Associations in Nigeria is a much more activist civil society group which promotes the participation and needs of Muslim women. Its members are involved in promoting education at all levels, access to reproductive health, micro-enterprise schemes, and Muslim women's interests in national deliberative bodies. Interviews with activists associated or employed by the federation confirm that they are effective advocates for women and have worked to defend women's rights under shariʻa.

The major controversies since the implementation of shariʻa emerged from the conviction and sentencing to death by stoning of two poor, rural, illiterate women   Amina Lawal and Safiya Hussaini—for the crime of *zina* (adultery, fornication) when they became pregnant out of wedlock. This set the stage for a vitriolic confrontation between international human rights and women's groups and the shariʻa advocates in Nigeria. Interestingly, one defendant was acquitted at the shariʻa appeals court level through the application of creative ijtihad (interpretation), whereby the fetus was determined to have been sleeping for years, so the conception could have occurred during the defendant's previous marriage. Of course, this pitted the conservative members of the shariʻa community against their adversaries in ways that made negotiations between progressive Muslims and the shariʻa court system extremely difficult. Women's rights groups like Baobab eventually asked Westerners not to sign petitions or attack the shariʻa system, because their criticism was fueling a siege mentality among Muslims in northern Nigeria. Human rights advocates have written extensively on the way in which men are exonerated and women are convicted of crimes that the women could not have committed by themselves. To be sure, these decisions reflect the poor training and preparation of rural judges at the lower levels and the class and gender bias of the system.

Space does not permit a more extensive discussion of the exemplary work performed by women's NGOs and civil society groups that have advocated for the rights of Muslim women in Nigeria. The refusal of women in cities like Kano to conform to dress codes and to accept harassment from *hisba* groups trying to prevent them from using motorcycle taxis also deserves greater attention than can be given here. While women have had to defend their constitutional rights in Islamic language, the educational trends and the commitment of professional women in civil society groups indicate that a spirited debate on the rights of women under shariʻa law in northern Nigeria is just beginning.

Interpreting the Politics of Restoration

In this final section I would like to present a typology of the different interpretations of the shariʻa movement that I and my research team recorded during formal interviews and informal conversations with northern Nigerians. In classifying interpretations I relied on the position each person took on shari'a restoration in general, on classical hudud punishments, and on the overall impact of shari'a restoration on northern Muslim society. To take the marginal positions first: non-Muslims generally believed that restoration violated their constitutional rights, especially by the vigilante activities of the *hisba* groups. Many feared the consequences of the politicization of religion and lamented the departure of many non-Muslims from the north. Alternatively, the more militant Shi'as and radical groups like Boko Haram opposed partial restoration at the state level and insisted that Nigeria should be transformed into a true Islamic state with full shari'a.

Professing secular Muslims were another outlying minority. Many had been active in the populist political parties and student movements of the 1970s and 1980s and lamented the triumph of what they referred to as Wahhabi authoritarianism, social backwardness, and "fanaticism." Many were employed in education, trade unions, international agencies, civil society groups, and independent professions. These secularists deplored the fact that shari'a had contributed to the north's economic and intellectual decline and to the departure of many productive southern Nigerians. They viewed shari'a as a xenophobic and reactionary response to Nigeria's economic and political crises. Since the real social problems of the majority of northern Muslims were not being addressed, they believed that pressures driven by the deprivation of the majority would eventually nurture a new movement to raise living standards, reignite democracy, and revitalize manufacturing industries.

The overwhelming majority of the people we interviewed, however, could be categorized under three headings: strict and full restorationists, ijtihad-minded restorationists, and enlightened Muslim modernists.

Strict and Full Restorationists

The full restorationists are the largest and most conservative group. They are also the one most influenced by neo-Salafi doctrines. They support the restoration of the "unchanging" shari'a as practiced in the nineteenth century, seeing it as a solution to what they perceive as lawlessness, criminality, Westernization, and moral decadence. A significant proportion have been the recipients of Islamic or Western education in Arabic, history, or Islamic studies. All denounced the performance of the Nigerian state, and they blamed backsliding Muslims for the corruption, waste, and indiscipline that characterizes contemporary Nigeria. They described many aspects of Nigerian national society as a Christian (colonial) imposition and represented the shari'a movement as a final and necessary stage of liberation from colonialism. They invoked conspiracy theories to explain away problems with shari'a implementation. While they supported democracy in principle, they did not put much weight on protecting minority rights. One volunteered, "We are an overwhelming majority in this state, so we have the right to democratically legislate our own legal system, one consistent with our customs, without interference from outsiders." Many echoed the conclusion reached by Tijani Naniya, a historian who is Kano State's commissioner for information and culture:

> There is a widespread feeling among Nigerians that the forty or so years of independence have brought nothing but corruption, degradation, and misery to the country's teeming populace. The new democratic dispensation introduced in 1999 is seen by many as the last chance for a change. While the solutions proposed by various ethno-cultural entities in the south range from redefinition of Nigeria federation, to recognizing regional autonomy and resource control, some states in northern Nigeria are opting for a return to the Shari'a. To these states, the strategies for social transformation and economic development induced by the West have failed. The alternative for them is for a return to their religio-cultural heritage represented by the Shari'a. (Naniya 2002, 31)

Ijtihad-Minded Restorationists

Most of the ijtihad-minded restorationists are public intellectuals who graduated from Western public universities and have credentials in shari'a law and Muslim subjects in general. Many belong to academic institutions with linkages to international Islamic university and foundation networks. Most are lawyers, academics, or consultants to international foundations and aid organizations because they can articulate the nuances of shari'a reform to a global audience. Known as "moderate Islamists" by the NGO community, they denounced the British corruption of shari'a and support its restoration in a humane way by staging educational campaigns, democratizing access to justice, supporting women's rights, raising the standard of shari'a court judges, and codifying shari'a. Many criticized the divisive effects of foreign-affiliated groups dependent on the patronage of foreign powers. They are hostile both to the imposing of cruel sentences by poorly trained judges and to the West's sensationalization of cases like that of Amina Lawal.

When discussing specific legal practices, these restorationists referred to the need to practice ijtihad to realize the public interest (*maslahah*) and suggested drawing on legal schools other than the Maliki or Hanbali, making such comments as "You know, there are actually sixteen different schools of shari'a law." They strongly favored implementing shari'a because citizens understand it and use its principles already in their daily lives. Several acknowledged that full restorationist positions were too harsh, and were applied unfairly to women and the weak. A provost of a medical college voiced his support for shari'a as an ideal, appropriate even for Christians, but was disillusioned with what he called "political shari'a" because it was corrupted by opportunistic, ambitious politicians. He and others rejected the effort of the state government to establish *zakat* commissions to collect and distribute alms, saying that this is the responsibility of individual Muslims, not the state. Most supported the continued funding of the religious police, the *hisba,* arguing that they acted as mediators and, if trained properly, functioned as a community police force. One articulate law professor, who has worked with British aid agencies to publish a handbook in Hausa and English defining the rights of women under shari'a (Centre for Islamic Legal Studies 2005), challenged the misguided intrusion of international NGOs into Muslim women's rights. "You Westerners think that you can transfer laws and customs that negatively impact women here. Really, Nigerian Muslim women will gain far more rights and freedoms if they understand their rights under shari'a law, because people in authority will listen to them but not to Westernized women from the NGOs." Interestingly, the ijtihad restorationists were optimistic that increasing outreach to women and improving women's education would shift the discourse of shari'a increasingly toward their interpretive framework.

Enlightened Muslim Modernists

The Muslim modernists favor the spirit of shari'a as a way of life but strongly believe that the militant restorationists are dogmatic and ill-equipped to perform the ijtihad required for a proper implementation of the law. They also decry the militant restorationists' dependence on Wahhabi patronage and doctrines. Their key point is that, before harsh punishments can be carried out, a just Islamic society and state must be established, an educated and compassionate judiciary must be put in place, and an informed Islamic citizenry must know its rights. Because none of these preconditions prevail, the implementation of shari'a by opportunistic politicians will only inflict injustice on women, the poor, and the weak. All spoke in favor of religious practice as a personal matter; most dismissed the politicians who are implementing "political shari'a" as backward, opportunistic, or corrupt. One thanked Allah that he lived in a secular state so that the full restorationists could be contained by the federal government. This is a small but intellectually influential group who are waiting for the tide to turn against what they see as a bumbling Islamist populism that has failed to meet societal needs.

Concluding Thoughts

A decade has passed since the governor of Zamfara restored shari'a criminal law. There is no doubt that the shari'a movement has transformed public life, especially in cities; improved security and public order along Islamist lines; and ignited an engaging debate within the Muslim public sphere on the proper application of the law. Yet, during this same period, the living conditions of the majority of the population have deteriorated significantly. It is readily apparent that Nigerian and international investors have not found conditions attractive, so the manufacturing industries of the shari'a states continue to decline, as do state infrastructures and services. Muslim modernists are very optimistic that the failure of the Islamist state governments to improve the lives of their citizens will lead to demands for more pragmatic policy choices. Overall, it appears that shari'a has become naturalized in different ways in each of the twelve states. It is noteworthy that in the federal presidential election of 2007, shari'a was not a divisive issue, as it had been in the 2003 election, even though the winning presidential candidate had overseen the introduction of shari'a criminal law when he was governor of Katsina. Whether the religious solidarity and Islamic discipline generated by the restoration of shari'a will help improve the life chances of the residents of the northern states remains an open issue.

Note

I would like to thank my co-researcher and colleague Mallam Ibrahim Muazzam, of Bayero University Kano, for his patience, insightful advice, and collaborative assistance in researching this paper. In addition, I would like to thank Professor Haruna Wakili of Mambayya House for his support and advice on many of the issues covered in this paper. And finally, I would like to acknowledge the advice and support I received from Dr. Mairo Mandara and Dr. Usman Bugaje on so many of complex issues dealt with in this paper. As always, all errors are my sole responsibility.

References Cited

Anderson, Norman. 1976. *Law Reform in the Muslim World*. London: Athlone.

Burgat, Francois. 2003. *Face to Face with Political Islam*. London: I. B. Tauris.

Centre for Islamic Legal Studies, Ahmadu Bello University. 2005. *Promoting Women's Rights through Sharia in Northern Nigeria*. London: British Council.

Christelow, Allan. 2002. "Islamic Law and Judicial Practice in Nigeria: An Historical Perspective." *Journal of Muslim Minority Affairs* 22 (1): 185–204.

Fourchard, Laurent. 2005. "Nigeria: A Missionary Nation." In *Entreprises religieuses transnationales en Afrique de l'Ouest*, ed. Laurent Fourchard, André Mary, and René Otayek, 117–243. Paris: Karthala.

Gwarzo, Tahir Haliru. 2003. "Activities of Islamic Civic Organizations in the Northwest of Nigeria with Particular Reference to Kano State." *Afrika Spectrum* 38:289–318.

———. 2006. "Islamic Civil Society Organizations and the State: A Kano Case Study." Ph.D. diss., Bayero University.

Hodgson, Marshall G. S. 1974. *The Venture of Islam.* Chicago: University of Chicago Press.

Human Rights Watch. 2004. "'Political Sharia'? Human Rights and Islamic Law in Northern Nigeria." http://www.hrw.org/reports/2004/nigeria0904/ (accessed August 19, 2008).

Ibrahim, Hauwa, and Princeton Lyman. 2004. *Reflections on the New Shari'a Law in Nigeria.* Washington, D.C.: Council on Foreign Relations.

Kane, Ousmane. 2003. *Muslim Modernity in Postcolonial Nigeria: A Study of the Society for the Removal of Innovation and Reinstatement of Tradition.* Leiden: Brill.

Last, Murray. 1973. "Reform in West Africa: The Jihad Movements of the Nineteenth Century." In *History of West Africa,* ed. J. F. Ade Ajayi and Michael Crowder, 3:1–29. New York: Columbia.

———. 2000. "La charia dans le Nord-Nigeria." *Politique africaine* 79:141–52.

———. 2008. "The Search for Security in Muslim Northern Nigeria." *Africa* 78:41–63.

Loimeier, Roman. 1997. *Islamic Reform and Political Change in Northern Nigeria.* Evanston, Ill.: Northwestern University Press.

———. 2005a. "Is There Something like 'Protestant Islam'?" *Die Welt des Islams* 45 (2): 216–54.

———. 2005b. "Playing with Affiliations: Muslims in Northern Nigeria in the 20th Century." In *Entreprises religieuses transnationales en Afrique de l'Ouest,* ed. Laurent Fourchard, André Mary, and René Otayek, 349–72. Paris: Karthala.

Lubeck, Paul, Michael Watts, and Ronnie Lipschutz. 2007. "Convergent Interests: US Energy Security and the 'Securing' of Nigerian Democracy." *International Policy Report.* Washington, D.C.: Center for International Policy.

Mack, Beverly, and Jean Boyd. 2000. *One Woman's Jihad: Nana Asma'u, Scholar and Scribe.* Bloomington: Indiana University Press.

Mahmoud, A. B. 2002. "The Shari'a Project in Northern Nigeria and Governance in a Federal Nigeria." Paper delivered at the Global Islam conference, UC Santa Cruz, March 2002. http://www2.ucsc.edu/cgirs/conferences/carnegie/papers/mahmoud.pdf (accessed November 8, 2008).

Marshall-Fratani, Ruth. 1998. "Mediating the Global and Local in Nigerian Pentecostalism." *Journal of Religion in Africa* 28 (3): 278–315.

Mohammed, Ahmed Rufai. 1993. "The Influence of the Niass Tijaniyya in the Niger-Benue Confluence Area of Nigeria." In *Muslim Identity and Social Change in Sub-Saharan Africa,* ed. Louis Brenner, 116–34. London: Hurst.

Naniya, Tijjani Muhammad. 2002. "History of the Shari'a in Some States of Northern Nigeria to circa 2000." *Journal of Islamic Studies* 13 (1): 14–31.

Paden, John N. 1973. *Religion and Political Culture in Kano.* Berkeley: University of California Press.

———. 2002. "Islam and Democratic Federalism in Nigeria." *Africa Notes* 8 (March). Published by the Center for Strategic and International Studies. http://www.csis .org/media/csis/pubs/anotes_0203.pdf (accessed August 2008).

———. 2008. *Faith and Politics in Nigeria: Nigeria as a Pivotal State in the Muslim World.* Washington, D.C.: U.S. Institute of Peace.

Pew Forum on Region and Public Life. 2006a. "Overview: Pentecostalism in Africa." Pew Forum. http://pewforum.org/Christian/Evangelical-Protestant-Churches/ Overview-Pentecostalism-in-Africa.aspx (accessed September 12, 2010).

———. 2006b. *Spirit and Power: A 10-Country Survey of Pentecostals.* Washington, D.C.: Pew Forum. http://pewforum.org/uploadedfiles/Orphan_Migrated_Content/ pentecostals-08.pdf (accessed September 12, 2010).

Sanusi, Sanusi Lamido. 2007. "Politics and Sharia in Northern Nigeria." In *Islam and Muslim Politics in Africa,* ed. Benjamin F. Soares and René Otayek, 167–92. New York: Palgrave Macmillan.

Spinoza, Jérome, and Olivier Vallée. 2008. "Nigeria: Is the End of Mafia Politics in Sight?" Egmont Paper 19. Brussels: Royal Institute for International Affairs.

Suberu, Rotimi. 2008. "Sharia and the Travails of Democratic Federalism in Nigeria." Unpublished paper. Washington, D.C.: U.S. Institute of Peace.

Sulaiman, Ibraheem. 2001. "Sharia Restoration in Nigeria: The Dynamics and the Process." Paper presented at the International Conference on Sharia at the Commonwealth Institute, London, April 14.

Tabiu, Muhammed. 2001. "Sharia, Federalism and the Nigerian Constitution." Paper presented at the International Conference on Sharia at the Commonwealth Institute, London, April 14.

Umar, Mohammad S. 1993. "Changing Islamic Identity in Nigeria from the 1960s to the 1980s: From Sufism to Anti-Sufism." In *Muslim Identity and Social Change in Sub-Saharan Africa,* ed. Louis Brenner, 154–78. London: Hurst.

———. 2004. "Mass Islamic Education and Emergence of Female 'Ulama' in Northern Nigeria." In *The Transmission of Learning in Islamic Africa,* ed. Scott S. Reese, 99–120. Leiden: Brill.

———. 2006. *Islam and Colonialism: Intellectual Responses of Muslims of Northern Nigeria to British Colonial Rule.* Leiden: Brill.

U.S. Department of State. 2009. "Background Note: Nigeria." http://www.state.gov/ r/pa/ei/bgn/2836.htm.

U.S. Department of Energy. 2009. "Nigeria." http://www.eia.doe.gov/cabs/Nigeria/ Background.html.

Vikør, Knut S. 2000. "Sufi Brotherhoods in Africa." In *The History of Islam in Africa,* ed. Nehemia Levtzion and Randall L. Pouwels, 441–76. Athens: Ohio University Press.

Wickham, Carrie Rosefsky. 2002. *Mobilizing Islam.* New York: Columbia University Press.

Yadudu, Auwalu H. 2001. "Sharia in Nigeria: Challenges and Benefits." Paper presented at the International Conference on Sharia at the Commonwealth Institute, London, April 14. Nigerian Muslims Network. http://www.shariah2001.nmnonline .net (accessed October 2006).

8. Indonesia

Shari'a Politics and
Democratic Transition

Robert W. Hefner

In May 1998, at the height of the Asian financial crisis, President Muhammad Soeharto of Indonesia was forced from office, bringing to an end some thirty-two years of authoritarian rule. The political movement that pushed Soeharto from power was an awkward and only temporary coalition of pro-democracy students, Muslim civic associations, and establishment politicians, as well as armed forces convinced that it was time to let their embattled patron go (Aspinall 2005b; Dijk 2001, 111–83). During the final months of Soeharto's rule, the country had suffered fierce outbreaks of ethnic and religious violence (Davidson 2008; Sidel 2006; Klinken 2007). The violence and the vacuum of power in Jakarta led many observers to conclude that this sprawling Southeast Asian nation was on the brink of, not democratic transition, but national disintegration.

Led by B. J. Habibie, a man hand-picked by Soeharto himself, the *Reformasi* (reform) government that succeeded Soeharto defended many of the old regime's privileges; however, in the face of mounting domestic and international pressure, it also implemented extensive democratic reforms. The new government freed political prisoners, liberalized press laws, authorized the establishment of independent trade unions, and issued sweeping legislation on human rights, the main elements of which were borrowed from the 1948 Universal Declaration of Human Rights (Lindsey 2002). In June 1999, the country also held the first free and fair elections since the parliamentary era of the 1950s. The results of these and subsequent elections in 2004 and 2009 were notable for their center-of-the-road moderation; voters shunned both authoritarian nationalist and radical Islamist appeals (Aspinall 2005a; Ufen 2008).

In 2007, the international democracy clearinghouse, Freedom House, identified Indonesia as the only country in Southeast Asia deserving the description "free" (Freedom House 2007). Seen as on the brink of collapse a few years earlier, Indonesia was now touted as one of the most promising democracies in the Muslim world.

In the first three years following the end of Soeharto's rule, however, the bright achievements of the political transition were darkened by widespread outbreaks of vigilantism and militia violence. Both were in part responses to the breakdown of law and order in cities after Soeharto's departure, leading frustrated citizens and opportunistic militia bosses to take anti-crime measures into their own hands (Schulte Nordholt 2002; MacDougall 2007). The vigilantism was not limited to Muslim-majority regions, but also took place in the country's mixed Christian-Muslim provinces (Aragon 2001; Davidson 2008; C. Wilson 2008). However, the largest and most aggressive militias boasted of their Islamic credentials and had a far broader agenda than just combating crime. Citing the Islamic ethical principle to "command right and forbid wrong" (see Cook 2000), militants in groups like the Islamic Defenders Front (Front Pembela Islam) took advantage of the post-Soeharto vacuum of power to ransack nightclubs, bars, and other alleged centers of vice (Ind. *tempat maksiat*). Some among the militia leaders also dismissed democracy as incompatible with Islam, and demanded that the state comprehensively implement the shari'a for the 88 percent of Indonesia's 240 million citizens who are Muslim (Feillard and Madinier 2006, 117–20; Hasan 2006; Hefner 2005; Jamhari and Jahroni 2004).

Notwithstanding repeated threats from Islamist militias demonstrating outside its chambers, in 2002 Indonesia's parliament voted down proposals that would have amended Article 29 of the constitution to require the state to enforce Islamic law for Muslim citizens. Some Indonesia observers imagined that this settled the question of state-enforced Islamic law once and for all. Over the next four years, however, Muslim activists joined forces with political parties—including some long regarded as "secular nationalist" rather than Islamist—to pass "shari'a-oriented regional regulations" (*peraturan daerah syariah Islam*) in 53 of the country's 470 districts and municipalities.

As Arskal Salim (2008) and Robin Bush (2008, 176) have observed, the content of some 45 percent of these regulations is not based in any strict sense on the shari'a or Islamic jurisprudence (fiqh). Acting in the name of public morality rather than Islamic law, the bylaws tighten controls on gambling, women's movement, and the consumption of alcohol. Notwithstanding their nonsectarian phrasing, they were widely perceived as shari'a-inspired, not least because their most ardent proponents included an alliance of conservative pro-shari'a groups, often working in collaboration with local branches of the semi-governmental Council of Indonesian Ulama (Majelis Ulama Indonesia, MUI). In the post-Soeharto era, the MUI had acquired a reputation for staking out anti-liberal positions on questions of doctrine, religious education, and interreligious relations. The council's growing conservatism in part reflected the fact that in the early post-Soeharto period it had attempted to counter the influence of liberal Muslim groupings by, for the first time, recruiting representatives of hardline Islamist organizations like the Indonesian Council of Jihad Fighters (Majelis Mujahidin Indonesia, MMI). However, as MUI officials themselves acknowledged,[1] the anti-liberal turn was also related to the leadership's determination to dispel the reputation the council had acquired during the Soeharto era of being insufficiently independent of the government (cf. Gillespie 2007; Ichwan 2005, 49; Porter 2002, 78–83).

The remaining 55 percent of the regional regulations did explicitly reference Islamic concerns, albeit in a language that owed less to classical fiqh than to the nation-making discourse of the postcolonial state. Although their precise phrasing varied from district to district, these bylaws shared the aim of making two categories of behavior mandatory for Muslim citizens: the performance of basic religious duties, such as reading the Qur'an and paying religious alms (*zakat*), and the wearing of dress deemed Islamic in schools, government offices, and other public spaces.

With the notable exception of the special province of Aceh,[2] none of the regional regulations sought to enforce Islamic criminal law; none applied the hudud penalties mandated in classical Islamic jurisprudence for theft, highway robbery, adultery, and other "crimes against God" (see my introduction to this volume). However, the more controversial features of Islamic law were by no means entirely absent from public discussion. Militants involved in the regional campaigns, like the Party of Liberation (Hizb ut-Tahrir) and the Indonesian Council of Jihad Fighters (MMI), continued to call for a totalizing and mandatory implementation of Islamic law, on the grounds that this alone could "save" (*selamatkan*) Indonesia from moral and political decline (cf. Fealy and Hooker 2006, 163–65, 178–80). Although less inclined to call for changes to the constitution, activist-minded members of the MUI also sought to extend the scope of shari'a-influenced legislation in specific directions. The council issued repeated calls for the criminal prosecution of non-conforming Islamic sects, including the three-hundred-thousand-strong Ahmadiyah, on the grounds that their profession of Islam was religiously deviant (ICG 2008; Olle 2009). In 2005, the MUI again startled many in the Muslim community by ruling that secularism, pluralism, and liberalism are antithetical to Islam (Gillespie 2007). The declaration was greeted with dismay by pro-democracy Muslims; several senior Muslim scholars, including Azyumardi Azra of the Hidayatullah State

Islamic University, described the statement as religiously indefensible.[3] But the declaration deepened the public debate over just what Islamic law requires and what its place should be in Indonesia's fledgling democracy.

It is against this unsettled backdrop that this essay aims to make sense of shari'a politics in post-Soeharto Indonesia by examining the history and social organization of movements aiming to bring about comprehensive state enforcement of shari'a law. The essay maps the main associations involved in the campaigns, and examines their roots in modern Indonesian history. More generally, it explores the implications of shari'a politics for the future of democracy in this sprawling Southeast Asian country.

Among the case studies discussed in this volume, Indonesia is of special interest for two reasons. First and most simply, it is the most populous Muslim-majority country in the world, one with a relatively impressive record of political and economic development. Although remote from the founding heartlands of Muslim civilization, Indonesia today is watched more closely than ever by the broader Muslim world. Second, and even more important, Indonesia is of special interest because it is in the throes of an unfinished but hopeful transition from authoritarian rule (cf. Bünte and Ufen 2009; Mietzner 2008; Mujani and Liddle 2007). Precisely because of the high-stakes nature of its transition, Indonesia highlights a tension pervasive in the public opinion of most Muslim-majority lands. The tension centers on the Muslim public's desire for democratically accountable government, on one hand, and its desire to give Islamic values and the shari'a greater public prominence, on the other (see the introduction). Indonesia offers special insights into the challenge of striking this balance, and into the circumstances that encourage democracy-friendly approaches to the shari'a—and those that do not.

Historical Antecedents

Several of the regionally based shari'a movements that arose after Soeharto's resignation justified their campaigns by asserting that in precolonial times Islamic law had already been implemented in their territories, and its modern absence was only the result of European colonialism. From a historical perspective, this argument has a measure of truth, but it greatly oversimplifies the history of Islamic law in Indonesia. Two centuries before the full Dutch assault on the archipelago, rulers in seventeenth-century Aceh, West Java, and south Sulawesi enforced a few elements of Islamic law (Peletz 2002, 26–38; Reid 1988, 142–43). However, the shari'a that was in force then differed greatly from modern jurists' understandings, as well as from the shari'a implemented in most Middle Eastern countries during this period. The law applied in these small states invoked a handful of Islamic legal principles but made no pretense of comprehensiveness or procedural consistency. For a few years, thieves' hands were cut off and adulterers executed. But most of the laws enforced by rulers were of a non-shari'a nature, not least because the legal and educational edifices so central to the transmission and understanding of the law in the Middle East were lacking. Moreover, after a generation, even these piecemeal attempts at state enforcement of the law came to an end. Muslim rulers intent on demonstrating their piety placed more emphasis on sponsoring grand religious ceremonies in which their own spiritual preeminence was highlighted than on enforcing the law (Burhanudin 2006, 57; Peletz 2002; Woodward 1989, 164–70).

There were three general reasons for the unelaborated state of Islamic legal affairs in the early modern archipelago. First, conversion to Islam was not the result of foreign conquerors bringing Islamic scholars and courts in their wake, but occurred in an incremental manner, with the greater portion of the process taking place during Southeast Asia's "Age of Commerce," from 1450 to 1680 (Reid 1993, 132). Although, in a few regions, the conversion of one or several rulers was followed by wars of conquest against non-Muslim neighbors, most of the conversion was brokered by the elite and served to sustain the existing political system. Not uncommonly, the shift to Islam occurred in the aftermath of a heretofore heathen ruler's having a religious dream or meeting a Muslim shaykh and, as a result of this experience, choosing to bring his people to Islam (Milner 1995, 186; Woodward 1989, 32–34). In most regions, too, the rulers who introduced Islam were of the same ethnic background as their non-Islamic predecessors.

This combination of ethnic commonality and elite-brokered conversion meant that there was considerable cultural continuity from the earlier, non-Muslim regime to the new. Certainly, the new Islamic states of the early modern period did away with the Hindu-Buddhist temple complexes once common in central portions of the archipelago, most famously in Java (see Hefner 1985; Pigeaud 1960–63). However, as the historian Anthony Milner (1995, 146, 217) has observed, Islam in island Southeast Asia displayed a "raja-centric" face not unlike that which had preceded it. Rulers were the pivot around which religiously inflected public ceremony was organized (cf. Woodward 1989, 164). Although sultans in a few states, most notably Aceh, displayed a measure of shari'a-mindedness, court rituals in Java, Malaya, and southern Sulawesi included the presentation of offerings to royal ancestors, as well as to spirits of the mountains and the sea. Although encompassed within a broader Islamic cosmology, both categories of spirit bore a striking resemblance to beings invoked in pre-Islamic ritual (cf. Laderman 1991, 16; Pelras 1996; Woodward 1989, 151). It was these grand rituals, more than it was madrasa study, that served as the primary medium for the production and consumption of an ostensibly Islamic ethic by the region's new Muslim publics.

The second circumstance that limited the scope of precolonial shari'a was the marginal place of Islamic legal writings in local Muslim literature. In a few parts of Muslim Southeast Asia, including remote portions of eastern Indonesia and the Cham territories of Vietnam and Cambodia (see Blengsli 2009, 174–81; Taylor 2007), the Muslim population adhered to what M. B. Hooker has aptly referred to as "a 'non-literary' Muslim culture." Apart from a confession of the faith, prayers, and fasting, "other elements of Islamic knowledge, including legal knowledge, are almost non-existent" (Hooker 1984, 1).

In the central territories of precolonial Indonesia, however, an Islamic literary tradition was established soon after the ruler's conversion. The tradition primarily produced written narratives known as *hikayat, babad,* or *serat,* as well as a much smaller assortment of theological tracts and legal digests (Day 1983, 144–59; Riddell 2001, 104–35, 172–92). The *hikayat* chronicles conveyed a measured sense of Islamic history and identity, but showed little concern for Islamic law. Equally important, these Islamic narratives coexisted with others that referred to normative traditions of a largely non-Islamic nature (see, e.g., Geertz 1960b; Gibson 2007).

The theological writings of this period had an even more restricted influence. The greatest works were composed in Aceh in the seventeenth century, and were "cast wholly in terms of the Sufi search to experience God" (Hooker 1984, 6). There were also several legal digests circulating in the archipelago, the first of which dates from the late sixteenth century. These showed a basic familiarity with some features of the law. However, the laws created by Muslim rulers either ignored the digests (as did Muslim Java's early legal texts) or stirred regulations from these works into a largely indigenous brew. The ruler's presence had a constraining influence on the process of law-making as well: Some digests dedicated more space to establishing the principles according to which status and rank in society were to be determined than they did to explicating legal issues (Hooker 1984, 10; Milner 1983, 27; Milner 1995, 148). Beyond courtly circles, legal disputes were handled by local notables and clan leaders, not classically trained scholars of the law. In resolving disputes, local officials usually drew on customary (*adat*) regulations only lightly laced with references to Islamic legal notions (cf. Peletz 2002, 26–38).

A third and especially important reason for the undeveloped nature of Islamic law in precolonial Indonesia was the elementary state of Islamic legal education. In the Middle East, the spread of madrasas from the eleventh century onward played a central role in generalizing and standardizing the study of Islamic law (Berkey 1992; Hallaq 2009, 135–46; Makdisi 1981). Lavishly patronized by ruling elites (Bulliet 1994; Chamberlain 1994), the colleges contributed to the consolidation of jurisprudence (fiqh) as the most important of Islamic sciences, and created a class of scholars with a vested interest in the law's enforcement. Although an earlier generation of Western scholars had assumed that Islamic colleges were established soon after the initial wave of conversion in Southeast Asia (Drewes 1969, 11; Geertz 1960a, 231), recent research has demonstrated that madrasa-like colleges (known locally as *pondok* or *pesantren;* see Dhofier 1999) became widespread in the central archipelago only in the nineteenth century (see Bruinessen 1995; Ricklefs 2007, 52–72). Indeed, in more marginal territories in Muslim Southeast Asia, including the southern Philippines and Cambodia, schools for the study of Islamic jurisprudence did not achieve a significant institutional presence until the middle decades of the twentieth century (Hefner 2009, 17).

The indigenous legal systems displaced by the Dutch colonial administration in the late nineteenth century, then, were not shari'a courts presided over by madrasa-trained jurists. The legal tradition in Muslim Southeast Asia was exuberantly multi-stranded; legal disputes were handled through an array of courtly, regional, and village agencies. Some of the legal traditions employed in these institutions blended bits and pieces of Islamic law into their regulations, but none did so in a way comparable in scope to the legal systems of the Middle East or South Asia (which were also pluralistic, but nonetheless had a more extensive infrastructure for transmitting and applying Islamic law). Faced with this diversity, and convinced that observant Muslims threatened their rule (Noer 1973), the Dutch rulers imposed an illiberal pluralism on their new subjects, one which highlighted region, race, and ethnic separation rather than religion or common citizenship (Burns 2004; cf. Furnivall 1944). Under the terms of what came to be known as "reception theory," Islamic regulations were acknowledged in the regional subsystems only to the degree that they already figured in local custom (*adat;* see Lev 1972, 196).

Applied to the populous islands of Java and Madura, the Priestcourt Regulation of 1882 qualified this marginalization of Islamic law by establishing an Islamic legal tribunal for marriage, divorce, and inheritance. The court also supervised pious endowments (Ar. *waqf;* Ind. *wakaf*). Even after its establishment, however, the court remained officially subordinate to the state's civil courts. Because the latter also claimed regulatory authority over endowments and inheritances, disputes over the respective jurisdictions of the two agencies were inevitable. In 1937 the colonial government attempted to ease the confusion by issuing directives that stipulated that the Dutch-imposed secular system had final jurisdiction in all legal conflicts. Where disputes occurred between Islamic and Native Courts, then, the matter was to be resolved by the governor general under the advice of the secular High Court and the Council of the Indies (Cammack 1997, 146; Hooker 1984, 251). As a result of arrangements like these, Islamic law never achieved the status of "personal law" for Indonesian Muslims as it did for Malay Muslims in the nearby British colony of Malaya (see Peletz 2002, 47–54).

In the late nineteenth and early twentieth centuries, however, Muslim society in island Southeast Asia underwent changes that contributed to a heightened interest in the shari'a. The flow of pilgrims to Arabia rose steadily from the 1820s on, and surged after the opening of the Suez canal in November 1869. In 1885, the Dutch scholar and colonial advisory officer Christiaan Snouck Hurgronje commented that Southeast Asian Muslims (of whom Indonesians were the majority) formed the largest community of pilgrims in Mecca (Hurgronje 1931, 215). For many travelers, pilgrimage to Arabia was not only a religious duty but an opportunity to study with learned Islamic scholars, including Indonesian scholars long resident in the Hijaz (Laffan 2003, 18–27; Ricklefs 2007, 58–70). The pilgrimage exposed Indonesians to new currents of Islamic reform and to the fiqh-centered curriculum long favored in Middle Eastern madrasas. Upon returning to Indonesia, many pilgrims established religious schools of their own, modeled on Middle Eastern and South Asian prototypes (Bruinessen 1994).

At the center of the curriculum for this expanding network of Islamic schools were the "yellow books" (kitab kuning), so called because of the color of the paper on which they were once printed (Bruinessen 1989). Most of these kitabs are commentaries in the local dialect or Arabic on an Arabic text which was itself a commentary or gloss on some older Arabic text. A study published in 1886 by the Dutch scholar L. W. C. van den Berg showed that, at this point in the building of Indonesia's Islamic school network, education in the Islamic sciences and jurisprudence remained elementary, to say the least. Among other things, the hadith collections so central to Middle Eastern legal training, and vital for a more comprehensive understanding of the law, were still rarely used (Berg 1886).

Over the next few decades, however, the scope and quality of legal education improved steadily. In boarding schools that taught jurisprudence, teachers began to devote greater attention to hadith study and the principles of Islamic jurisprudence (usul al-fiqh), rather than just the study of particular cases or rulings (furu). The new methodology facilitated a more dynamic engagement with the law (Bruinessen 1994, 129). The changes also brought the curriculum in Indonesian religious schools in line with the fiqh-centered madrasa curriculum long dominant in the Middle East, especially that associated with centers of Shafi'i legal learning. In this manner, the religious schools laid the foundation for the movements of Islamic reform that arose across Indonesia in the first half of the twentieth century. Not coincidentally, these movements were to make a comprehensive implementation of Islamic law a priority.

Postcolonial Contestations

The period from 1870 to 1930, then, saw the spread of institutions of higher Islamic learning, a deeper scholarly engagement with classical Islamic jurisprudence, and the emergence of a Muslim leadership dedicated to a more shari'a-conscious profession of Islam. In the 1910s and 1920s, the Islamic ascent was given added organizational impetus with the establishment of two mass-based Muslim welfare associations, the Muhammadiyah (1912) and Nahdlatul Ulama (1926), as well as the country's first mass-based political organization, Sarekat Islam (SI). SI was founded in 1911 as an Islamic nationalist organization whose initial concern was to protect native businesses from Chinese competition. Especially in Java, however, the organization soon attracted anti-colonial socialists to its ranks. In 1921, the organization's "red" SI members were forced out by Muslim "whites," on the grounds that membership in organizations other than SI, not least the recently established Indonesian Communist Party, was prohibited (Shiraishi 1990, 218–31).

The tension seen in the SI's red-white fission was indicative of a growing socio-religious divide in native society. Outside of eastern Indonesia and interior portions of western and central Indonesia, the great majority of native Indonesians saw themselves as Sunni Muslims. But local cultures of Islamic observance varied greatly in style and orthodoxy. In regions like Aceh and West Sumatra, most Muslims already professed what was by international standards a mainstream and "reformed" Sunnism (Bowen 1993, 11–16). As a result, the primary divide among believers did not pit pious Muslims against heterodox syncretists, but "New Group" (*kaum muda*) reformists against "Old Group" (*kaum tua*) traditionalists (Abdullah 1971; Peletz 2002, 53–55; Roff 1994, 56–90). Elsewhere, however, as in Lombok, South Sumatra, southern Sulawesi, and, most importantly, Java, the main divide pitted observant Muslims (both reformist and traditionalist) against a disparate assortment of syncretic peasants (most of whom regarded themselves as Muslims), pantheist aristocrats, and secular nationalists (Cederroth 1981; Geertz 1960b; Ricklefs 2007; cf. Gibson 2007, 169–82). The hiving off of Marxist socialists from SI, the rise of the Communist Party, and the formation of the Indonesian Nationalist Party (1927) signaled that this religious tension was of great political consequence. As it turned out, the divide was to serve as a key organizing principle for mass politics over the next half-century (Anderson 1983; Feith 1963).

This, then, was the background against which the struggle to implement the shari'a in a comprehensive and state-based manner unfolded in postcolonial Indonesia. There were four peak periods to the campaign. The first was at the end of the Japanese occupation in 1945 and the onset of Indonesia's war of independence (1945–49); the second took place during the convocation of the Constituent Assembly, from 1957 to 1959, when the country's political parties tried to write a new constitution and resolve the question of the place of the shari'a in the republic; the third occurred during the special session of the Provisional People's Consultative Assembly at the beginning of Soeharto's "New Order" regime, from 1966 to 1968; and the fourth has taken place during the post-Soeharto period, from 1998 to today (see Salim 2008, 85). Each of these periods had its own political dynamics, but events during the first period, at the end of the Japanese occupation and during the independence war, set the terms for later contests.

At the end of April 1945, the Japanese command in occupied Indonesia realized that an Allied invasion was imminent. Some in the upper ranks of the occupying command were sympathetic to Indonesians' nationalist aspirations. On April 29, then, the Japanese established the Investigating Committee for the Preparation of Independence (BPUK), to which they appointed both secular and Islamic nationalists. One of the issues over which the BPUK delegates immediately disagreed was whether Indonesia was to become an Islamic state.

In July 1945, a special subcommittee of the BPUK devised a compromise answer to this question. The preamble of the constitution was to contain five principles of governance, known as the Pancasila ("five principles"). After negotiations, it was resolved that the first principle would be "belief in God with the obligation to implement Islamic shari'a for its adherents." The latter portion of this principle, with its stipulation that the state was to enforce the shari'a, came to be known as the Jakarta Charter; it has remained at the center of contention over shari'a to this day. The charter's wording offered no details on who had the authority to formulate the law or the mechanisms for its implementation. Nonetheless, Muslim parties saw the declaration as an important first step toward establishing Islam as the basis of the state

Events soon dashed this hope. On August 18, 1945, one day after Indonesia's leaders declared their country's independence, the first principle of the Pancasila was altered by the removal of the seven Indonesian words that mention the state's obligation to implement Islamic law for Muslims. The change was made after a Japanese naval officer reported that Christians in eastern Indonesia were threatening to secede if the clause was not deleted. The amendment was approved by the twenty-seven members of the preparatory committee, which included representatives from Muslim organizations. For the next half-century, however, Islamist parties would remember the charter's deletion as a last-minute betrayal of the Muslim majority by the Christian and secularist "minority."[4]

Another incident during the Indonesian war of independence had no less momentous consequences for shari'a politics in postcolonial Indonesia. In 1948, at the height of the war, the country's nationalist leaders signed an agreement with the Dutch forces ceding control of much of West Java to the Dutch, and allowing an orderly retreat of Indonesian fighters to republican territories to the east. Angered by the agreement (and several other disputes with republican leaders), a prominent Muslim commander in West Java by the name of Kartosuwiryo announced the establishment of a Darul Islam (DI) nation, independent of both Dutch and republican authority. The DI state, Kartosuwiryo declared, was to be based not on secular law but on the shari'a. As in earlier periods, however, the questions of just what was meant by "shari'a" and how it was to be enforced were left unanswered (Dijk 1981, 95–97; cf. Soebardi 1983).

Notwithstanding the DI's lack of detail on matters of Islamic law, at the height of the rebellion DI commanders cut off thieves' hands, stoned adulterers, and executed peasants who had paid taxes to the republican government, an act the rebels deemed tantamount to apostasy.[5] All of these measures were justified with reference to the shari'a. However, in the context of political rebellion, those enforcing the law paid little attention to classical jurisprudence's careful reasoning and handling of evidence. The law was "functionalized" (Starrett 1998, 9; see my introduction to this volume) with an eye toward, not respect for fiqh proceduralism, but efficiency in delimiting the boundaries of the Darul Islam community and mobilizing against political enemies. Although the DI movement never posed a grave threat to the republic, it did attract significant armed support in Aceh, South Sulawesi, a few portions of northern Central Java, and South Kalimantan. In South Sulawesi and West Java, armed resistance continued for more than a decade, ending only in 1962 with the killing of Kartosuwiryo.

The DI rebellion left two legacies for later struggles over Islamic law. First, by taking up arms against the republic at a time of great peril, the movement convinced many Indonesian nationalists, including many otherwise observant Muslims, that extreme proponents of Islamic law lacked a sense of loyalty to the nation, and would defy the wishes of the majority to get their way. Until well into the 1980s—when a growing Islamic resurgence convinced them that they needed to reach a new accommodation with the proponents of Islamic law (Effendy 2003, 149–77; Hefner 2000; Kim 1998)—many nationalists associated the effort to make the shari'a the basis of the state with what they regarded as DI treachery.

The other legacy of the DI rebellion concerned the insurgent organization itself. By 1962, most Darul Islam commanders had either surrendered or been killed. For many years, Indonesian observers have assumed that DI survivors had given up and reconciled with the republic. During Soeharto's New Order period (1966–98), a number of prominent DI activists, like Shaykh Abdussalam Rasyidi Panji Gumilang, the well-known leader of the al-Zaytun mega-*pesantren* in West Java (Simanullang 2005), became outspoken supporters of the president and the ruling party, Golkar. However, in the early 2000s, after some former DI activists were linked to acts of terrorist violence, researchers revisited Darul Islam territories and were surprised to discover that a rejectionist underground had survived the movement's military defeat. Most of its membership was no longer interested in taking up arms against the Pancasila state. But many dreamed of a time when they might again struggle for God's law (ICG 2005).

Research also revealed that, in the early 1990s, a dissident DI faction known as the Jemaah Islamiyah (JI) had broken with the DI organization and established an underground military wing dedicated to the cause of making Islamic law the basis of the state in Indonesia and neighboring areas of Muslim Southeast Asia. Led by two Central Javanese religious teachers of Arab-Indonesian descent, the Jemaah Islamiyah was far more internationalist in orientation than the Darul Islam leadership had ever been. Several of the most prominent JI military leaders, like Hambali (associated with the 2002 bombing of resorts in Bali), had received military training in the early 1990s in Afghanistan (ICG 2002a, 2002b).

Little more than a year after Soeharto's resignation, the armed wing of the JI launched a bombing campaign, beginning with attacks on Christian churches in thirteen cities on Christmas Eve 2000; sixteen churchgoers died and a hundred were injured. When, in 1999 and 2000, violence flared between Muslims and Christians in the eastern Indonesian provinces of Maluku (the Moluccas) and North Maluku, the Jemaah Islamiyah mobilized fighters for armed jihad in the troubled province. Militants associated with the group went on to carry out a number of attacks on high-profile Western targets, including bombings at a beachfront pub in Bali in October 2002, the Marriott Hotel in Jakarta in August 2003, the Australian embassy in September 2004, and a tourist restaurant in Bali in October 2005. Already in 2002, some in the mainline JI leadership were having second thoughts about the tactical benefits of the bombing campaign. However, a faction under the leadership of the Malaysian-born military strategist Noordin Mohammad Top broke with the main organization and continued the armed struggle. After a four-year lapse, the group carried out a spectacular attack on the Marriott and Ritz-Carlton hotels in Jakarta on July 17, 2009 (ICG 2009).

Inevitably, these incidents captured the attention of international news media and created the impression that armed insurgents with ties to al-Qaʿida were attempting to open a second front in Southeast Asia, centered in Indonesia and the southern Philippines. Al-Qaʿida operatives may well have had just such an ambition, and investigative reports issued by the International Crisis Group have confirmed that the military wing of the Jemaah Islamiyah did have intermittent contact with al-Qaʿida (ICG 2005). Notwithstanding these meetings, both the Jemaah Islamiyah and the splinter group led by Noordin Mohammad Top were primarily regionally organized, rather than franchises of a centralized terrorist *internationale*.

Equally important, neither the Jemaah Islamiyah nor Noordin's faction ever posed a serious threat to the broader post-Soeharto transition. In fact, by pressing forward with their violent adventurism despite loud protests from the broader Muslim leadership, the radical fringe of the shariʿa movement handed the government the proof that it needed to convince a skeptical public that the threat posed by the Jemaah Islamiyah was real. After the second Bali bombing in October 2005, the police intensified their campaign against the group's violent faction. Over the next three years, they arrested more than two hundred militants and broke up numerous bomb-making cells. In September 2009, the Indonesian police succeeded in cornering and killing the splinter group's master strategist, Noordin Top.

Constitutional Accommodations

Accounts that highlight the activities of radical proponents of the shariʿa inevitably risk overlooking the diversity of the social actors supportive of efforts to heighten the role of the shariʿa, however defined, in state and society. As Clark B. Lombardi (2006) has shown and as Nathan Brown explains in this volume, Egypt in the 1980s witnessed outbreaks of armed violence initiated by radical proponents of Islamic law. However, most shariʿa proponents in Egypt wanted nothing to do with the violence, or with the radicals' authoritarian understandings of the shariʿa. More remarkably, in the 1990s, the Supreme Constitutional Court of Egypt took steps to implement a theory and practice of Islamic law that was "capable of co-existing with liberal constitutional philosophy" (Lombardi 2006, 7). As Brown explains, these developments laid the foundation for a new consensus on how to integrate elements of the shariʿa into a constitutional order.

Efforts to nudge Indonesia in a similar direction, toward a new constitutional accommodation with elements of the shariʿa, acquired fresh momentum during the early post-Soeharto period. However, these efforts would not have been possible were it not for several accommodations reached in the last decade of the New Order era. In purely political terms, the accommodations were a response to far-reaching changes in Indonesian society, including the rise of an educated Muslim middle class and Soeharto's efforts to reach out to Muslim associations so as to undercut challenges to his rule made by his former allies in the armed forces (Liddle 1996; Hefner 2000, 130–66). However, the impact of the changes went well beyond the fickle posturings of New Order politics.

The accommodations the Soeharto government made to Muslim interests have been discussed elsewhere (Effendy 2003, 149–71; Hefner 2000, 129–43), but two are of special note here, since they represented a significant shift on the part of New Order elites with regard to Islamic law. The first accommodation was Law 7/1989, which reformed Indonesia's existing system of Islamic courts. The legislation extended the courts' jurisdiction in matters of Islamic marriage, divorce, and inheritance to the whole of the country and strengthened their standing relative to civil courts. As Mark Cammack has noted, "Most observers in the 1970s would have found it unthinkable that in the 1990s the Suharto government would be actively promoting state enforcement of Islamic doctrine" (Cammack 1989, 144). In May 2006, a revised law on religious courts (No. 3/2006) extended the courts' jurisdiction to Islamic banking, which had been legalized in 1992 but not placed under the authority of Islamic courts.

The second and equally startling accommodation to the proponents of Islamic law was the creation and subsequent dissemination of a volume entitled Compilation of Islamic Laws in Indonesia (*Kompilasi hukum Islam di Indonesia*, KHI), a codification of Islamic law for use in Islamic courts (Hooker 2008, 17–25; Mawardi 2003). It was created on the basis of interviews with leading Indonesian religious scholars, as well as thirty-eight fiqh texts long studied in Indonesia's Islamic schools. It dealt only with those matters adjudicated in Islamic courts as stipulated under the 1989 law: marriage and divorce, inheritance, and pious endowments (*waqf*). The compilation caused some controversy in liberal Muslim circles, because, among other things, it incorporated a ruling made in 1980 by the Council of Indonesian Ulama banning interreligious marriages. Although the law formally restricted husbands' rights to polygyny and divorce and imposed a minimum age for marriage, liberals and Muslim feminists in the post-Soeharto period argued forcefully that the compilation did not go far enough toward equalizing the rights of men and women, and of Muslims and non-Muslims (see Mulia 2006; Mulia and Cammack 2007). Nonetheless, from the perspective of the history of Islamic law in Indonesia, the compilation was reform-minded and modernist in spirit, and, "as an original attempt of codification," has proved "remarkably successful" (Hooker 2008, 26).

In the early years of the post-Soeharto period, the mainstream proponents of a more comprehensive state enforcement of Islamic law hoped to build on these late–New Order reforms. Although foreign news reports sometimes made it appear as if bomb-throwing jihadists were the primary actors behind the push for a greater implementation of Islamic law, they actually played a marginal role in the movement. The effort's main promoters were found instead in two broader groupings: 1) conservative Islamist parties who from 1999 to 2002 sought to amend Article 29 of the Indonesian constitution so as to require state enforcement of Islamic law; and 2) a coalition of militant Muslim associations, including the Party of Liberation (Hizb ut-Tahrir), the Islamic Defenders Front (FPI), and the Indonesian Council of Jihad Fighters (MMI), as well as a number of smaller, regionally based groupings.

After Indonesia's June 1999 elections, the campaign to implement the shari'a came to focus on a constitutional amendment that would mandate state enforcement of Islamic law. Two of Indonesia's larger political parties made the issue their *cause célèbre:* the United Development Party (PPP) and the Crescent Moon and Star Party (PBB). Both parties proposed to add the seven words of the Jakarta Charter to Article 29, so that in addition to stating that "the state is based on belief in a unitary God," the article would stipulate that the state was obliged "to implement Islamic shari'a for its adherents."

The PPP and PBB's sponsorship of the amendment was central to each party's political strategy in the post-Soeharto era. Both parties faced unexpected challenges in the period. Earlier, during the New Order era, the PPP had been the sole state-authorized Islamic party, and in the post-Soeharto era the PPP leadership had hoped that it could retain its dominant role. In the months following Soeharto's ouster, however, dozens of new Islamic parties were formed. Faced with an unexpectedly competitive political market, the PPP decided that its comparative advantage lay in emphasizing a single-minded commitment to state enforcement of Islamic law. The party also differentiated itself from its rivals by rallying support in the country's two largest and often opposed Muslim constituencies, "traditionalists" in groups like the Nahdlatul Ulama, and "modernists" in groups like the Muhammadiyah. The PPP's internal diversity, however, made its leadership wary of sponsoring serious discussion of the details of shari'a implementation, for fear that such discussion might cause division in its own ranks. The smaller PBB placed a similar emphasis on state enforcement of Islamic law. But the PBB's base was much narrower than the PPP's, since the former was grounded in the conservative wing of the modernist community, especially that portion linked to the Saudi-backed predication organization, the Indonesian Council for Islamic Appeal (Dewan Dakwah Islamiyah Indonesia, DDII; see Hefner 2000, 106–13).

To the surprise of party leaders, the shari'a-first strategy of the PPP and PBB did not prove an effective mobilizational instrument. In the 1999 elections, the two parties' combined share of seats in the national assembly came to just 12 percent. Their share of the national vote declined even further after the 2004 and 2009 elections, as a result of intraparty bickering, allegations of corruption, and the electorate's cooling toward proposals to change the constitutional basis of the state. The small share of the pro-shari'a parties in all three of the national elections stands in marked contrast to the outcome of the 1955 elections, when parties dedicated to the establishment of some manner of "Islamic state" won more than 40 percent of the national vote (Feith 1963; cf. Ufen 2008).

The lack of popular interest in state-enforced shari'a is all the more curious in that, although only these two parties (and two other tiny Islamic parties) supported the amendment to Article 29, some 40 percent of the parties in the national assembly after 1999 had their primary base in the organized wing of the Muslim community. A moderately conservative Islamist party committed to da'wa (Islamic predication) as well as electoral democracy, the Justice Party (Partai Keadilan, PK; known today as the Prosperous Justice Party or PKS) had its roots in the Muslim Brotherhood–influenced tarbiyah (education) student movement of the late 1990s (Bubalo, Fealy, and Mason 2008, 49–74; Machmudi 2006; Salman 2006). The National Mandate Party (PAN), led by Amien Rais, the former leader of the modernist welfare organization Muhammadiyah, recruited primarily from the ranks of that twenty-five-million-strong organization (Alfian 1989). The National Awakening Party (Partai Kebangkitan Bangsa, PKB) had been established by representatives from the (relatively) progressive wing of Indonesia's largest traditionalist Muslim organization, the Nahdlatul Ulama, which had some thirty-five million supporters (Bush 2009, 118–25; Feillard and Madinier 2006, 84–86).

Notwithstanding their deep roots in Muslim constituencies, none of these parties supported the effort to amend the constitution so as to mandate state-enforced shari'a. The twenty-two interviews I conducted in Jakarta, Yogyakarta, Medan, and West Java (Tangerang) from 2001 to 2007 confirmed that there was strong support for state-mandated Islamic law among the rank and file of the Prosperous Justice Party. National leaders with whom I spoke, however, were convinced that prioritizing the issue would only hurt the party's electoral prospects and the long-term hopes for shari'a law itself. The leadership concluded that the better strategy was to educate Indonesian Muslims about the aims and meaning of the shari'a, on the assumption that an educated public would gradually come to support its enforcement by the state (cf. Fahmi 2006).

Leaders of both the PKB and the PAN whom I interviewed in Jakarta and Yogyakarta in July 2001 and 2002 (and on related matters from 2003 to 2008) were of the opinion that focusing on the shari'a would jeopardize their parties' outreach to non-Muslims and secular Muslims. Especially in PAN, however, party leaders were aware that some among their rank and file supported state-enforced shari'a. After the party's performance in the 1999 elections fell short of expectations, PAN refurbished its Islamic credentials. However, as Muhammadiyah intellectuals had long done (see Hooker 2008, 28), the party leadership continued to speak, not of the need to enforce specific punishments mandated by Islamic law, but of the need to abide by the "higher objectives" of the shari'a (*maqasid al-shari'a;* see my introduction to this volume). Through a rather less complex process of public reasoning, the PKB leadership—intent as it was on extending its base into the more or less "nationalist" wing of the electorate—reached a similar conclusion. In the end, both parties opted not to support a constitutional amendment mandating the law's enforcement by the state.

Not surprisingly, the strongest opposition to the proposed constitutional amendment came from two parties not based in Muslim associations, and usually portrayed as the core of Indonesia's "secular nationalist" community. These were the Indonesian Democracy Party-Struggle (PDI-P) and Golkar, the governing party during Soeharto's New Order (Tomsa 2008). Although for years Indonesian observers have described both parties as secular nationalist, both in fact occupy a middle ground often overlooked in discussions of Muslim politics. They combine a broad commitment to multi-confessional nationalism with acceptance of a state role in promoting religion.

Although both agree that it is legitimate for the state to involve itself in religious affairs, today these two parties differ on the question of just how far that support should go. For the first twenty years of the New Order, Golkar officials interpreted the Pancasila much as the PDI-P still does today. In particular, Golkar in the early New Order affirmed that the state should actively promote religious education and observance. However, notwithstanding the fact that 88 percent of Indonesians are Muslim, Golkar officials in these years emphasized that the state was to treat equally all five of the religions officially recognized since the 1960s (Islam, Protestantism, Catholicism, Hinduism, and Buddhism; see Kim 1998). With Soeharto's celebrated "Islamic turn" in the early 1990s, however, Golkar gradually retreated from this equal-treatment principle to a position that gave pride of place to Islam. The ideological shift had an organizational concomitant, first seen in the establishment in 1990 of an in-government Muslim lobby known as the All-Indonesia Association of Muslim Intellectuals (ICMI; see Hefner 2000, 128–66; Porter 2002, 110–54). The policy shift was also reflected in struggles among Golkar elites. From the early 1990s on, the once-dominant "Pancasila nationalists" who had favored equal treatment of all state-recognized religions were pushed aside in favor of a moderate Islamic leadership with ties to the Islamic Students Association (HMI; see Dijk 2001, 334; on HMI; see Sitompul 1997).

Despite their ideological differences, during 2001–2002 Golkar and the PDI-P joined forces to oppose the proposal to amend Article 29. They were eventually joined by PAN and PKB; the Justice Party (PK) abstained from the final vote. Importantly, however, the actions of all of these parties showed that their leaders were not secularists interested in erecting a high wall between religion and state. At one point representatives from PAN, the PKB, and the PK flirted with proposing an alternative amendment to Article 29, affirming "the obligation upon the followers of each religion to carry out its respective teachings." One party official commented that it was "the state's task to persuade, and not compel, people to be loyal or observant to their respective religious duties" (Salim 2008, 102). PKB officials eventually backed off from this amendment, concerned, as they told me in August 2001, that amending Article 29 would only complicate cooperation with allies in the nationalist camp and the military. As support for even a modified amendment to Article 29 waned, PAN too concluded that the most prudent tack was not to support any amendment.

In the end, opposition to amending Article 29 carried the day, and the effort to enforce an encompassing version of the shari'a through constitutional amendment failed. Secular nationalists breathed a deep sigh of relief. Nonetheless, the debate that raged from 2001 into 2002 revealed that the majority of representatives in the national assembly were not high-wall secularists opposed to state involvement in religious affairs. Indeed, as it became clear that their efforts to amend Article 29 were doomed, the promoters of state-enforced shari'a (particularly those in the PPP) shifted their attention to a second possible constitutional amendment, of Article 31 on education. The PPP proposed that the article be amended so as to describe the aims of national education as including the effort "to increase faith and people's consciousness of God" (Salim 2008, 105). In one sense, there was nothing new to this proposal. The Pancasila has always affirmed belief in God, and in the New Order period this affirmation was interpreted to mean that the state had a right and duty to promote religion among its citizens (Kim 1998). But the proposed amendment to Article 31 gave a new institutional twist to the state's role, making clear that state schools should play a leading role in the religionization of society. Although the PDI-P opposed it, the amendment passed with a solid majority.

A year later, in October 2003, Muslim parties cited the amendment to press for the passage of another law that stiffened the requirement that all schools with Muslim students, including Christian schools, take measures to provide courses on Islam for those students. The proposed legislation was bitterly opposed by Christian groups, who saw it as yet another example of government meddling in their affairs. (Christian schools had long allowed their Muslim students to opt out of Christian religion classes, but most did not have Muslim teachers to teach courses on Islam to those students.) Nonetheless, the legislation was approved. Islamist activists associated with the PPP whom I interviewed in Jakarta and Yogyakarta in July 2004 were delighted with the outcome, describing it (as one activist told me) as "a great step forward in the struggle to educate citizens on the importance of shari'a" (cf. Sirozi 2004). Although their constitutional efforts had reached an impasse, the proponents of more ambitious state enforcement of the shari'a were by no means ready to retire from politics. They were soon to discover another field of struggle for their cause.

Decentralizing Shari'a: The Bylaw Campaigns

The debate over constitutional amendments was just one example of the free-wheeling nature of Indonesian politics during the first years of the post-Soeharto era. B. J. Habibie's *Reformasi* government, which remained in power until October 1999, passed laws expanding press freedoms, legalizing independent political parties, and authorizing a referendum in East Timor, which had been forcefully integrated into Indonesia in 1976. One month before the June 1999 elections, the Habibie government also rushed through two laws (Nos. 22 and 25/1999) designed to devolve an array of powers from the nation's capital to districts (*kabupaten*) and municipalities (Aspinall and Fealy 2003, 3–4). In the dizzying manner typical of legislation in this period, the law stipulated that the decentralized administration was to be operative by January 1, 2001. Breaking with Soeharto's pattern of centralized rule, Habibie and Golkar hoped that by acknowledging regional aspirations they could hold their own in the forthcoming elections in the country's "outer islands," even if (as indeed proved to be the case) Golkar suffered electoral setbacks in Java and Bali.

Article 7 of Law 22/1999 stipulated that five administrative functions were to remain under the control of the central government: foreign relations, security and defense, justice, fiscal and monetary policy, and, most important for the present discussion, religion. Primary responsibility for eleven other jurisdictions, including agriculture, public health, environmental affairs, public works, transportation, cooperatives, foreign investment, and education and culture, was devolved to the regions. Although pushed through with little legislative discussion (see Bünte 2009), Law 22/1999 was intended to bring government closer to the people. In keeping with this ambition, provincial governors, district heads, and mayors were to be elected rather than appointed, at first by the provincial assembly and through direct elections after 2004.

Although the international media often assumed that radical Islamist insurgents were the greatest threat to Indonesia's post-Soeharto transition, the backdraft caused by the rapid devolution of powers from Jakarta to the regions was vastly more destabilizing. Although devolution was premised on the idea of strengthening civil society and deepening democracy, the policy's immediate consequence was a "decentralization of corruption, collusion, and political violence" (Schulte Nordholt and Klinken 2007, 18). Faced with an intensified struggle over local resources, regional party bosses, business elites, and militia chiefs jockeyed to create coalitions capable of winning control of the regional state apparatus and the nebulous "shadow state" that ran alongside it (Klinken 2007, 33, 51). With control of government the most coveted prize, local politicians also pressed to subdivide districts to create new political units and, therefore, new opportunities for rent-seeking spoils. In just a few years, the number of districts (*kabupaten*) in the country increased by almost 50 percent, to 440.

It was in this highly unsettled context that the locally based militias mentioned at the beginning of this chapter took on a politically consequential role. Although some of the larger Islamist militias declared their allegiance to the cause of implementing Islamic law, others signaled that they had more practical priorities. Many, like the celebrated Betawi Brotherhood Forum (Forum Betawi Rembug; see I. Wilson 2006, 2008) in metropolitan Jakarta, had been established in the early months of the post-Soeharto transition and were known to have close ties to the old New Order elite. They were vaguely nationalist and "Islamic," then, but not particularly concerned with Islamic law. In the fiercely competitive circumstances of the post-Soeharto era, however, groups like the Brotherhood Forum quickly discovered that they had to be ready to change their stripes. In 2001 and 2002, when the Brotherhood Forum found itself challenged on its home turf by a radical Islamist militia, the Islamic Defenders Front (FPI), the Brotherhood Forum quickly added the struggle to implement Islamic law to its charter.

Another consequence of decentralization was that aspiring politicians in the provinces felt emboldened to distance themselves from New Order principles of national unity and rally support by appealing to regional and ethnic interests. Where a district was dominated by a particular ethnic group, a common technique was to wrap oneself in the flag of ethno-regional solidarity against the interests of Jakarta, the Javanese, and whatever other immigrant group happened to have recently taken up residence in one's territory. The pressure to localize and ethnicize led many regional elites to invent "indigenous" (*asli*), customs, including new forms of dress, entertainment, and even male and female beauty contests (*sans* sexually alluring clothing; see Long 2008, 191–220). However, one theme stood out above all others in these campaigns, as it would also in subsequent shari'a-oriented bylaws: "Women have been the main objects in this process, particularly through applying a dress code" (Setyawati 2008, 79).

Where the local population was majority Muslim, then, the "indigenous" culture highlighted in this way was usually Islamic, but not typically Islamist or shari'a-minded. Nonetheless, the recourse to religious symbolism often strained interreligious relations, especially where sectarian appeals were made by rival, and religiously distinct, elites struggling to seize control of local state bureaus. The coincidence of resource competition and ethno-religious mobilization proved especially volatile in the few districts where Christians and Muslims lived side by side in near-equal numbers: parts of Maluku and North Maluku, Central Sulawesi, and West and Central Kalimantan. In the early years of the post-Soeharto period, all of these regions witnessed fierce outbreaks of communal and religious violence (Davidson 2008; Klinken 2007). In provinces where Muslims constituted the great majority, riots also broke out on occasion, but they rarely reached the intensity seen in these religiously polarized regions. Fortunately, by 2002, violence even in the core conflict zones had peaked. By 2003, the armed forces were again cooperating with their civilian president, new governing coalitions were in place, and mass violence in most provinces had declined dramatically.

These regional rivalries in the context of decentralization also provided the backdrop to the campaigns for the implementation of shari'a bylaws. Although radical organizations like the Hizb ut-Tahrir, the Indonesian Council of Jihad Fighters (MMI), and the Islamic Defenders Front (FPI)—working hand in hand with local branches of the Council of Indonesian Ulama (MUI)—had hoped to transform these regional struggles into a nationwide campaign, the initiative's supporters succeeded at getting legislation passed in only about one-ninth (53) of the country's 470 districts and municipalities (see Bush 2008, 176; Salim 2008, 128–29).

As noted above, the regulations implemented in these regions were actually comparatively modest in scope. Although in some sense "shari'a-informed" and aimed primarily at Muslims, in their derivation and implementation the laws were not really shari'a; they were closer in spirit to the coercive social controls favored in many authoritarian postcolonial states. The regulations tightened controls on alcohol, gambling, and women's movement (ostensibly to crack down on prostitution); they also mandated the performance of certain Islamic devotional duties.

However limited their scope, the bylaws proved enormously controversial, for three reasons. First, Christians and nationalist-minded Muslims decried the mandating of Islamic dress and ritual behaviors as violations of the citizen equality enshrined in Indonesia's Pancasila and constitution (cf. Wahid Institute 2006). Although support for the Pancasila remained strong among Indonesians (as discussed below), this particular criticism did not prove particularly effective at mobilizing opposition to the bylaws. Its limited appeal reflected the fact that many Indonesians had long assumed that the Pancasila was a nonsecularist charter, compatible with state promotion of religion.

The second source of controversy was that, in crafting the bylaws, regional legislators had often placed greater emphasis on getting them passed quickly than they had on working out the details of their enforcement. In South Sulawesi, for example, proponents of the law had advised that devoting too much time to the details of enforcement would only undermine chances for the bylaws' passage. Members therefore rushed them through the local assembly, explaining that the details of enforcement could be worked out later (see Hooker 2008, 263). While acknowledging that bylaws dealing with sexual trafficking and violence against women had been well intended, the government-sponsored National Commission on Women observed that the haste with which the regional bylaws had been drawn up often led them to undermine women's civil rights (*Jurnal Perempuan* 2006).

The third reason the bylaws generated controversy was that, with the mechanisms of enforcement put in place so hastily, the most frequent targets of the ill-trained young men charged with implementing them were local women and the poor. As in Tangerang, West Java, the morals police's arrests of innocent women out after dark generated bitter protests from civil society and women's groups, both of whom saw the laws as blatantly discriminatory (Mulia 2006). Although many of the more ardent proponents of shari'a law, like the Party of Liberation (Hizb ut-Tahrir) and the Indonesian Council of Jihad Fighters (MMI), claimed the shari'a could be a weapon with which to fight government corruption, none of the regional bylaws addressed the issue, and few if any of the individuals punished under them came from the ranks of the well-off.

Notwithstanding these criticisms, the momentum for the crafting of shari'a-inflected bylaws at first grew briskly, peaking in 2003. But opposition to the bylaws grew as well, with the result that, as Robin Bush has noted (2008, 179), the number of new bylaws dropped precipitously between 2003 and 2007. As shown by the passage of the anti-pornography law by the national assembly in 2008, legislation of a vaguely religious nature can still win considerable public support. However, at the national level, the proponents of such legislation have found that they can best make their case on the grounds of public ethics rather than shari'a (see Kitley 2008; White and Anshor 2008).

The brevity of the period during which shari'a bylaws proved popular suggests that, where they gained traction, the bylaw campaigns benefited from the sense of crisis and public ethical panic unleashed by the sudden collapse of the New Order, the rushed effort at decentralization, and a spike in criminality and communal violence. Several Indonesia observers have pointed out that there was an additional influence on the regional bylaw campaigns. The movements gained greatest traction in districts which two generations earlier had been strongholds of the Darul Islam movement. Indeed, half of the districts that implemented bylaws had been centers of Darul Islam resistance (Bush 2008, 183). The DI districts, including Bulukumba in South Sulawesi and Garut, Ciamis, and Tasikmalaya in West Java, also gave rise to some of the largest and most aggressive shari'a militias. In South Sulawesi, the head of the Committee for the Implementation of Islamic shari'a (KPSI) was none other than Abdul Aziz Kahar Muzakkar, the son of Kahar Muzakkar, the leader of the Darul Islam rebels in South Sulawesi in the 1950s (Halim 2005; Juhannis 2007).

Although they played a key role in organizing Islamist militias, it is important not to exaggerate the DI activists' actual power. Many of the district chiefs who sponsored the bylaws, including government officials in Tangerang, Ciamis, and Garut in West Java and Bulukumba in South Sulawesi, were affiliated with the Golkar party, whose national leadership had opposed efforts to amend Article 29 of the constitution so as to allow state enforcement of the shari'a. As Michael Buehler (2008) has noted, in areas where established elites faced new electoral challenges, shari'a appeals often proved an attractive instrument for mobilizing support and new economic resources.

In the unsteady world of post-Soeharto Indonesia, however, even this political tactic had its limits, not least for some in the regional Golkar leadership. In interviews that I conducted in December 2007 in Tangerang, West Java, local Golkar officials acknowledged that recently they had been gently "reminded" by the national party leadership that the Tangerang regulations restricting unescorted women's movement after dark "went too far." The city's vice-mayor told me in no uncertain terms that the bylaws had "nothing to do with shari'a" but "were concerned with public morals and had been welcomed by non-Muslims as well as Muslim citizens." My interviews with Tangerang Christians confirmed that several groups *had* welcomed a crackdown on Tangerang's out-of-control prostitution industry, in which elements of the local police were thought to be involved. But from the start Christian groups and a local alliance of women's organizations had also objected to the regulations that forbade women from going out of the house unescorted after 10:00 PM.[6]

In Bulukumba, South Sulawesi, Golkar officials had also backed the shari'a-influenced bylaws, in what critics claimed was a shameless effort to burnish their Islamic credentials in the face of growing popular unrest over corruption allegations (see Buehler 2008). By the time I conducted interviews in that district in 2007 and 2008, several mid-level Golkar officials seemed to have developed second thoughts about the wisdom of such burnishing. One volunteered that some of his regional superiors had been "too quick to support" the legislation, and added that he thought that it was time for local Golkar officials to "pay attention again" to the national leadership. The national chair of Golkar at this time was none other than vice-president Jusuf Kalla, a Buginese native son of South Sulawesi. As early as 2005, Kalla had spoken out against the shari'a-influenced bylaws. Two officials I interviewed in Makassar two years later reported that "underlings of the vice-president" had communicated his and the national party's displeasure with party leaders in the province and asked other local officials to rein in their colleagues. I was never able to confirm these reports with the vice-president's office. However, the commentaries were consistent with information provided by Golkar officials interviewed in Jakarta, Yogyakarta, Medan, and Makassar in 2006, 2007, and 2008. One Jakarta official summarized the situation this way: "Of course we support the efforts of citizens and fellow Muslims to abide by the aims [Ind. *maksud*] of Islamic law. But playing the 'shari'a card' for simple political gain is another matter. It's fine to support public morality and the suppression of vice [*maksiat*]. But it really should be done in a way consistent with the national interest."

The shift in sentiment in upper-echelon party circles, including Golkar, may well have played a role in the growing opposition after 2003 to the shari'a-oriented regional bylaws. Other developments deepened the public's reservations. After 2002–2003, communal violence in eastern Indonesia declined dramatically, eliminating an issue that radicals in groups like the Islamic Defenders' Front, the Laskar Jihad, and the Hizb ut-Tahrir had used to discredit nationalist opponents of shari'a legislation. Around this same time, Indonesia's economy began to recover from the lingering effects of the Asian financial crisis. Much of the public seemed tired of the post-Soeharto bickering and wanted the nation's politicians to get back to the business of development and job creation. In the national assembly, more than 40 percent of parliamentarians elected in 2004 had business backgrounds, while "the number of former military officers, bureaucrats, and nationalist political activists, as well as people with backgrounds in Islamic mass organizations, has fallen" (Ufen 2008, 26). The "technocratic" trend in politics was confirmed in the 2004 election of Susilo Bambang Yudhoyono, the first directly elected president in Indonesian history. Although Yudhoyono has a background in the military, he has long been regarded as a reform-minded technocrat, and a politely mannered Javanese at that.

The developmentalist trend was also apparent in the relative slackening of public interest in the old, religion-based ideological divides of the 1950s and 1960s, and in the greater fluidity of political affiliation seen generally (see Aspinall 2005a, 121). Certainly, as the 2002 debates on constitutional amendments had revealed, the parties still differed on some matters of principle, not least the question of the place of Islamic law in public life. However, most party leaders sensed that the public had reservations about efforts to enforce elements of Islamic law in a manner that appeared narrowly sectarian. Rather than highlighting shari'a issues, then, Muslim-oriented parties joined their nationalist counterparts to engage in "a fight for the middle ground" (Ufen 2008, 28; cf. Hefner 2009). In preparing for that contest, Muslim-based parties emphasized their commitment to good governance and social services rather than the specific commands of Islamic law.

In 2005, the first direct popular elections for governors, district heads, and mayors took place. In the run-up to the elections, Indonesians had feared the campaigning might tempt some provincial politicians to reemphasize sectarian divides, not least by pushing for the implementation of shari'a-influenced bylaws. But the expected sectarian outbidding did not materialize, as voters once again signaled their preference for development-oriented politicians of a pragmatic and public ethical rather than sectarian cast (Mietzner 2009, 142).

This combination of influences meant that, by 2007, efforts in the provinces to implement shari'a-oriented legislation on the model of the 2001–2003 period had slowed. The decline has led some observers to conclude that efforts to implement Islamic shari'a are now a thing of the past. But that conclusion is almost certainly premature, or sociologically misleading. It is not that the Muslim public in Indonesia has lost interest in religiously influenced ethics. Rather, the Muslim public appears to be exploring new and more practically efficacious ways of putting religious values into practice.

Pious Publics and Shari'a Ambiguity

The limited success of parties that campaigned on the basis of state-enforced shari'a was confirmed in every one of post-Soeharto Indonesia's elections. No party advocating the comprehensive implementation of Islamic law ever received more than 12 percent of the national vote, and the combined shares of such parties came only to about 20 percent. This outcome surprised many Indonesian observers. They had speculated that, because Muslim Indonesians appeared more religiously observant than ever, it was just a matter of time before efforts to promote some variety of state-enforced shari'a would prevail.

This impression was reinforced by the results of several public opinion surveys conducted in the 2000s by highly regarded survey institutes, including the Indonesian Survey Institute (Lembaga Survei Indonesia, LSI) and the Center for the Study of Islam and Society (Pusat Pengkajian Islam dan Masyarakat, PPIM) at the Hidayatullah State Islamic University in Jakarta. These and other surveys all suggested that somewhere between 60 and 75 percent of Muslim Indonesians endorsed the idea that the state should implement shari'a law for all Muslim citizens. Support declined when respondents were asked about such harsh hudud penalties as the amputation of thieves' limbs or the stoning of adulterers, but even these punishments were endorsed by a sizable portion of the population (LSI 2007; PPIM 2007). The PPIM and LSI surveys have also indicated that since 2006 support for state-enforced shari'a has dipped somewhat—but the result still stands above 50 percent.

Other studies have confirmed these findings, showing that, when responding to survey questions, Indonesian Muslims voice strong support for state enforcement of the shari'a. However, other research suggests that the responses reflect surprisingly complex, conditional judgments rather than values singularly determinative of political choices. In a 2007 survey, LSI researchers asked more than a thousand Indonesians whether they supported a "Pancasila" state or would prefer one built on some other basis (LSI 2007). Indonesians understand that a Pancasila state is one based on multi-confessional principles rather than just the shari'a, an issue that harks back to debates at the republic's founding. According to this survey, 90 percent of the respondents indicated that they preferred a Pancasila state to any alternative. This finding is interesting because the figure is comparable to (just 10 percent greater than) the percentage of voters who since 1999 have chosen parties supportive of Pancasila nationalism rather than state-enforced shari'a.

My own survey, interview, and ethnographic research from 2005 to 2009 on Indonesian attitudes toward the shari'a also underscores the importance of contextualizing Indonesians' expressed support for state-enforced Islamic law. In January 2006 and January 2007, I worked with staff at the PPIM at the Hidayatullah National Islamic University to carry out two surveys, each of some one thousand Muslim educators. The survey had 184 questions, on an array of topics too complex to present here. But on matters of the shari'a and democracy, our findings were broadly consistent with those of the PPIM and the LSI in earlier studies of public opinion in the general Muslim population. In particular, and quite remarkably, more than 80 percent of the respondents agreed that democracy is the best form of government for Indonesia. Their support for democracy was not merely general, but extended to high levels of support for citizen equality before the law (94.2 percent), freedom to join political organizations (82.5 percent), protection of the media from arbitrary government action (92.8 percent), and a host of other democratic values. However, when asked their views on the shari'a, the level of support reported by these educators was again comparable to (in fact, a bit higher than) that of the general Muslim public: 72.2 percent believed the state should be based on the Qur'an and Sunna and to some degree advised by religious experts, and 82.8 percent of educators thought the state should work to implement the shari'a. As in the surveys conducted among the general Muslim public, support for the shari'a slipped a bit on controversial matters like the amputation of thieves' hands (59.1 percent support), the stoning of adulterers (48 percent agree), and government compulsion in the performance of the Ramadan fast (only 49.9 percent agree).

Notwithstanding the educators' and the Muslim public's support for state-enforced shari'a, my one-on-one interviews with a hundred respondents to the surveys provided a far more complex sense of how these respondents square their views of the shari'a with real-world political choices. Although 72.2 percent of my survey respondents had expressed support for establishing a state based on the Qur'an and Sunna, fewer than 30 percent indicated that they had actually voted for a party in any sense dedicated to that end. Equally striking, two-thirds of that group had voted for the Prosperous Justice Party (PKS), which had made clear that it had no intention of pressing for immediate implementation of shari'a law. Only 10 percent of the educators voted for a party like the PPP or the PBB that made state-enforced shari'a an urgent priority.

Asked in open-ended interviews why they chose not to make implementation of the law their first priority in choosing a party, interviewees offered a number of observations. Moderately conservative Islamists, including many regional supporters of the PKS, explained that they felt that the Indonesian people were not "ready" for the full implementation of the shari'a, and that any step in such a direction had to be gradual. However, the more fiqh-savvy among the respondents often commented that what is important with regard to the law is not its formal letter but its higher "objectives" (Indo. *maksud,* Ar. *maqasid;* see my introduction to this volume) as understood through a comprehensive reading of the Qur'an, the Sunna, and classical commentaries on the law. Interestingly, a simpler version of this last comment was also the most common response among the less legally literate. These respondents emphasized that they too were devoted to shari'a values. But those values have to be implemented in such a way that, as one Makassar interviewee put the matter in August 2008, "they make a positive difference in our lives, rather than just causing social discord."

As discussed in the introduction to this volume, survey and interview findings like these are not unique to Indonesia. They suggest that in Indonesia and many other Muslim-majority societies the public's views on democracy and the shari'a are in tension, but not necessarily irreconcilably so. Here in Indonesia especially, the public seems subtly aware of the tension between its commitment to the shari'a and its desire for good governance and social peace. Rather than rushing to support radical programs for state enforcement of Islamic law, then, most Muslims contextualize their commitment to the shari'a. While still subscribing to the notion that some variety of the shari'a is religiously required, they reference an ethicalized understanding of the law, one that focuses on social harmony and the public good rather than individual regulations or inflexible punishments. In the minds of most Muslim Indonesians, this ethicalized understanding of Islamic law also happens to be consistent with democracy.

Moving Forward: Centripetal or Centrifugal Shariʻa?

Modern Indonesian history offers a panoply of trends with regard to Islamic law. On one hand, since the 1940s, Indonesia has hosted a variety of radical groups committed to singular and authoritarian variants of Islamic law—to be implemented by any means necessary. Notwithstanding repeated setbacks, the radicals have survived, coming up from underground in the post-Soeharto period, although not winning broad support.

On the other hand, Indonesia also has one of the largest and most sophisticated traditions of pro-democracy Muslim scholarship in the world (Feener 2007, 182–221; cf. Hooker 2008). In the late 1980s and early 1990s, Indonesia's State Islamic Colleges (IAIN) produced an array of gifted scholars who, while well versed in Islamic fiqh, provided strong religious arguments for democracy and the rule of law (Abdillah 1997). In the 1990s, some among these scholars played a key role in mobilizing Muslim support for the democracy movement challenging President Soeharto. No less impressive is the fact that the democratic efflorescence was not just the purview of a few intellectuals. The most striking characteristic of the three national elections conducted since 1999 has been the electorate's "inclination to reject candidates who campaigned on exclusivist platforms" (Mietzner 2009, 141). Contrary to the situation of the 1950s, no party making state-commanded shariʻa a priority has won broad electoral support.

Two things make the larger landscape of shariʻa politics especially interesting. The first is that these political developments have taken place against the backdrop of, from 1999 to 2003, a severe economic downturn, communal violence, and, in urban areas, a pervasive "fear of extortion, harassment, or violence at the hands of *preman* [gangsters]" (I. Wilson 2008, 192). In this context, radical Islamists mounted a ferocious campaign to discredit democracy, widen the divide between Christians and Muslims, and present a shariʻa understood as singular and unchanging as a panacea for the nation's ills. Notwithstanding these framing efforts, voters opted for candidates of the center promising good government, economic growth, and Islamic values expressed in an ethicalized and adaptive rather than formalistic and uncontextualized way.

The second fact that makes this larger landscape interesting is that, by any measure, the 1990s and 2000s have been characterized by a great surge in Islamic observance. Regional social histories, ethnographic studies, and survey data all testify to the depth and breadth of the pietistic turn. But the piety has not translated into support for the modern Islamist dogma—itself a break with the classical tradition of Islamic law (see my introduction)—that the shari'a is best realized by giving primary responsibility for its definition and enforcement to state elites or self-appointed shari'a activists in society.

There is an interesting parallel in all this between the political and religious fields. The German political scientist Marcus Mietzner has spoken, I think correctly, of the prevalence of "centripetal" trends in political party competition today, as opposed to the "centrifugal" instability of the 1950s. Interparty rivalries during the earlier period, Mietzner observes, became so polarized that the crucial disputes "took place at the far ends of the ideological spectrum" (cf. Geertz 1960b, 1965). Today, by contrast, and despite the anti-systemic appeals of some radicals, "the vast majority of Indonesians, and Indonesian Muslims, do not favour a change in the political system" (Mietzner 2008, 431). This generalization applies broadly to public arguments about the shari'a as well. The major parties differ only marginally on questions of shari'a and democracy. They agree in part because their leadership is aware that most members of the Muslim public have a pragmatic interest in Islamic law, preferring good government and the law's higher objectives to a narrow formalization of it.

It goes without saying that not everyone has joined the rush to the political center. A small but well-organized flank continues to demand state enforcement of a shari'a understood in authoritarian terms. Some among these groups, like the Party of Liberation (Hizb ut-Tahrir) and the Islamic Defenders Front (FPI), have grown in recent years, building a network of militias, schools, and economic patronage. Statistically speaking, these groups still do not have a large mass following. However, as the history of the Darul Islam demonstrates, movements do not need huge numbers of supporters to mount regular challenges to the political order. Even if their numbers remain small, these movements have the dedication and organizational skill to guarantee themselves a role in Indonesian shari'a politics for some years to come. But if political and moral crises on a scale like that of 1998–2002 can be avoided, they are not likely to make great headway.

Perhaps the more decisive question as regards the future of shari'a politics in Indonesia, however, concerns points of articulation between state institutions and strategically placed Islamic groupings. Here the Indonesian case offers a sobering lesson. One of the most striking features of shari'a politics in the post-Soeharto period is that, although radical proponents of state-enforced shari'a have been repeatedly rebuffed, some were able to exercise influence by trading support for local political bosses (most of whom were not of radical Islamist disposition) for influence on the crafting of shari'a bylaws. Interestingly, much of the public and even some among the political elite have cooled to this sort of deal-making. They object, not to the bringing of shari'a values into public life, but to varieties of the law that fail to address serious public problems.

A few other non-democratic Islamists have extended their influence by gaining a perch in the executive of the semi-governmental MUI (see Olle 2009). Early on in the post-Soeharto era, some in the MUI leadership lent their support to authoritarian understandings of the shari'a. These MUI officials called for the state to take action against "deviationist" currents in Indonesian Islam (Gillespie 2007). Militants in groups like the Islamic Defenders Front and the Hizb ut-Tahrir have cited MUI declarations to justify violence against minority Muslim sects, including the Ahmadiyah, whose mosques have been shuttered and homes burned (ICG 2008). Although the MUI is not fully state-based, its ties to the bureaucracy afford it great influence. After the failed effort to amend Article 29 in 2002, regional MUI councils lent their backing to local efforts to craft shari'a bylaws and to criminalize religious non-conformism. Local councils also winked at the radical militias who used threats and violence to promote their aims (cf. Olle 2009, 111–16).

The striking of deals with party bosses and the capturing of state bureaus by well-organized activist groups are commonplace events in modern polities, including democracies. Arrangements like these allow the members of "uncivil society" (Keane 1996, 14; cf. Hefner 2003) to scale up their influence well beyond their representation in society. This strategy was a key feature of political developments in late modern Sudan and Iran, where actors with authoritarian understandings of shari'a law made their way to power, despite the fact that they did not enjoy the backing of most citizens. Such undemocratic collaborations across the state-society divide may well remain an aim of the radical flank of the Islamist movement here in Indonesia. The effort will not likely jeopardize Indonesia's broader political transition. As the MUI example shows, however, the capture of even small perches in or around the state can provide the proponents of authoritarian variants of Islamic law with an influence disproportionate to their numbers in society.

This last example points to what may be, for the future of shari'a politics in Indonesia, the truly decisive matter. It is not the breadth of theological or jurisprudential divides that presents the greatest challenge to Indonesian Islam in the post-Soeharto period. It is the task of building a political, legal, and public-ethical framework with sufficient legitimacy and reward to continue to bring people to a democracy-reinforcing center. Notwithstanding the violence of the early post-Soeharto period, the results of Indonesia's elections suggest that such a framework is slowly taking form. The consolidation of this cultural and institutional framework will depend on the state's ability to deliver on the promise of prosperity and justice for most citizens. The state's efforts in this sphere will also be key to Muslim reformists' efforts to take the shariʿa to the center rather than the fringes of national politics, demonstrating that democracy and the shariʿa are indeed compatible.

Notes

1. Din Syamsuddin, MUI general secretary, personal interview, March 17, 2007. In our conversation, Syamsuddin explained that the outreach was also intended to discourage militants from going outside established political channels and "becoming more radical."

2. With its long history of struggle against outside rule, Aceh, in northwestern Sumatra, is a special case in Indonesia's shariʿa politics; its full analysis would require a longer discussion than space allows in this essay. At the dawn of the Indonesian republic in 1945, ulama played a role in Acehnese politics greater than in those of any other region in Indonesia. The ulama also insisted that the implementation of shariʿa was a precondition for their region's joining the new republic. However, early on Indonesia's leaders made clear they had no intention of allowing the implementation of Islamic law in the restless territory. In the 1950s, a rebellion against Jakarta made enforcement of Islamic law a core demand. But the revolt's collapse in the early 1960s undermined ulama power and put the shariʿa campaign on hold. During the New Order, a government-created council managed to coopt most ulama even as political resistance to Jakarta's authority surged. With the end of the New Order in May 1998, an alliance of religious students and rural ulama established a new ulama body and called again for the implementation of Islamic law. Locked in a bitter armed conflict with the Indonesian military, the Free Aceh independence movement (Gerakan Aceh Merdeka, GAM) regarded the ulama organization warily and never endorsed its demand for Islamic law. In 1999, in an effort to win the favor of the ulama and undercut support for the rebels, the central government passed a law (No. 44/1999) recognizing Aceh's special status. Two years later, Law 18/2001 on Special Autonomy went further, authorizing the establishment of shariʿa courts. The national law portrays Aceh's shariʿa courts as part of the national court system, and thus subject to Supreme Court review. However, Aceh's Council of Ulama (Majelis Permusyawaratan Ulama, MPU) has insisted that the region's special status allows a fuller array of shariʿa laws (qanun) than the national system allows. In 2002, Acehnese authorities passed regulations banning Shiʿism, the Ahmadiyah sect, and Muʿtazila rationalists. Groups and individuals identified as "deviationist" are also subject to whipping and prison. Alcohol consumption and the illicit proximity (khalwat) of unmarried males and females are punished by caning. Some religious leaders have proposed imposing a poll tax (jizya) on non-Muslims in the province. On September 14, 2009, the outgoing parliament of Aceh passed legislation making adultery punishable by stoning to death. The law was a direct challenge to the incoming Aceh Party, which has roots in the Free Aceh movement and had been swept to power in elections a few weeks earlier. Although careful not to take on the ulama, the Aceh Party was opposed to strict-constructionist implementation of Islamic law. At present, the constitutional legality of Aceh's shariʿa legislation remains unclear; some

legal experts insist that many *qanun* violate Indonesian law and must be amended. However, Jakarta authorities have yet to rule on this question. On the history and current situation of shari'a in Aceh, see Bowen 2003; Hooker 2008, 246–64; Lindsey and Hooker 2007; and Salim 2008, 143–67.

3. Personal communication, February 7, 2006.

4. For a particularly vivid presentation of this argument, written by the executive director of the Indonesian Council of Jihad Fighters, see Awwas 2008.

5. Indeed, memories of such incidents loomed large in the interviews I conducted with ten senior ulama in South Sulawesi in December 2007 and November 2008.

6. Tangerang Women's Coalition, personal interview, November 3, 2008.

References Cited

Abdillah, Masykuri. 1997. *Responses of Indonesian Muslim Intellectuals to the Concept of Democracy (1966–1993)*. Hamburg: Abera Verlag Meyer.

Abdullah, Taufik. 1971. *Schools and Politics: The Kaum Muda Movement in West Sumatra (1927–1933)*. Ithaca: Cornell Modern Indonesia Project, Cornell University.

Alfian. 1989. *Muhammadiyah: The Political Behavior of a Muslim Modernist Organization under Dutch Colonialism*. Yogyakarta, Java, Indonesia: Gadjah Mada University Press.

Anderson, Benedict. 1983. "Old State, New Society: Indonesia's New Order in Comparative Historical Perspective." *Journal of Asian Studies* 42 (3): 477–96.

Aragon, Lorraine V. 2001. "Communal Violence in Poso, Central Sulawesi: Where People Eat Fish and Fish Eat People." *Indonesia* 72: 45–79.

Aspinall, Edward. 2005a. "Elections and the Normalization of Politics in Indonesia." *South East Asia Research* 13 (2): 117–56.

———. 2005b. *Opposing Suharto: Compromise, Resistance, and Regime Change in Indonesia*. Stanford: Stanford University Press.

Aspinall, Edward, and Greg Fealy. 2003. "Decentralisation, Democratisation, and the Rise of the Local." Introduction to *Local Power and Politics in Indonesia: Decentralizations*, ed. Edward Aspinall and Greg Fealy, 1–11. Singapore: Institute of Southeast Asian Studies.

Awwas, Irfan S. 2008. *Trilogi kepemimpinan negara Islam Indonesia: Menguak perjuangan umat Islam dan pengkhianatan kaum nasionalis-sekuler*. Yogyakarta, Java, Indonesia: Uswah Press.

Berg, L. W. C. van den. 1886. "Het Mohammedaansche godsdienstonderwijs op Java en Madoera en de daarbij gebruikt Arabische Boeken." *Tijdschrift voor Indische Taal-, Land-, en Volkenkunde* (Batavia) 31:519–55.

Berkey, Jonathan. 1992. *The Transmission of Knowledge in Medieval Cairo: A Social History of Islamic Education*. Princeton: Princeton University Press.

Blengsli, Bjorn Atle. 2009. "Muslim Metamorphosis: Islamic Education and Politics in Contemporary Cambodia." In *Making Modern Muslims: The Politics of Islamic Education in Southeast Asia*, ed. Robert W. Hefner, 172–204. Honolulu: University of Hawaii Press.

Bowen, John R. 1993. *Muslims through Discourse: Religion and Ritual in Gayo Society*. Princeton: Princeton University Press.

———. 2003. *Islam, Law and Equality in Indonesia: An Anthropology of Public Reasoning*. Cambridge: Cambridge University Press.

Bruinessen, Martin van. 1989. "*Kitab Kuning*: Books in Arabic Script Used in the Pesantren Milieu." *Bijdragen tot de Taal-, Land-, en Volkenkunde* 146 (2–3): 225–69.

———. 1994. "Pesantren and *Kitab Kuning*: Maintenance and Continuation of a Tradition of Religious Learning." In *Texts from the Islands: Oral and Written Traditions of Indonesia and the Malaya World*, ed. Wolfgang Marschall, 121–45. Berne: University of Berne Press.

———. 1995. "*Shari'a* Court, *Tarekat* and *Pesantren*: Religious Institutions in the Banten Sultanate." *Archipel* 50:165–200.

Bubalo, Anthony, Greg Fealy, and Whit Mason. 2008. *Zealous Democrats: Islamism and Democracy in Egypt, Indonesia, and Turkey*. Double Bay, N.S.W., Australia: Lowy Institute for International Policy.

Buehler, Michael. 2008. "The Rise of Shari'a Bylaws in Indonesian Districts: An Indication for Changing Patterns of Power Accumulation and Political Corruption." *South East Asia Research* 16 (2): 255–85.

Bulliet, Richard W. 1994. *Islam: The View from the Edge*. New York: Columbia University Press.

Bünte, Marco. 2009. "Indonesia's Protracted Decentralization: Contested Reforms and Their Unintended Consequences." In *Democratization in Post-Suharto Indonesia*, ed. Marco Bünte and Andreas Ufen, 102–23. London and New York: Routledge.

Bünte, Marco, and Andreas Ufen. 2009. *Democratization in Post-Suharto Indonesia*. London and New York: Routledge.

Burhanudin, Jajat. 2006. "*Kerajaan*-Oriented Islam: The Experience of Pre-colonial Indonesia." *Studia Islamika* 13 (1): 33–66.

Burns, Peter. 2004. *The Leiden Legacy: Concepts of Law in Indonesia*. Leiden: KITLV Press.

Bush, Robin. 2008. "Regional Sharia Regulations in Indonesia: Anomaly or Symptom?" In *Expressing Islam: Religious Life and Politics in Indonesia*, ed. Greg Fealy and Sally White, 174–91. Singapore: Institute of Southeast Asian Studies.

———. 2009. *Nahdlatul Ulama and the Struggle for Power within Islam and Politics in Indonesia*. Singapore: Institute of Southeast Asian Studies.

Cammack, Mark. 1997. "Indonesia's 1989 Religious Judicature Act: Islamization of Indonesia or Indonesianization of Islam?" *Indonesia* 63:143–68.

Cederroth, Sven. 1981. *The Spell of the Ancestors and the Power of Mekkah: A Sasak Community on Lombok*. Göteborg, Sweden: Acta Universitatis Gothoburgensis.

Chamberlain, Michael. 1994. *Knowledge and Social Practice in Medieval Damascus, 1190–1350*. Cambridge Studies in Islamic Civilization. Cambridge: Cambridge University Press.

Cook, Michael. 2000. *Commanding Right and Forbidding Wrong in Islamic Thought*. Cambridge: Cambridge University Press.

Davidson, Jamie S. 2008. *From Rebellion to Riots: Collective Violence on Indonesian Borneo*. Madison: University of Wisconsin Press.

Day, Anthony. 1983. "Islam and Literature in South-East Asia: Some Pre-modern, Mainly Javanese Perspectives." In *Islam in South-East Asia,* ed. M. B. Hooker, 130–59. Leiden: Brill.

Dhofier, Zamakhsyari. 1999. *The Pesantren Tradition: The Role of the Kyai in the Maintenance of Traditional Islam in Java.* Tempe: Monograph Series, Program for Southeast Asian Studies, Arizona State University.

Dijk, C. van. 1981. *Rebellion under the Banner of Islam: The Darul Islam in Indonesia.* Verhandelingen van Het KITLV no. 94. The Hague: Martinus Nijhoff.

———. 2001. *A Country in Despair: Indonesia between 1997 and 2000.* Leiden: KITLV Press.

Drewes, G. W. J. 1969. *The Admonitions of Seh Bari.* The Hague: Martinus Nijhoff.

Effendy, Bahtiar. 2003. *Islam and the State in Indonesia.* Singapore: Institute of Southeast Asian Studies.

Fahmi, Nashir. 2006. *Menegakkan syariat Islam ala PKS.* Solo, Java, Indonesia: Era Intermedia.

Fealy, Greg, and Virginia Hooker, eds. 2006. *Voices of Islam in Southeast Asia: A Contemporary Sourcebook.* Singapore: Institute of Southeast Asian Studies.

Feener, R. Michael. 2007. *Muslim Legal Thought in Modern Indonesia.* Cambridge: Cambridge University Press.

Feillard, Andrée, and Rémy Madinier. 2006. *La fin de l'innocence? L'Islam indonésien face à la tentation radicale de 1967 à nos jours.* Paris: Les Indes Savantes.

Feith, Herbert. 1963. "Dynamics of Guided Democracy." In *Indonesia,* ed. Ruth T. McVey, 309–409. New Haven: Southeast Asia Studies, Yale University, by arrangement with HRAF Press.

Freedom House. 2007. "Map of Freedom in the World: 2007 Edition." http://www .freedomhouse.org/template.cfm?page=363&year=2007 (accessed February 24, 2008).

Furnivall, J. S. 1944. *Netherlands India: A Study of Plural Economy.* New York: Macmillan.

Geertz, Clifford. 1960a. "The Javanese Kijaji: The Changing Role of a Cultural Broker." *Comparative Studies in Society and History* 2 (2): 228–49.

———. 1960b. *Religion of Java.* Glencoe, Ill.: Free Press.

———. 1965. *The Social History of an Indonesian Town.* Cambridge, Mass: MIT Press.

Gibson, Thomas. 2007. *Islamic Narrative and Authority in Southeast Asia: From the 16th to the 21st Century.* New York: Palgrave Macmillan.

Gillespie, Piers. 2007. "Current Issues in Indonesian Islam: Analysing the 2005 Council of Indonesian Ulama Fatwa No. 7 Opposing Pluralism, Liberalism, and Secularism." *Journal of Islamic Studies* 18 (2): 202–40.

Halim, Wahyuddin. 2005. "Shari'ah Implementation in South Sulawesi: An Analysis of the KPPSI Movement." *Future Islam,* July–August. http://www.futureislam .com/20050701/insight/Wahyuddin_Halim/Shariah_Implementation_in_South_ Sulawesi_prn.asp (accessed June 15, 2007).

Hallaq, Wael B. 2009. *Shari'a: Theory, Practice, Transformations.* Cambridge: Cambridge University Press.

Hasan, Noorhaidi. 2006. *Laskar Jihad: Islam, Militancy, and the Quest for Identity in Post– New Order Indonesia.* Ithaca: Southeast Asia Program, Cornell University.

Hefner, Robert W. 1985. *Hindu Javanese: Tengger Tradition and Islam*. Princeton: Princeton University Press.

———. 2000. *Civil Islam: Muslims and Democratization in Indonesia*. Princeton: Princeton University Press.

———. 2003. "Civic Pluralism Denied? The New Media and *Jihadi* Violence in Indonesia." In *New Media in the Muslim World: The Emerging Public Sphere*, ed. Dale F. Eickelman and Jon W. Anderson, 158–79. Bloomington: Indiana University Press.

———. 2005. "Muslim Democrats and Islamist Violence in Post-Soeharto Indonesia." In *Remaking Muslim Politics: Pluralism, Contestation, Democratization*, ed. Robert W. Hefner, 273–301. Princeton: Princeton University Press.

———. 2009. "The Politics and Cultures of Islamic Education in Southeast Asia." In *Making Modern Muslims: The Politics of Islamic Education in Southeast Asia*, ed. Robert W. Hefner, 1–54. Honolulu: University of Hawaii Press.

Hooker, M. B. 1984. *Islamic Law in South-East Asia*. Singapore: Oxford University Press.

———. 2008. *Indonesian Syariah: Defining a National School of Islamic Law*. Singapore: Institute of Southeast Asian Studies.

Hurgronje, C. Snouck 1931. *Mekka in the Latter Part of the 19th Century*. Leiden: Brill.

ICG (International Crisis Group). 2002a. "Al-Qaeda in Southeast Asia: The Case of the 'Ngruki Network' in Indonesia." Jakarta and Brussels: Asia Briefing no. 20.

———. 2002b. "Indonesia Backgrounder: How the *Jemaah Islamiyah* Terrorist Network Operates." Jakarta and Brussels: Asia Report no. 43.

———. 2005. "Recycling Militants in Indonesia: Darul Islam and the Australian Embassy Bombing." Jakarta and Brussels: Asia Report no. 92.

———. 2008. "Indonesia: Implications of the Ahmadiyah Decree." Jakarta and Brussels: Asia Briefing no. 78.

———. 2009. "Indonesia: The Hotel Bombings." Jakarta and Brussels: Asia Briefing no. 94.

Ichwan, Moch. Nur. 2005. "'*Ulama*, State and Politics: Majelis Ulama Indonesia after Suharto." *Islamic Law and Society* 12 (1): 45–72.

Jamhari, and Jajang Jahroni. 2004. *Gerakan salafi radikal di Indonesia*. Jakarta: Rajawali Press.

Juhannis, Hamdan. 2007. "Komite Persiapan Penegakan Syariat Islam: A South Sulawesi Formalist Islamic Movement." *Studia Islamika* 14 (1): 47–84.

Jurnal Perempuan. 2006. "Komnas Perempuan Menuntut Adanya Penertiban Perda-Perda Diskriminatif." June 20. http://www.jurnalperempuan.com/index.php/jpo/comments/komnas_perempuan_menuntut_adanya_penertiban_perda_perda_diskriminatif/ (accessed December 17, 2007).

Keane, John. 1996. *Reflections on Violence*. London and New York: Verso.

Kim, Hung-Jun. 1998. "The Changing Interpretation of Religious Freedom in Indonesia." *Journal of Southeast Asian Studies* 29 (2): 357–73.

Kitley, Philip. 2008. "*Playboy Indonesia* and the Media: Commerce and the Islamic Public Sphere on Trial in Indonesia." *South East Asia Research* 16 (1): 85–116.

Klinken, Gerry van. 2007. *Communal Violence and Democratization in Indonesia: Small Town Wars*. London and New York: Routledge.

Laderman, Carol. 1991. *Taming the Wind of Desire: Psychology, Medicine, and Aesthetics in Malay Shamanistic Performance*. Berkeley: University of California Press.

Laffan, Michael Francis. 2003. *Islamic Nationhood and Colonial Indonesia: The Umma below the Winds*. London and New York: RoutledgeCurzon.

Lev, Daniel. 1972. *Islamic Courts in Indonesia: A Study in the Political Bases of Legal Institutions*. Berkeley: University of California Press.

Liddle, R. William. 1996. "The Islamic Turn in Indonesia: A Political Explanation." *Journal of Asian Studies* 7 (2): 52–63.

Lindsey, Tim. 2002. "Indonesian Constitutional Reform: Muddling towards Democracy." *Singapore Journal of International and Comparative Law* 6:244–301.

Lindsey, Tim, and M. B. Hooker. 2007. "Shari'a Revival in Aceh." In *Islamic Law in Contemporary Indonesia: Ideas and Institutions*, ed. R. Michael Feener and Mark E. Cammack, 216–54. Islamic Legal Studies Program, Harvard University Cambridge, Mass.: Harvard University Press.

Lombardi, Clark B. 2006. *State Law as Islamic Law in Modern Egypt: The Incorporation of the Shari'a into Egyptian Constitutional Law*. Leiden: Brill.

Long, Nicholas. 2008. "Urban, Social and Personal Transformations in Tanjung Pinang, Kepulauan Riau, Indonesia." Ph.D. diss., Cambridge University.

LSI (Lembaga Survei Indonesia). 2007. "Trend Dukungan Nilai Islamis versus Nilai Sekular di Indonesia." http://www.lsi.or.id/riset/310/trend-dukungan-nilai-islamis-versus-nilai-sekular (accessed November 20, 2007).

MacDougall, John M. 2007. "Criminality and the Political Economy of Security in Lombok." In *Renegotiating Boundaries: Local Politics in Post-Suharto Indonesia*, ed. Henk Schulte Nordholt and Gerry van Klinken, 291–303. Leiden: KITLV Press.

Machmudi, Yon. 2006. "Islamizing Indonesia: The Rise of Jemaah Tarbiyah and the Prosperous Justice Party (PKS)." Ph.D. diss., Australian National University.

Makdisi, George. 1981. *The Rise of Colleges: Institutions of Learning in Islam and the West*. Edinburgh: Edinburgh University Press.

Mawardi, Ahmad Imam. 2003. "The Political Backdrop of the Enactment of the Compilation of Islamic Laws in Indonesia." In *Shari'a and Politics in Modern Indonesia*, ed. Arskal Salim and Azyumardi Azra, 125–47. Singapore: Institute of Southeast Asian Studies.

Mietzner, Marcus. 2008. "Comparing Indonesia's Party Systems of the 1950s and the Post-Suharto Era: From Centrifugal to Centripetal Inter-party Competition." *Journal of Southeast Asian Studies* 39 (3): 431–53.

———. 2009. "Indonesia and the Pitfalls of Low-Quality Democracy: A Case Study of Gubernatorial Elections in North Sulawesi." In *Democratization in Post-Suharto Indonesia*, ed. Marco Bünte and Andreas Ufen, 124–49. London and New York: Routledge.

Milner, Anthony. 1983. "Islam and the Muslim State." In *Islam in South-East Asia*, ed. M. B. Hooker, 23–49. Leiden: Brill.

———. 1995. *The Invention of Politics in Colonial Malaya: Contesting Nationalism and the Expansion of the Public Sphere*. Cambridge: Cambridge University Press.

Mujani, Saiful, and R. William Liddle. 2007. "Leadership, Party, and Religion: Explaining Voting Behavior in Indonesia." *Comparative Political Studies* 40 (7): 832–57.

Mulia, Siti Musdah. 2006. "Perda syariat dan peminggiran perempuan." Paper presented at the Indonesian Conference on Religion and Peace, August 11. http://kompilasiriset.blogspot.com/2007/03/icrp-perda-syariat-dan-peminggiran.html (accessed September 1, 2010).

Mulia, Siti Musdah, with Mark E. Cammack. 2007. "Toward a Just Marriage Law: Empowering Indonesian Women through a Counter Legal Draft to the Indonesian Compilation of Islamic Law." In *Islamic Law in Contemporary Indonesia: Ideas and Institutions,* ed. R. Michael Feener and Mark E. Cammack, 128–45. Islamic Legal Studies Program, Harvard University. Cambridge, Mass.: Harvard University Press.

Noer, Deliar. 1973. *The Modernist Muslim Movement in Indonesia, 1900–1942.* Oxford: Oxford University Press.

Olle, John. 2009. "The Majelis Ulama Indonesia versus 'Heresy': The Resurgence of Authoritarian Islam." In *State of Authority: The State in Society in Indonesia,* ed. Gerry van Klinken and Joshua Barker, 95–116. Ithaca: Southeast Asia Program, Cornell University.

Peletz, Michael G. 2002. *Islamic Modern: Religious Courts and Cultural Politics in Malaysia.* Princeton: Princeton University Press.

Pelras, Christian. 1996. *The Bugis.* Oxford: Blackwell.

Pigeaud, Th. G. Th. 1960–63. *Java in the 14th Century.* 5 vols. The Hague: Martinus Nijhoff.

Porter, Donald J. 2002. *Managing Politics and Islam in Indonesia.* London and New York: RoutledgeCurzon.

PPIM. 2007. "Indonesian Muslim Attitudes on Islamism and Democracy." Unpublished research report, Project on Islam and Education in Southeast Asia. Boston, Mass.: Institute on Culture, Religion, and World Affairs, Boston University.

Reid, Anthony. 1988. *The Lands below the Winds.* Vol. 1 of *Southeast Asia in the Age of Commerce, 1450–1680.* New Haven: Yale University Press.

———. 1993. *Expansion and Crisis.* Vol. 2 of *Southeast Asia in the Age of Commerce, 1450–1680.* New Haven: Yale University Press.

Ricklefs, M. C. 2007. *Polarizing Javanese Society: Islamic and Other Visions c. 1830–1930.* Honolulu: University of Hawaii Press.

Riddell, Peter. 2001. *Islam and the Malay-Indonesian World.* London: Hurst.

Roff, William R. 1994. *The Origins of Malay Nationalism.* 2nd ed. Kuala Lumpur: University of Malaya Press.

Salim, Arskal. 2008. *Challenging the Secular State: The Islamization of Law in Modern Indonesia.* Honolulu: University of Hawaii Press.

Salman. 2006. "The Tarbiyah Movement: Why People Join This Indonesian Contemporary Islamic Movement." *Studia Islamika* 13 (2): 171–240.

Schulte Nordholt, Henk. 2002. "A Genealogy of Violence." In *Roots of Violence in Indonesia,* ed. Freek Colombijn and J. Thomas Lindblad, 33–61. Leiden: KITLV Press.

Schulte Nordholt, Henk, and Gerry van Klinken. 2007. Introduction to *Renegotiating Boundaries: Local Politics in Post-Suharto Indonesia,* ed. Henk Schulte Nordholt and Gerry van Klinken, 1–29. Leiden: KITLV Press.

Setyawati, Lugina. 2008. *"Adat,* Islam and Womanhood in the Reconstruction of Riau Malay Identity." *Indonesian Islam in a New Era,* ed. Susan Blackburn, Bianca J. Smith, and Siti Syamsiyatun, 69–96. Clayton, Victoria, Australia: Monash University Press.

Shiraishi, Takashi. 1990. *An Age in Motion: Popular Radicalism in Java, 1912–1926.* Ithaca and London: Cornell University Press.

Sidel, John. 2006. *Riots, Pogroms, Jihad: Religious Violence in Indonesia.* Ithaca and London: Cornell University Press.

Simanullang, Robin. 2005. *Ma'had al-Zaytun: Pusat Pendidikan dan Pengembangan Budaya Toleransi dan Perdamaian.* Jakarta: Gramedia.

Sirozi, Muhammad. 2004. "Secular-Religious Debates on the Indonesian National Education System: Colonial Legacy and a Search for National Identity in Education." *Intercultural Education* 15 (2): 123–39.

Sitompul, H. Agussalim. 1997. *HMI: Mengayuh di antara cita dan kritik.* Yogyakarta, Java, Indonesia: Aditya Media.

Soebardi, S. 1983. "Kartosuwiryo and the Darul Islam Rebellion in Indonesia." *Journal of Southeast Asian Studies* 13 (3): 109–33.

Starrett, Gregory. 1998. *Putting Islam to Work: Education, Politics, and Religious Transformation in Egypt.* Berkeley: University of California Press.

Taylor, Philip. 2007. *Cham Muslims of the Mekong Delta: Place and Mobility in the Cosmopolitan Periphery.* Singapore: NUS Press.

Tomsa, Dirk. 2008. *Party Politics and Democratization in Indonesia: Golkar in the Post-Suharto Era.* London and New York: Routledge.

Ufen, Andreas. 2008. "From *Aliran* to Dealignment: Political Parties in Post-Suharto Indonesia." *South East Asia Research* 16 (1): 5–41.

Wahid Institute. 2006. "Perda SI: Aspirasi atau Komodoti?" *Nawala* 1 (1): 1–6.

White, Sally, and Maria Ulfah Anshor. 2008. "Islam and Gender in Contemporary Indonesia: Public Discourses on Duties, Rights and Morality." In *Expressing Islam: Religious Life and Politics in Indonesia,* ed. Greg Fealy and Sally White, 137–58. Singapore: Institute of Southeast Asian Studies.

Wilson, Chris. 2008. *Ethno-religious Violence in Indonesia: From Soil to God.* London and New York: Routledge.

Wilson, Ian Douglas. 2006. "Continuity and Change: The Changing Contours of Organized Violence in Post–New Order Indonesia." *Critical Asian Studies* 38 (2): 265–97.

———. 2008. "'As Long as It's Halal': Islamic *Preman* in Jakarta." In *Expressing Islam: Religious Life and Politics in Indonesia,* ed. Greg Fealy and Sally White, 192–210. Singapore: Institute of Southeast Asian Studies.

Woodward, Mark R. 1989. *Islam in Java: Normative Piety and Mysticism in the Sultanate of Yogyakarta.* Tucson: University of Arizona Press.

Contributors

Bahman Baktiari is Director of the Middle East Center at the University of Utah and the author of numerous works on Iranian politics and history, including *Parliamentary Politics in Revolutionary Iran.*

T. Barfield is President of the American Institute of Afghanistan Studies and Director of the Institute for the Study of Muslim Societies and Civilizations at Boston University. His most recent book is *Afghanistan: A Cultural and Political History.*

Nathan J. Brown is Professor of Political Science and International Affairs at George Washington University and the author of many works on law and governance in the Middle East, including *Constitutions in a Nonconstitutional World: Arab Basic Laws and the Prospects for Accountable Government.*

Robert W. Hefner is Director of the Institute on Culture, Religion, and World Affairs at Boston University and was President of the Association for Asian Studies. His most recent book is *Muslims and Modernity: Culture and Society since 1800,* volume 6 in the *New Cambridge History of Islam.*

Paul M. Lubeck is Professor of Sociology at the University of California, Santa Cruz, and the author of numerous works on Islamic revival and social movements, including "The Challenge of Islamic Networks and Citizenship Claims."

Frank E. Vogel is an Honorary Fellow at and the founding director (1991–2006) of the Islamic Legal Studies Program at Harvard Law School as well as the author of several books on Islamic law, including *Islamic Law and Legal System: Studies of Saudi Arabia.*

M. Hakan Yavuz is Professor of Political Science and a Fellow at the Middle East Center at the University of Utah. His most recent book is *Secularism and Muslim Democracy in Turkey.*

Muhammad Qasim Zaman is Robert H. Niehaus '77 Professor of Near Eastern Studies and Religion at Princeton University. He is author of *The Ulama in Contemporary Islam,* among other works on Islamic history, thought, and politics.

Index